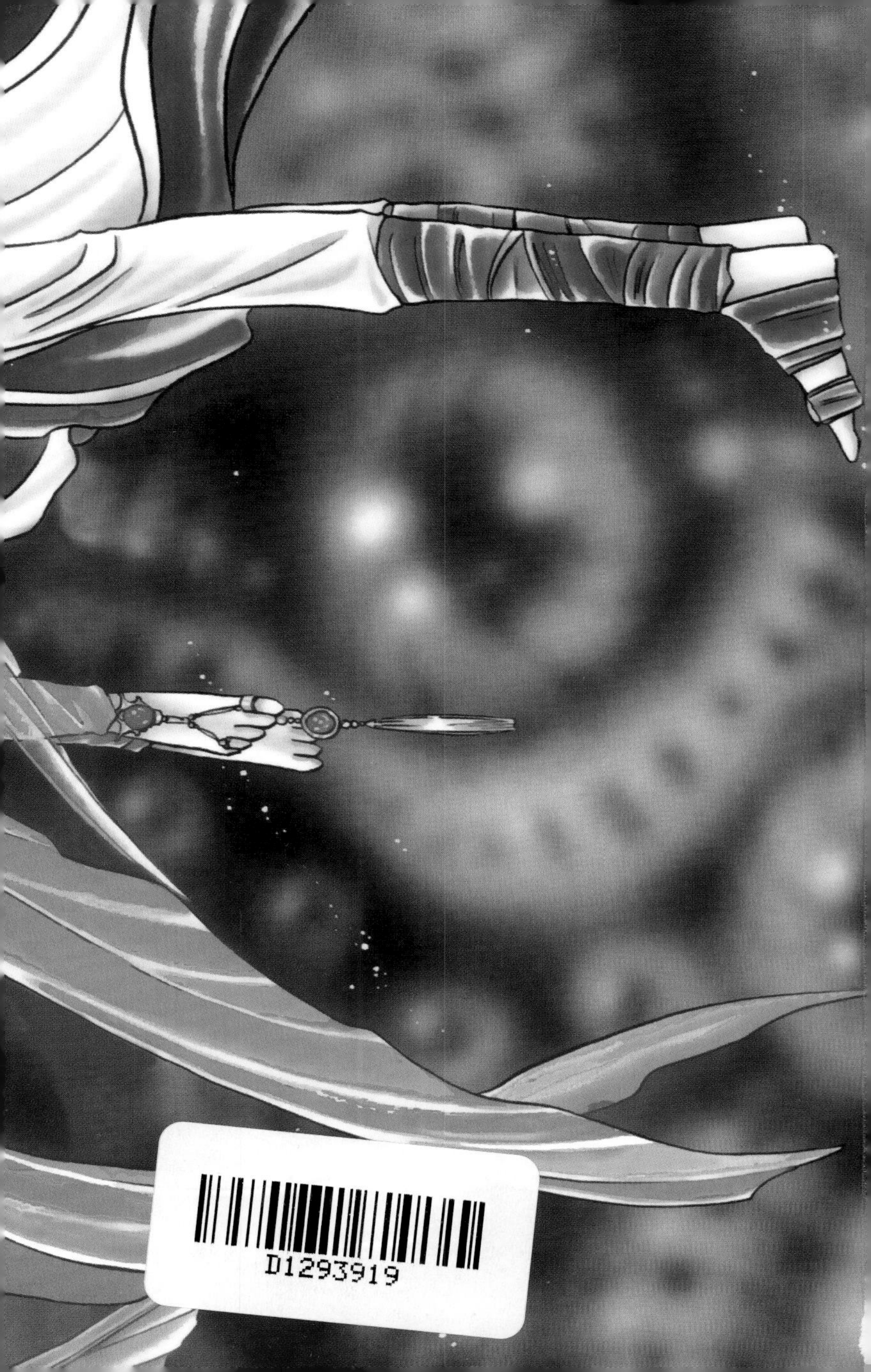

魍魎
姫
伝

Mouryou Kiden: Legend of The Nymph Vol. 3
Created by Tamayo Akiyama

Translation - Ray Yoshimoto
English Adaptation - Jake Forbes
Retouch and Lettering - Gloria Wu
Production Artist - Jose Macasocol, Jr.
Cover Design - Jennifer Nunn-Iwai

Editor - Lillian Diaz-Przybyl
Digital Imaging Manager - Chris Buford
Pre-Press Manager - Antonio DePietro
Production Managers - Jennifer Miller and Mutsumi Miyazaki
Art Director - Matt Alford
Managing Editor - Jill Freshney
VP of Production - Ron Klamert
Editor-In-Chief - Mike Kiley
President and C.O.O. - John Parker
Publisher and C.E.O. - Stuart Levy

A  Manga

TOKYOPOP Inc.
5900 Wilshire Blvd. Suite 2000
Los Angeles, CA 90036

E-mail: info@TOKYOPOP.com
Come visit us online at www.TOKYOPOP.com

MOURYOU KIDEN 3 ©TAMAYO AKIYAMA 1995 All rights reserved. No portion of this book may be
First published in Japan in 1995 by reproduced or transmitted in any form or by any means
KADOKAWA SHOTEN PUBLISHING CO., LTD., Tokyo. without written permission from the copyright holders.
English translation rights arranged with This manga is a work of fiction. Any resemblance to
KADOKAWA SHOTEN PUBLISHING CO., LTD., Tokyo actual events or locales or persons, living or dead, is
through TUTTLE-MORI AGENCY, INC., Tokyo. entirely coincidental.

English text copyright © 2005 TOKYOPOP Inc.

ISBN: 1-59532-247-7

First TOKYOPOP printing: June 2005
10 9 8 7 6 5 4 3 2 1
Printed in the USA

Mouryou Kiden
Legend of the Nymph

Volume 3

by
Tamayo Akiyama

HAMBURG // LONDON // LOS ANGELES // TOKYO

The Story So Far... Mouryou Kiden

Legend of the Nymph

Long ago, in the Age of Legends, the world was shrouded in fog. Mouryou Spirits, monsters in the service of the goddess Reiki, roamed the land unchecked, leaving chaos and destruction in their wake. But the Shiki Goddess Mikage of Fuyo-Den used her power to imprison Reiki and erect the Mi-Hashira pillar. The magical field emitted by the pillar kept the evil spirits and their mistress at bay for a thousand years. However, over time the power of the Mi-Hashira waned and the spirits began to awaken. And so it was that the world was plunged into chaos once more. Then, a most unlikely encounter occurred: Ayaka the nymph, daughter of Reiki, and Kai, heir to the Shiki demon clan, fell in love. But fate was not kind to the young lovers. Reiki convinced the love-struck Kai to give his own life to destroy the pillar. Ayaka traveled to the land of her blood rivals, the Shiki Demons, in hopes of seeing her dead lover one last time. The Shiki pitied the nymph and granted her wish, opening the gates to Hades so that his spirit might appear. It did not. The only answer—Kai was not dead! Together with Kurama, one of the Eight Shiki Lords, Ayaka set out in search of Kai. They were soon joined by a most unusual companion, Little Mikage, of the Kagero clan. Just who is she and why does she share the missing Goddess' name? Ayaka finds Kai, but he is no longer the man she fell in love with. Kai is dead after all, his body being used by Reiki to further her schemes. Now, the evil goddess has constructed the new Mi-Hashira of the moon, to fortify her strength. The end of the world seems inevitable...but Ayaka has much to learn. And during a lunar eclipse, with Reiki's moon-based powers weakened, the Mouryou Nymph receives a message from the goddess Mikage...

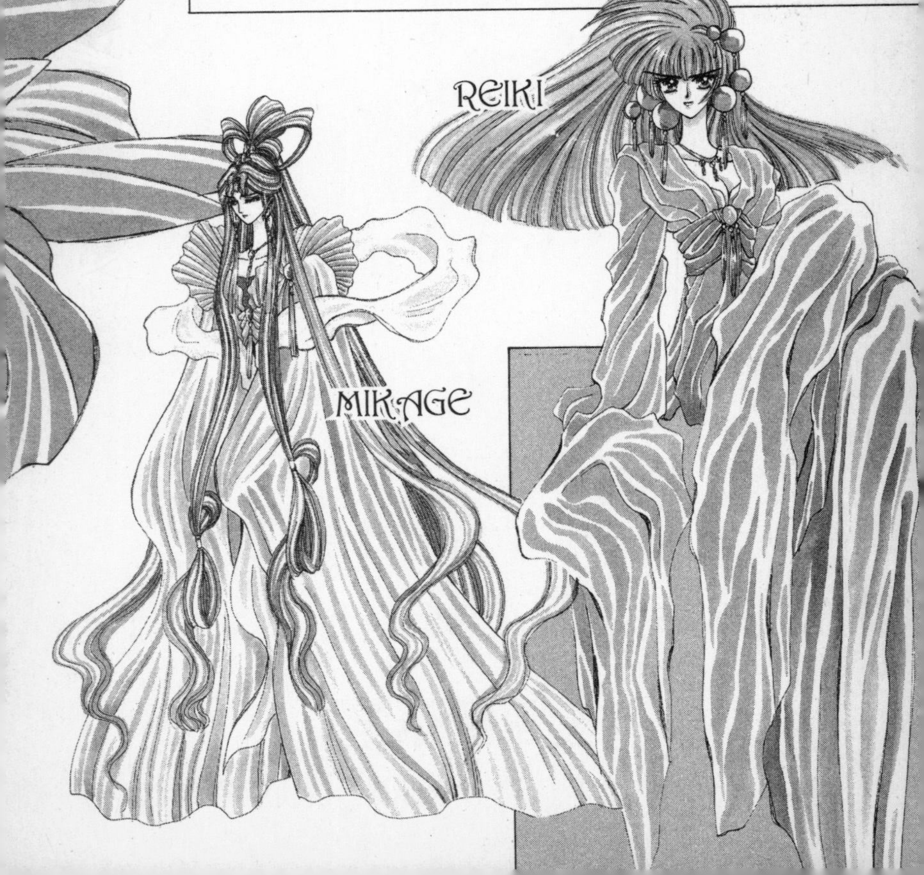
REIKI
MIKAGE

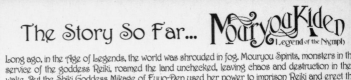

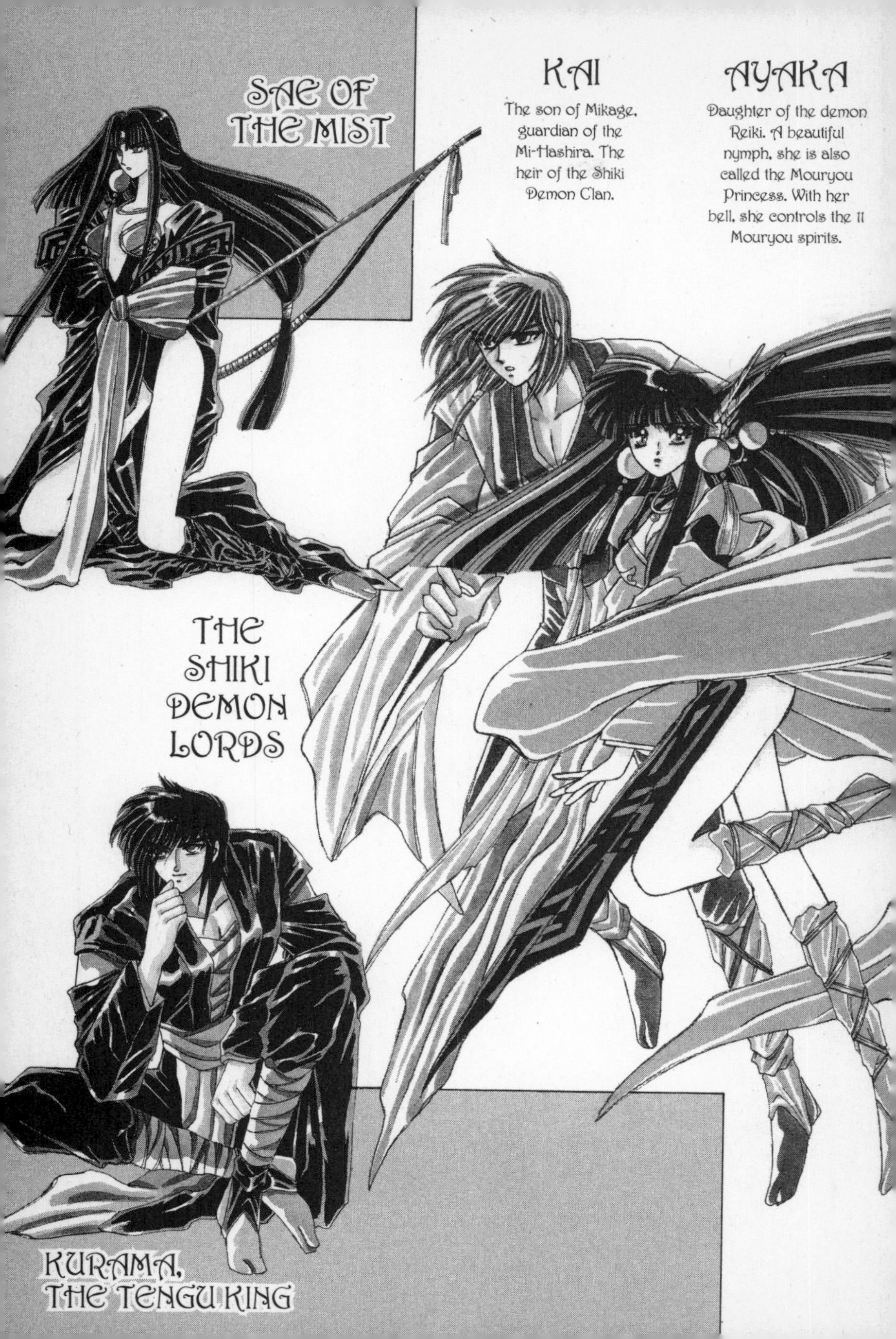
AYAKA
Daughter of the demon Reiki. A beautiful nymph, she is also called the Mouryou Princess. With her bell, she controls the 11 Mouryou spirits.
KAI
The son of Mikage, guardian of the Mi-Hashira. The heir of the Shiki Demon Clan.
SAE OF THE MIST
THE SHIKI DEMON LORDS
KURAMA, THE TENGU KING

魍魎姫伝

MouryouKiden
Legend of the Nymph

The Mouryou
(Demons of Darkness)

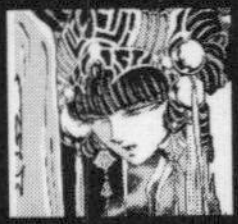

Reiki
(Goddess)

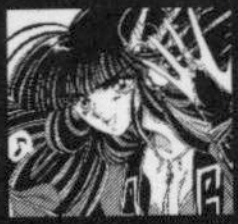

Ayaka
(Nymph; Mouryou Princess)

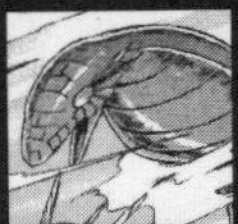

11 Mouryou
(Mountain Spirits)

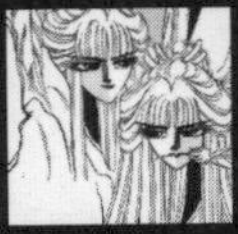

Meiki Devils
(Spirits of Hades)

The Shiki
(Demons of Light)

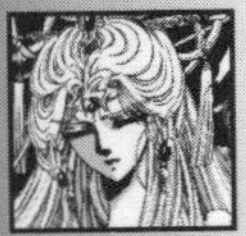

Mikage
(Goddess)

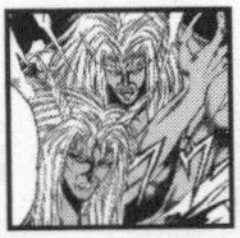

En & Haku
(Ogre Demons)

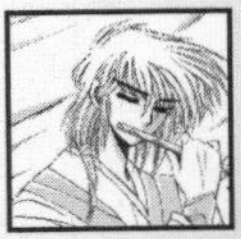

Kai
(Half-Blood Prince;
Leader of the Eight Clans)

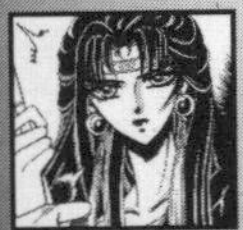

Sae of the Mists
(One of the Eight Shiki Lords)

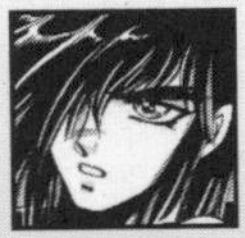

Kurama, the Tengu King
(One of the Eight Shiki Lords)

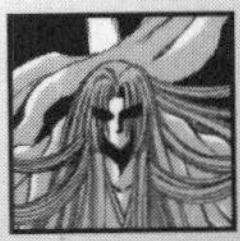

Rajin of the Hundred Eyes
(One of the Eight Shiki Lords)

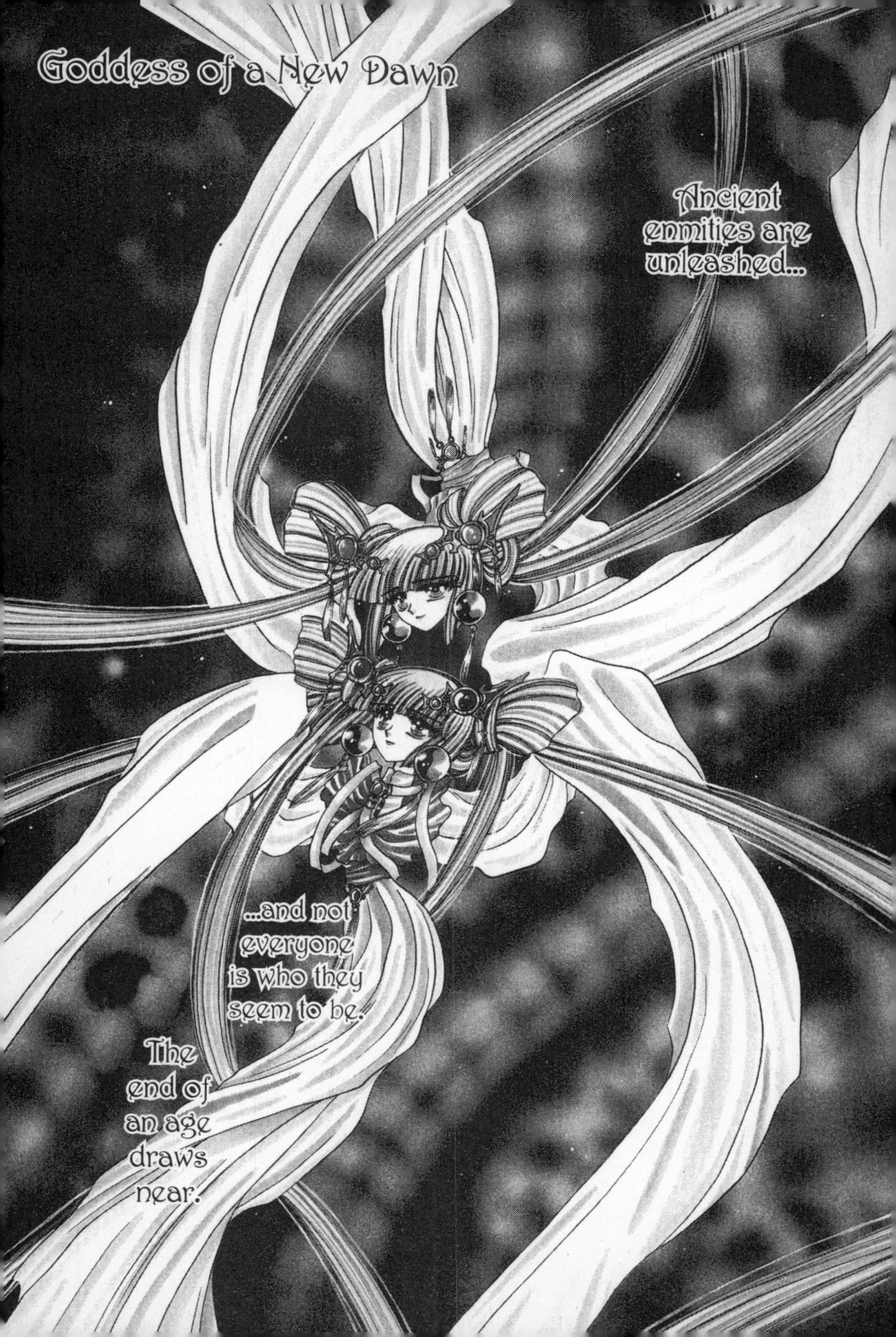
Goddess of a New Dawn
Ancient enmities are unleashed...
...and not everyone is who they seem to be.
The end of an age draws near.

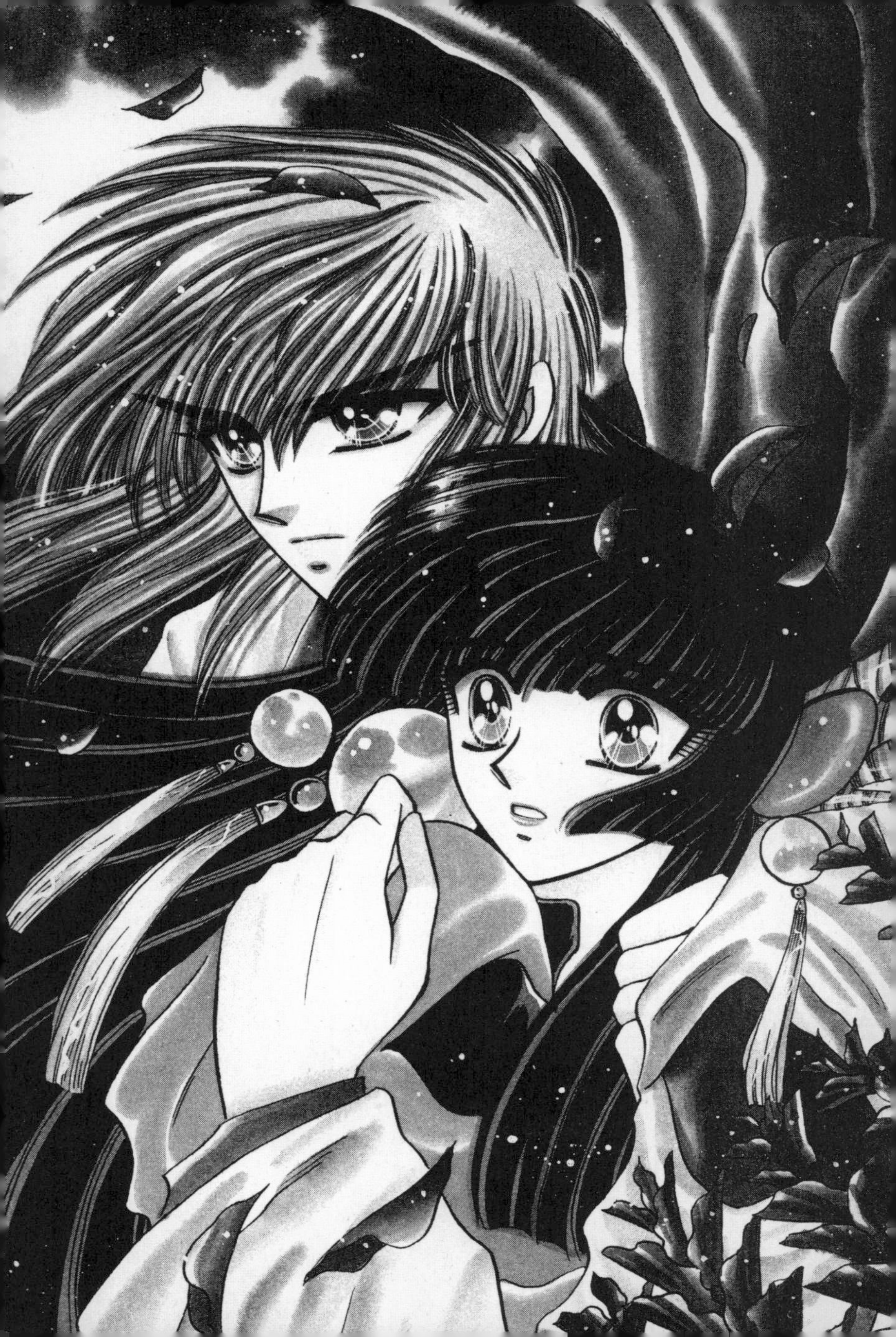

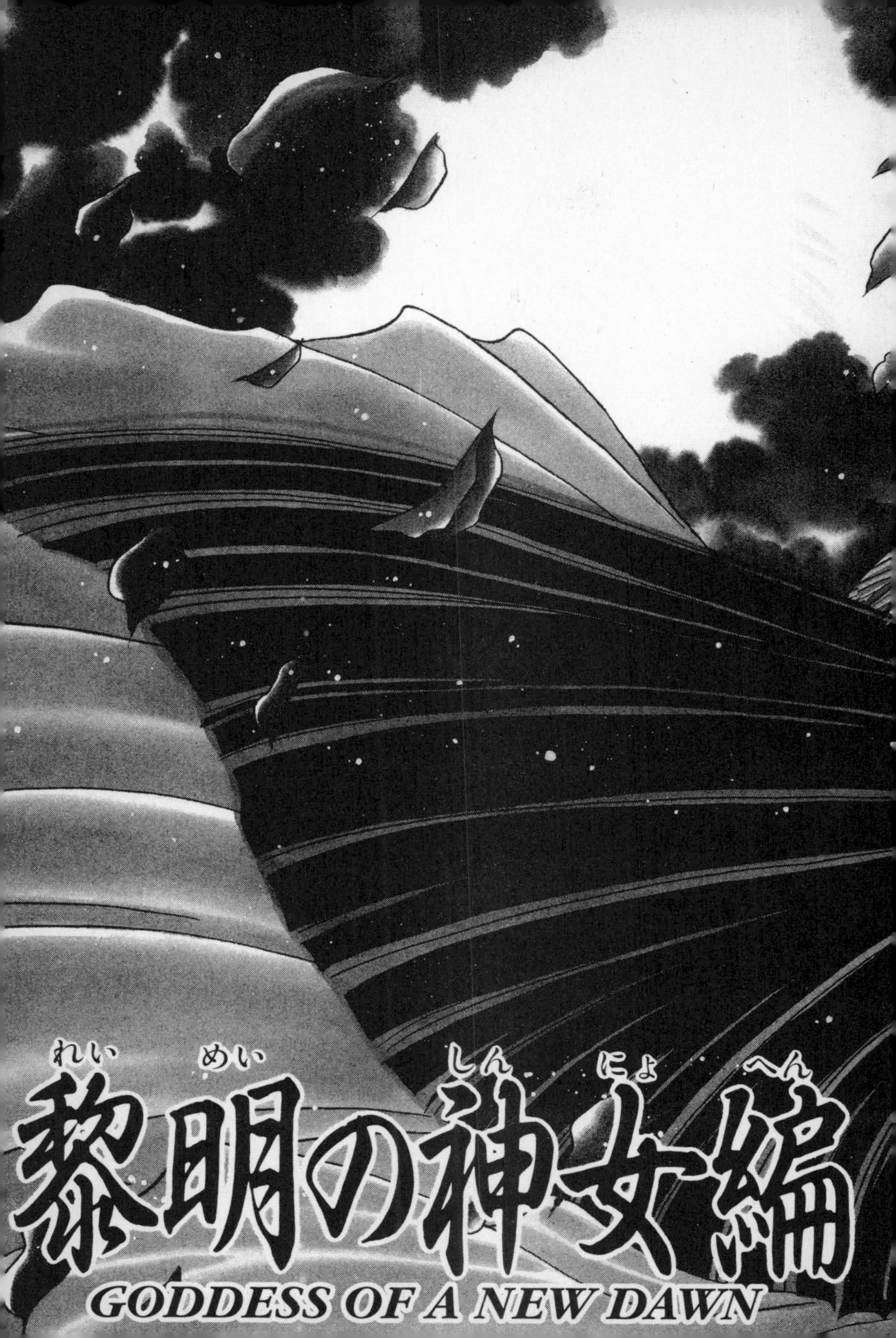
黎明の神女編
GODDESS OF A NEW DAWN

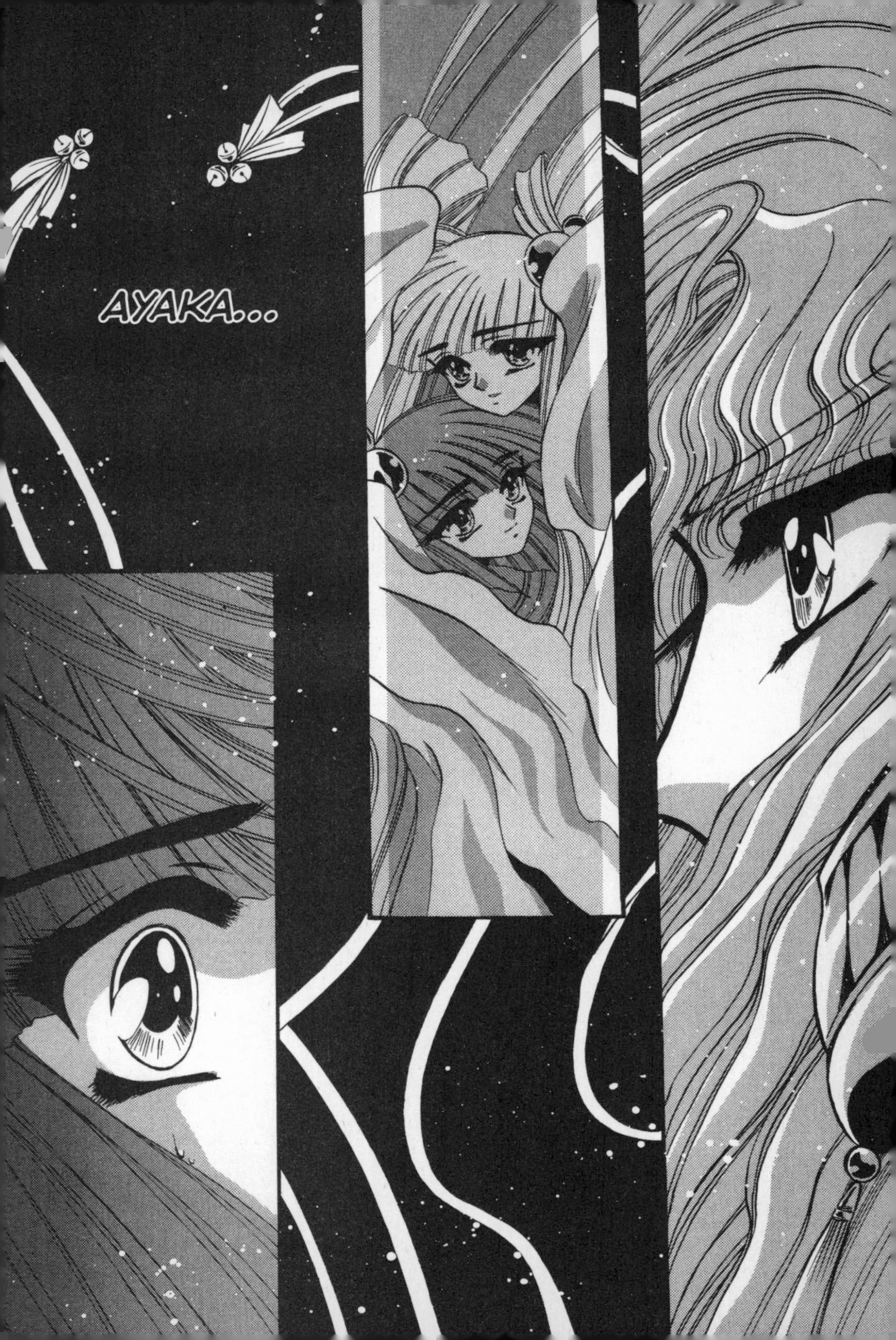
AYAKA...

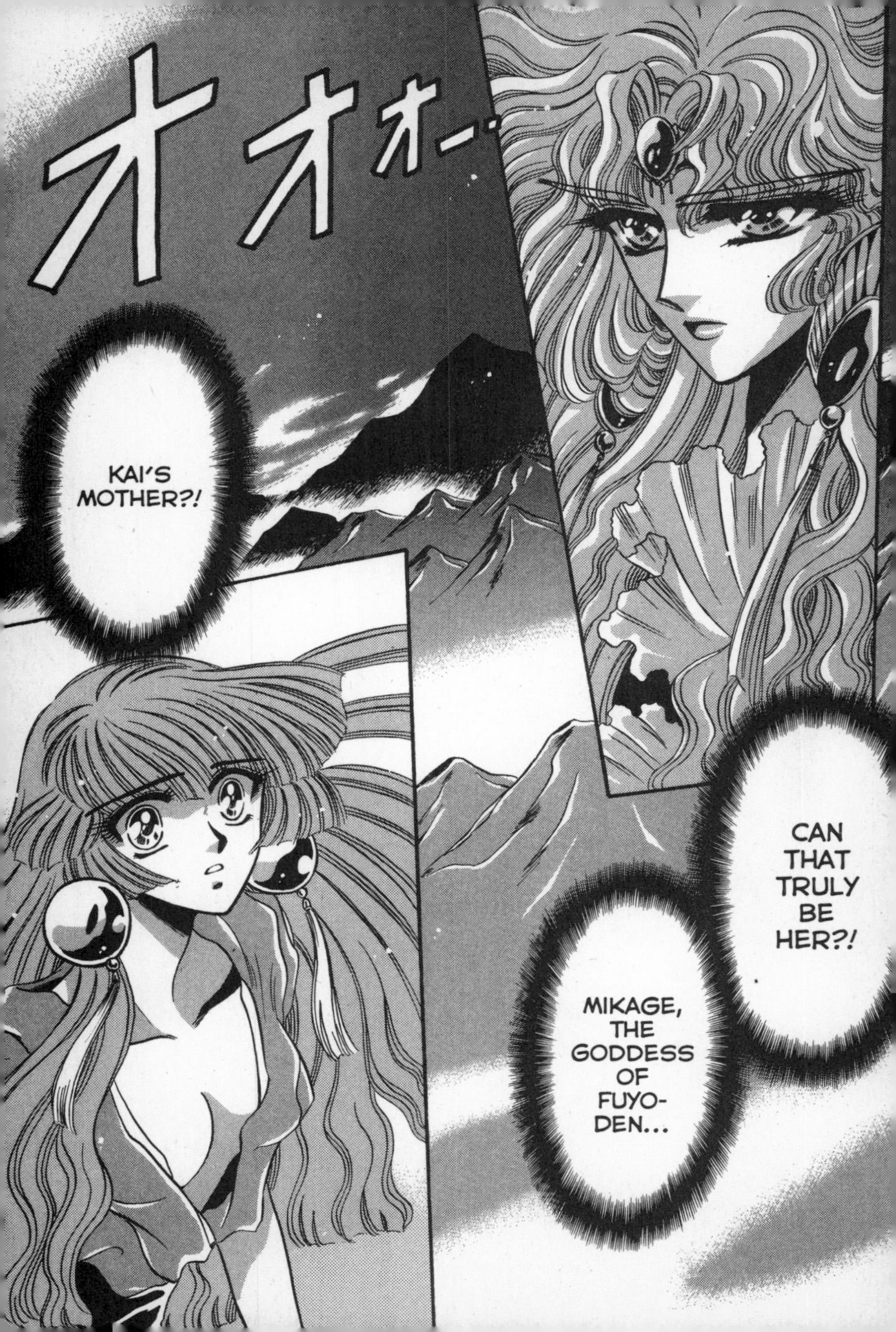
オオォー・・
KAI'S MOTHER?!
CAN THAT TRULY BE HER?!
MIKAGE, THE GODDESS OF FUYO-DEN...

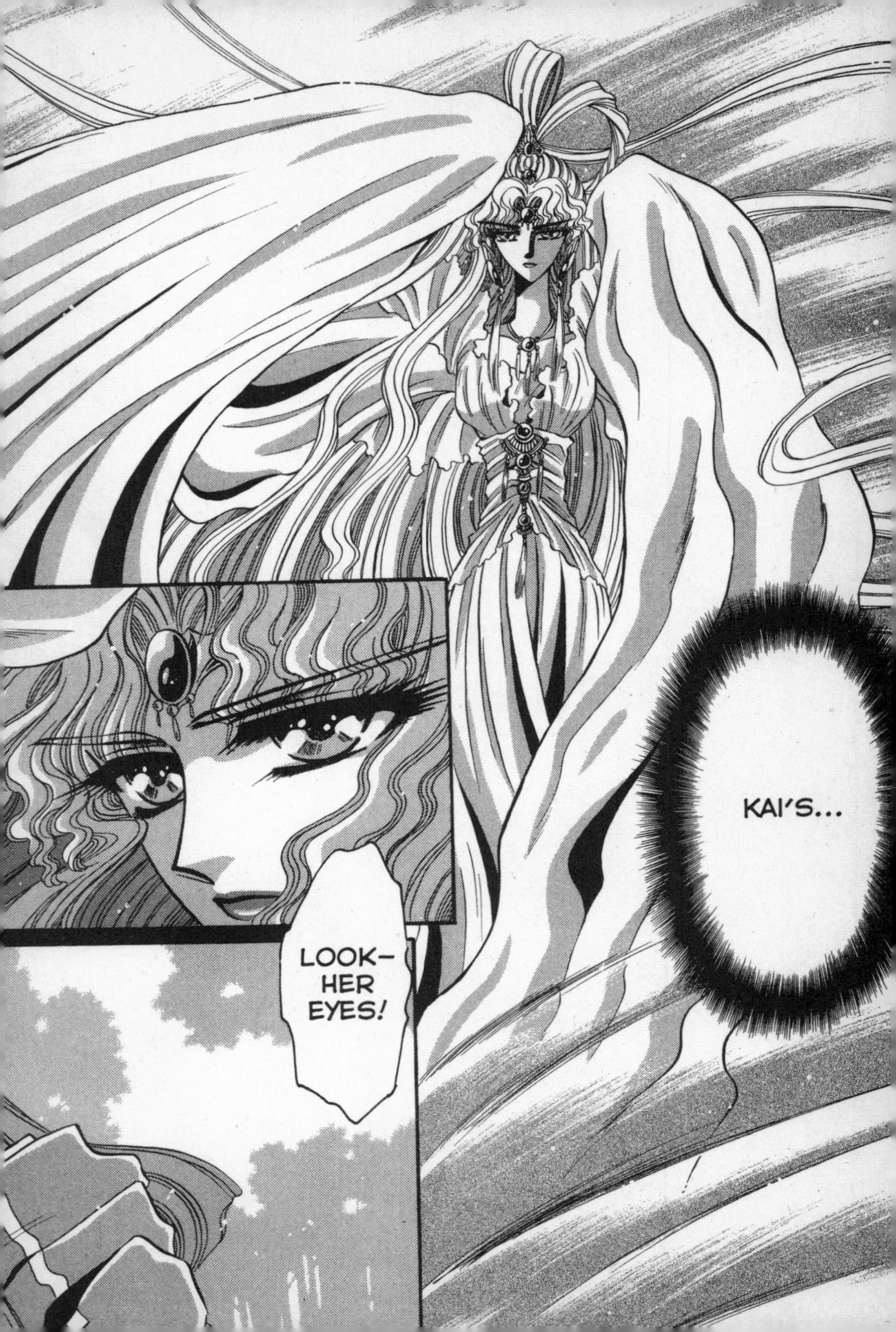
KAI'S...
LOOK— HER EYES!

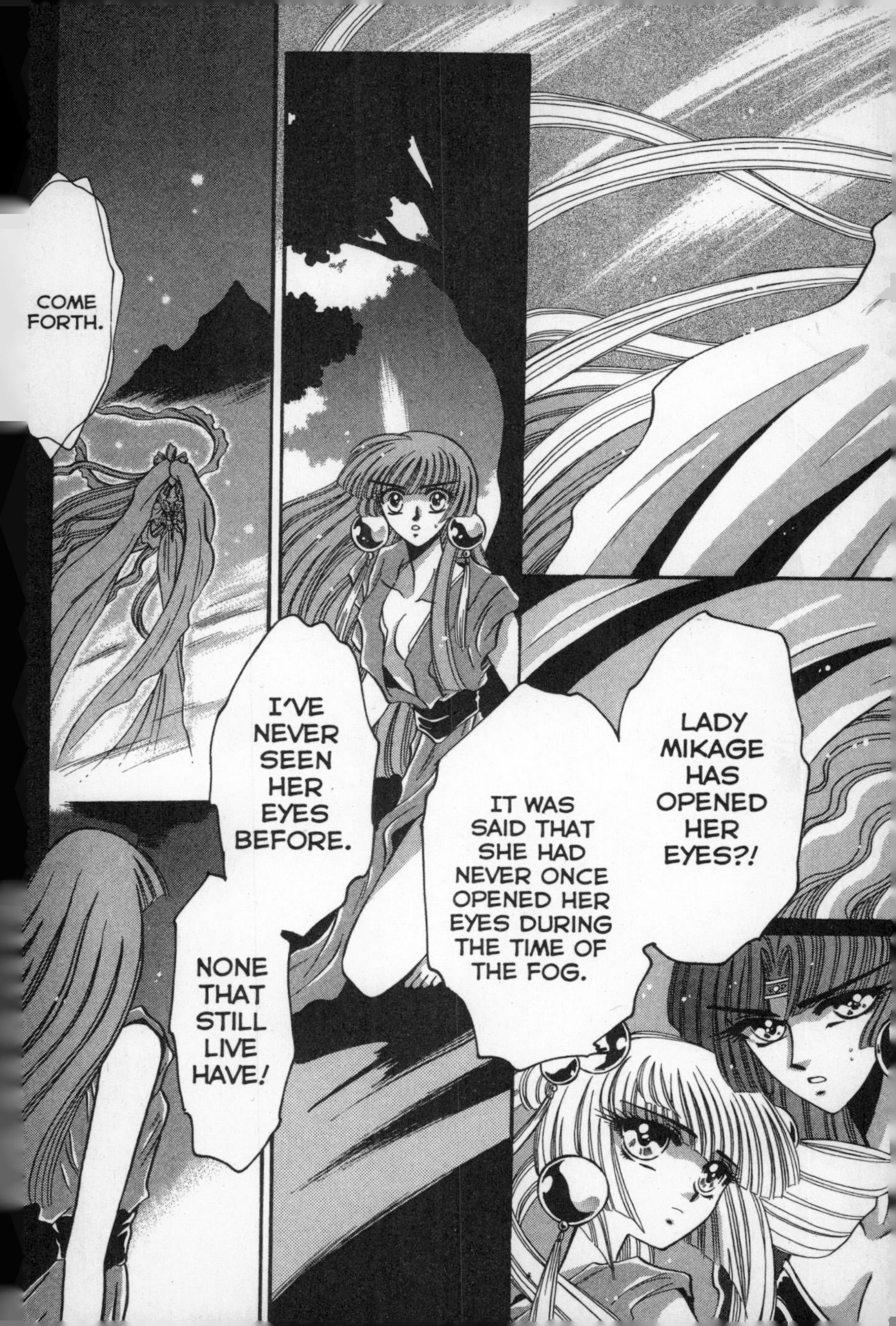
COME FORTH.
LADY MIKAGE HAS OPENED HER EYES?!
IT WAS SAID THAT SHE HAD NEVER ONCE OPENED HER EYES DURING THE TIME OF THE FOG.
I'VE NEVER SEEN HER EYES BEFORE.
NONE THAT STILL LIVE HAVE!

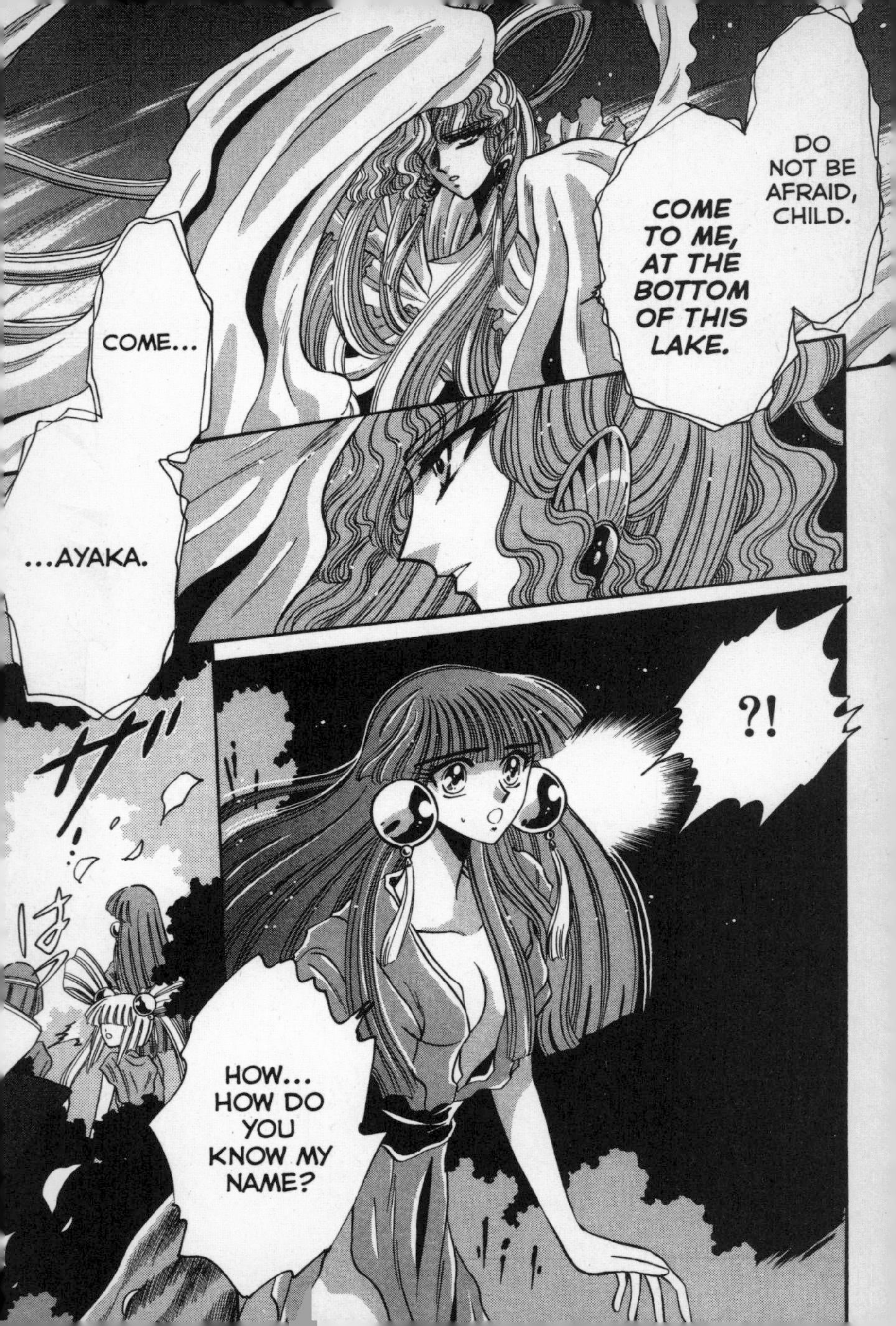
DO NOT BE AFRAID, CHILD.
COME TO ME, AT THE BOTTOM OF THIS LAKE.
COME...
...AYAKA.
?!
HOW... HOW DO YOU KNOW MY NAME?

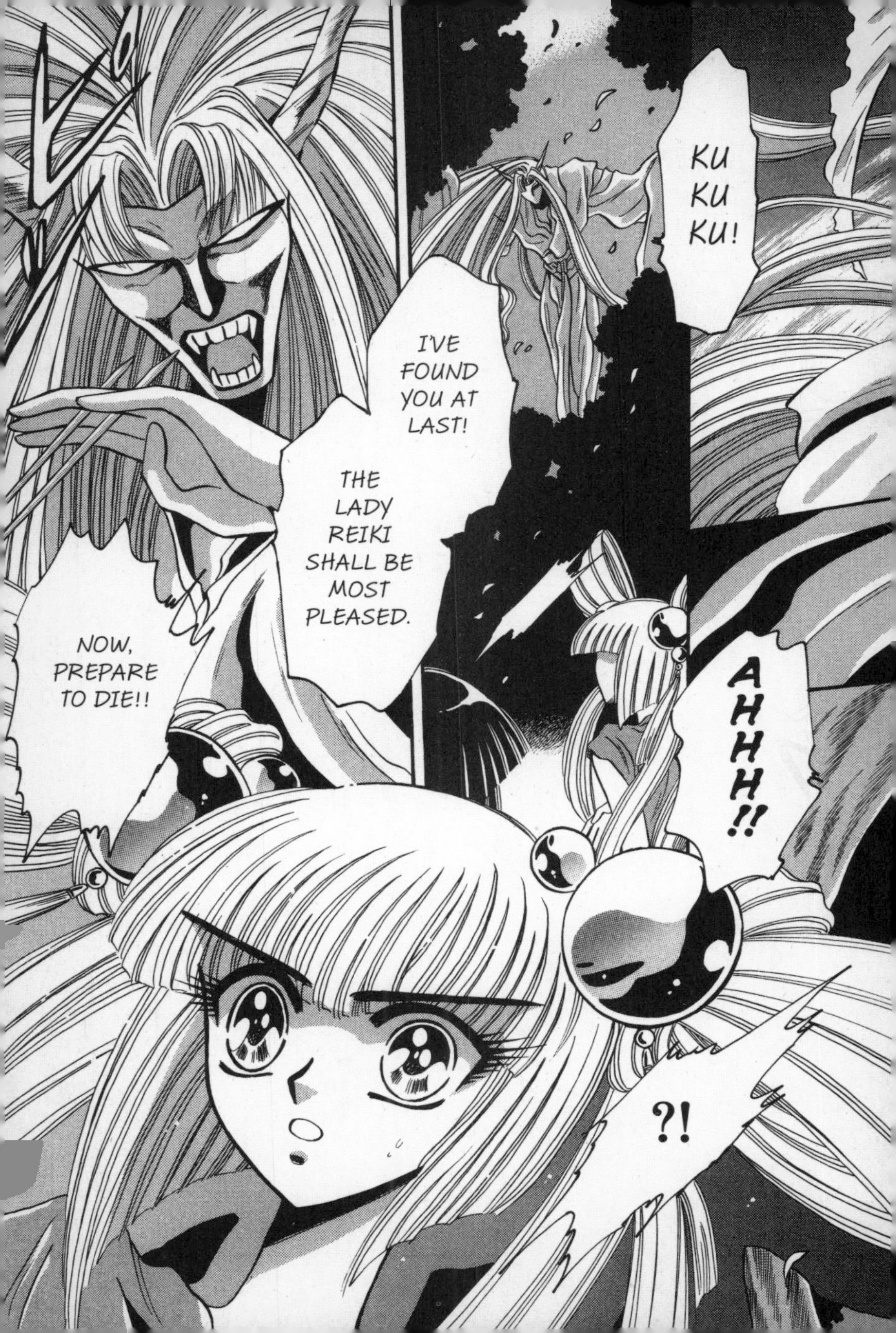
KU KU KU!
I'VE FOUND YOU AT LAST!
THE LADY REIKI SHALL BE MOST PLEASED.
NOW, PREPARE TO DIE!!
AHHHH!!
?!

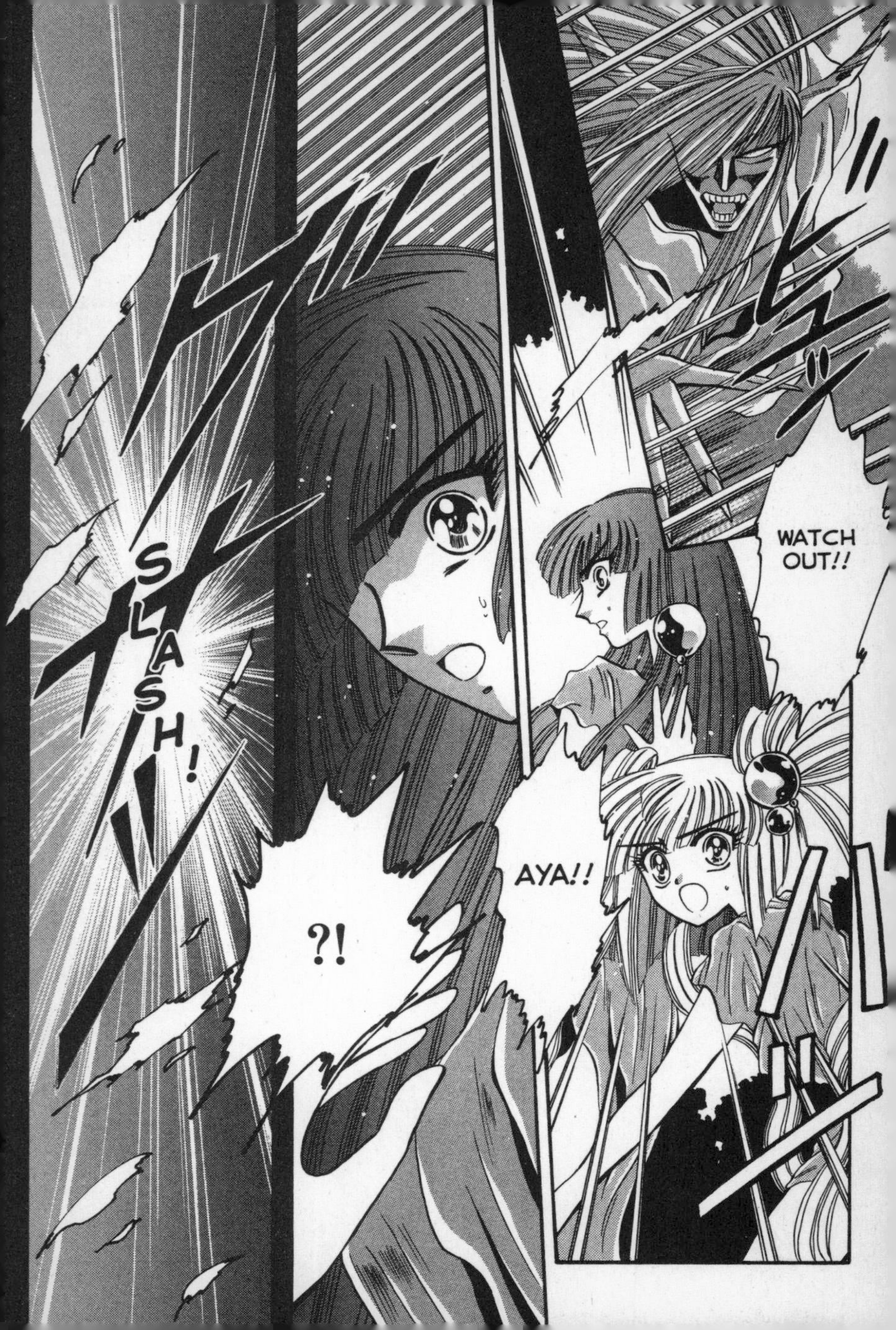
WATCH OUT!!
AYA!!
?!
SLASH!

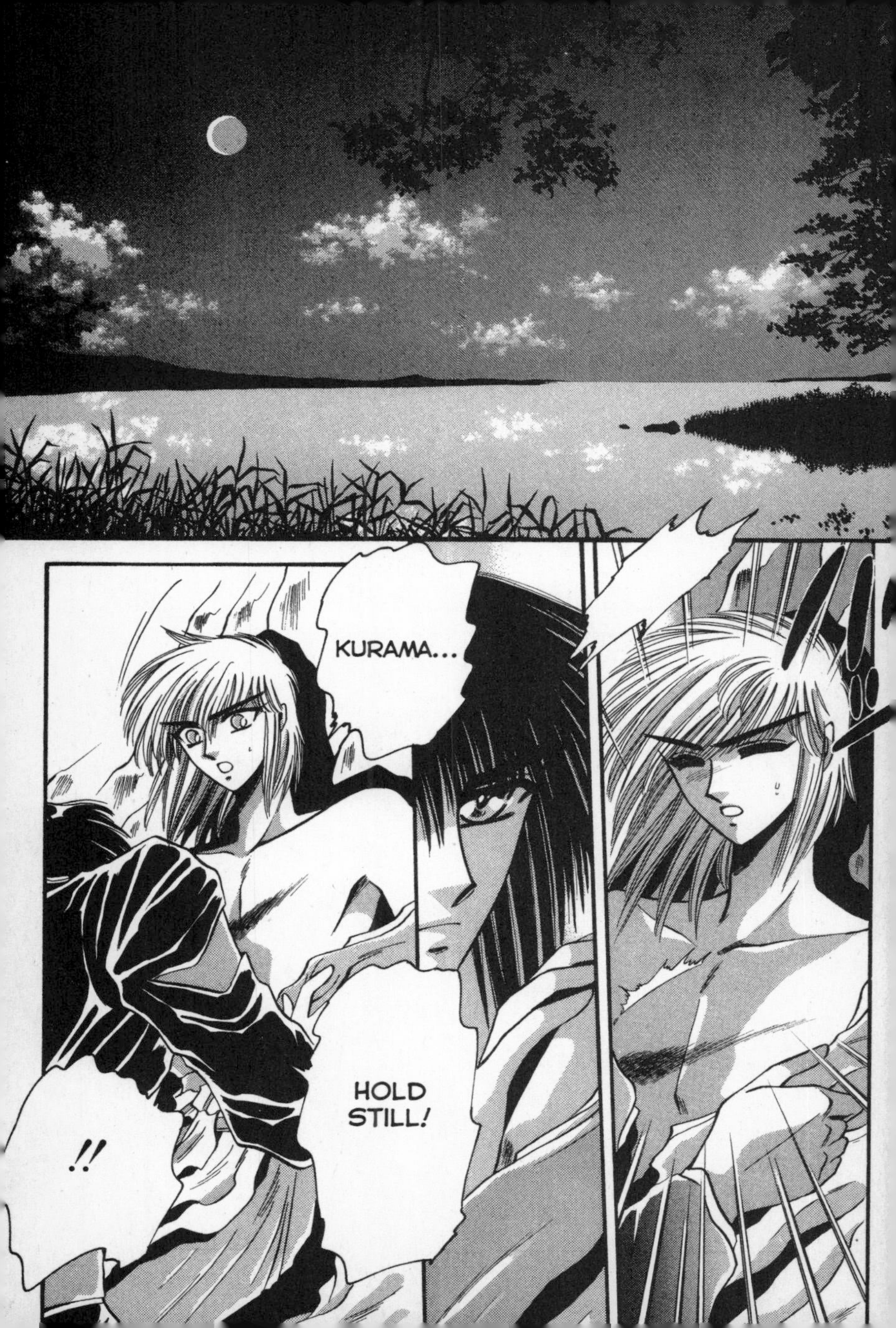
KURAMA...
HOLD STILL!
!!

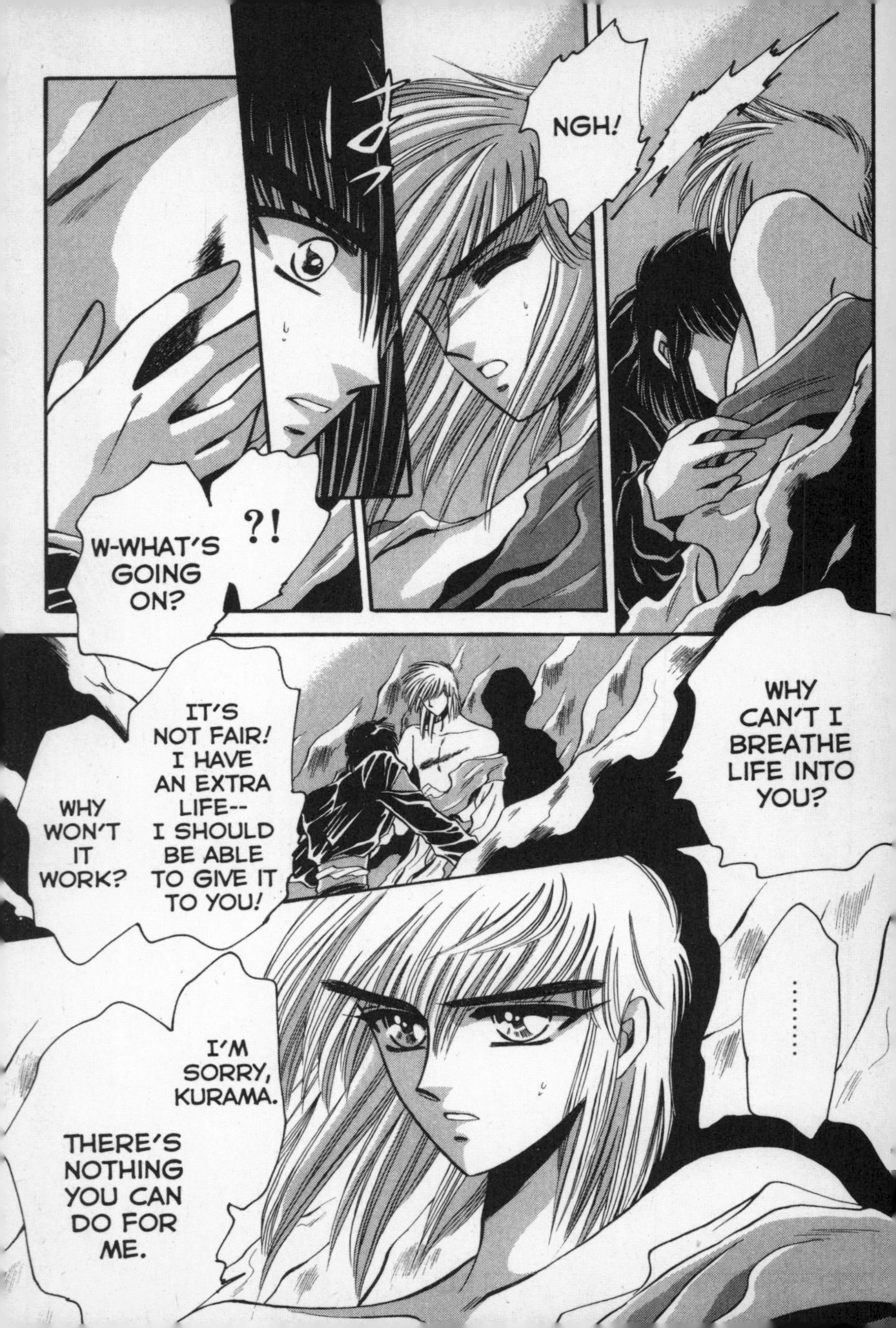

NGH!
はっ
?!
W-WHAT'S GOING ON?
WHY CAN'T I BREATHE LIFE INTO YOU?
IT'S NOT FAIR! I HAVE AN EXTRA LIFE-- I SHOULD BE ABLE TO GIVE IT TO YOU!
WHY WON'T IT WORK?
......
I'M SORRY, KURAMA.
THERE'S NOTHING YOU CAN DO FOR ME.

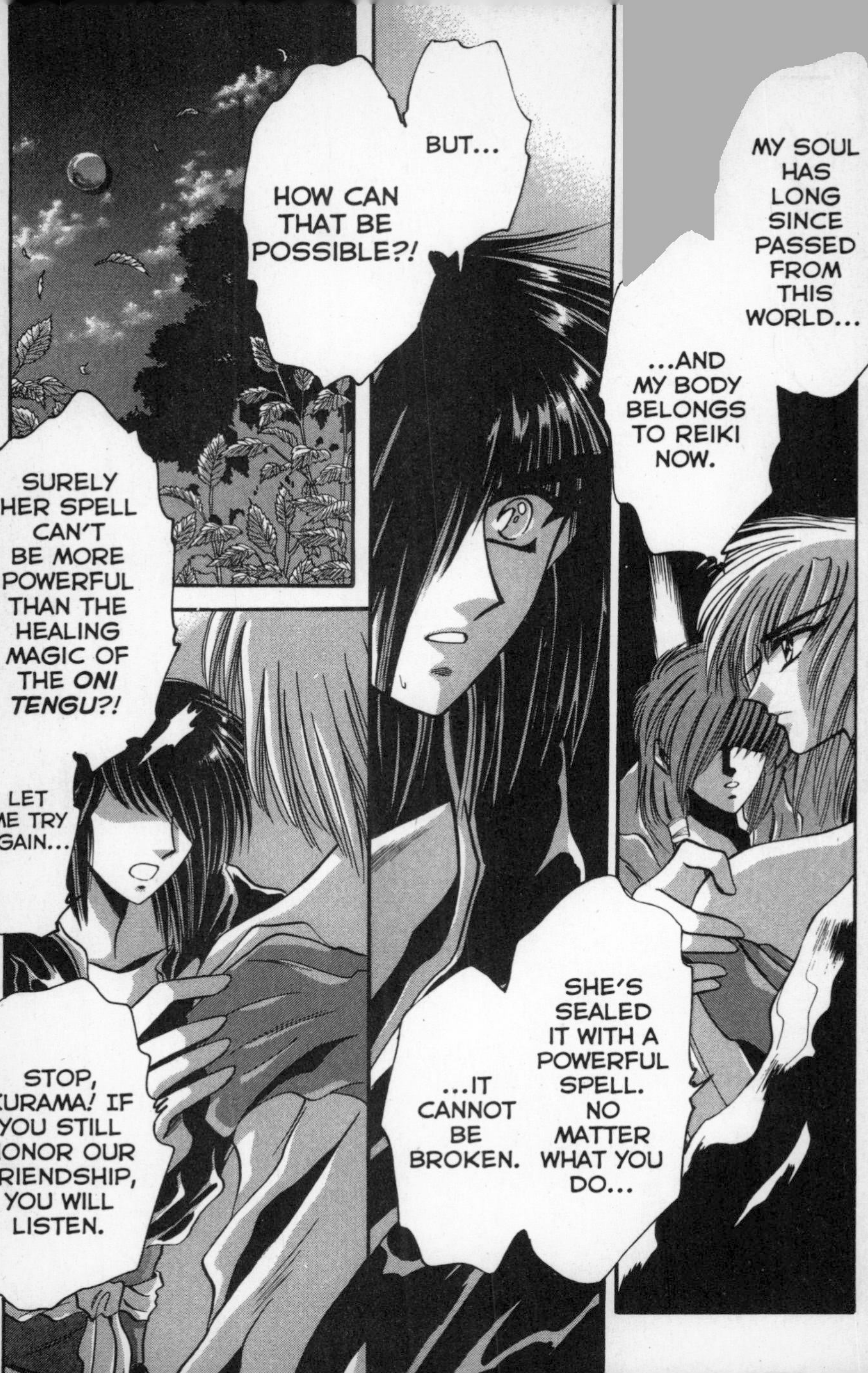
MY SOUL HAS LONG SINCE PASSED FROM THIS WORLD...
...AND MY BODY BELONGS TO REIKI NOW.
BUT...
HOW CAN THAT BE POSSIBLE?!
SURELY HER SPELL CAN'T BE MORE POWERFUL THAN THE HEALING MAGIC OF THE *ONI TENGU*?!
LET ME TRY AGAIN...
STOP, KURAMA! IF YOU STILL HONOR OUR FRIENDSHIP, YOU WILL LISTEN.
SHE'S SEALED IT WITH A POWERFUL SPELL. NO MATTER WHAT YOU DO...
...IT CANNOT BE BROKEN.

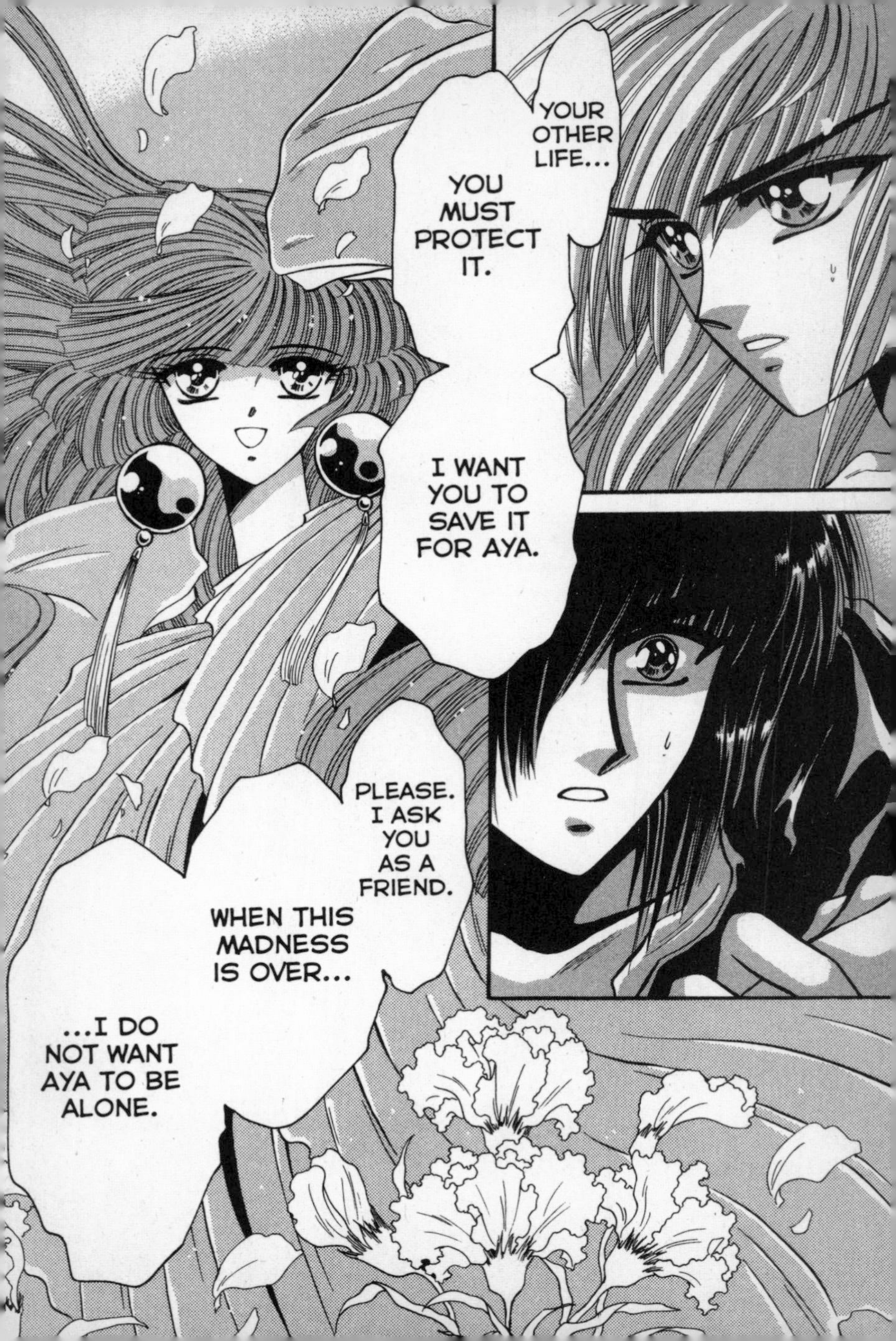
YOUR OTHER LIFE...
YOU MUST PROTECT IT.
I WANT YOU TO SAVE IT FOR AYA.
PLEASE. I ASK YOU AS A FRIEND.
WHEN THIS MADNESS IS OVER...
...I DO NOT WANT AYA TO BE ALONE.

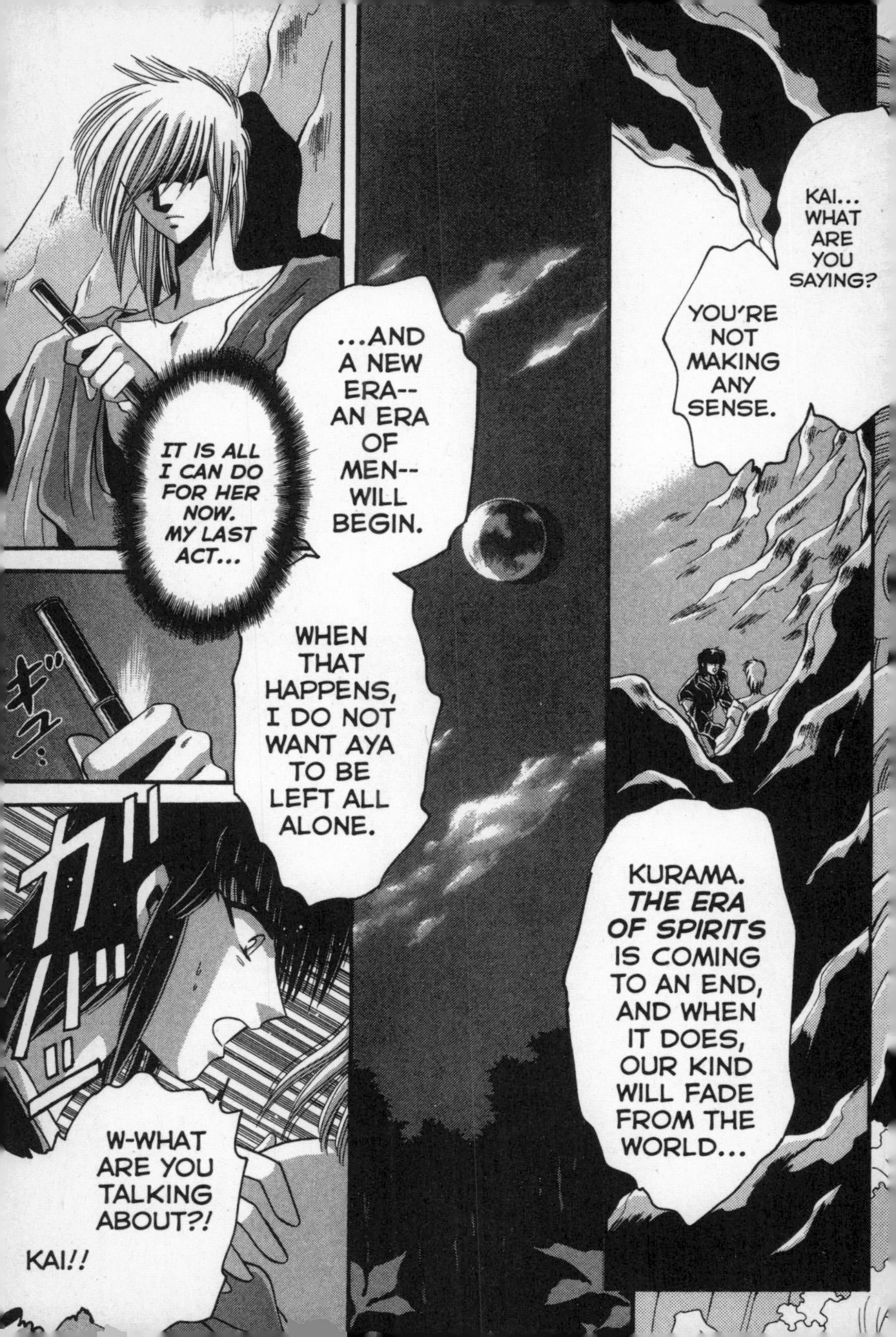
KAI... WHAT ARE YOU SAYING?
YOU'RE NOT MAKING ANY SENSE.
KURAMA. *THE ERA OF SPIRITS* IS COMING TO AN END, AND WHEN IT DOES, OUR KIND WILL FADE FROM THE WORLD...
...AND A NEW ERA-- AN ERA OF MEN-- WILL BEGIN.
WHEN THAT HAPPENS, I DO NOT WANT AYA TO BE LEFT ALL ALONE.
IT IS ALL I CAN DO FOR HER NOW. MY LAST ACT...
W-WHAT ARE YOU TALKING ABOUT?!
KAI!!

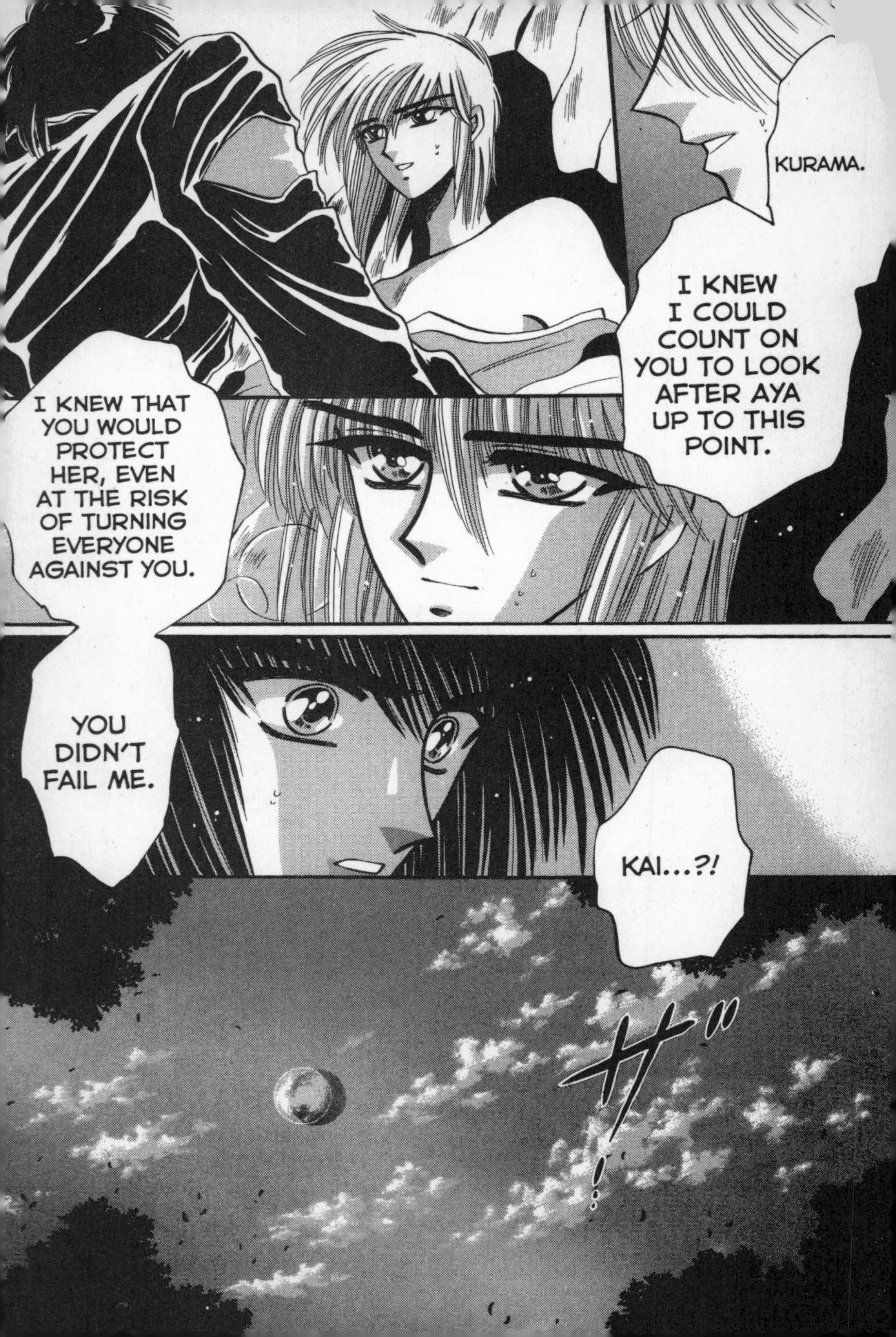
KURAMA.
I KNEW I COULD COUNT ON YOU TO LOOK AFTER AYA UP TO THIS POINT.
I KNEW THAT YOU WOULD PROTECT HER, EVEN AT THE RISK OF TURNING EVERYONE AGAINST YOU.
YOU DIDN'T FAIL ME.
KAI...?!
ザ!!

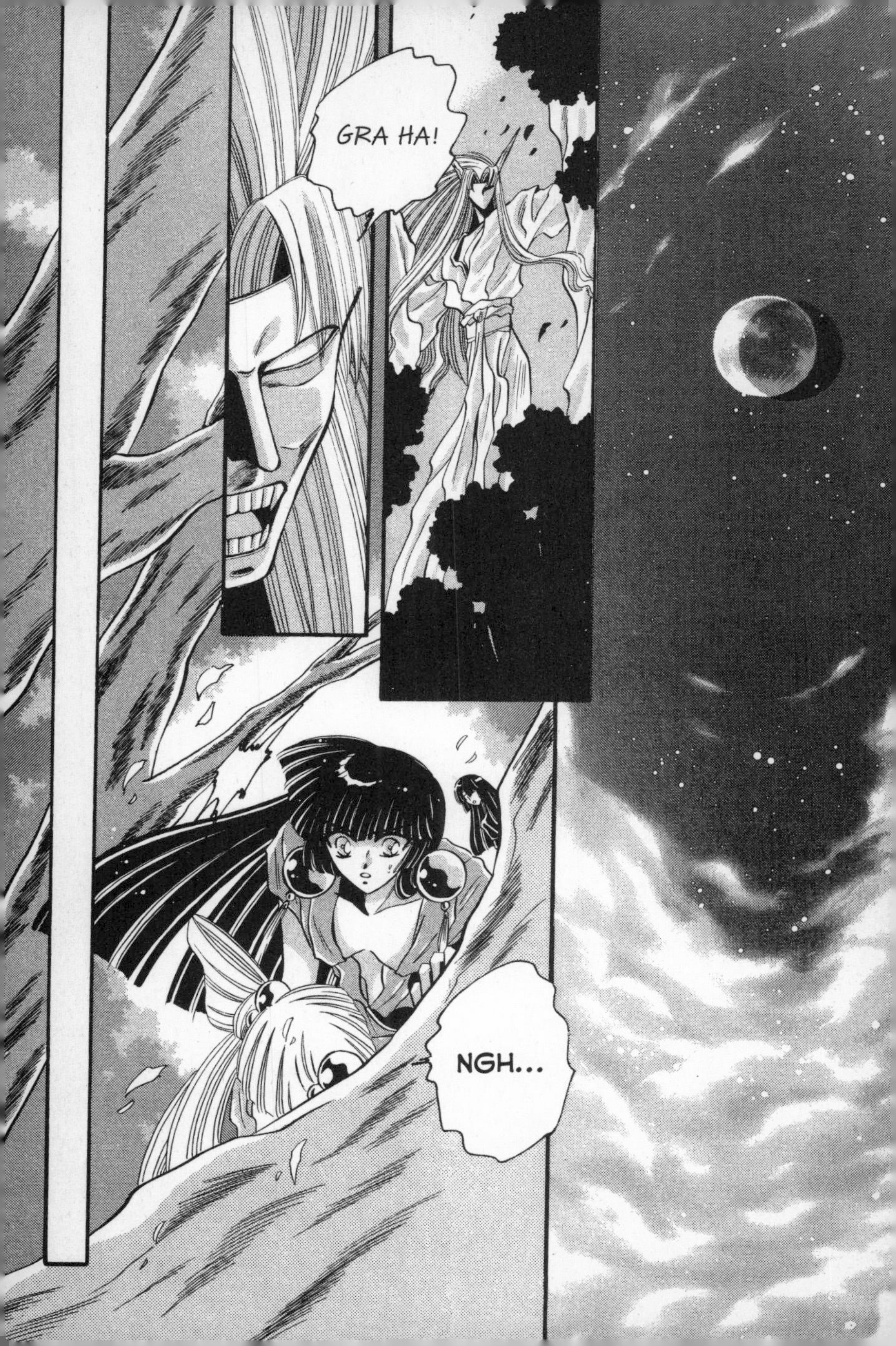
GRA HA!
NGH...

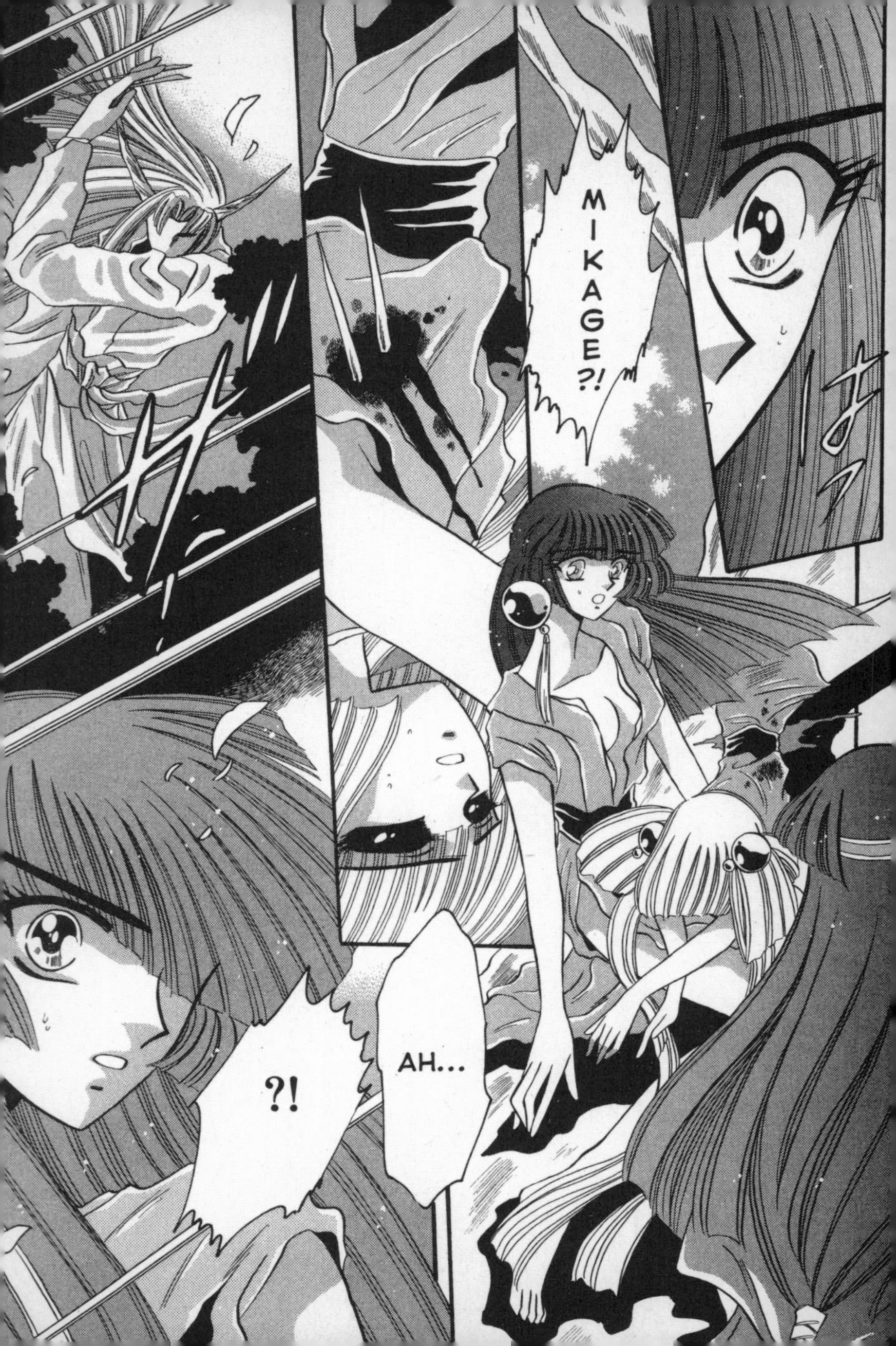
はっ
MIKAGE?!
AH...
?!

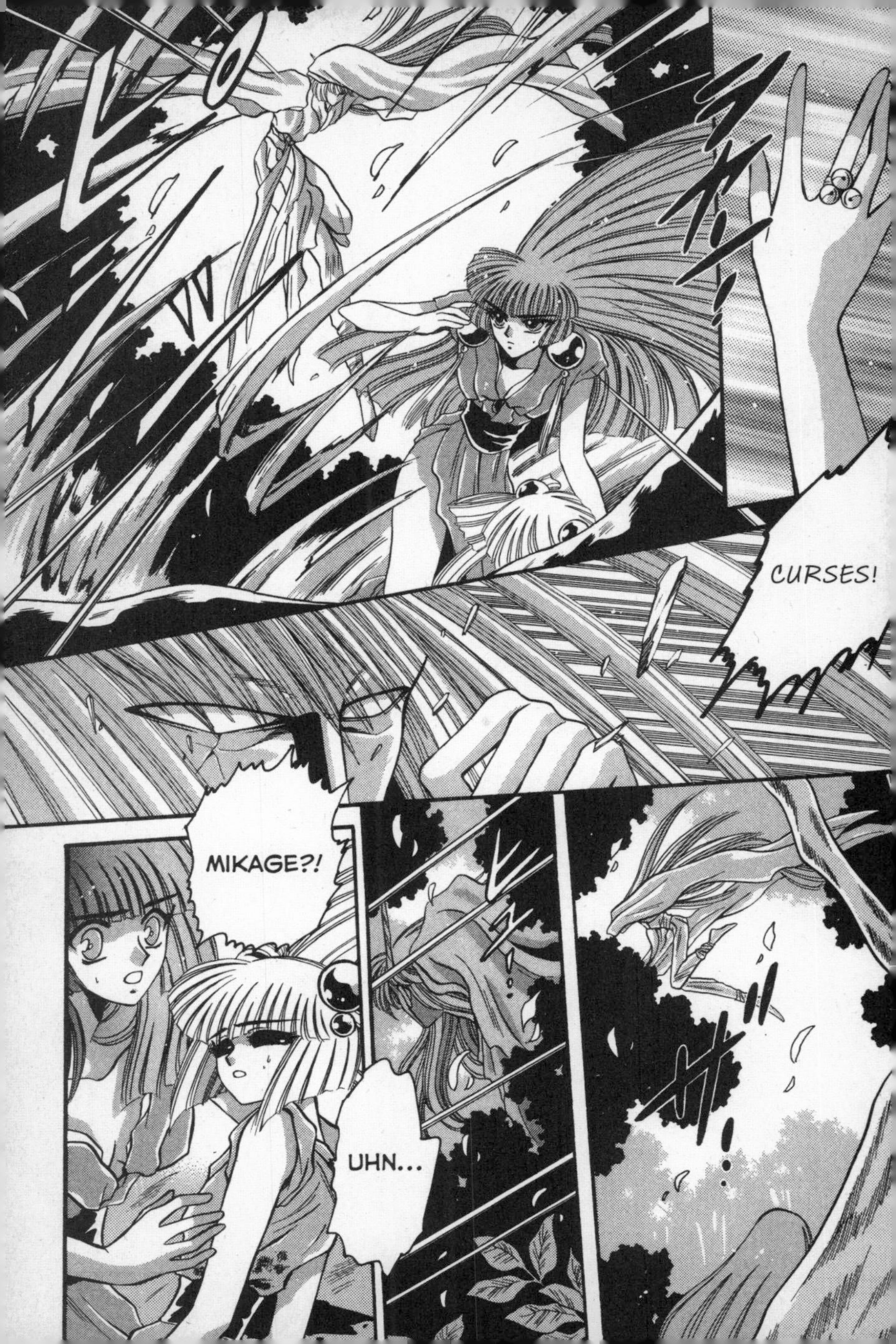
CURSES!
MIKAGE?!
UHN...

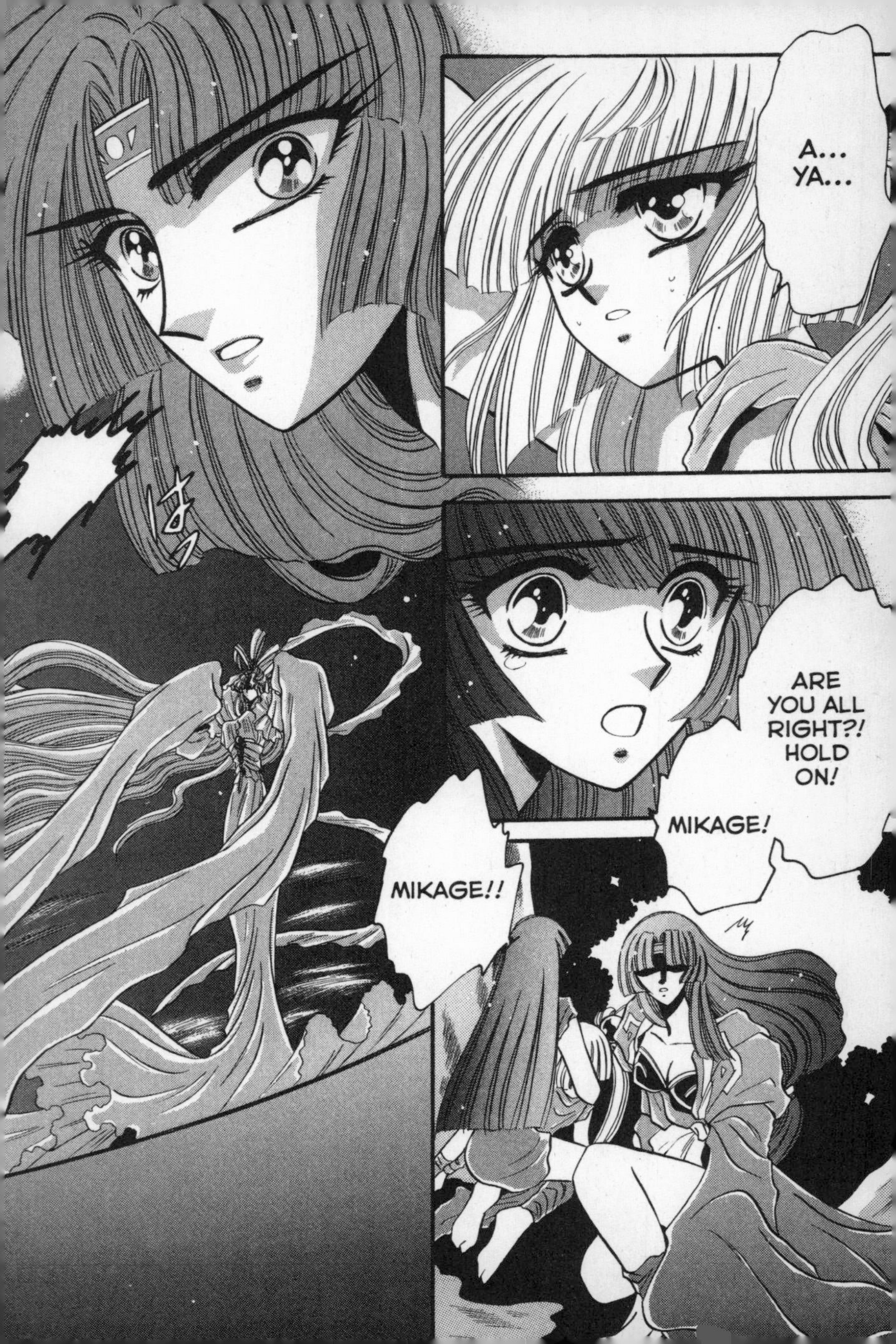

A... YA...
ARE YOU ALL RIGHT?! HOLD ON!
MIKAGE!
MIKAGE!!
はっ

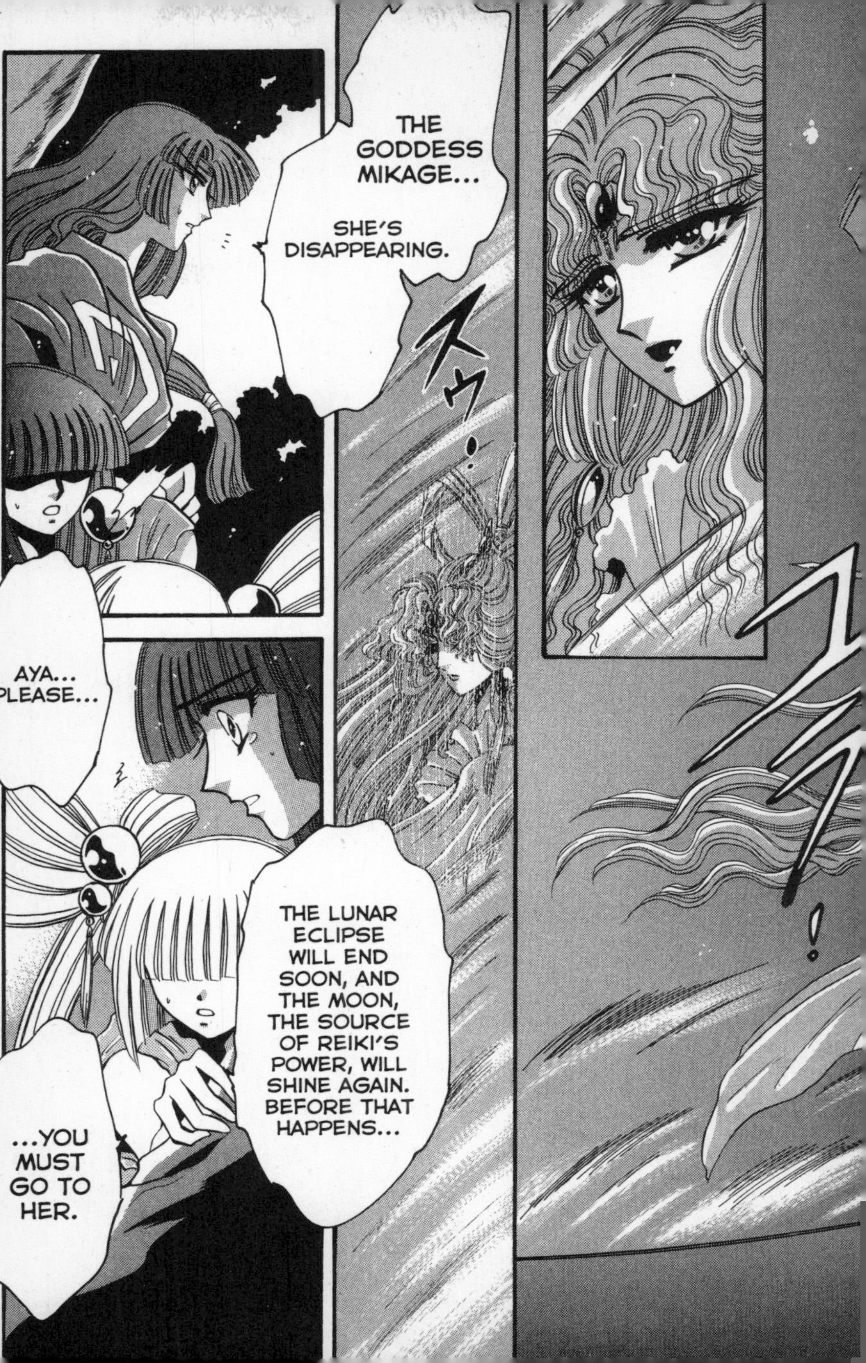
THE GODDESS MIKAGE...
SHE'S DISAPPEARING.
AYA... PLEASE...
THE LUNAR ECLIPSE WILL END SOON, AND THE MOON, THE SOURCE OF REIKI'S POWER, WILL SHINE AGAIN. BEFORE THAT HAPPENS...
...YOU MUST GO TO HER.

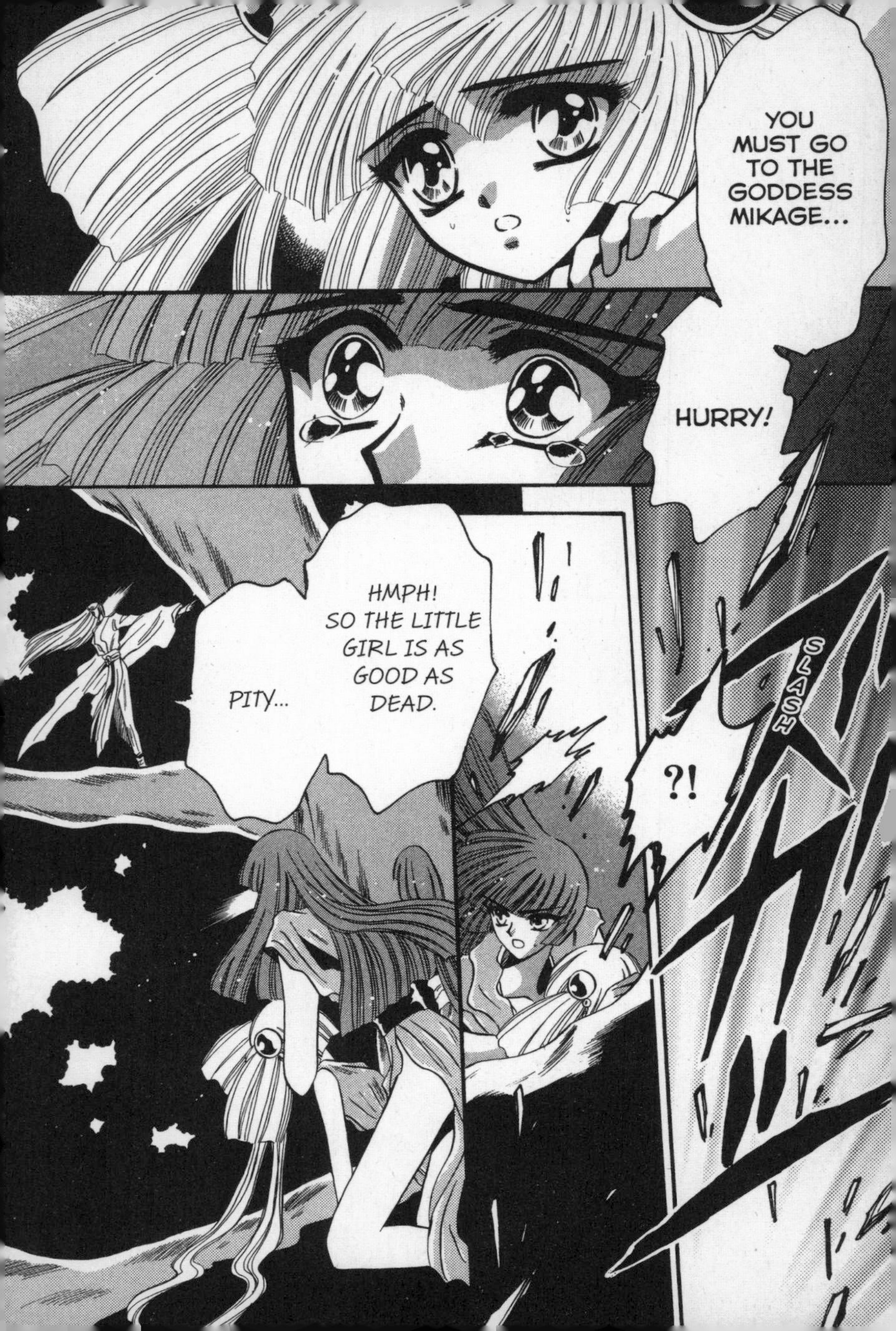
YOU MUST GO TO THE GODDESS MIKAGE...
HURRY!
SLASH
?!
HMPH! SO THE LITTLE GIRL IS AS GOOD AS DEAD.
PITY...

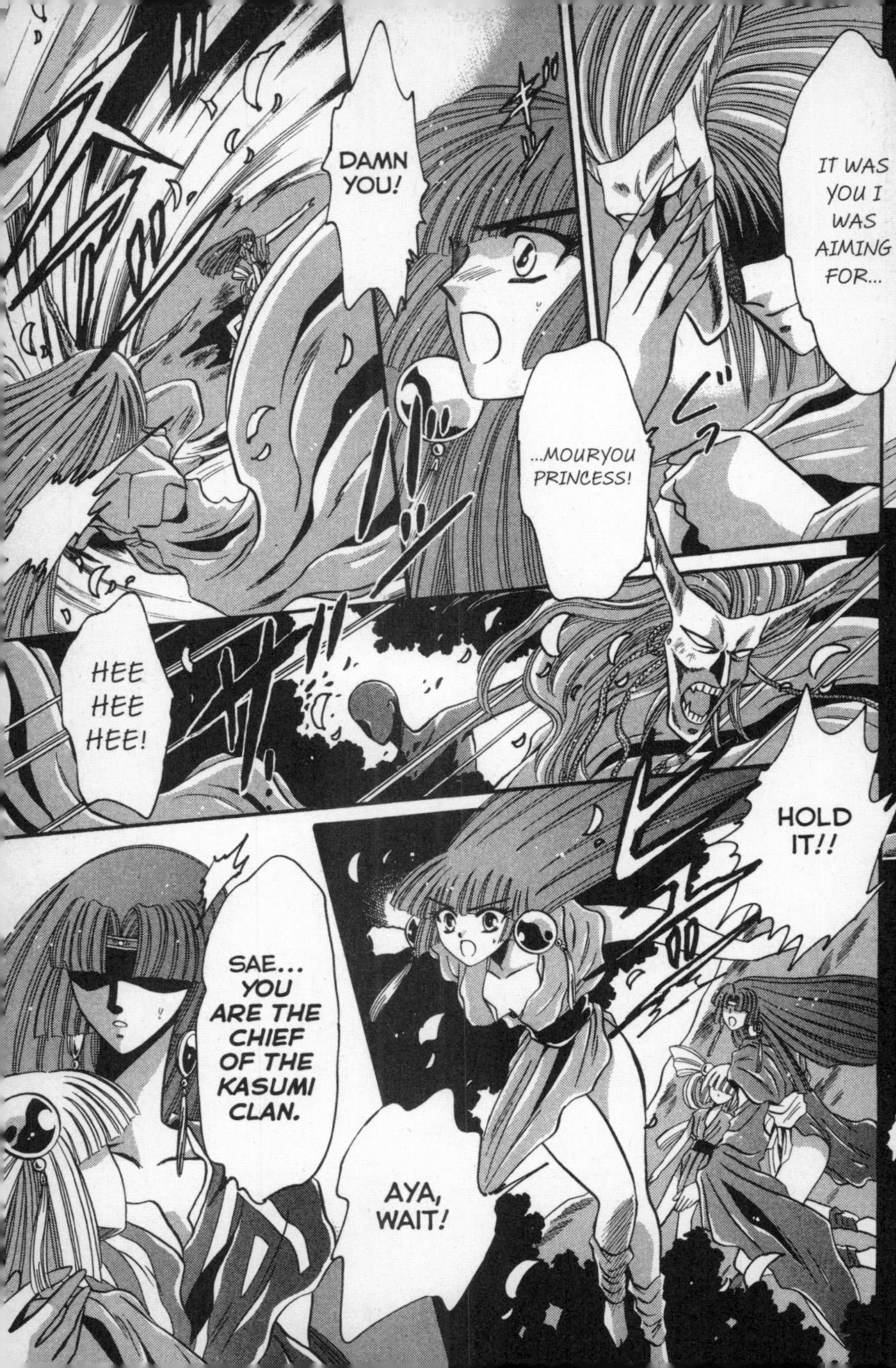
IT WAS YOU I WAS AIMING FOR...
DAMN YOU!
...MOURYOU PRINCESS!
HEE HEE HEE!
HOLD IT!!
AYA, WAIT!
SAE... YOU ARE THE CHIEF OF THE KASUMI CLAN.

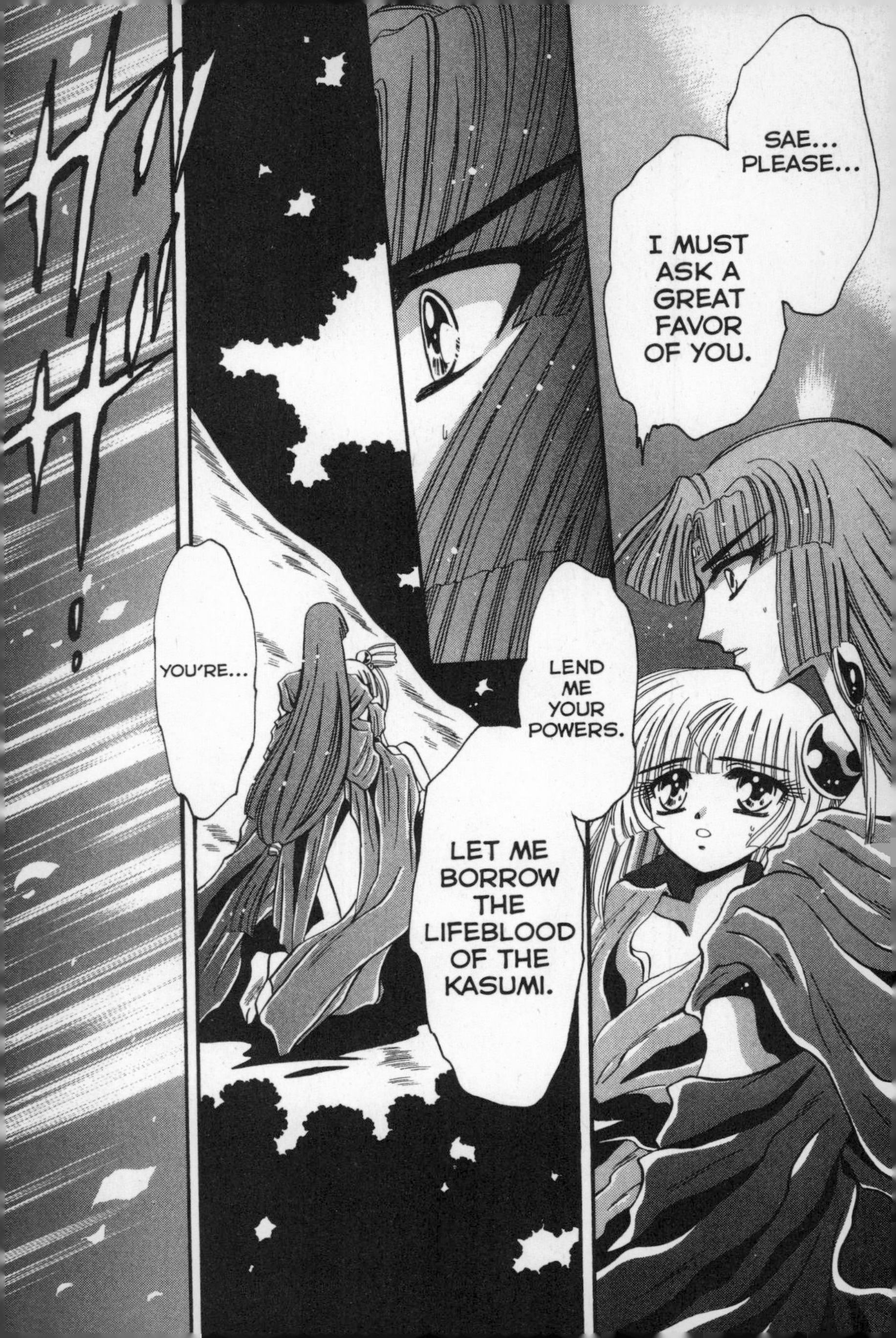
SAE... PLEASE...
I MUST ASK A GREAT FAVOR OF YOU.
LEND ME YOUR POWERS.
LET ME BORROW THE LIFEBLOOD OF THE KASUMI.
YOU'RE...

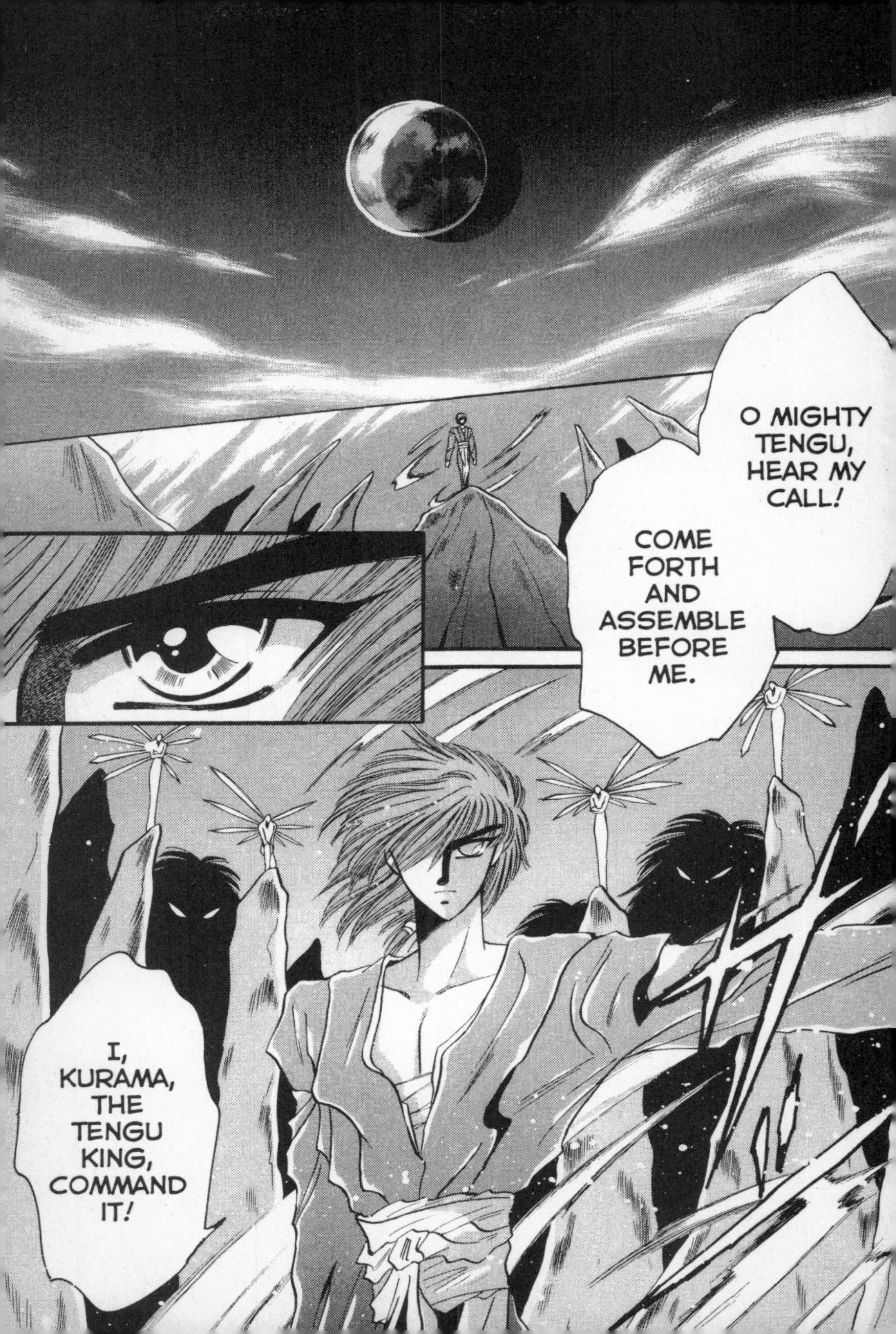
O MIGHTY TENGU, HEAR MY CALL!
COME FORTH AND ASSEMBLE BEFORE ME.
I, KURAMA, THE TENGU KING, COMMAND IT!

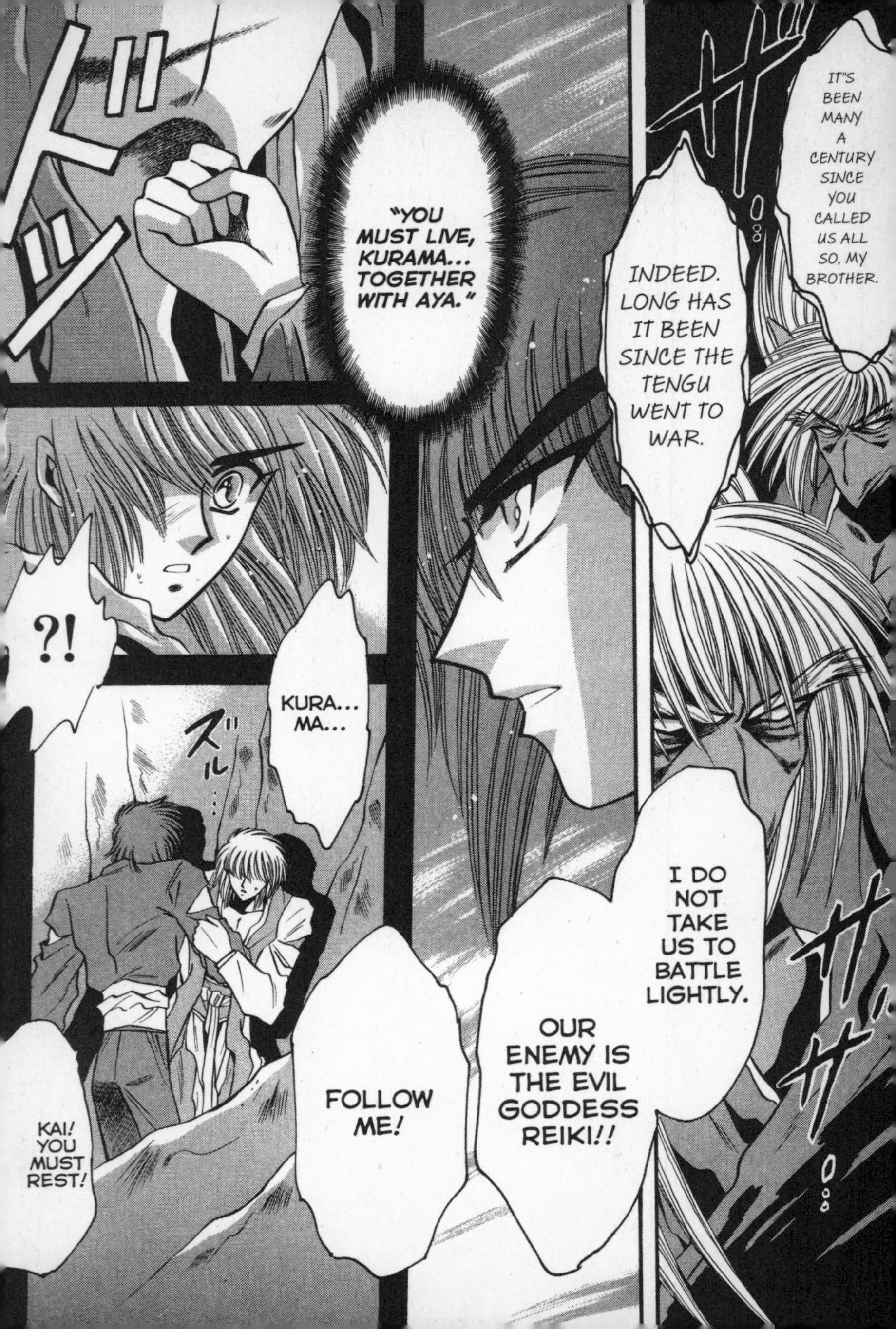
IT'S BEEN MANY A CENTURY SINCE YOU CALLED US ALL SO, MY BROTHER.
INDEED. LONG HAS IT BEEN SINCE THE TENGU WENT TO WAR.
I DO NOT TAKE US TO BATTLE LIGHTLY.
OUR ENEMY IS THE EVIL GODDESS REIKI!!
FOLLOW ME!
"YOU MUST LIVE, KURAMA... TOGETHER WITH AYA."
?!
KURA... MA...
KAI! YOU MUST REST!

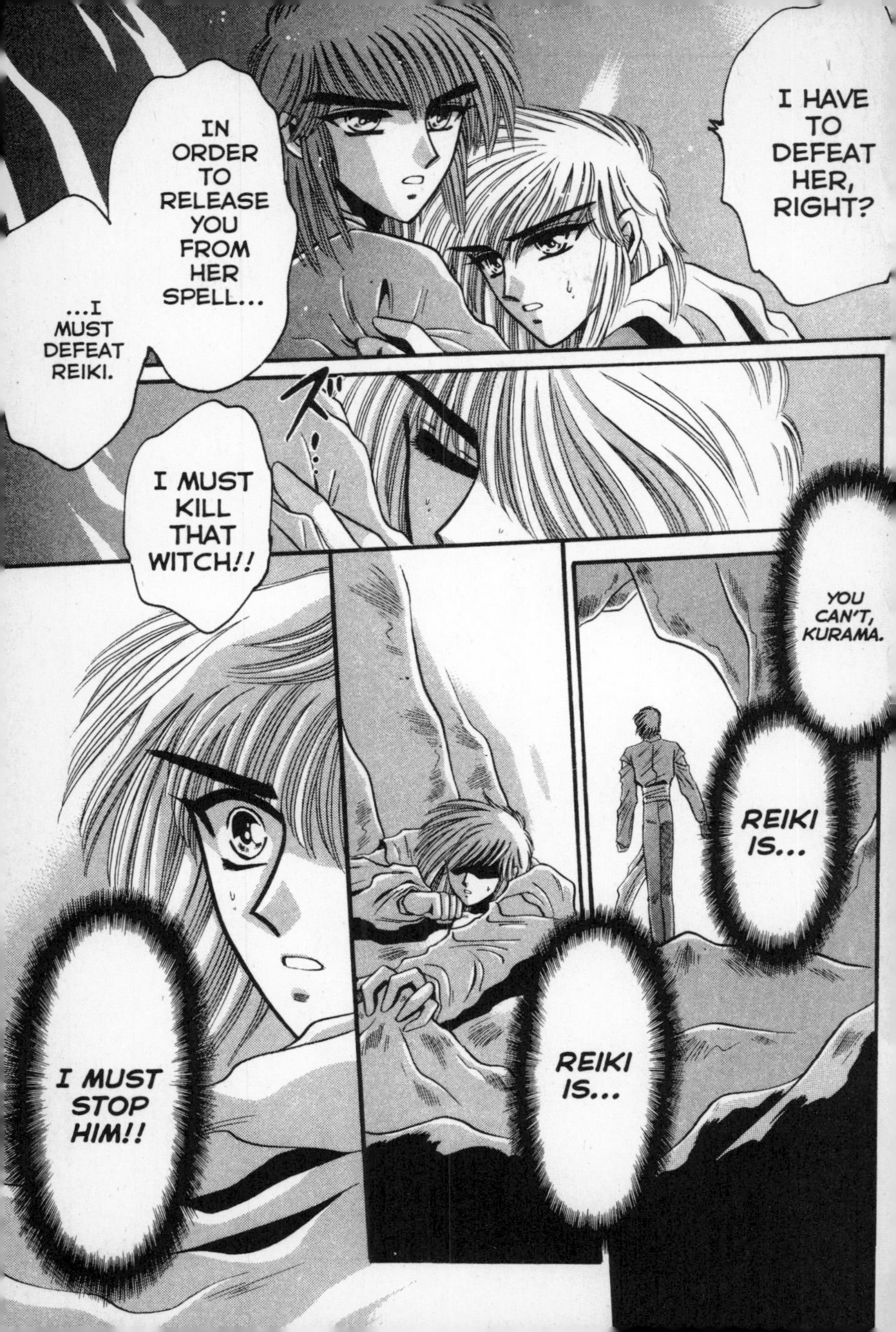
I HAVE TO DEFEAT HER, RIGHT?
IN ORDER TO RELEASE YOU FROM HER SPELL...
...I MUST DEFEAT REIKI.
I MUST KILL THAT WITCH!!
YOU CAN'T, KURAMA.
REIKI IS...
REIKI IS...
I MUST STOP HIM!!

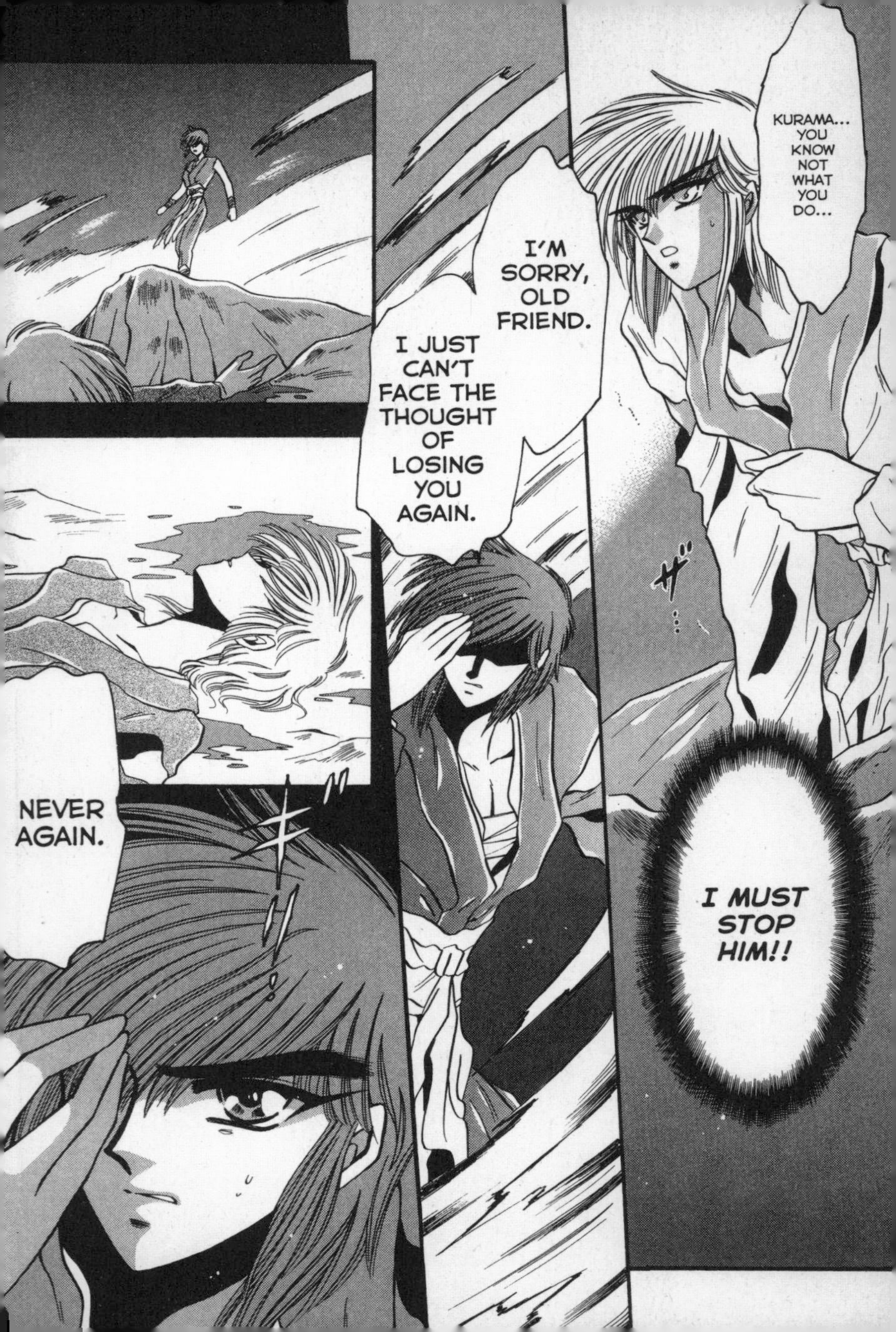
KURAMA... YOU KNOW NOT WHAT YOU DO...
I MUST STOP HIM!!
I'M SORRY, OLD FRIEND.
I JUST CAN'T FACE THE THOUGHT OF LOSING YOU AGAIN.
NEVER AGAIN.

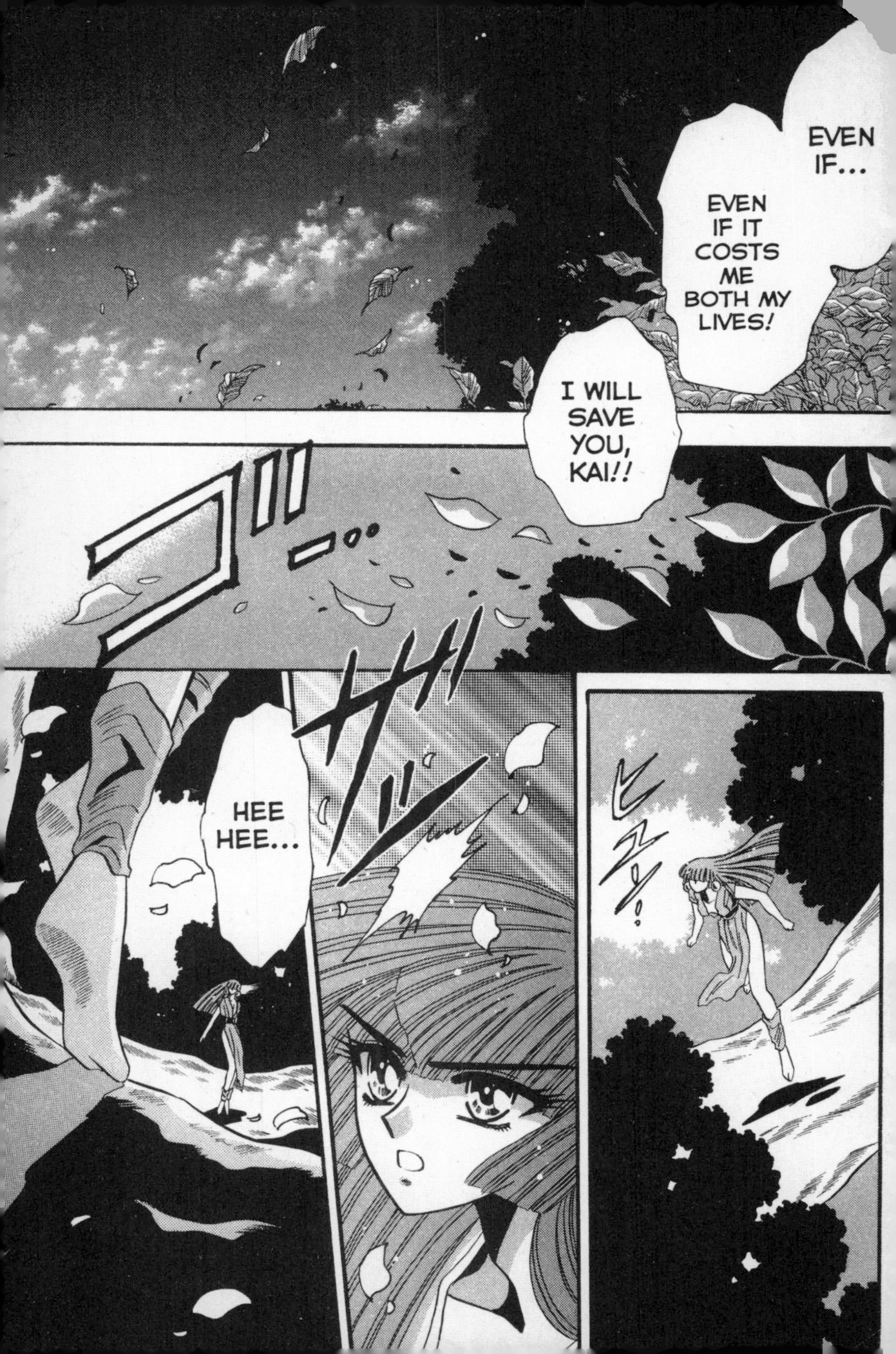
EVEN IF...
EVEN IF IT COSTS ME BOTH MY LIVES!
I WILL SAVE YOU, KAI!!
HEE HEE...

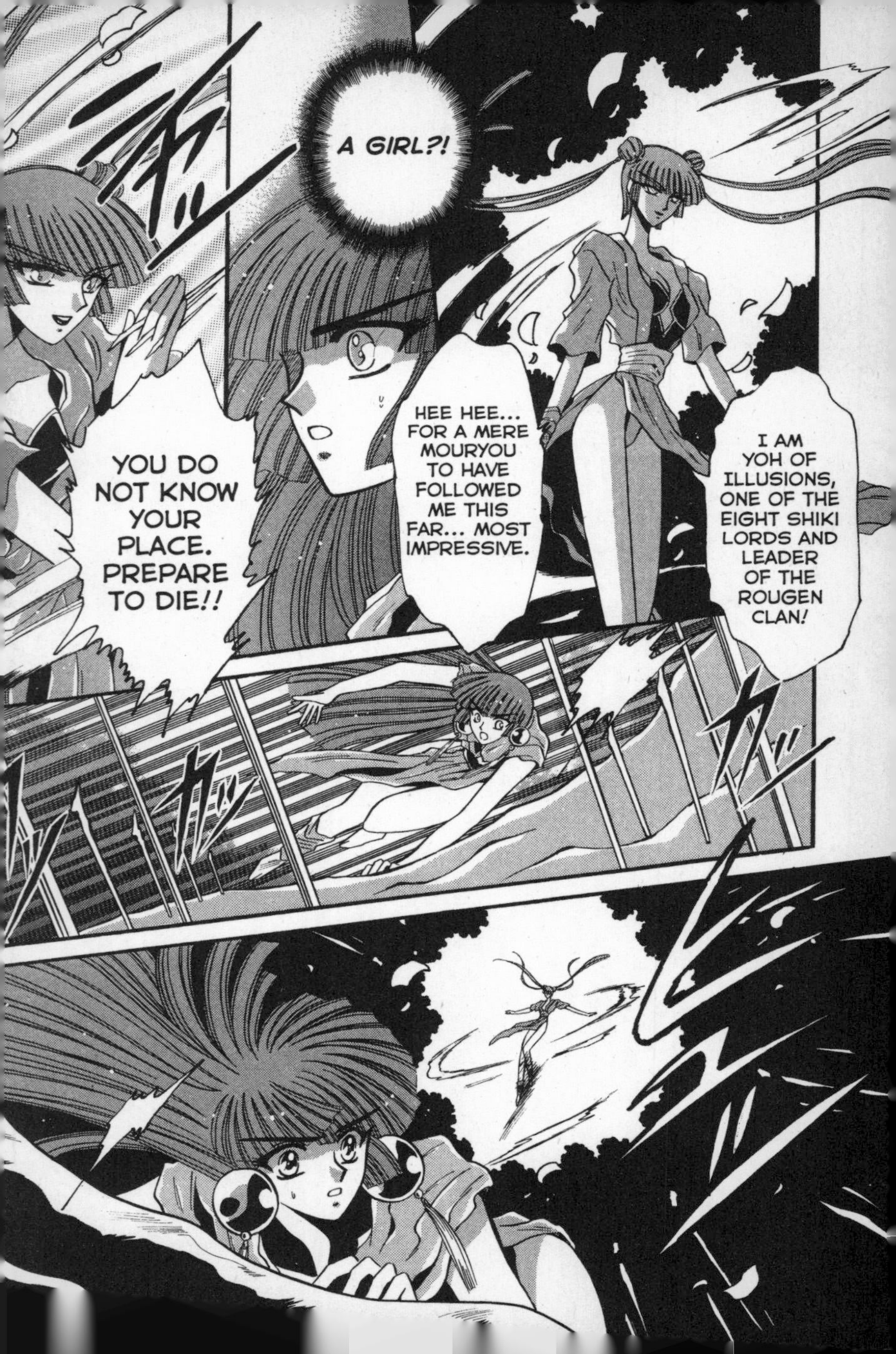
A GIRL?!
I AM YOH OF ILLUSIONS, ONE OF THE EIGHT SHIKI LORDS AND LEADER OF THE ROUGEN CLAN!
HEE HEE... FOR A MERE MOURYOU TO HAVE FOLLOWED ME THIS FAR... MOST IMPRESSIVE.
YOU DO NOT KNOW YOUR PLACE. PREPARE TO DIE!!

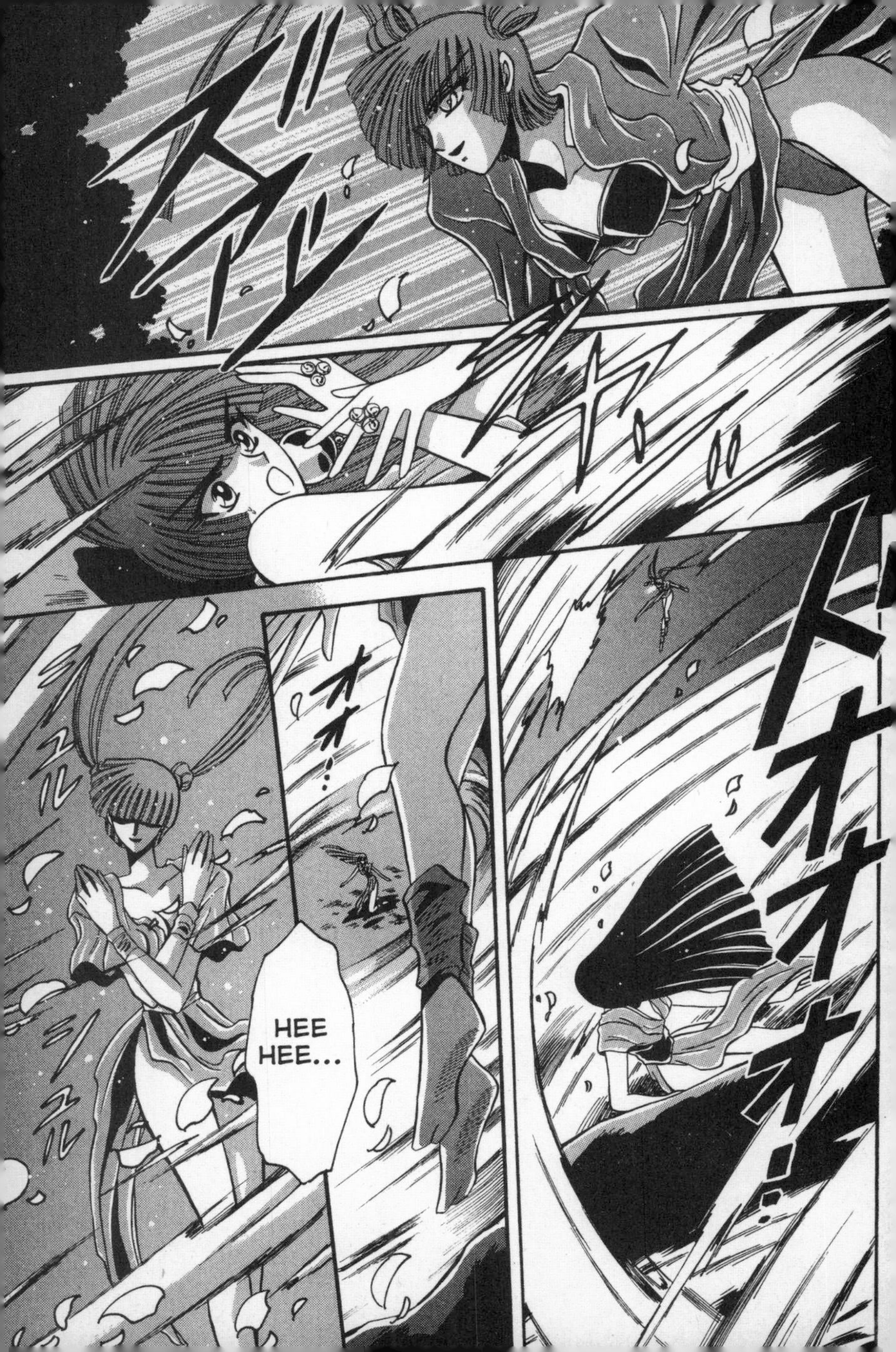
HEE
HEE...

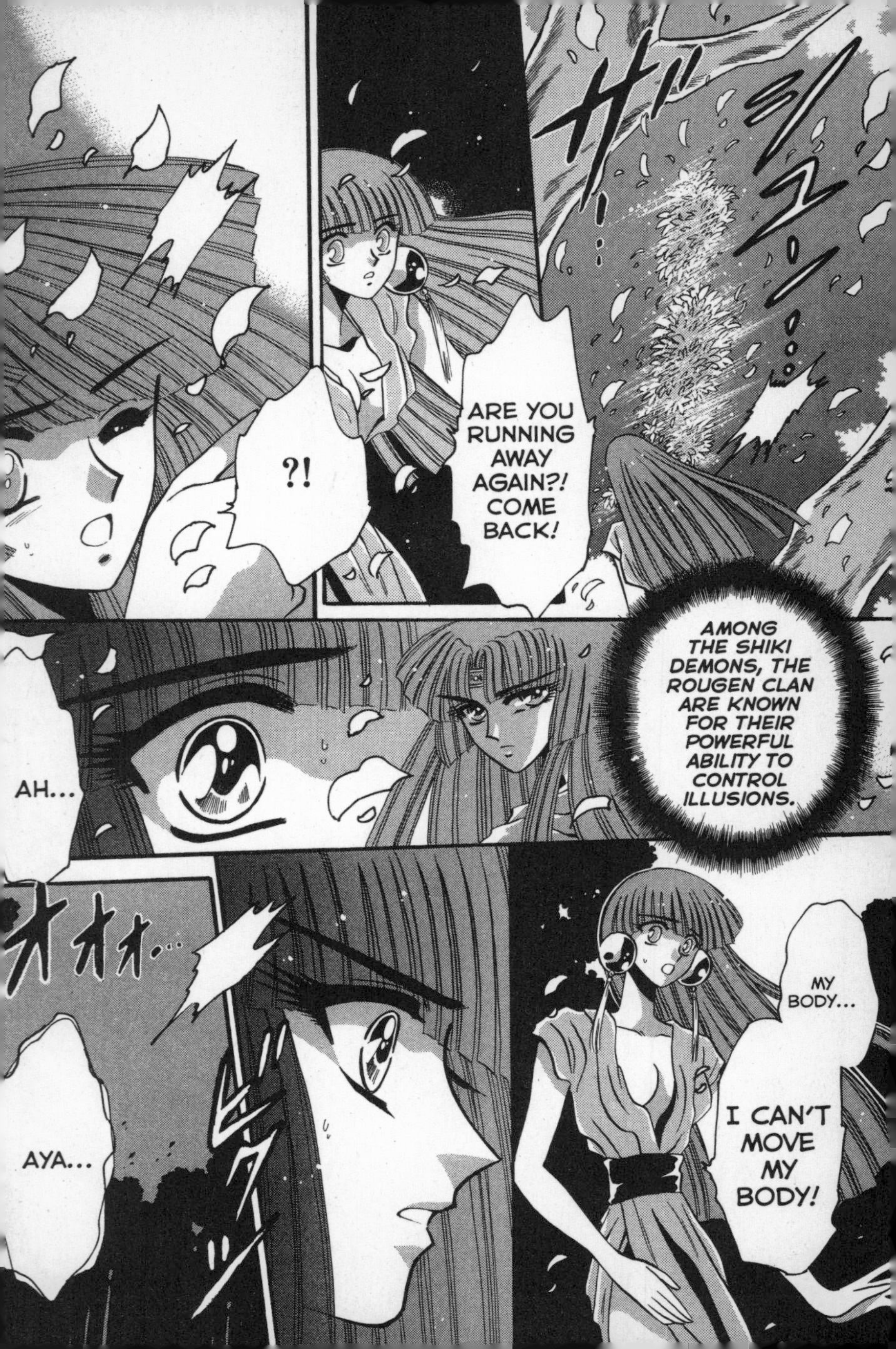
ARE YOU RUNNING AWAY AGAIN?! COME BACK!
?!
AMONG THE SHIKI DEMONS, THE ROUGEN CLAN ARE KNOWN FOR THEIR POWERFUL ABILITY TO CONTROL ILLUSIONS.
AH...
MY BODY...
I CAN'T MOVE MY BODY!
オオオ...
AYA...

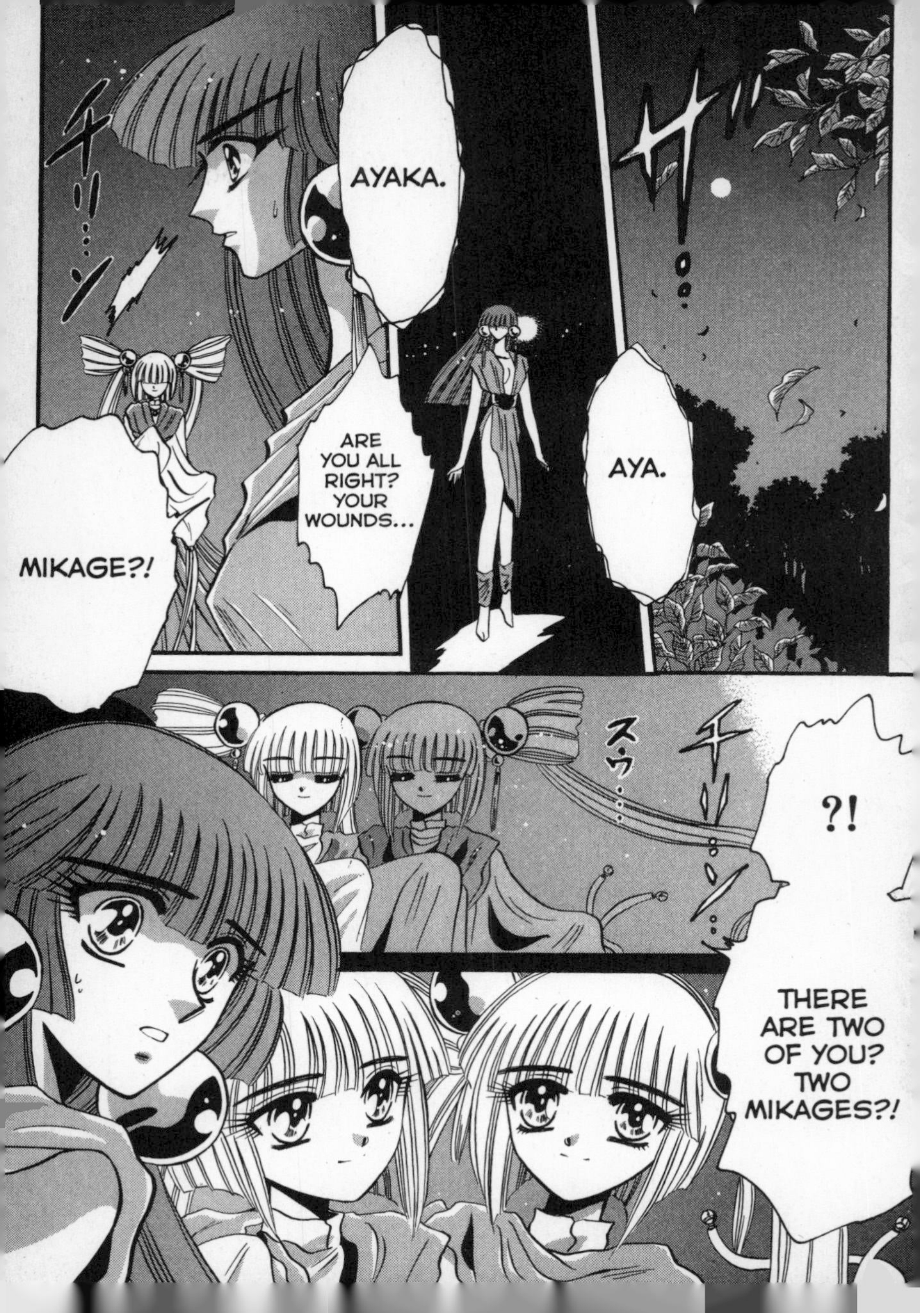
AYA.
AYAKA.
ARE YOU ALL RIGHT? YOUR WOUNDS...
MIKAGE?!
?!
THERE ARE TWO OF YOU? TWO MIKAGES?!

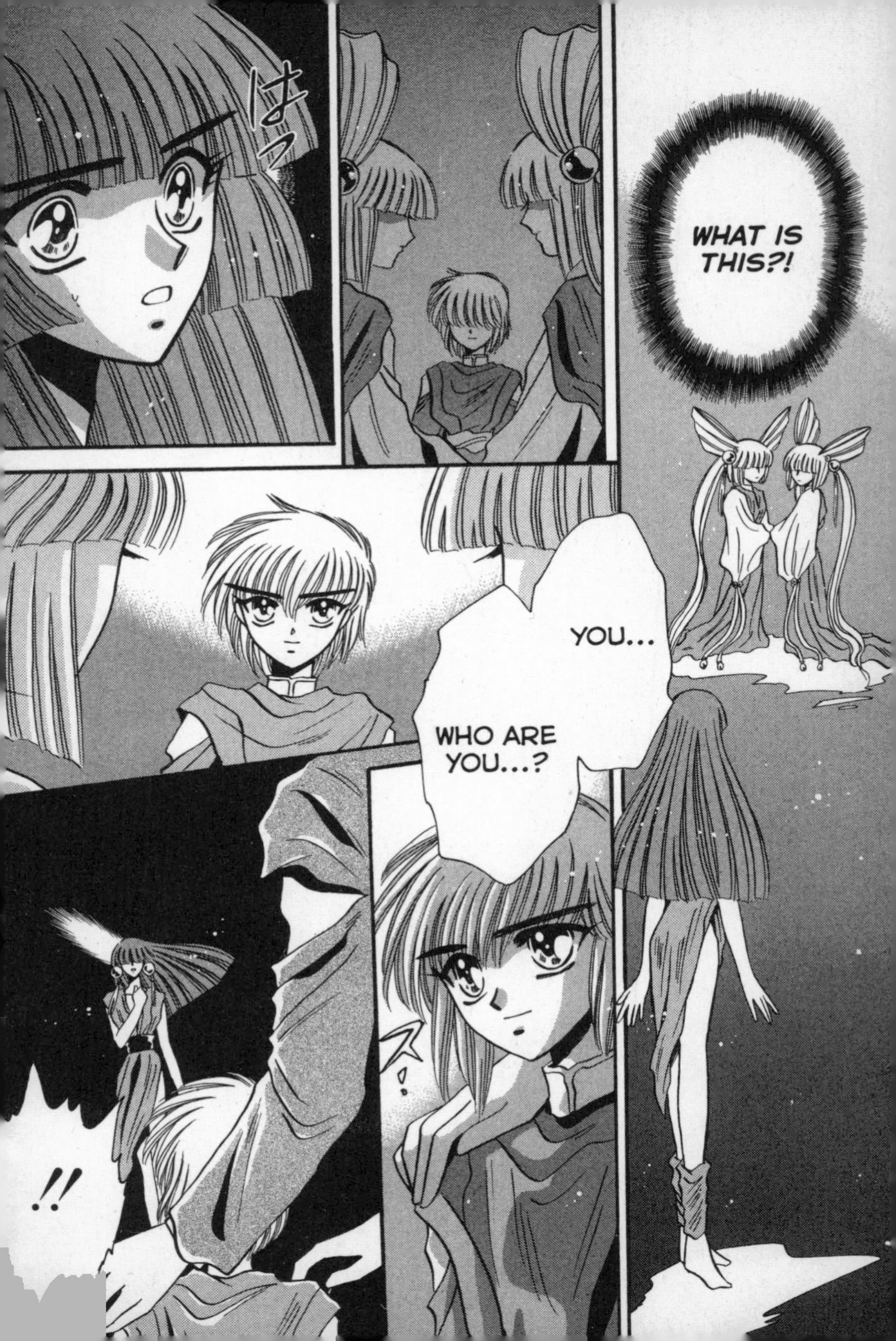
WHAT IS THIS?!
はっ
YOU...
WHO ARE YOU...?
!
!!

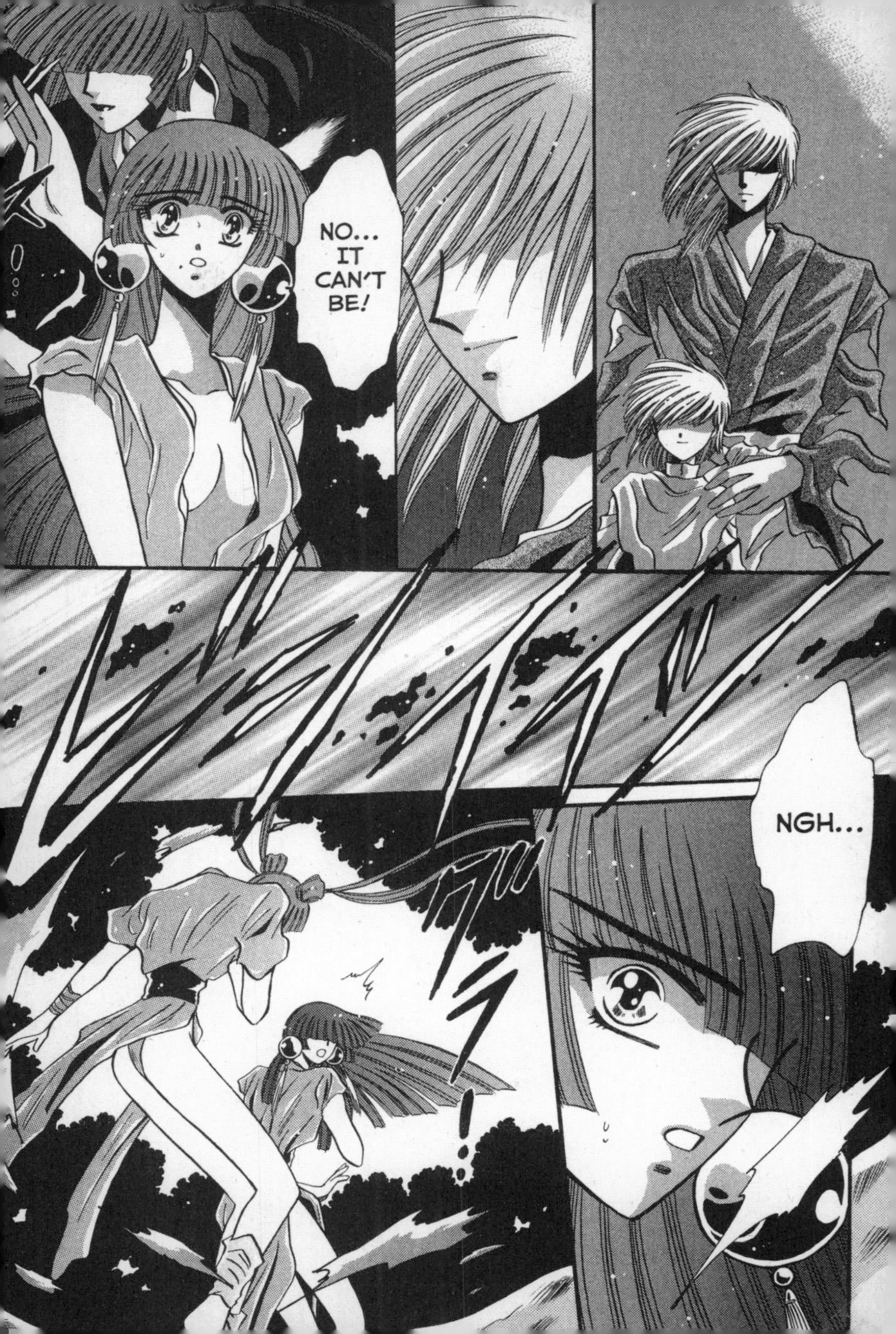
NO... IT CAN'T BE!
NGH...

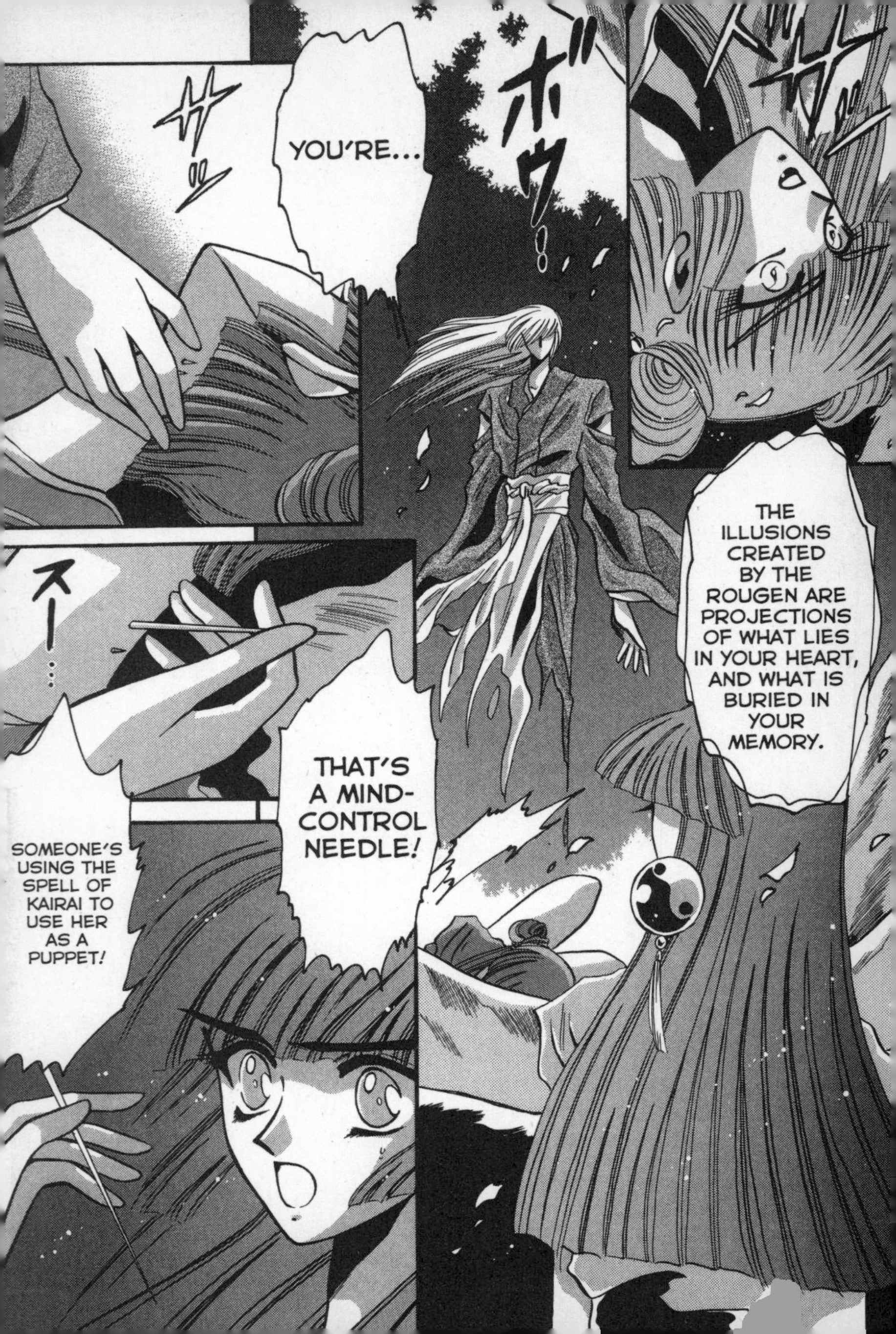
THE ILLUSIONS CREATED BY THE ROUGEN ARE PROJECTIONS OF WHAT LIES IN YOUR HEART, AND WHAT IS BURIED IN YOUR MEMORY.
ボウ!!
YOU'RE...
ザッ
スー…
THAT'S A MIND-CONTROL NEEDLE!
SOMEONE'S USING THE SPELL OF KAIRAI TO USE HER AS A PUPPET!

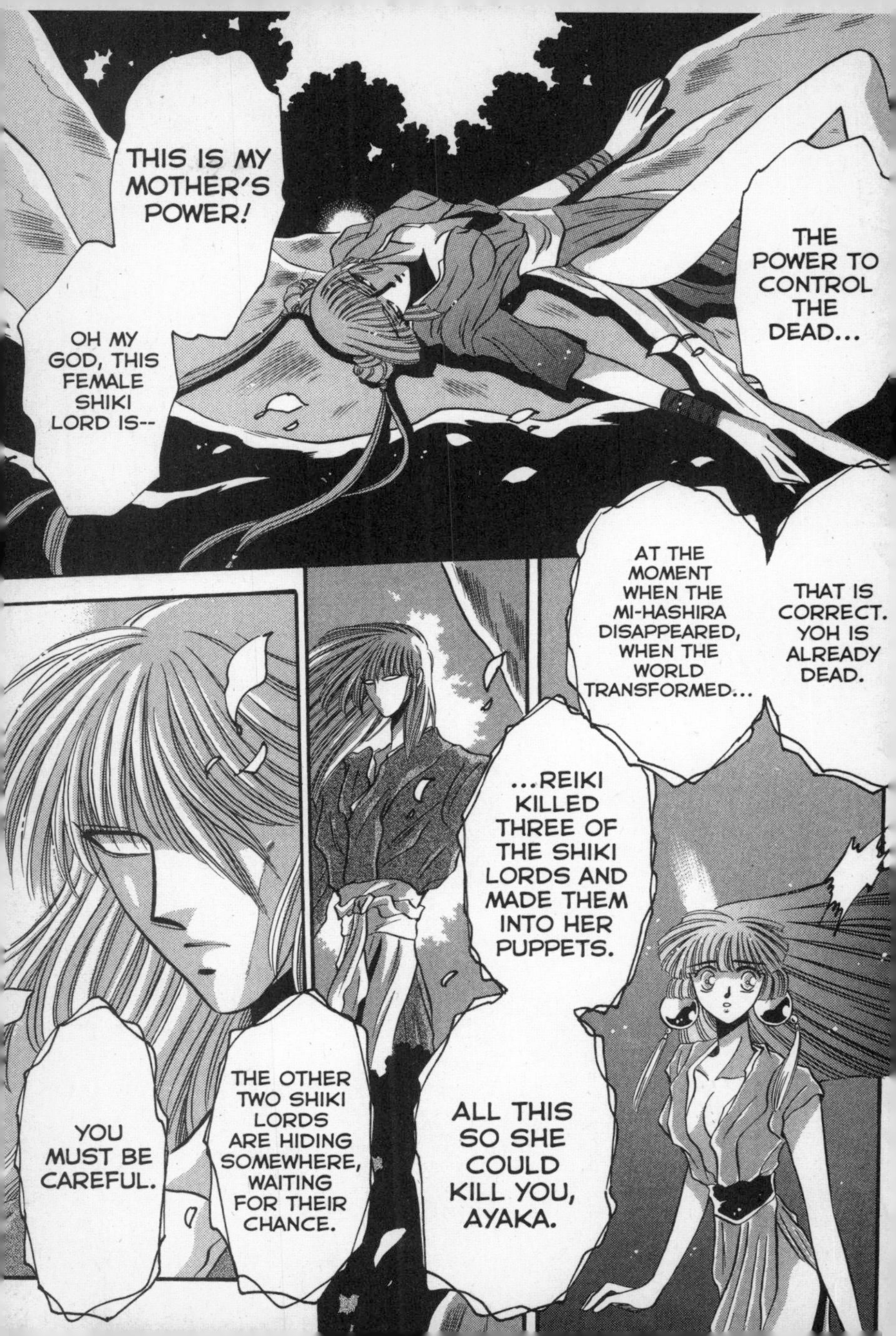
THIS IS MY MOTHER'S POWER!
THE POWER TO CONTROL THE DEAD...
OH MY GOD, THIS FEMALE SHIKI LORD IS--
THAT IS CORRECT. YOH IS ALREADY DEAD.
AT THE MOMENT WHEN THE MI-HASHIRA DISAPPEARED, WHEN THE WORLD TRANSFORMED...
...REIKI KILLED THREE OF THE SHIKI LORDS AND MADE THEM INTO HER PUPPETS.
ALL THIS SO SHE COULD KILL YOU, AYAKA.
THE OTHER TWO SHIKI LORDS ARE HIDING SOMEWHERE, WAITING FOR THEIR CHANCE.
YOU MUST BE CAREFUL.

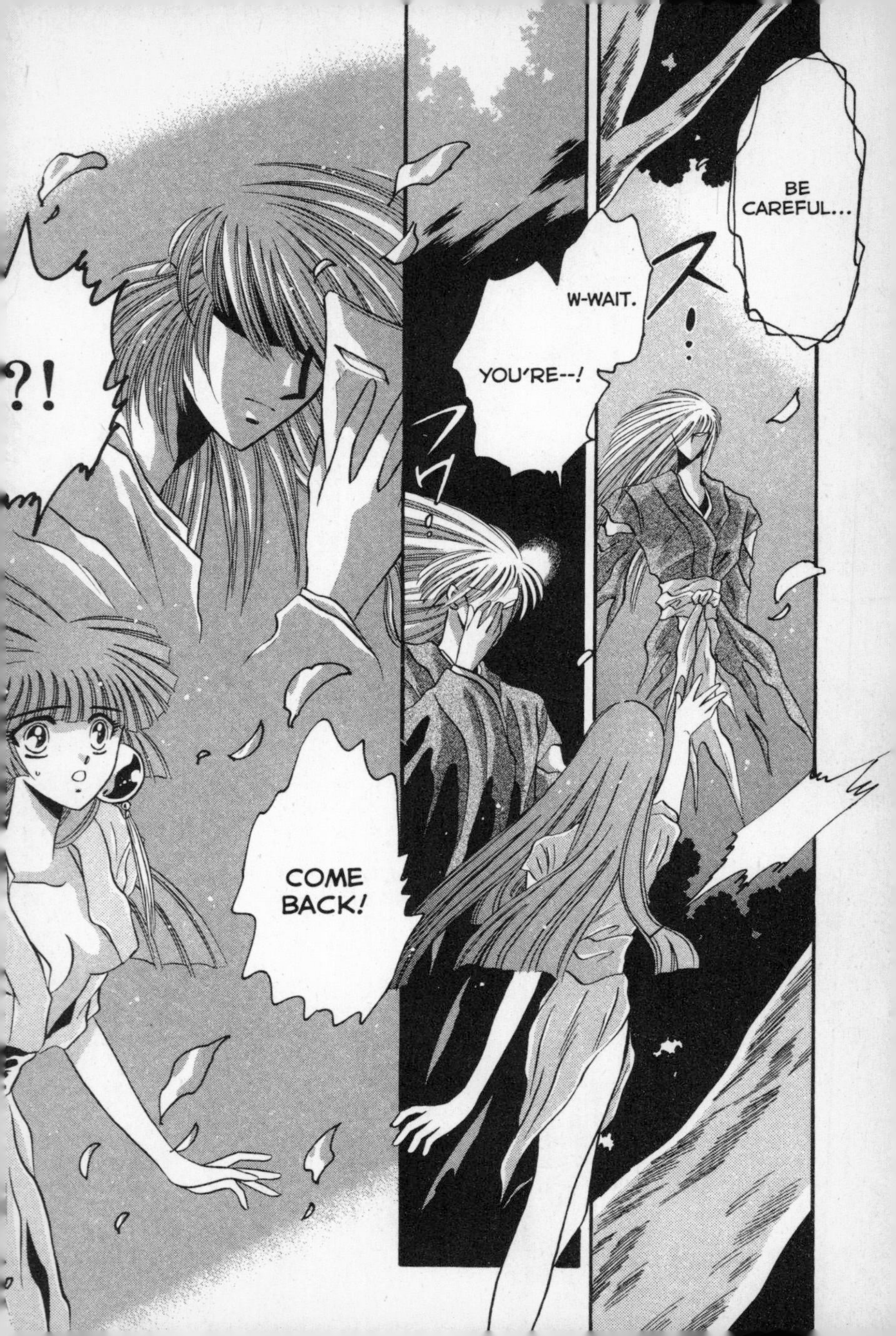
BE CAREFUL...
W-WAIT.
YOU'RE--!
?!
COME BACK!

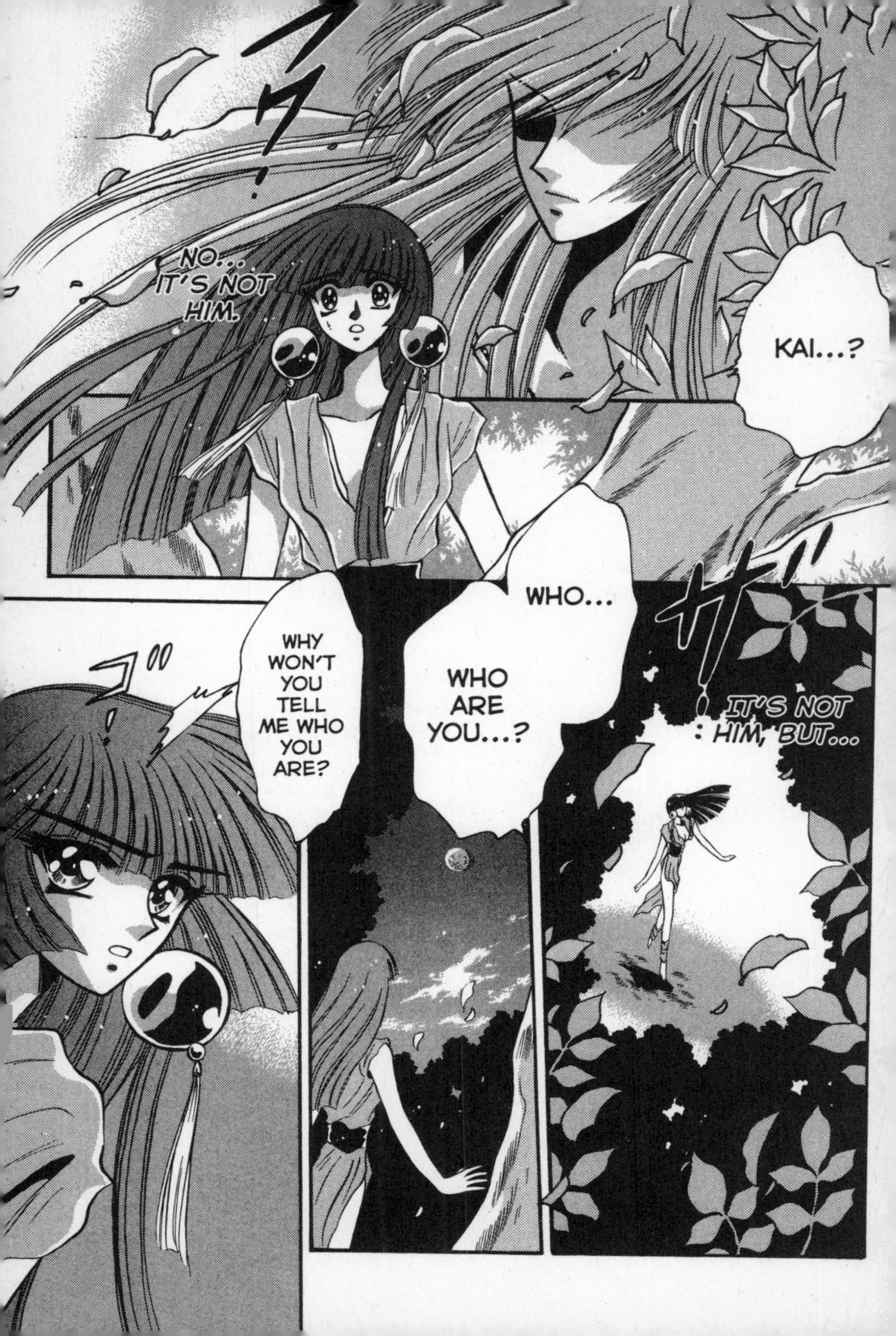
KAI...?
NO... IT'S NOT HIM.
WHO...
IT'S NOT HIM, BUT...
WHO ARE YOU...?
WHY WON'T YOU TELL ME WHO YOU ARE?

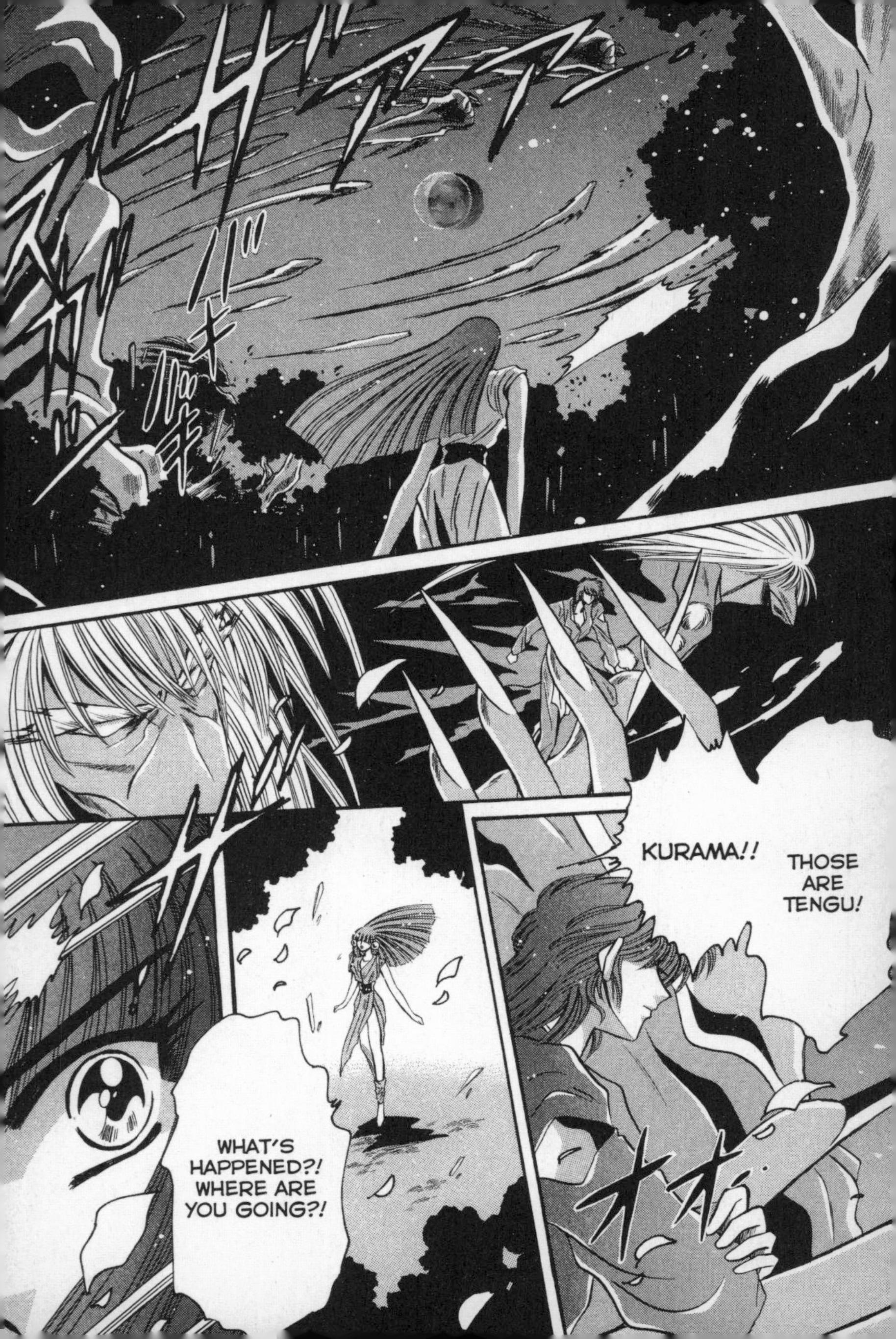
THOSE ARE TENGU!
KURAMA!!
WHAT'S HAPPENED?! WHERE ARE YOU GOING?!

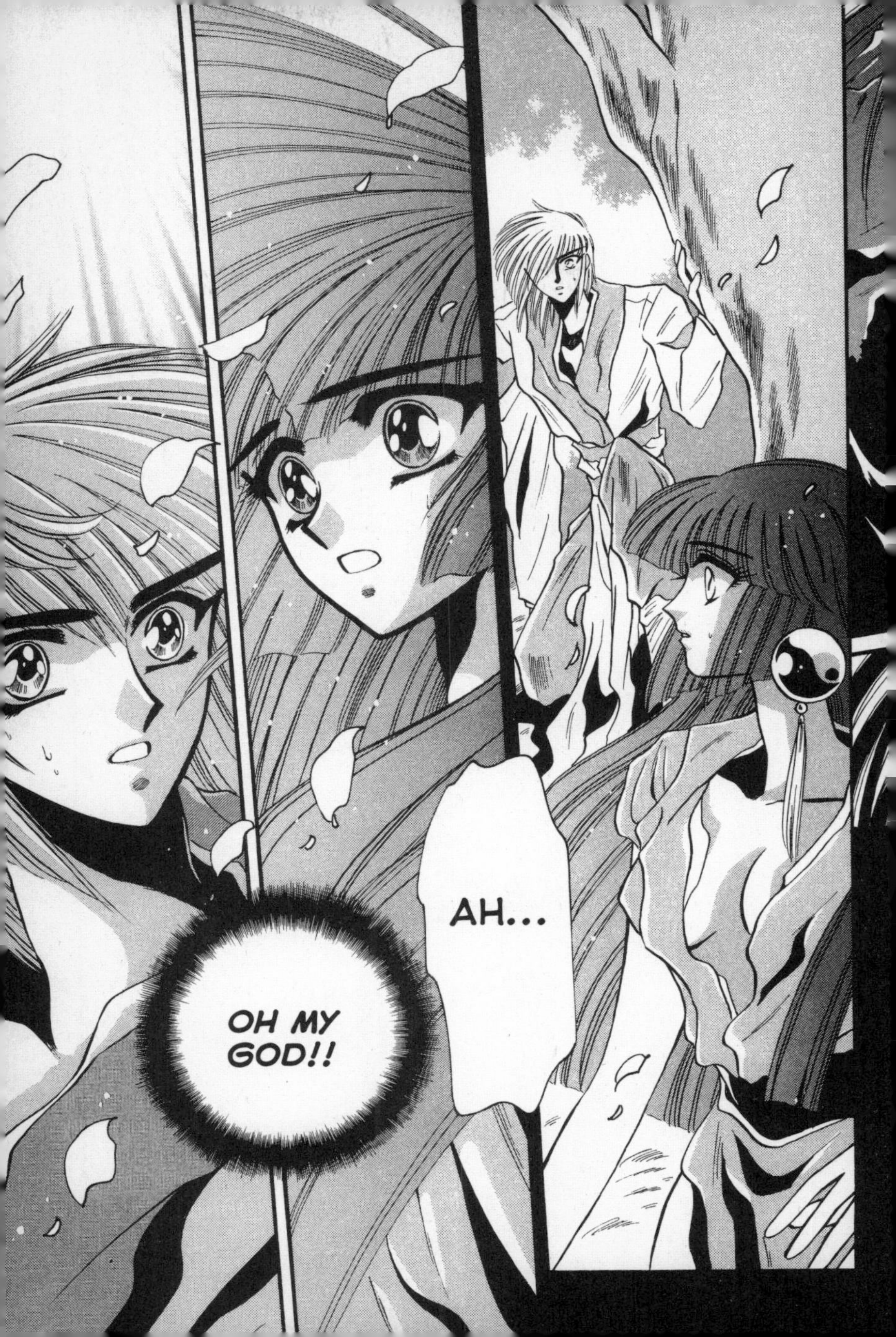
AH...
OH MY GOD!!

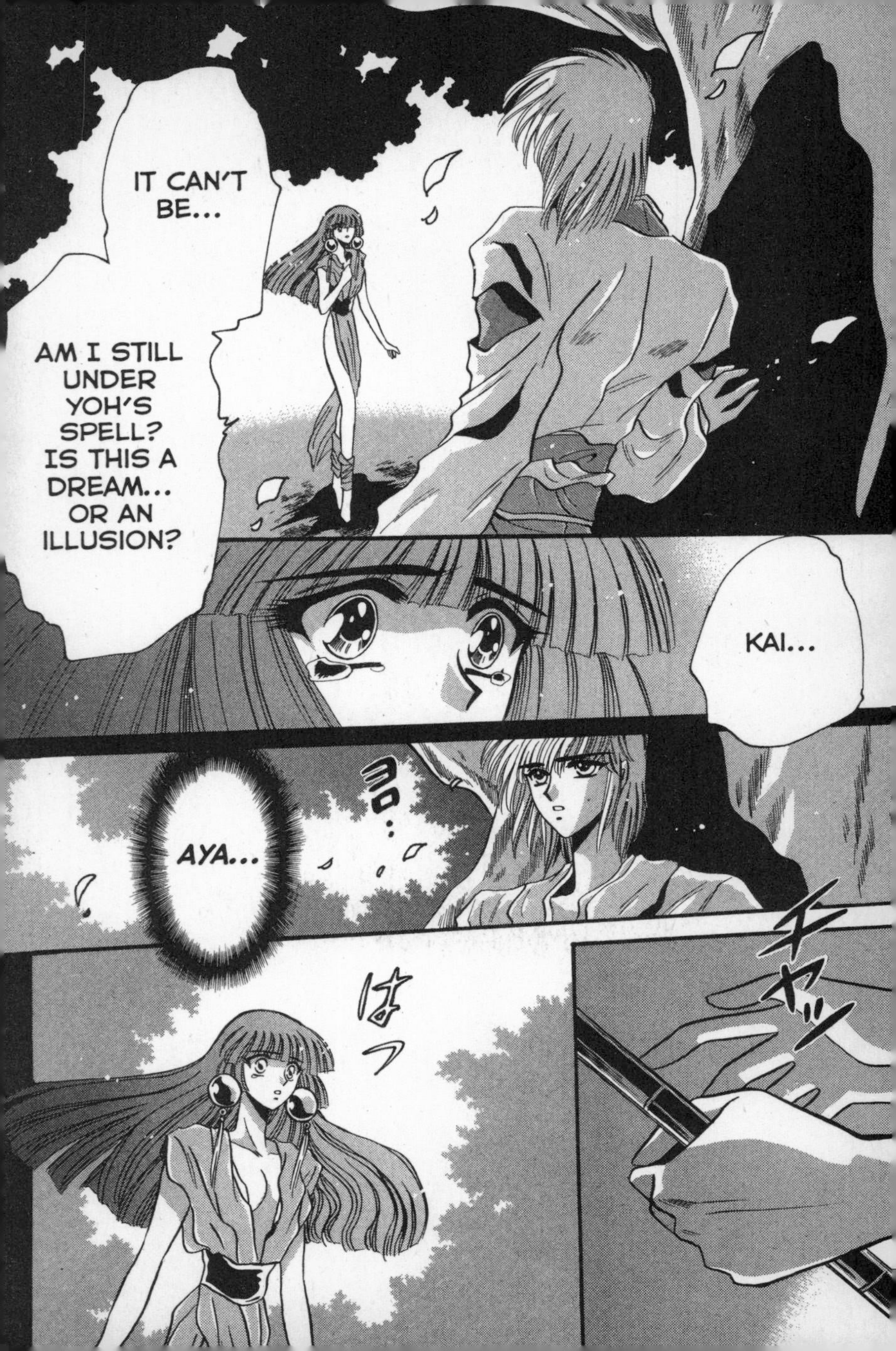
IT CAN'T BE...
AM I STILL UNDER YOH'S SPELL? IS THIS A DREAM... OR AN ILLUSION?
KAI...
ヨロ‥
AYA...
キャッ
はっ

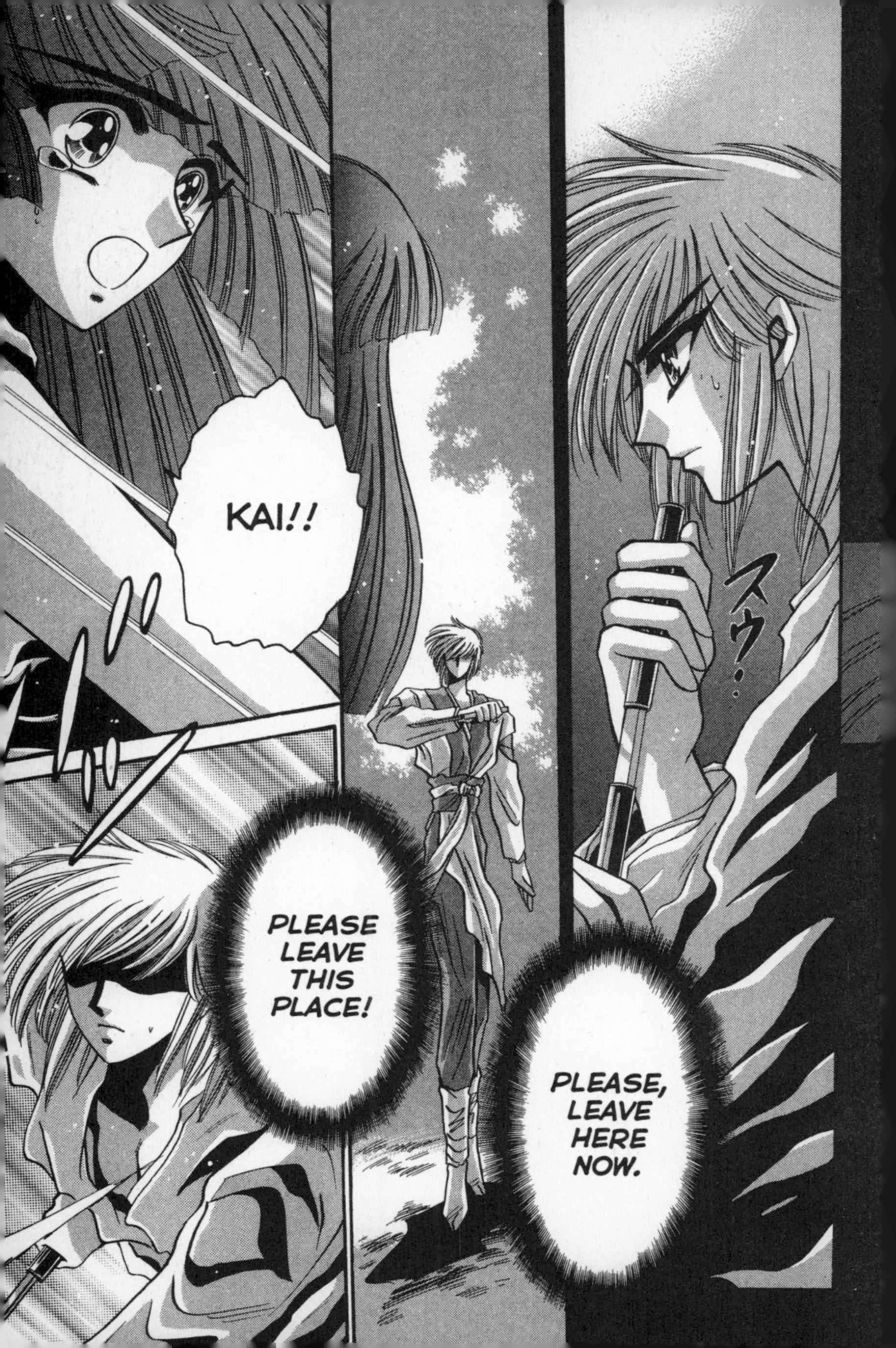
スウ・・
PLEASE, LEAVE HERE NOW.
PLEASE LEAVE THIS PLACE!
KAI!!

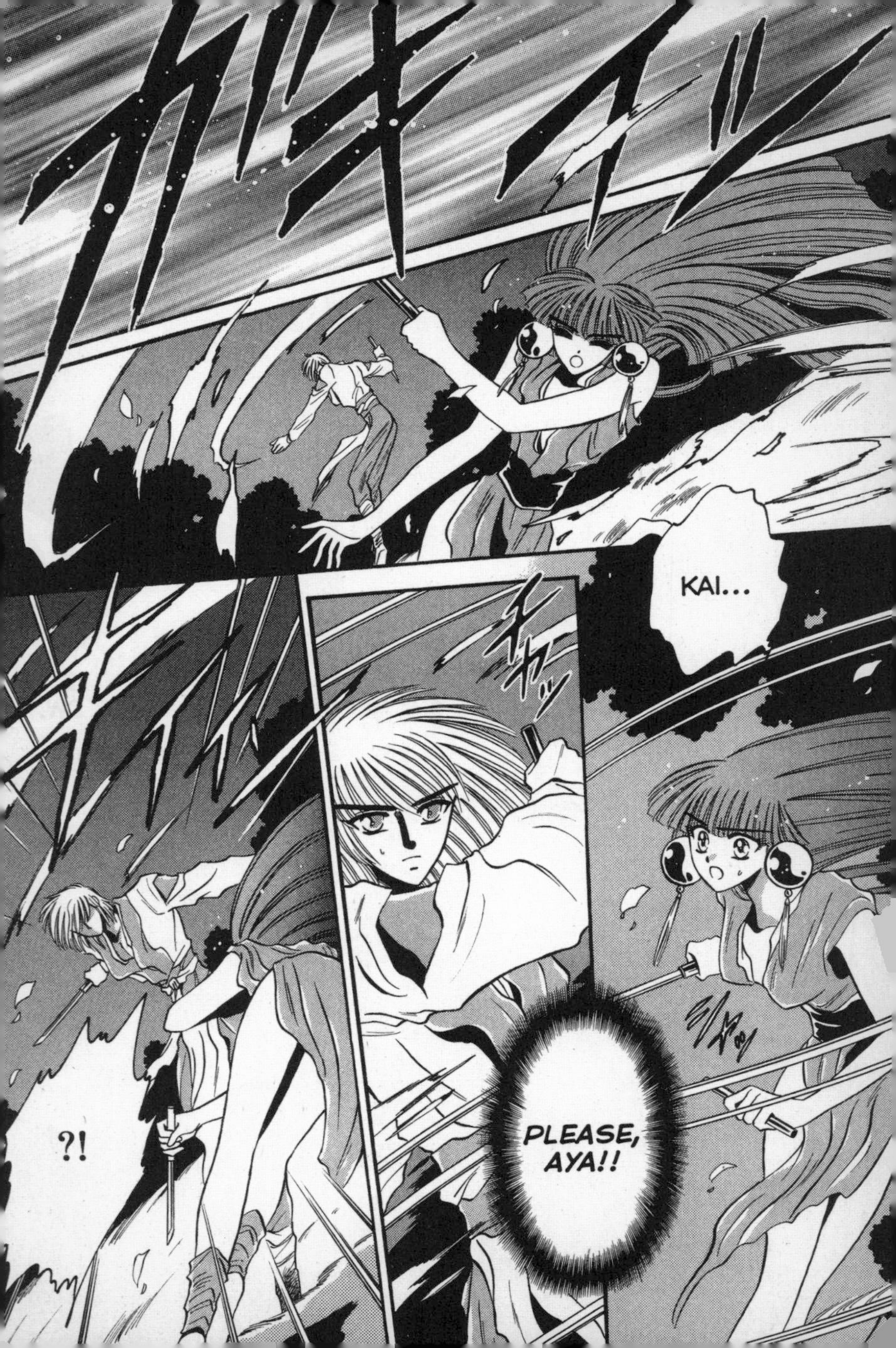
KAI...
PLEASE, AYA!!
?!

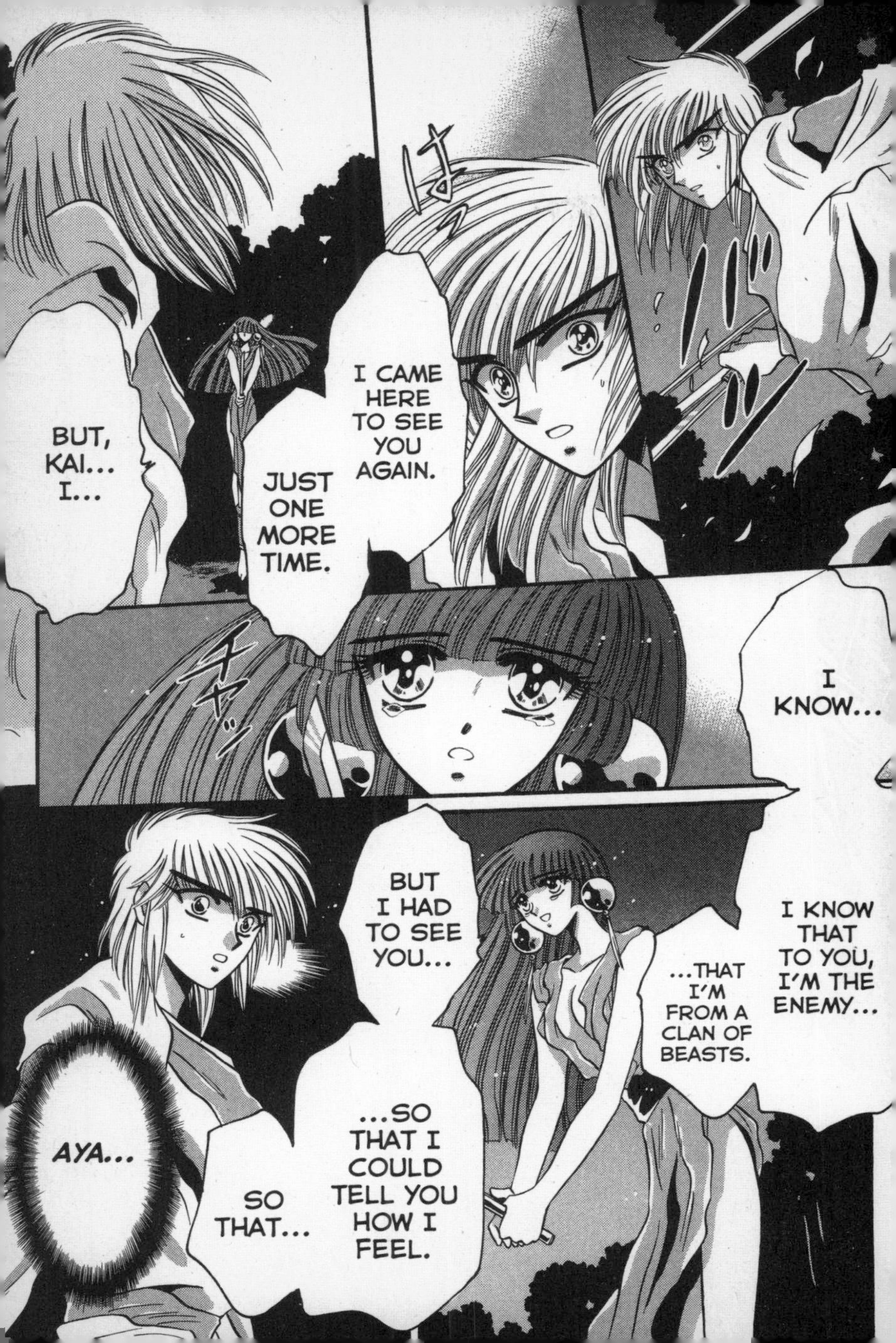
はっ
I CAME HERE TO SEE YOU AGAIN.
JUST ONE MORE TIME.
BUT, KAI... I...
I KNOW...
チャッ
I KNOW THAT TO YOU, I'M THE ENEMY...
...THAT I'M FROM A CLAN OF BEASTS.
BUT I HAD TO SEE YOU...
...SO THAT I COULD TELL YOU HOW I FEEL.
SO THAT...
AYA...

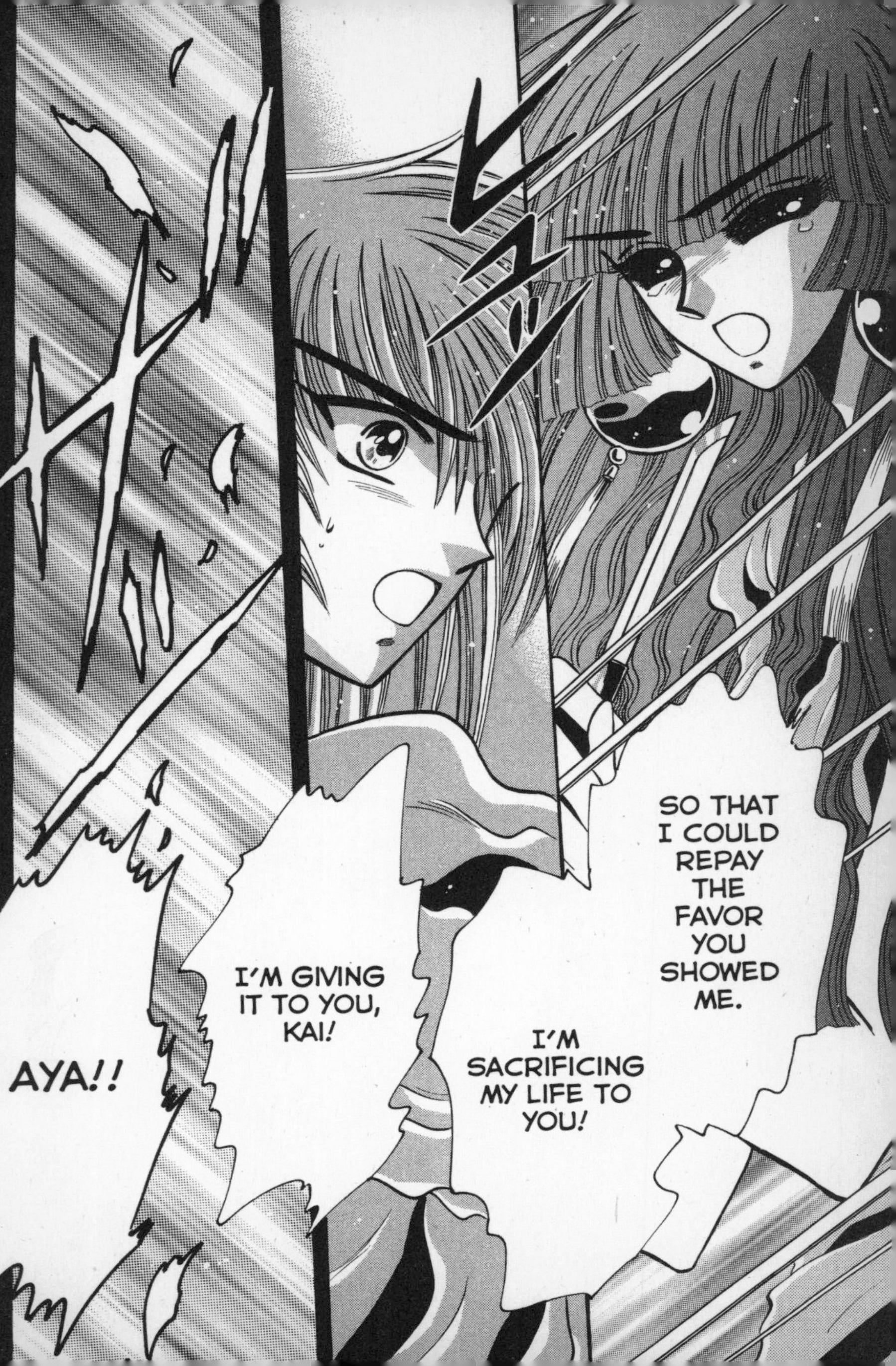
SO THAT I COULD REPAY THE FAVOR YOU SHOWED ME.
I'M SACRIFICING MY LIFE TO YOU!
I'M GIVING IT TO YOU, KAI!
AYA!!

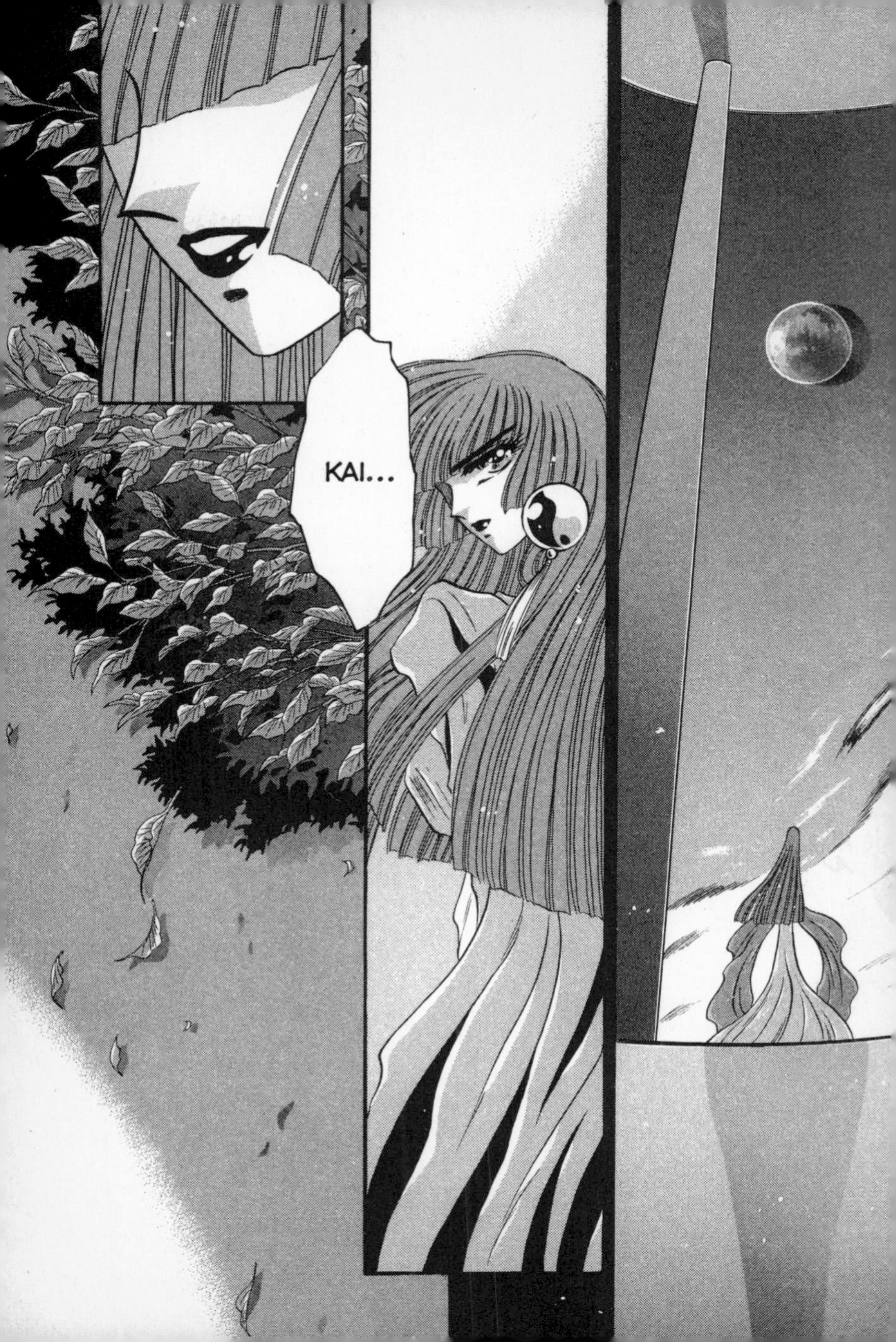
KAI...

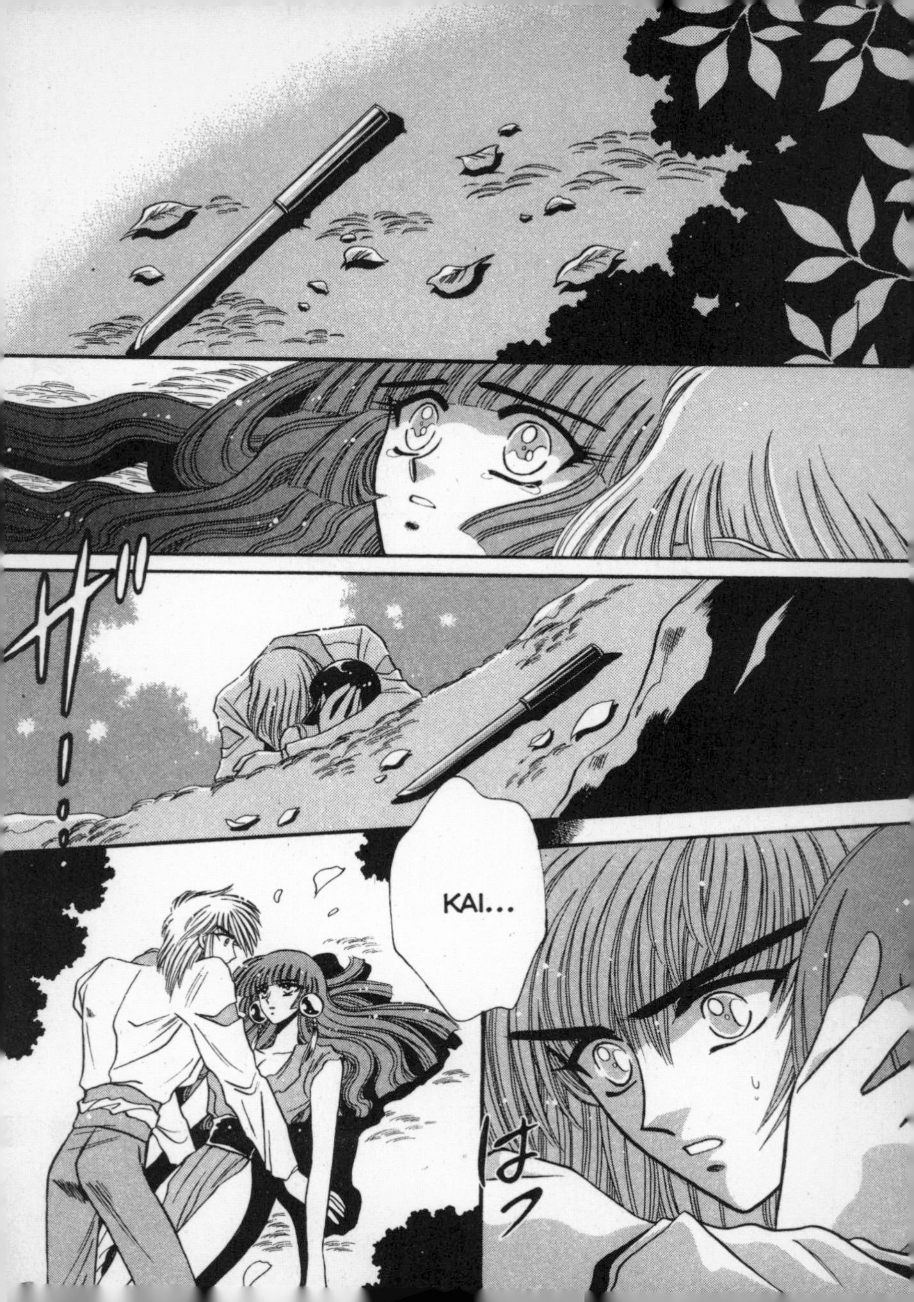
KAI...
はっ

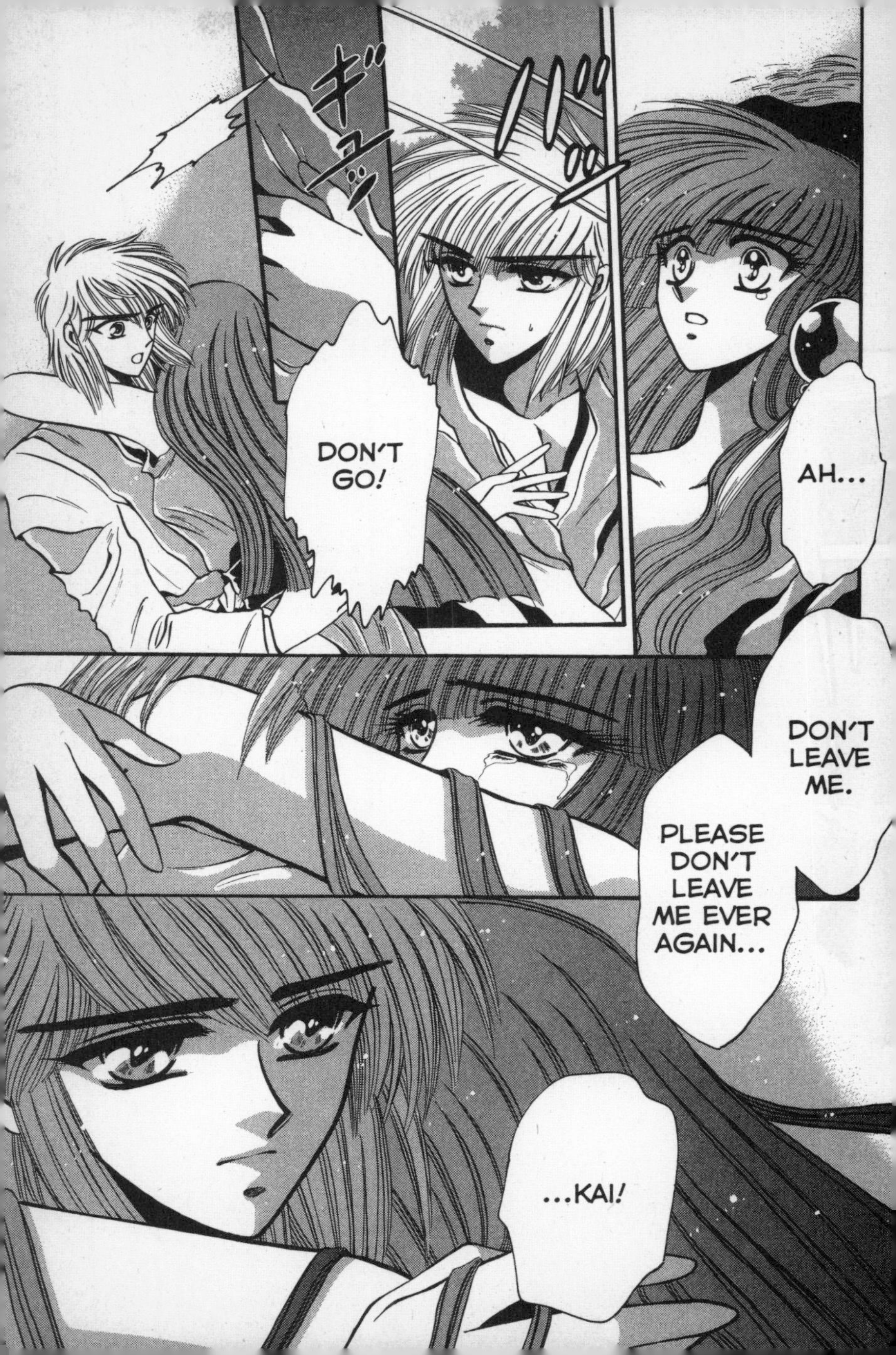

AH...
バッ
ギュッ
DON'T GO!
DON'T LEAVE ME.
PLEASE DON'T LEAVE ME EVER AGAIN...
...KAI!

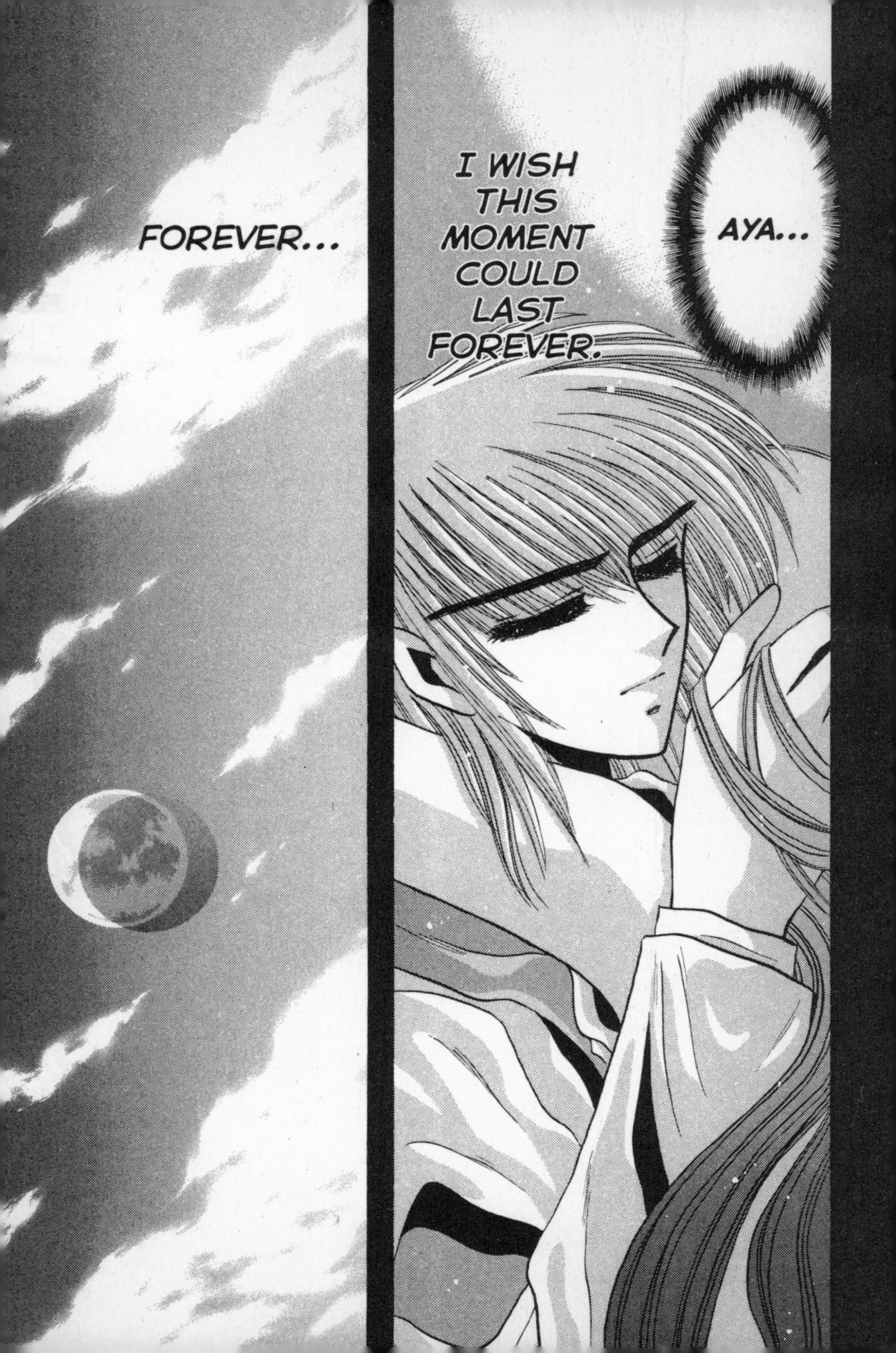
AYA...
I WISH THIS MOMENT COULD LAST FOREVER.
FOREVER...

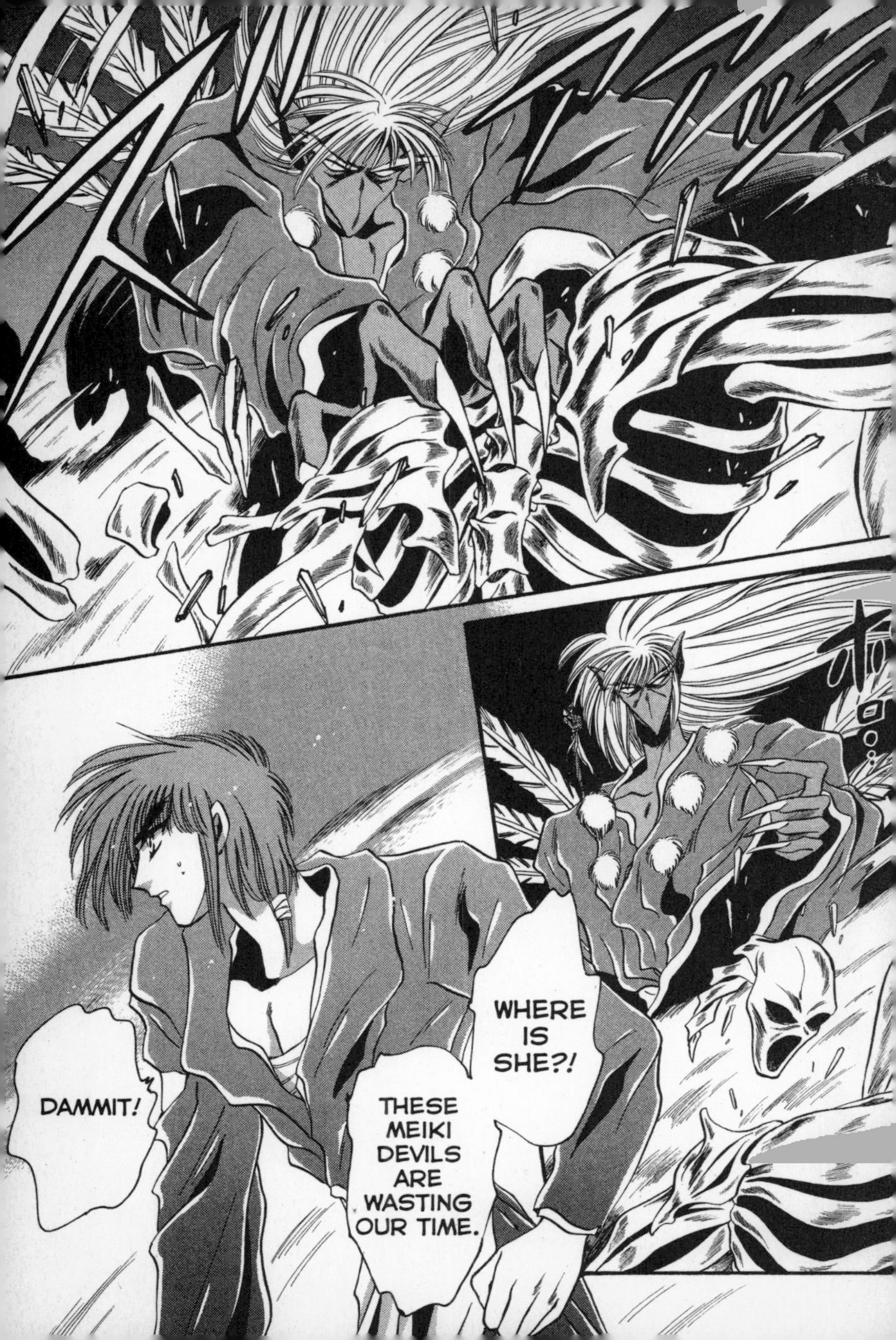
WHERE IS SHE?!
THESE MEIKI DEVILS ARE WASTING OUR TIME.
DAMMIT!

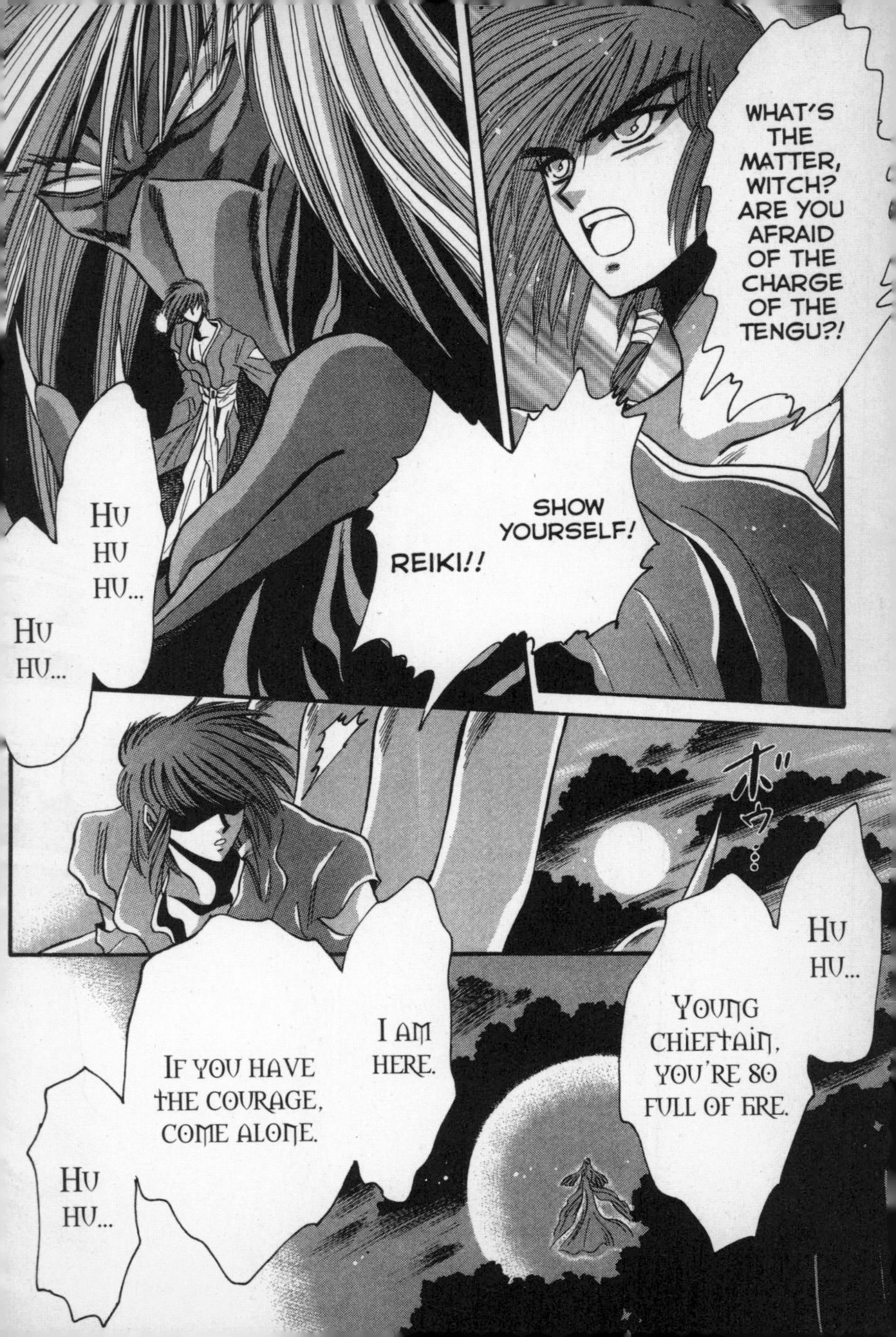
WHAT'S THE MATTER, WITCH? ARE YOU AFRAID OF THE CHARGE OF THE TENGU?!
SHOW YOURSELF!
REIKI!!
HU HU HU...
HU HU...
ボウ…
HU HU...
YOUNG CHIEFTAIN, YOU'RE SO FULL OF FIRE.
I AM HERE.
IF YOU HAVE THE COURAGE, COME ALONE.
HU HU...

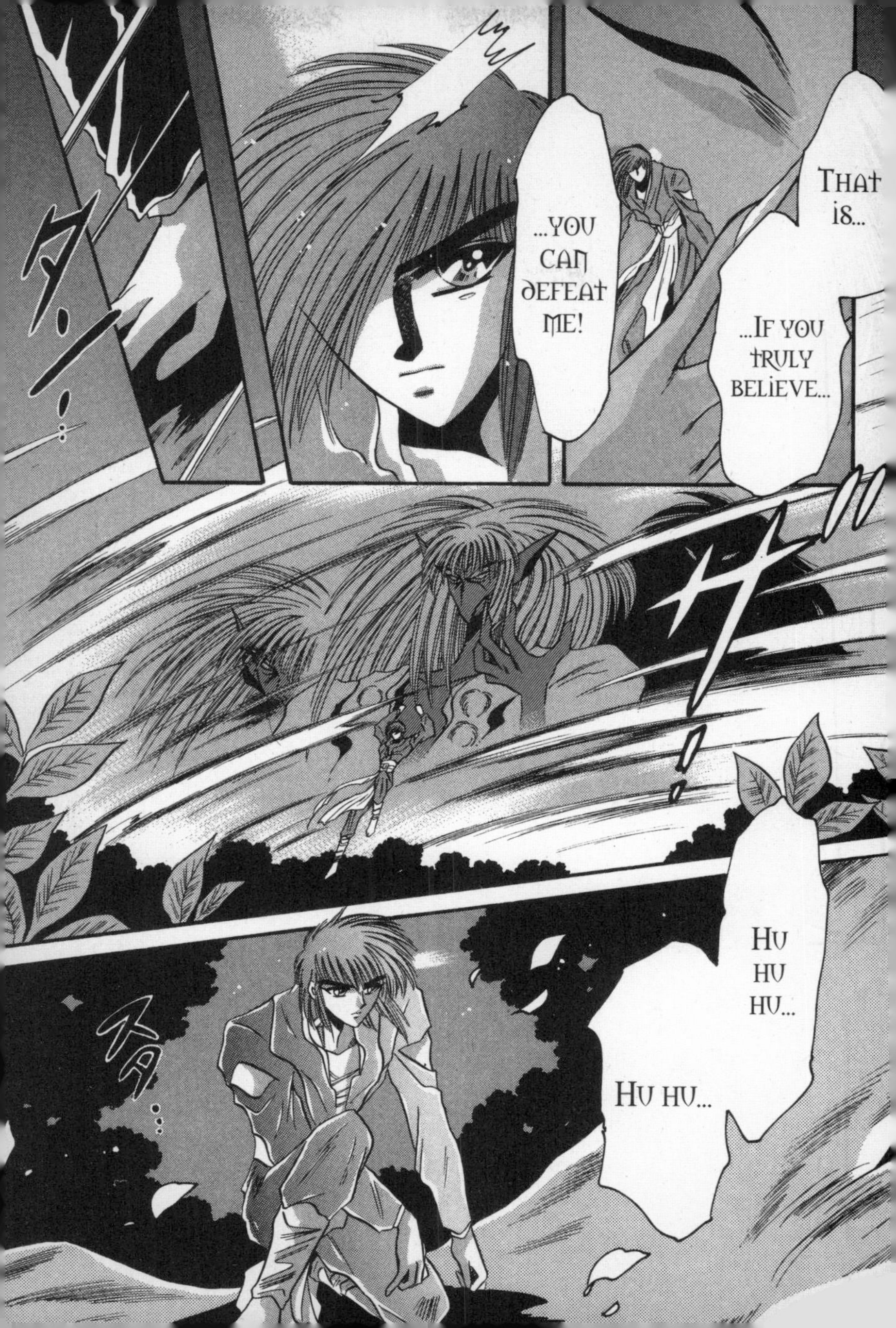
That is...
...If you truly believe...
...you can defeat me!
Hu hu hu...
Hu hu...

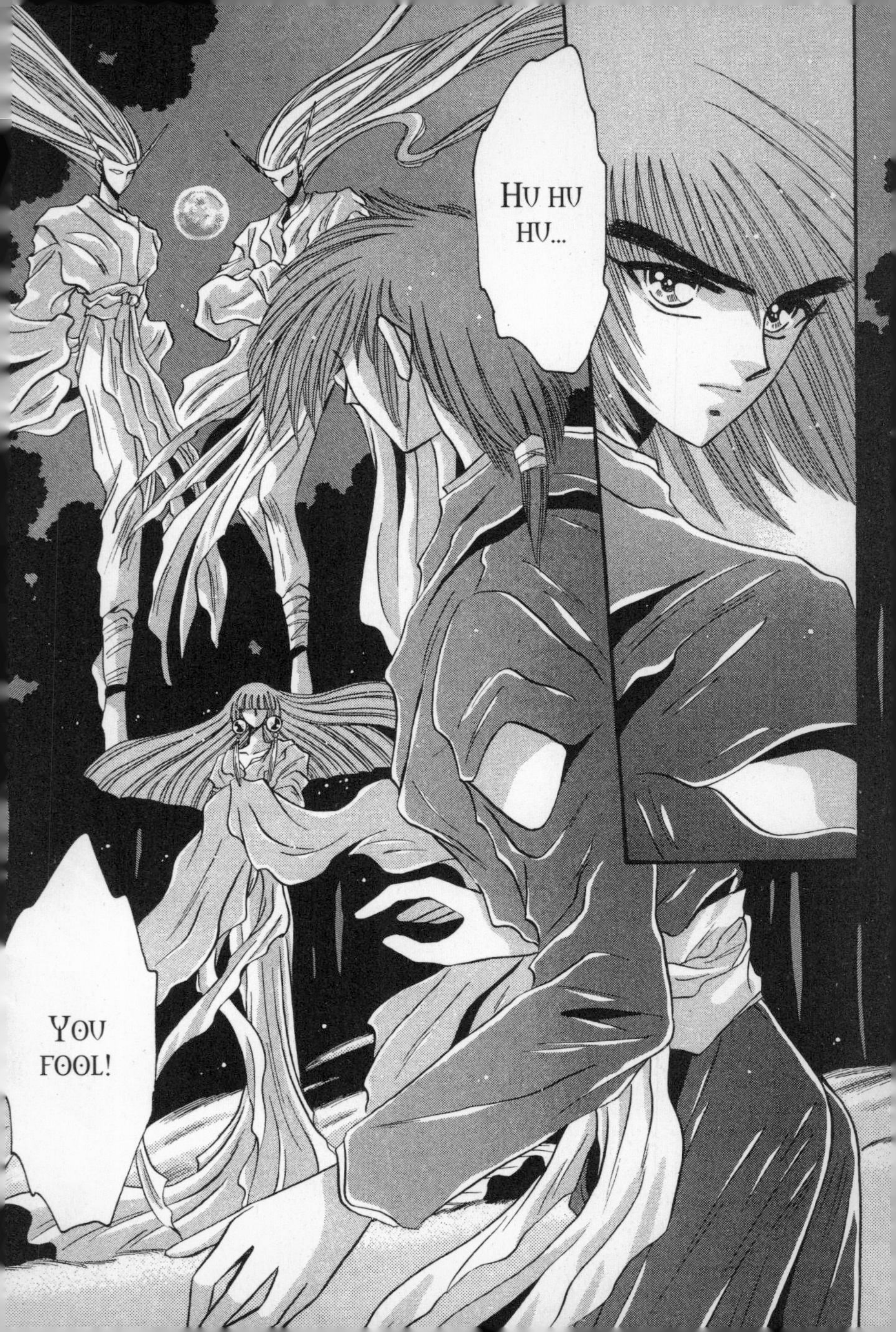
Hu hu hu...
You fool!

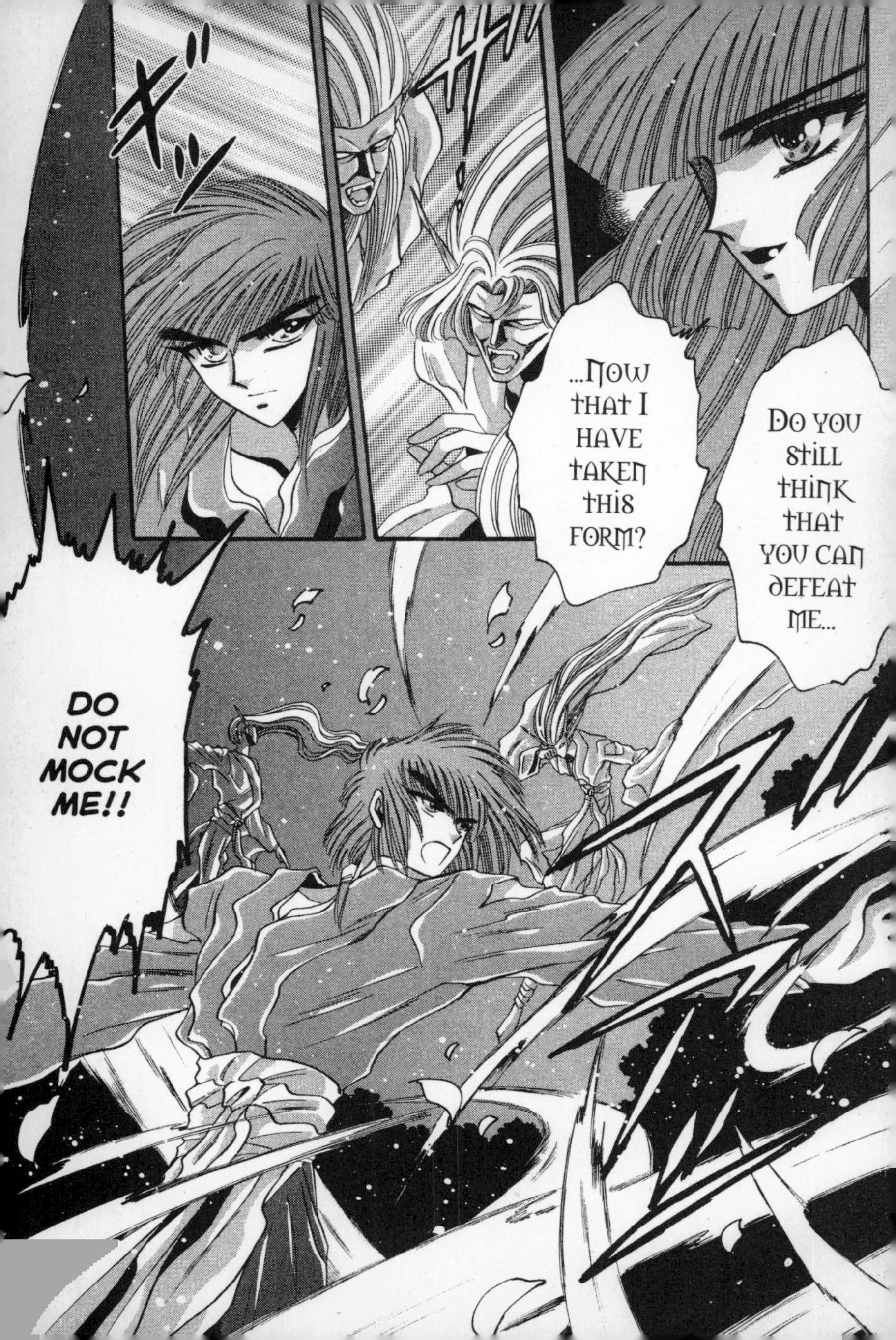
Do you still think that you can defeat me...
...Now that I have taken this form?
DO NOT MOCK ME!!

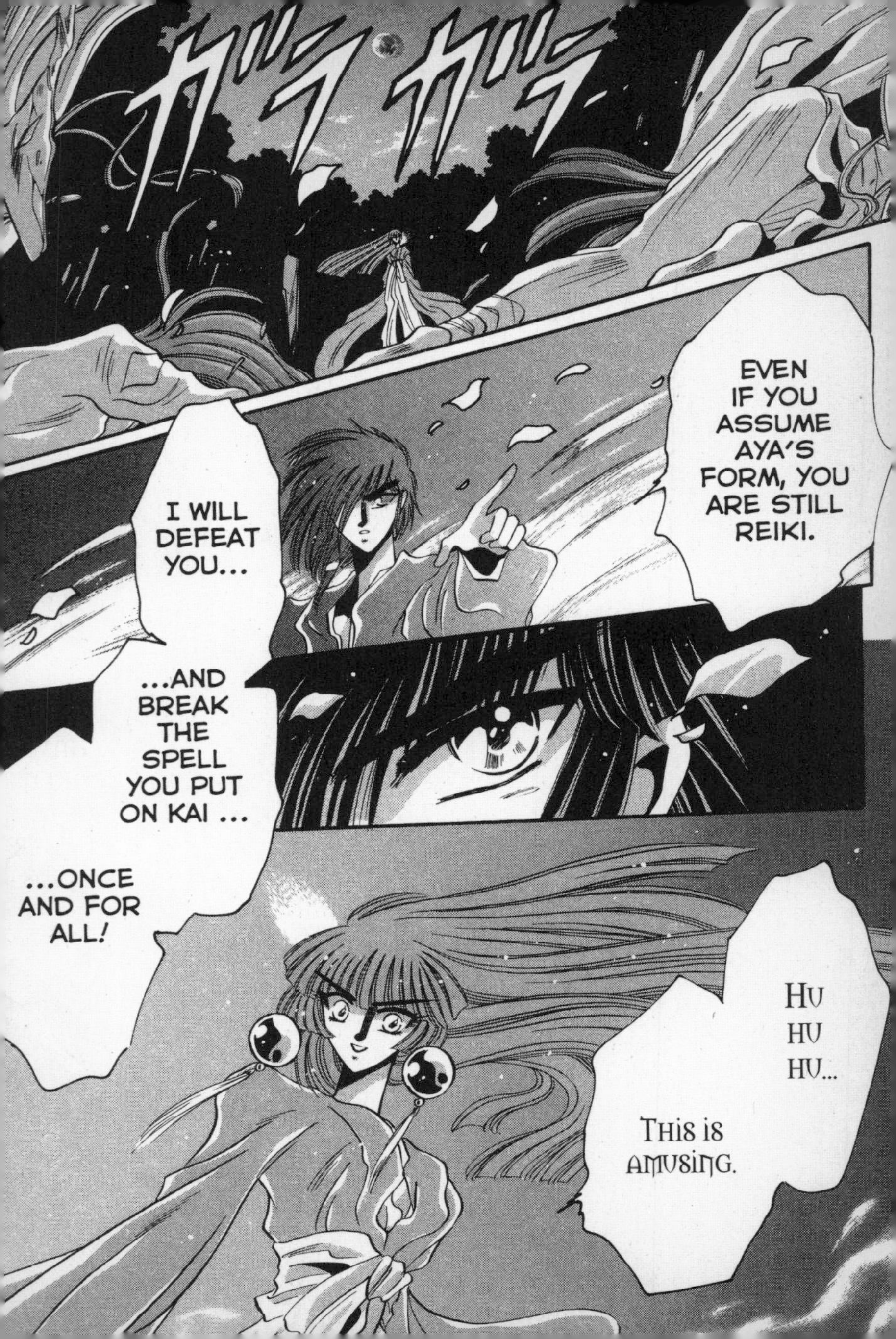

EVEN IF YOU ASSUME AYA'S FORM, YOU ARE STILL REIKI.
I WILL DEFEAT YOU...
...AND BREAK THE SPELL YOU PUT ON KAI ...
...ONCE AND FOR ALL!
HU HU HU...
THIS IS AMUSING.

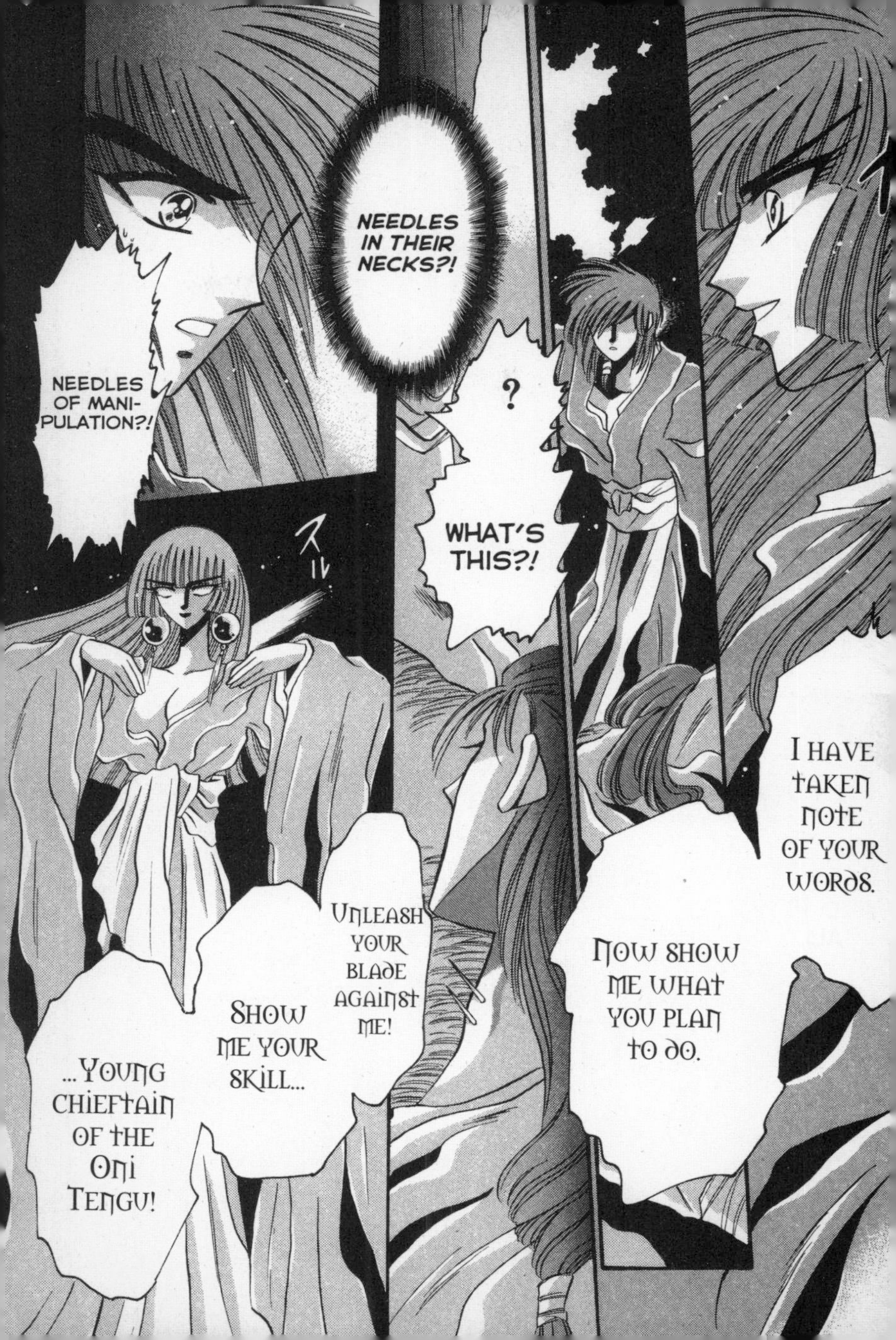
I HAVE TAKEN NOTE OF YOUR WORDS.
NOW SHOW ME WHAT YOU PLAN TO DO.
?
WHAT'S THIS?!
NEEDLES IN THEIR NECKS?!
NEEDLES OF MANIPULATION?!
スル
UNLEASH YOUR BLADE AGAINST ME!
SHOW ME YOUR SKILL...
...YOUNG CHIEFTAIN OF THE ONI TENGU!

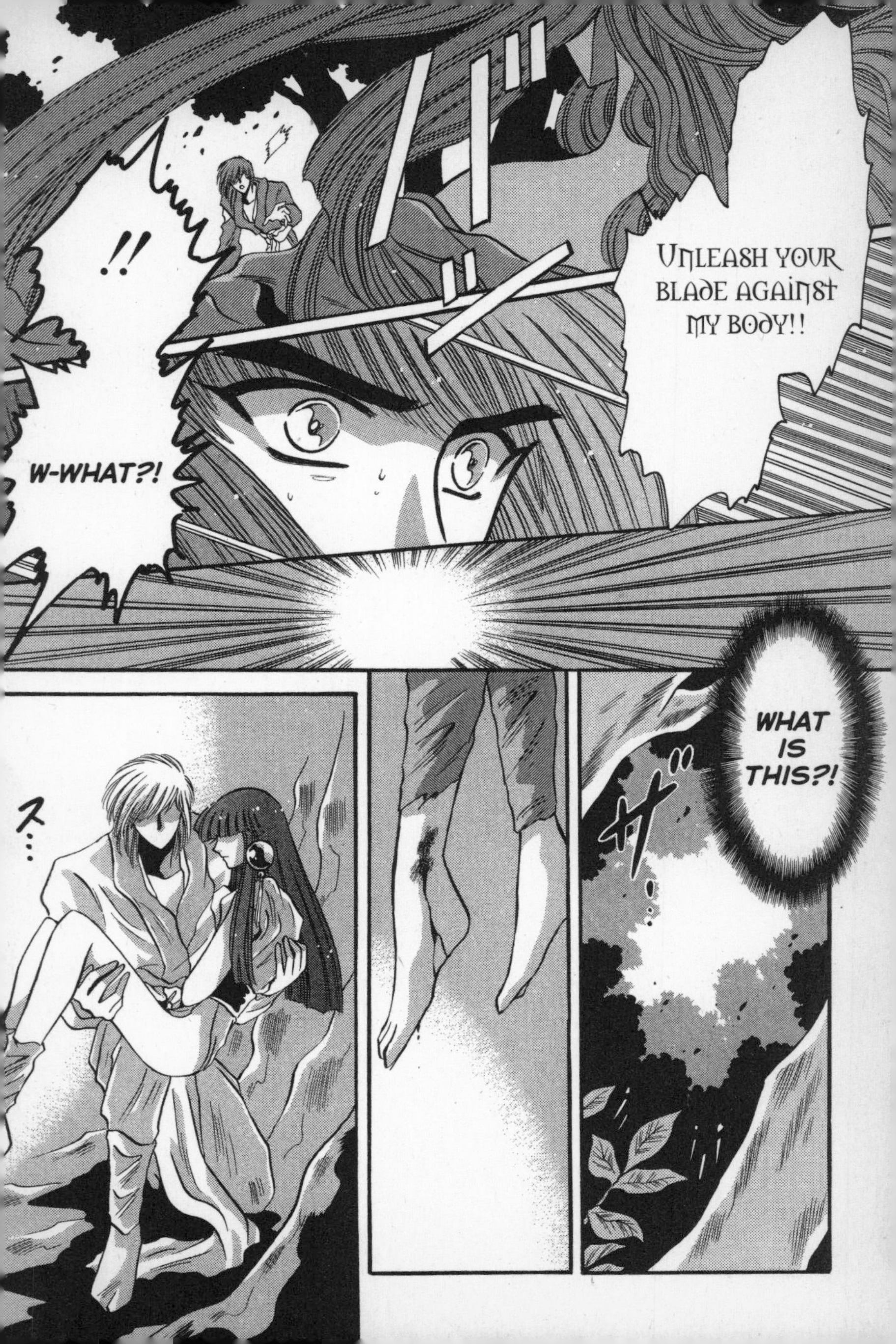
UNLEASH YOUR BLADE AGAINST MY BODY!!
!!
W-WHAT?!
WHAT IS THIS?!
ザ…
ス…

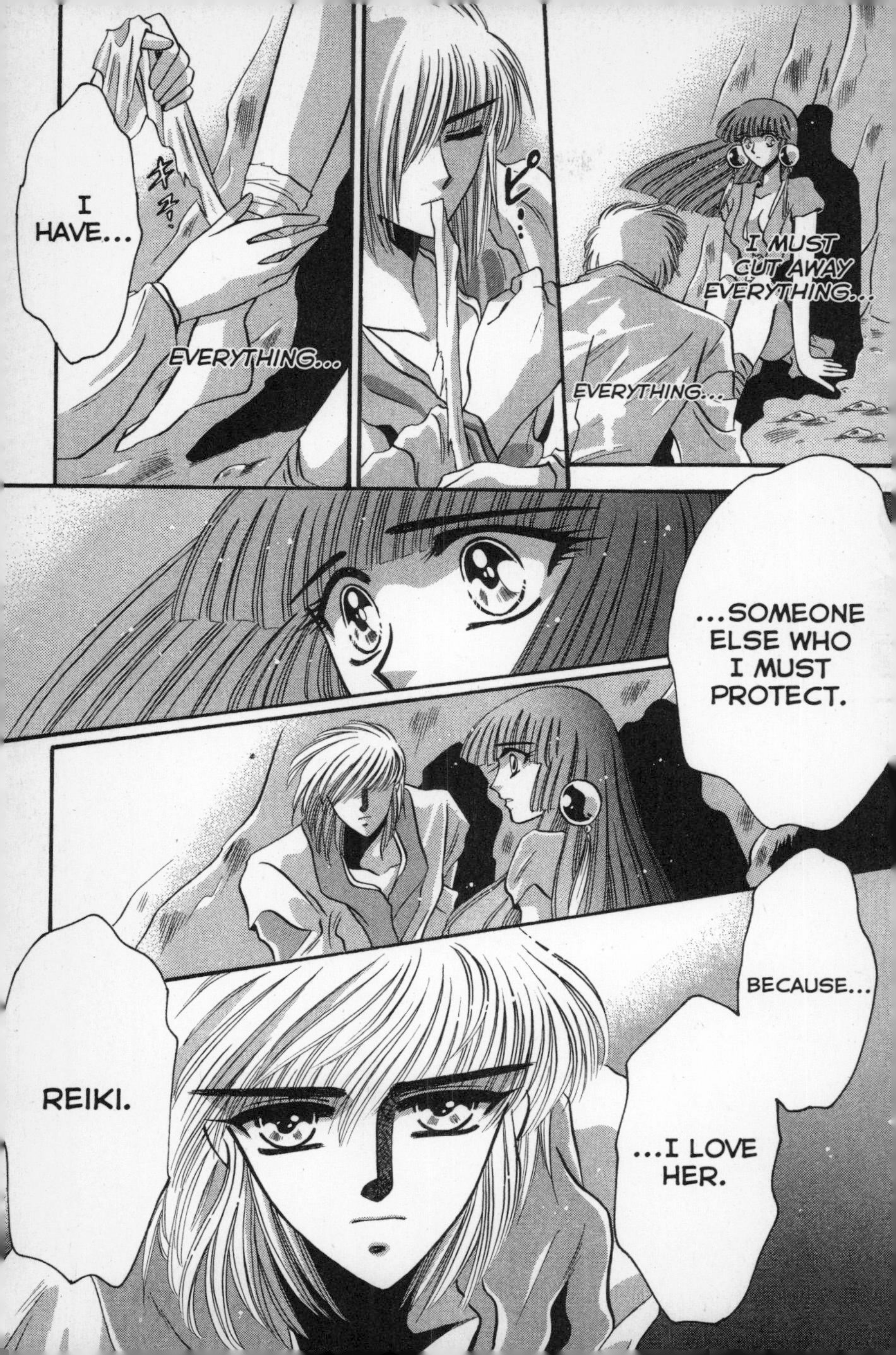
I MUST CUT AWAY EVERYTHING...
EVERYTHING...
ピ…
I HAVE...
EVERYTHING...
...SOMEONE ELSE WHO I MUST PROTECT.
BECAUSE...
...I LOVE HER.
REIKI.

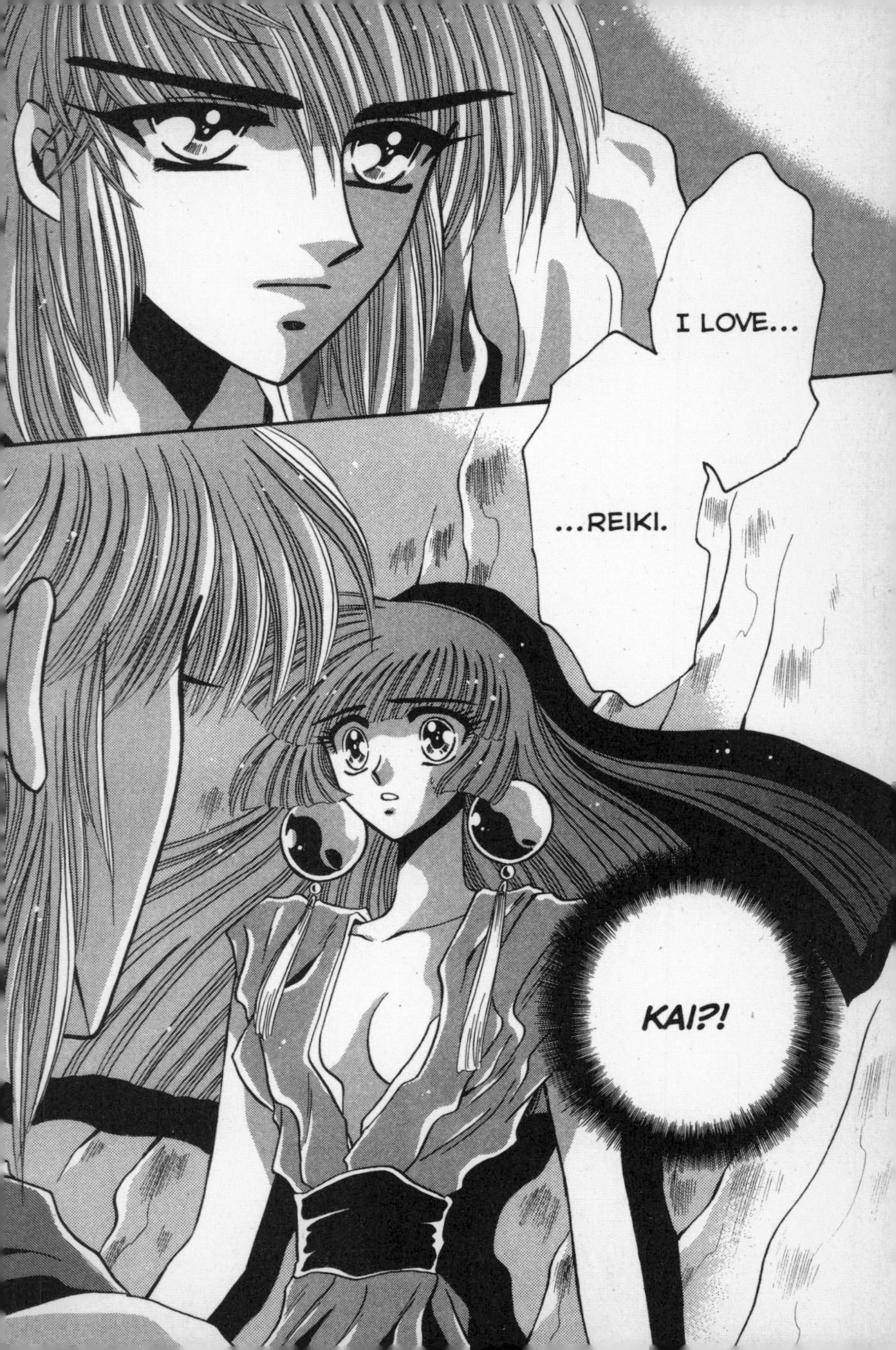
I LOVE...
...REIKI.
KAI?!

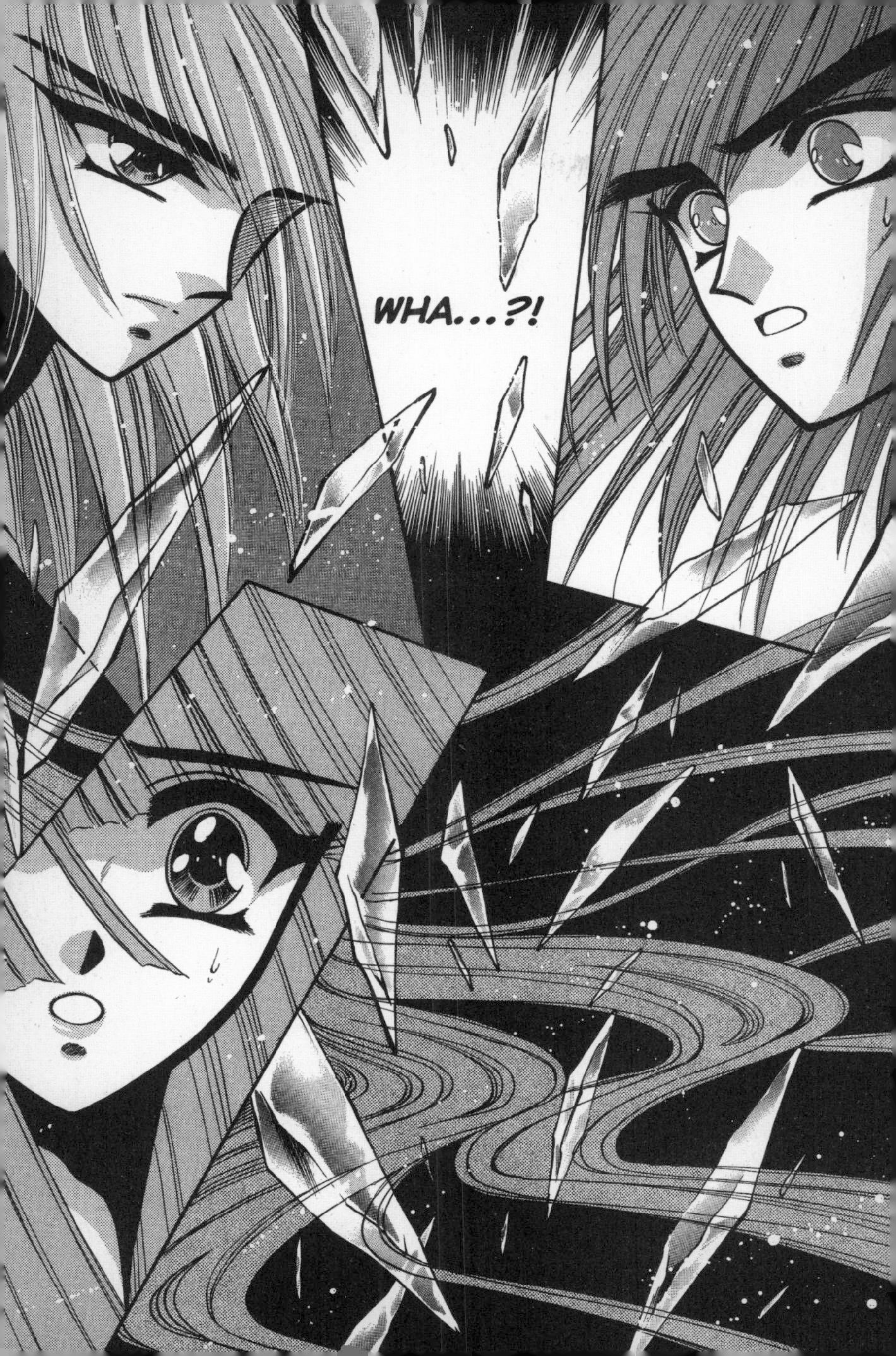
WHA...?!

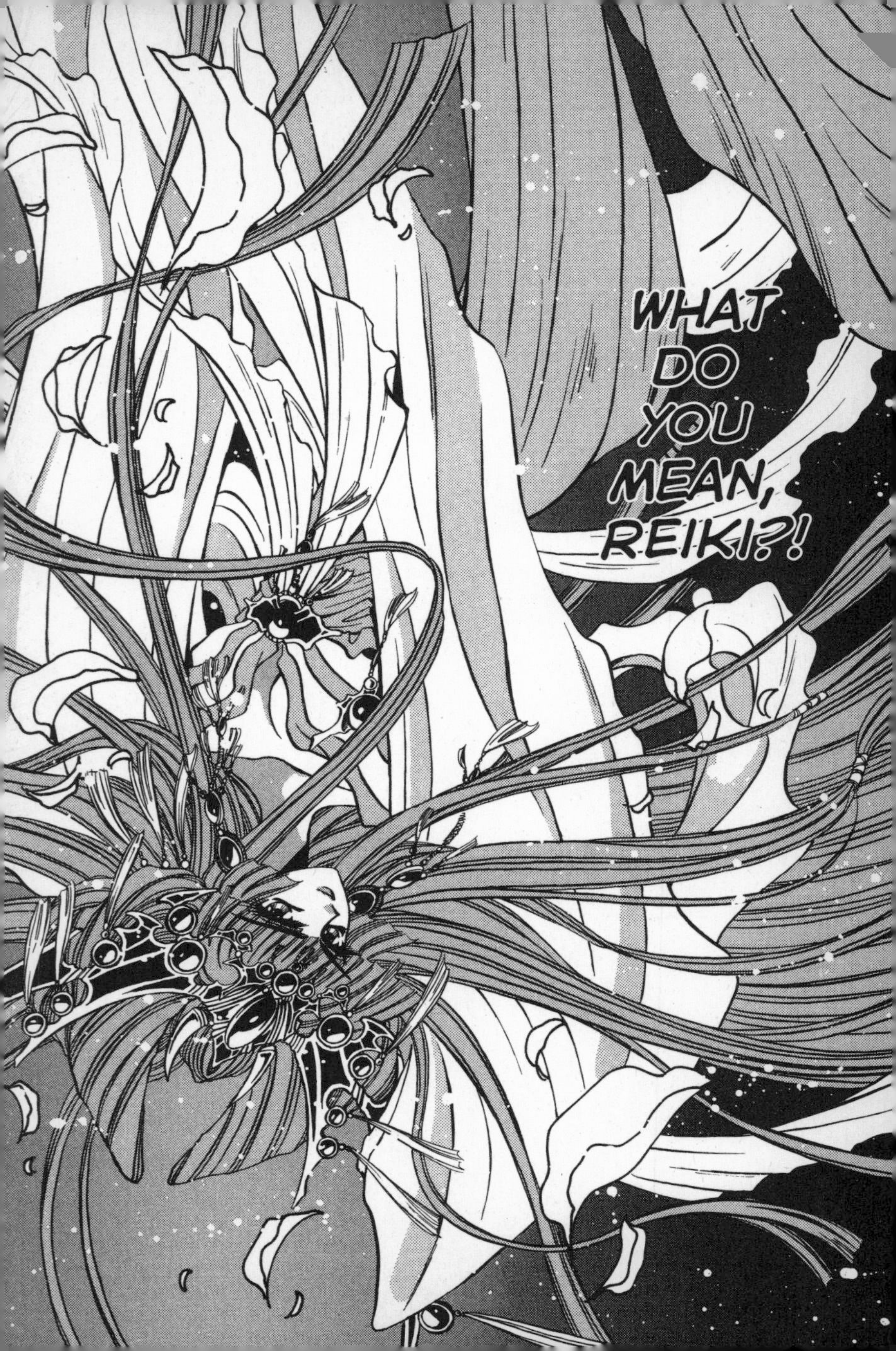
WHAT DO YOU MEAN, REIKI?!

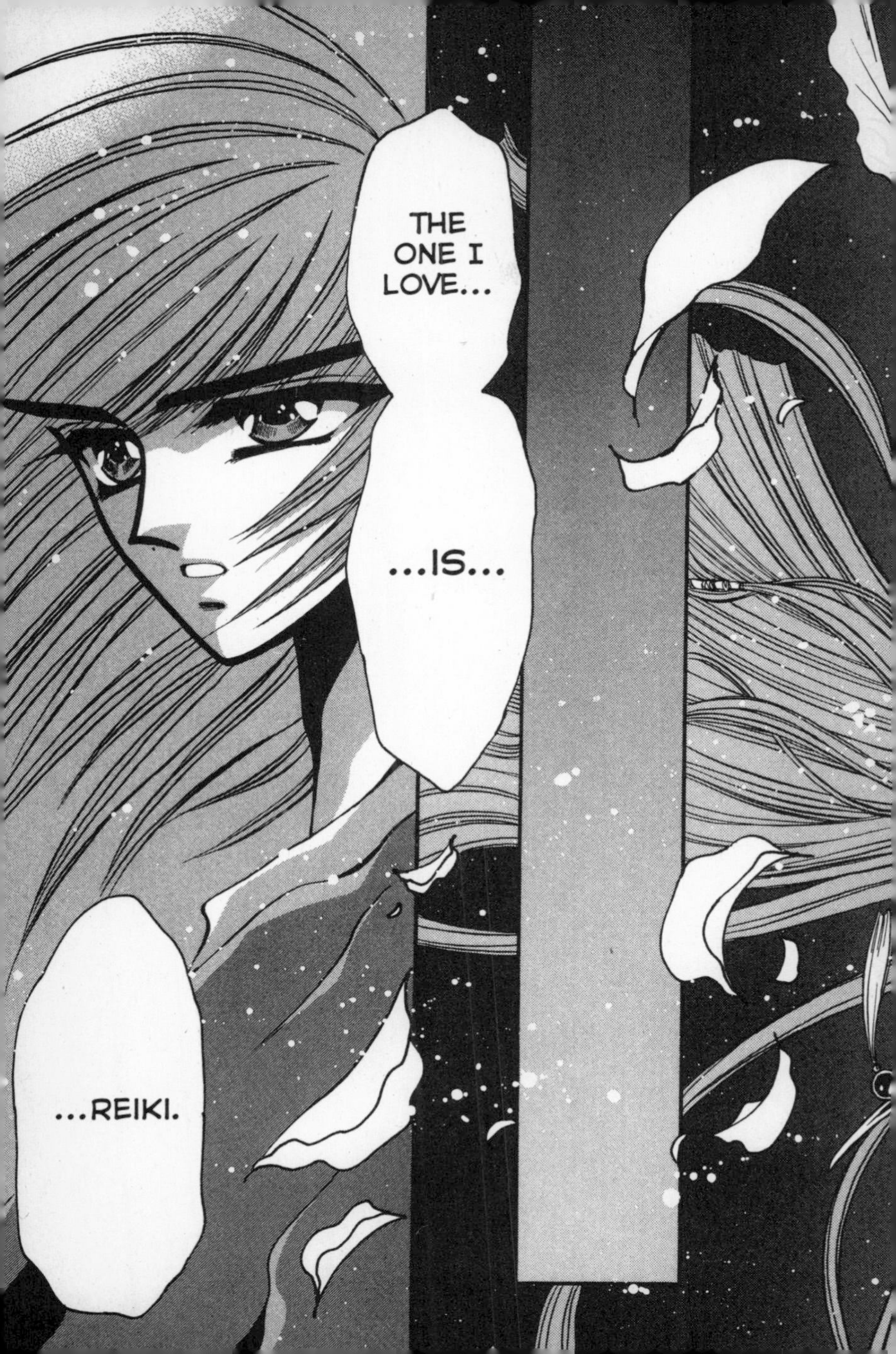
THE ONE I LOVE...
...IS...
...REIKI.

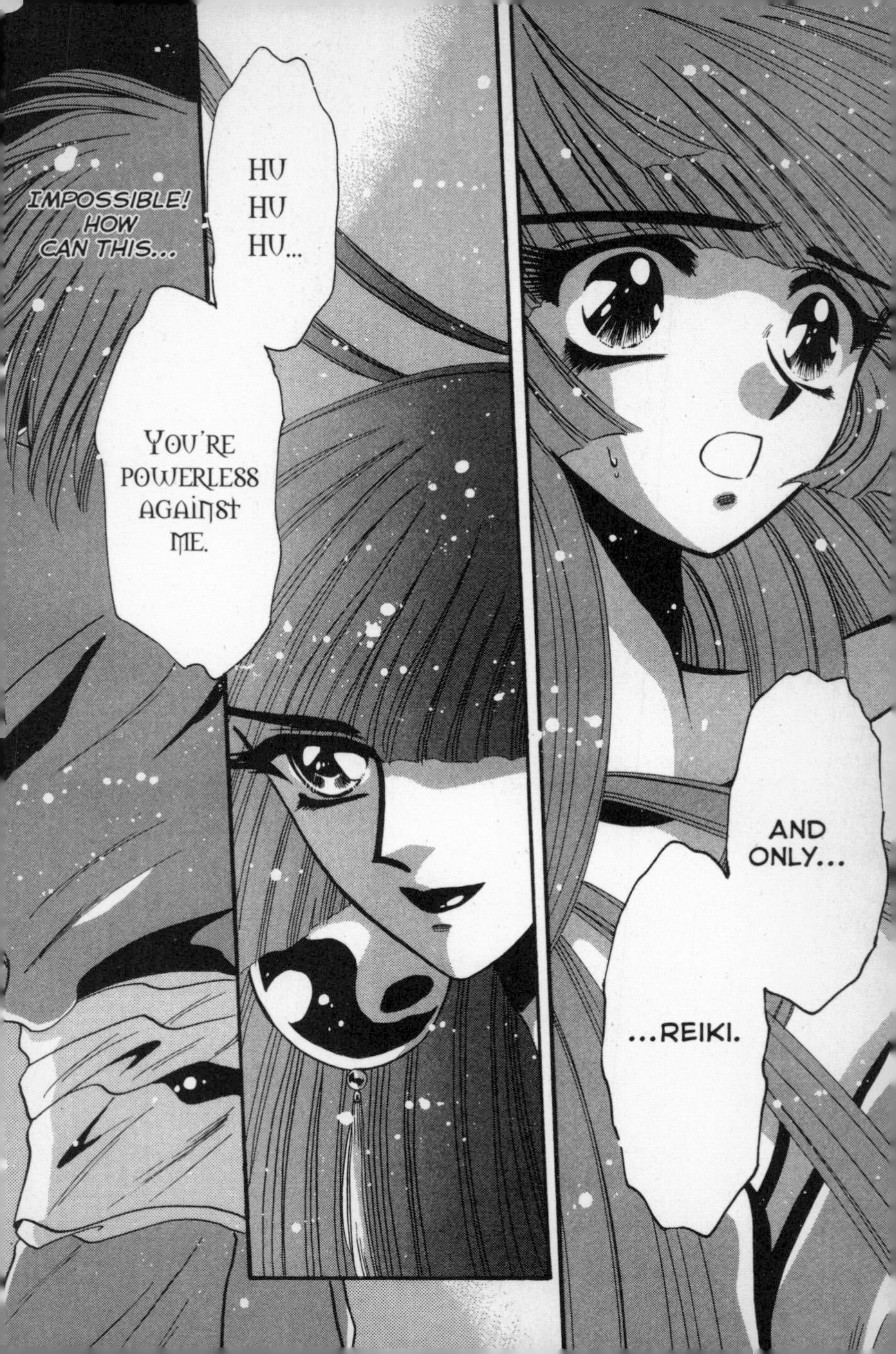
AND ONLY...
...REIKI.
HU HU HU...
YOU'RE POWERLESS AGAINST ME.
IMPOSSIBLE! HOW CAN THIS...

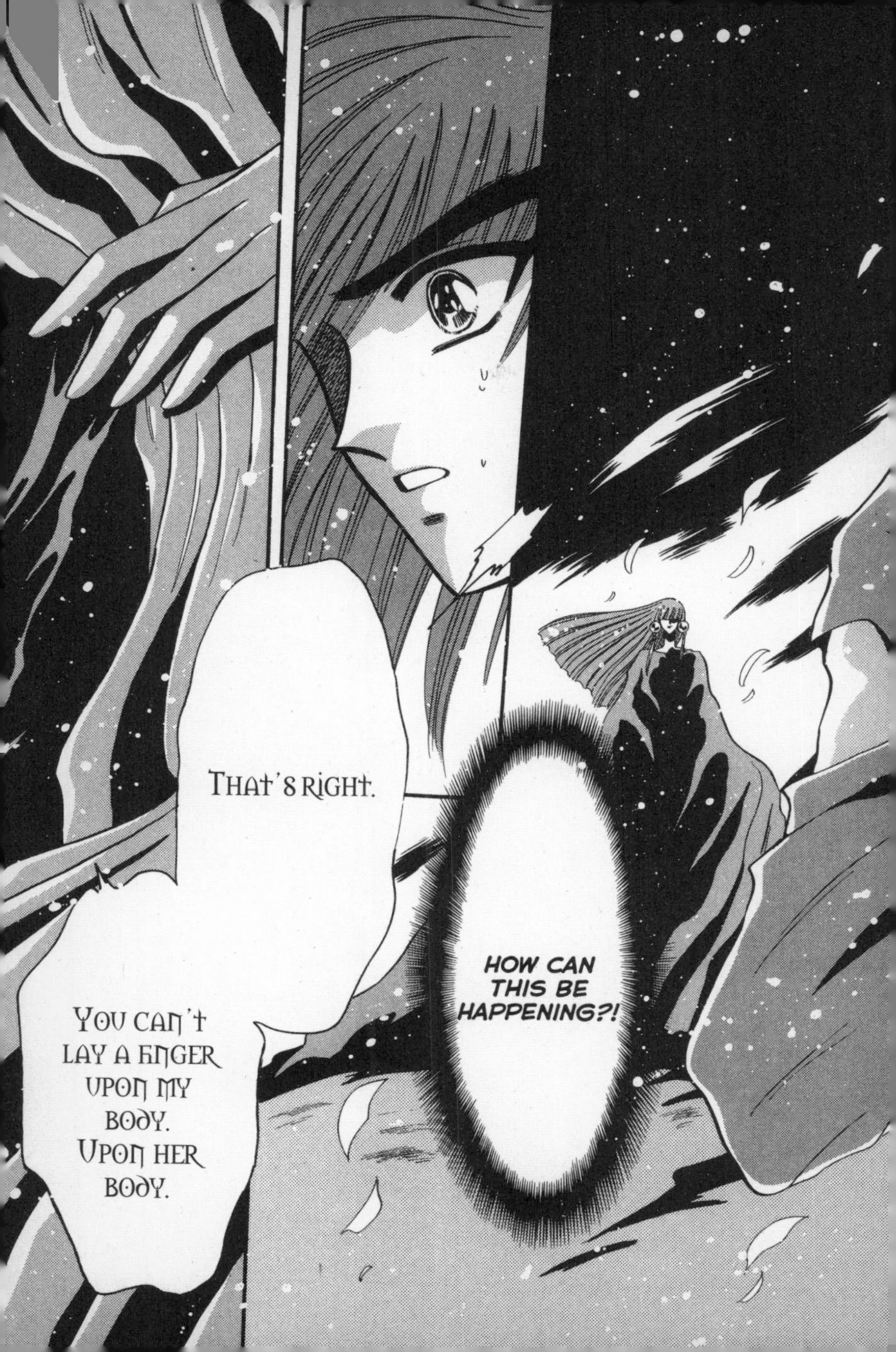
HOW CAN THIS BE HAPPENING?!
THAT'S RIGHT.
YOU CAN'T LAY A FINGER UPON MY BODY. UPON HER BODY.

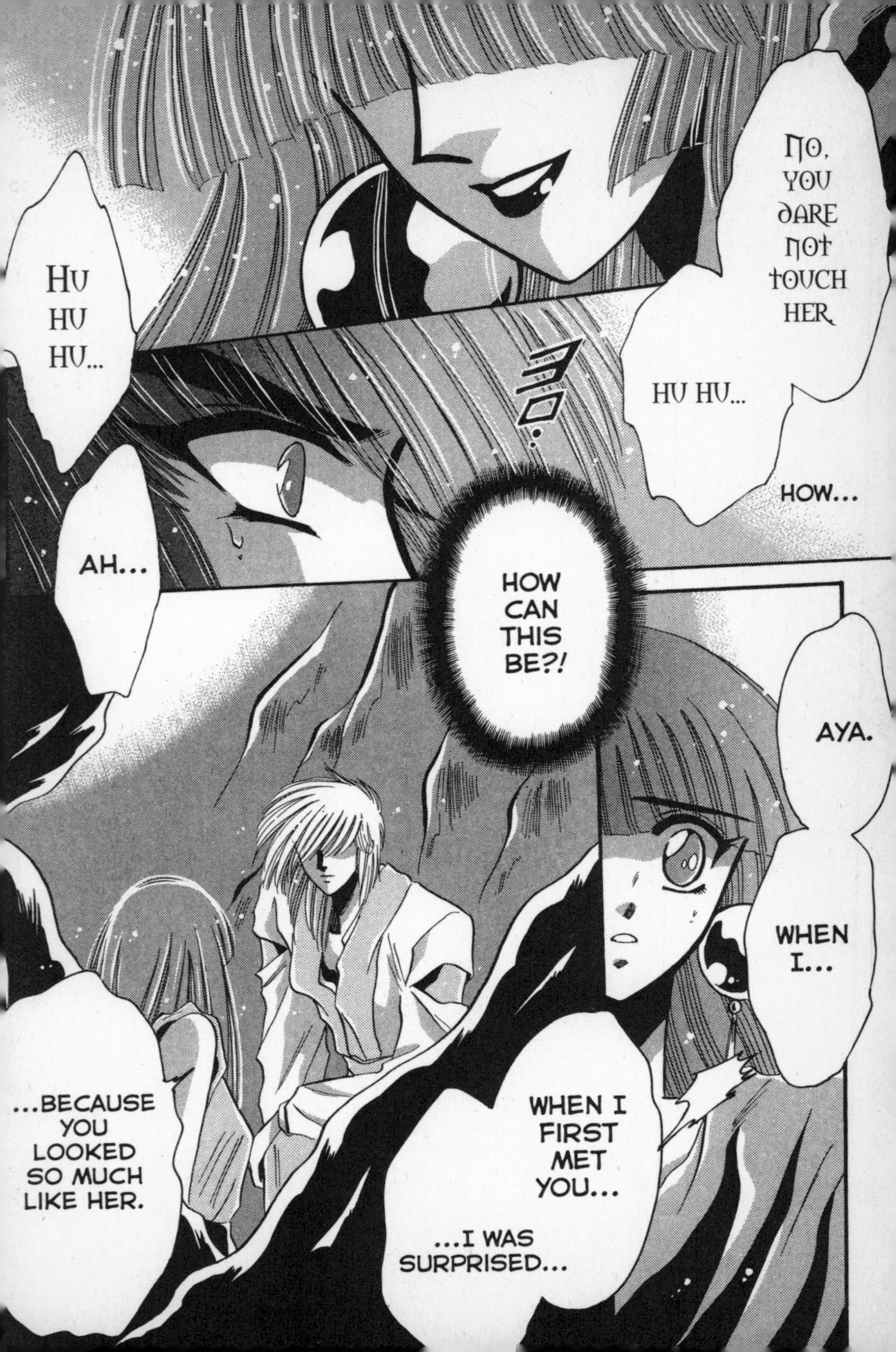

No, you dare not touch her.
Hu hu hu...
Hu hu...
How...
Ah...
How can this be?!
Aya.
When I...
When I first met you...
...I was surprised...
...because you looked so much like her.

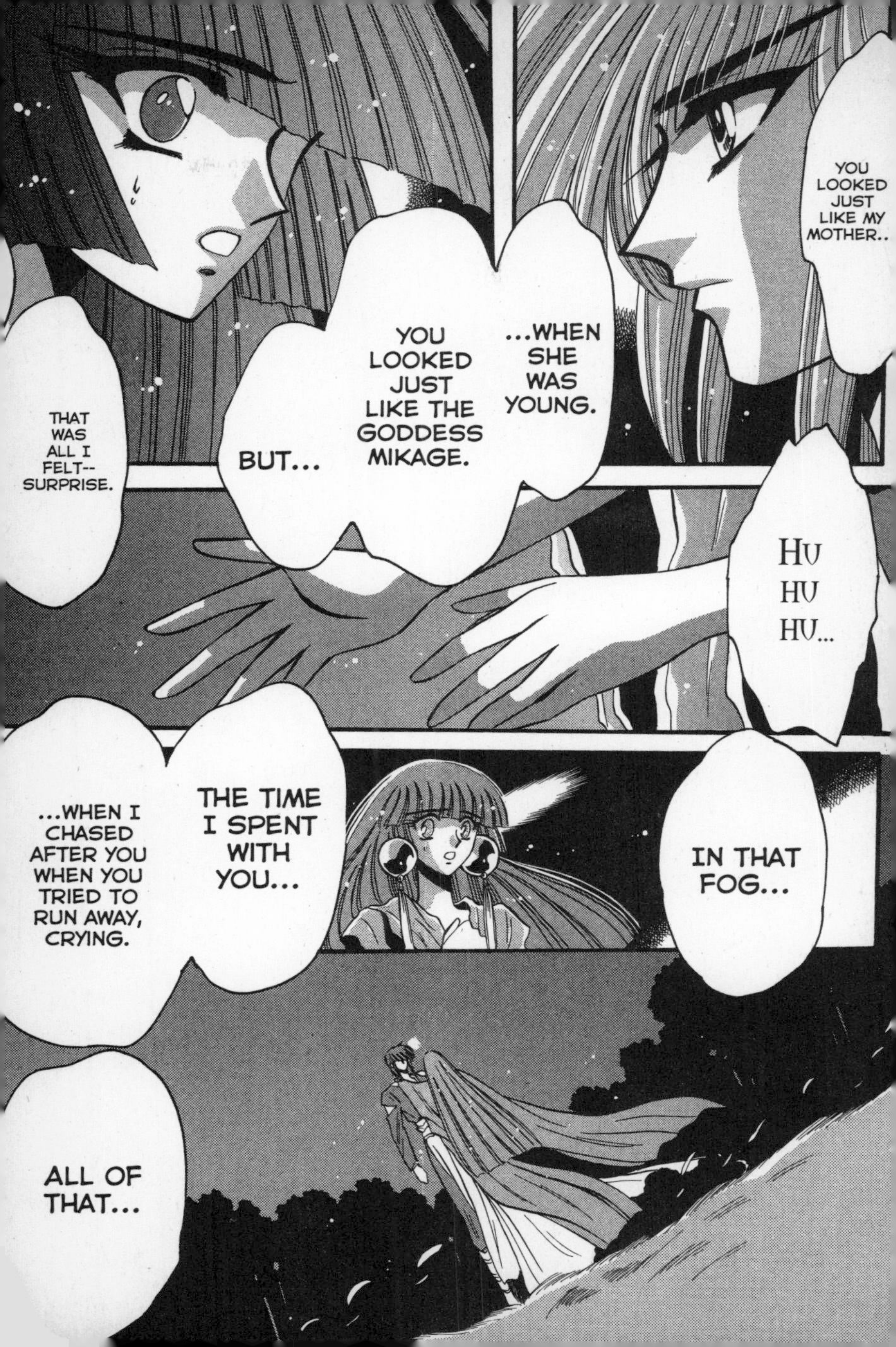
YOU LOOKED JUST LIKE MY MOTHER..
...WHEN SHE WAS YOUNG.
YOU LOOKED JUST LIKE THE GODDESS MIKAGE.
BUT...
THAT WAS ALL I FELT-- SURPRISE.
HU HU HU...
IN THAT FOG...
THE TIME I SPENT WITH YOU...
...WHEN I CHASED AFTER YOU WHEN YOU TRIED TO RUN AWAY, CRYING.
ALL OF THAT...

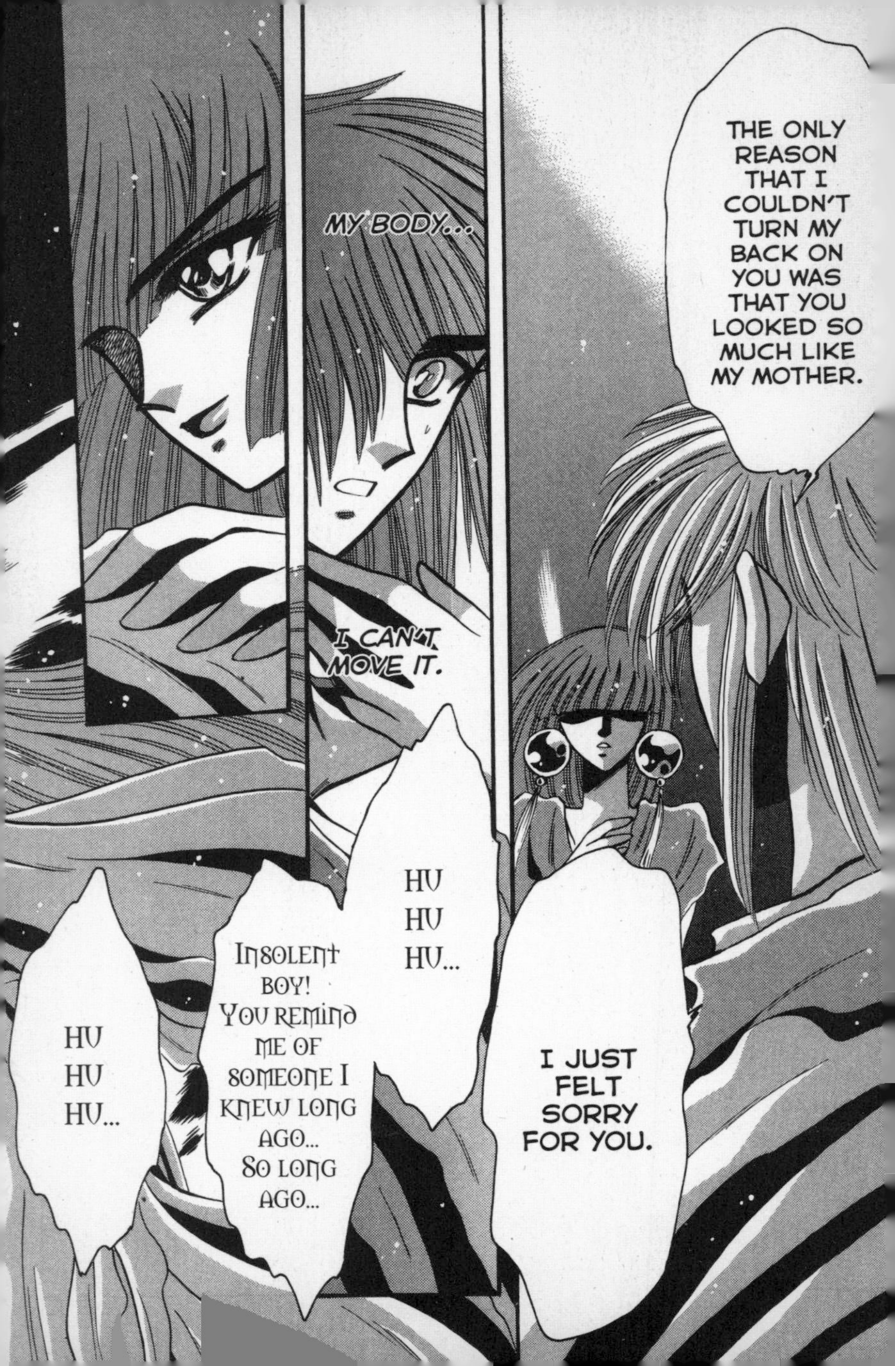
THE ONLY REASON THAT I COULDN'T TURN MY BACK ON YOU WAS THAT YOU LOOKED SO MUCH LIKE MY MOTHER.
MY BODY...
I CAN'T MOVE IT.
I JUST FELT SORRY FOR YOU.
HU HU HU...
INSOLENT BOY! YOU REMIND ME OF SOMEONE I KNEW LONG AGO... SO LONG AGO...
HU HU HU...

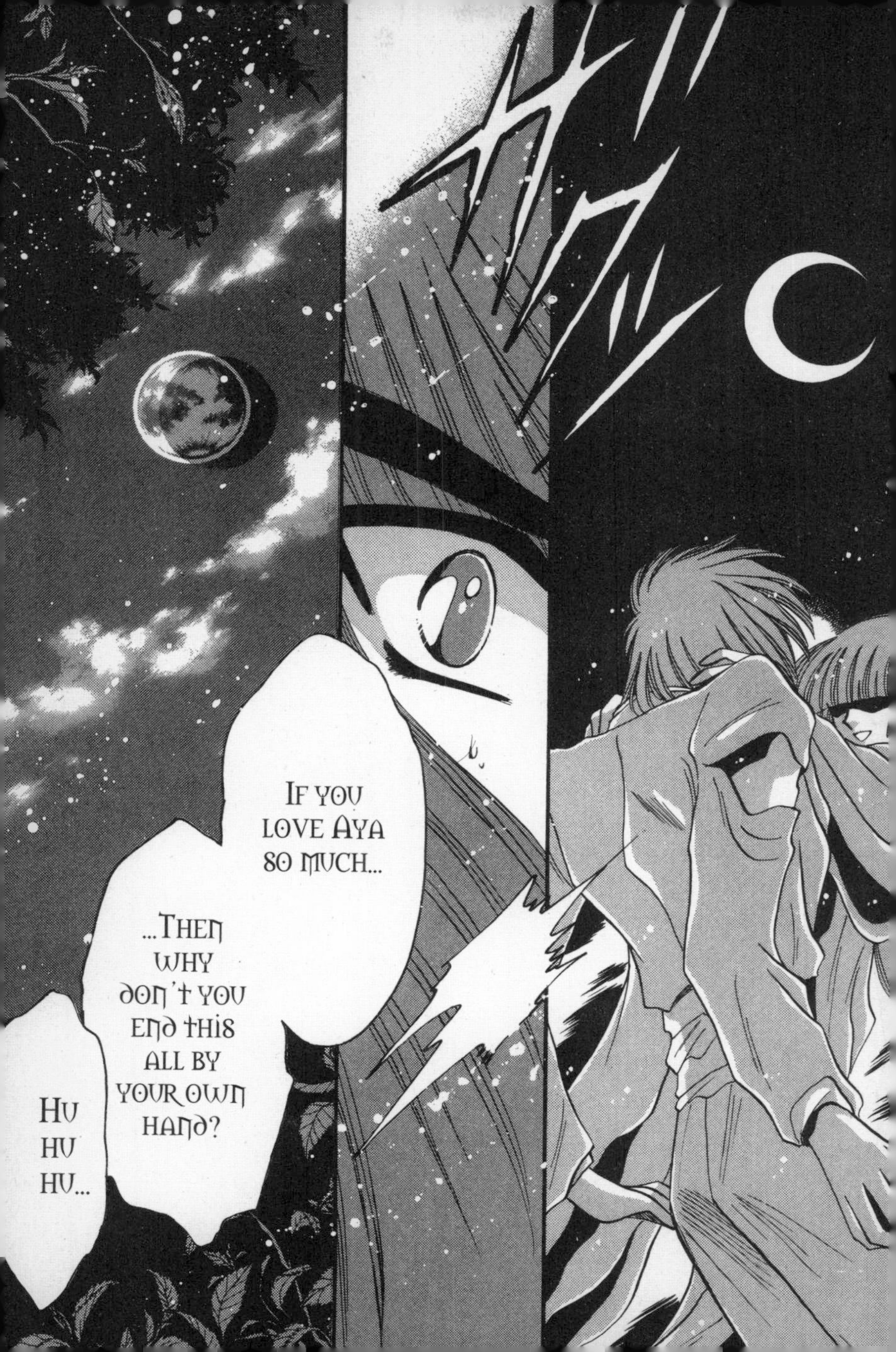
If you love Aya so much...
...Then why don't you end this all by your own hand?
Hu hu hu...

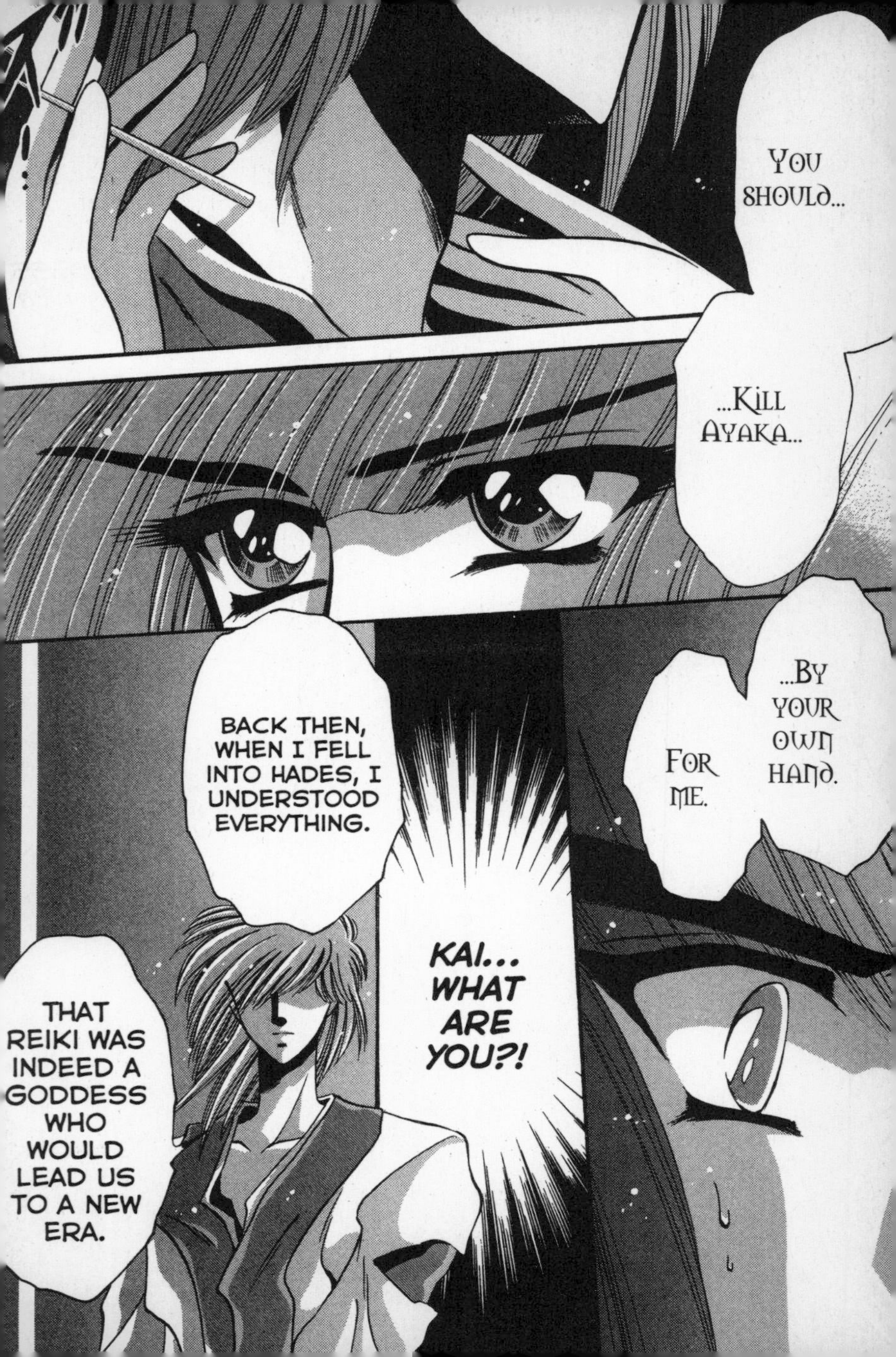
You should...
...Kill Ayaka...
...By your own hand.
For me.
Kai... what are you?!
Back then, when I fell into Hades, I understood everything.
That Reiki was indeed a goddess who would lead us to a new era.

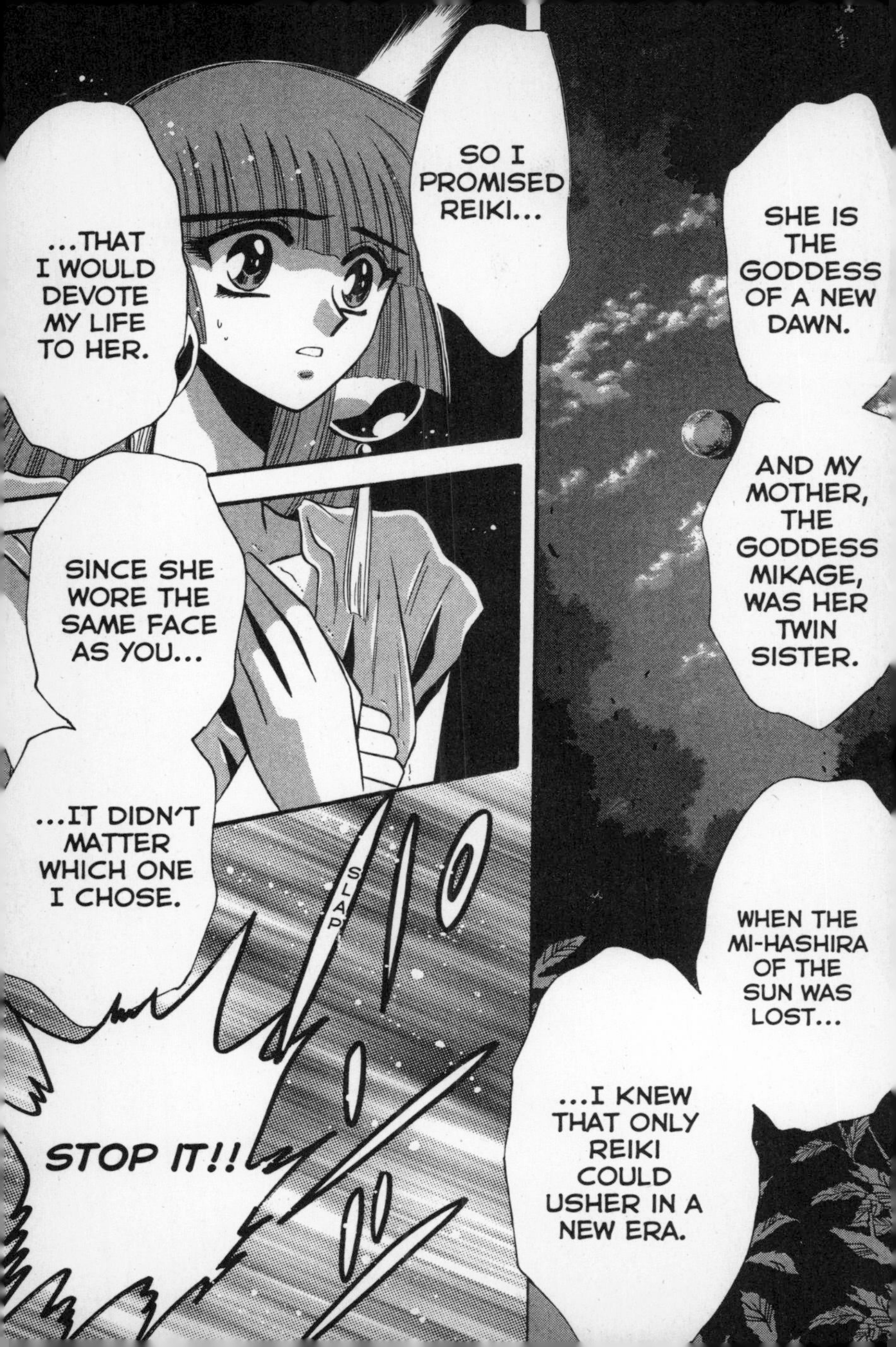
SHE IS THE GODDESS OF A NEW DAWN.
AND MY MOTHER, THE GODDESS MIKAGE, WAS HER TWIN SISTER.
WHEN THE MI-HASHIRA OF THE SUN WAS LOST...
...I KNEW THAT ONLY REIKI COULD USHER IN A NEW ERA.
SO I PROMISED REIKI...
...THAT I WOULD DEVOTE MY LIFE TO HER.
SINCE SHE WORE THE SAME FACE AS YOU...
...IT DIDN'T MATTER WHICH ONE I CHOSE.
STOP IT!!
SLAP

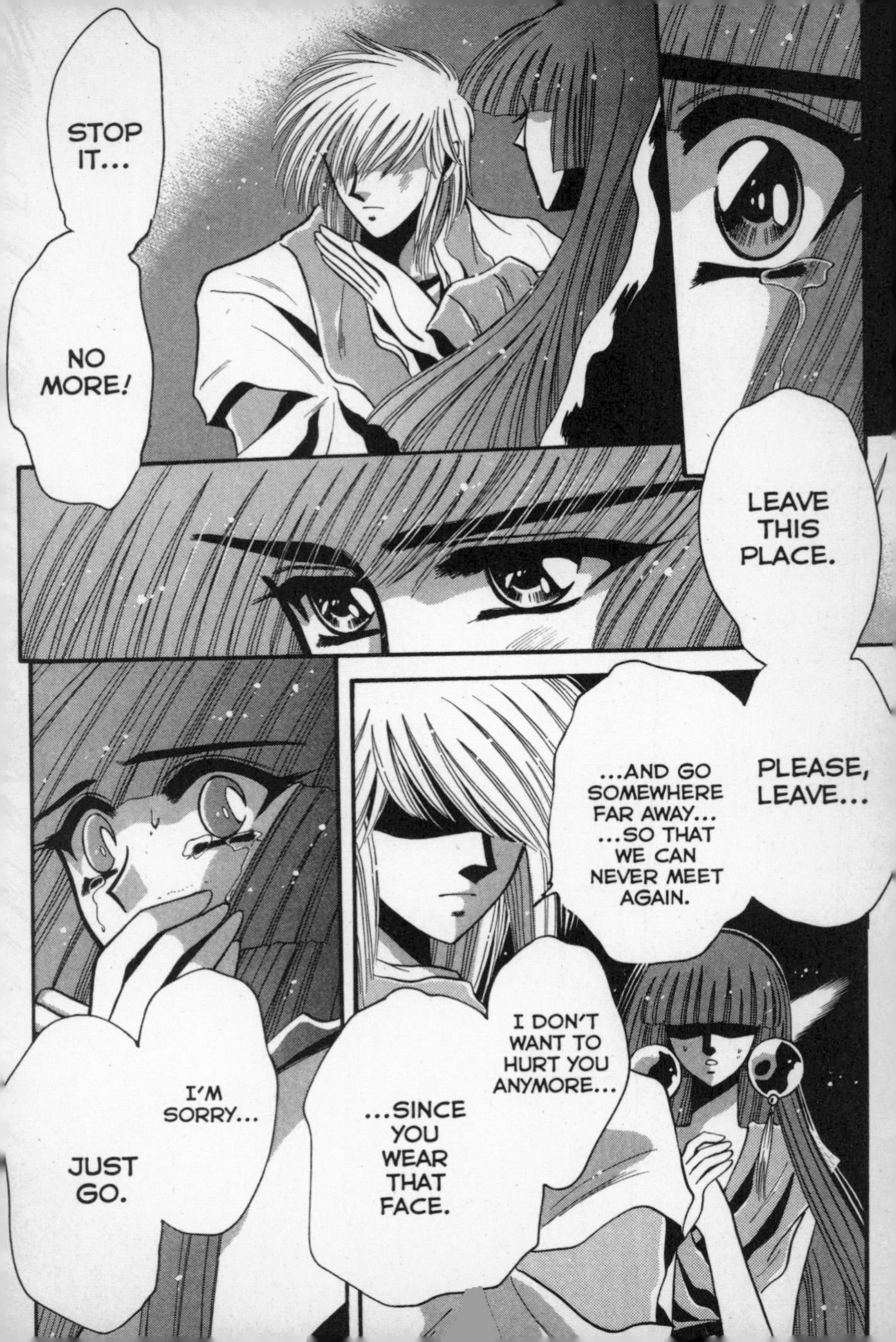
STOP IT...
NO MORE!
LEAVE THIS PLACE.
PLEASE, LEAVE...
...AND GO SOMEWHERE FAR AWAY... ...SO THAT WE CAN NEVER MEET AGAIN.
I DON'T WANT TO HURT YOU ANYMORE...
...SINCE YOU WEAR THAT FACE.
I'M SORRY...
JUST GO.

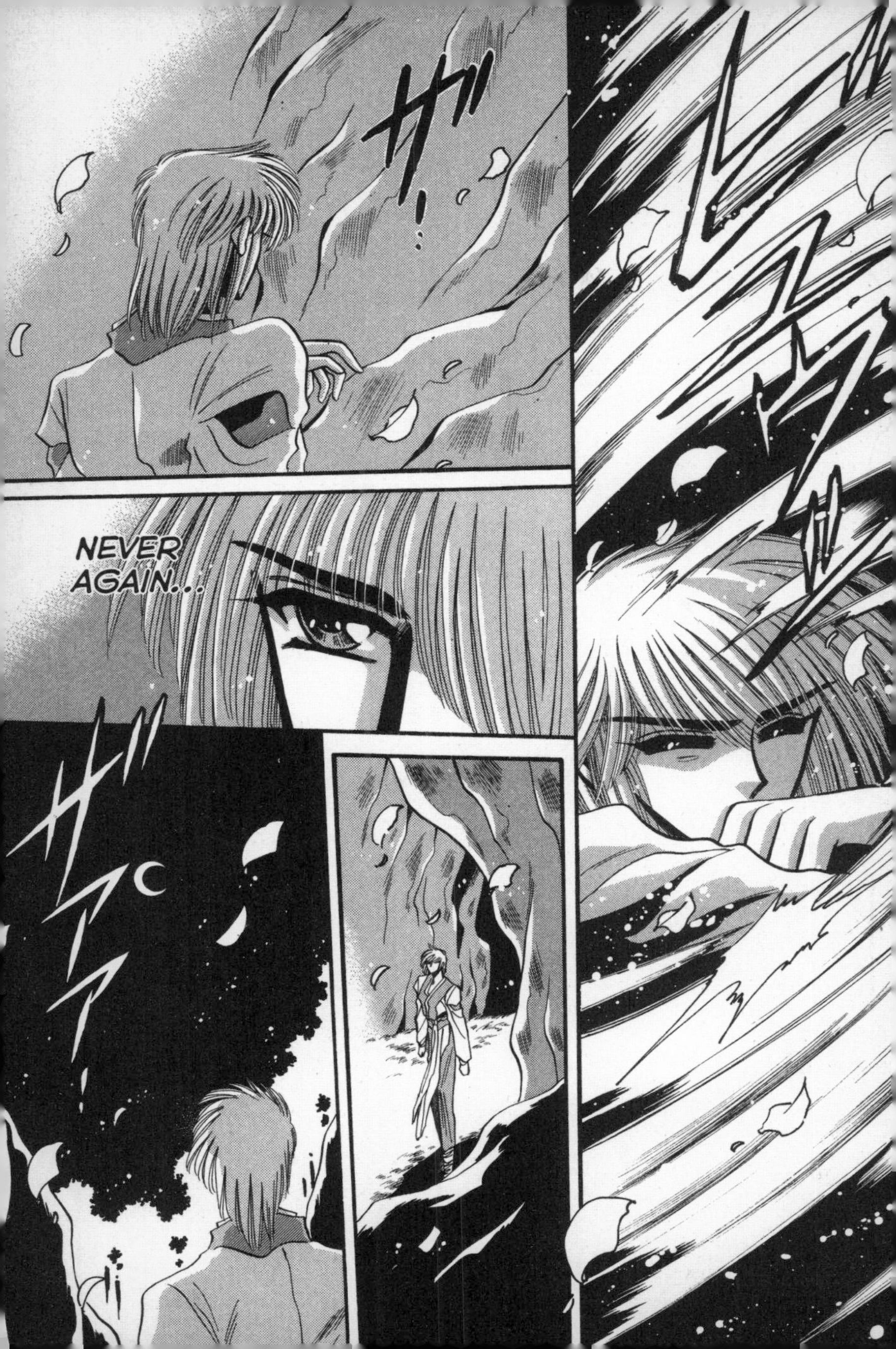
NEVER AGAIN...

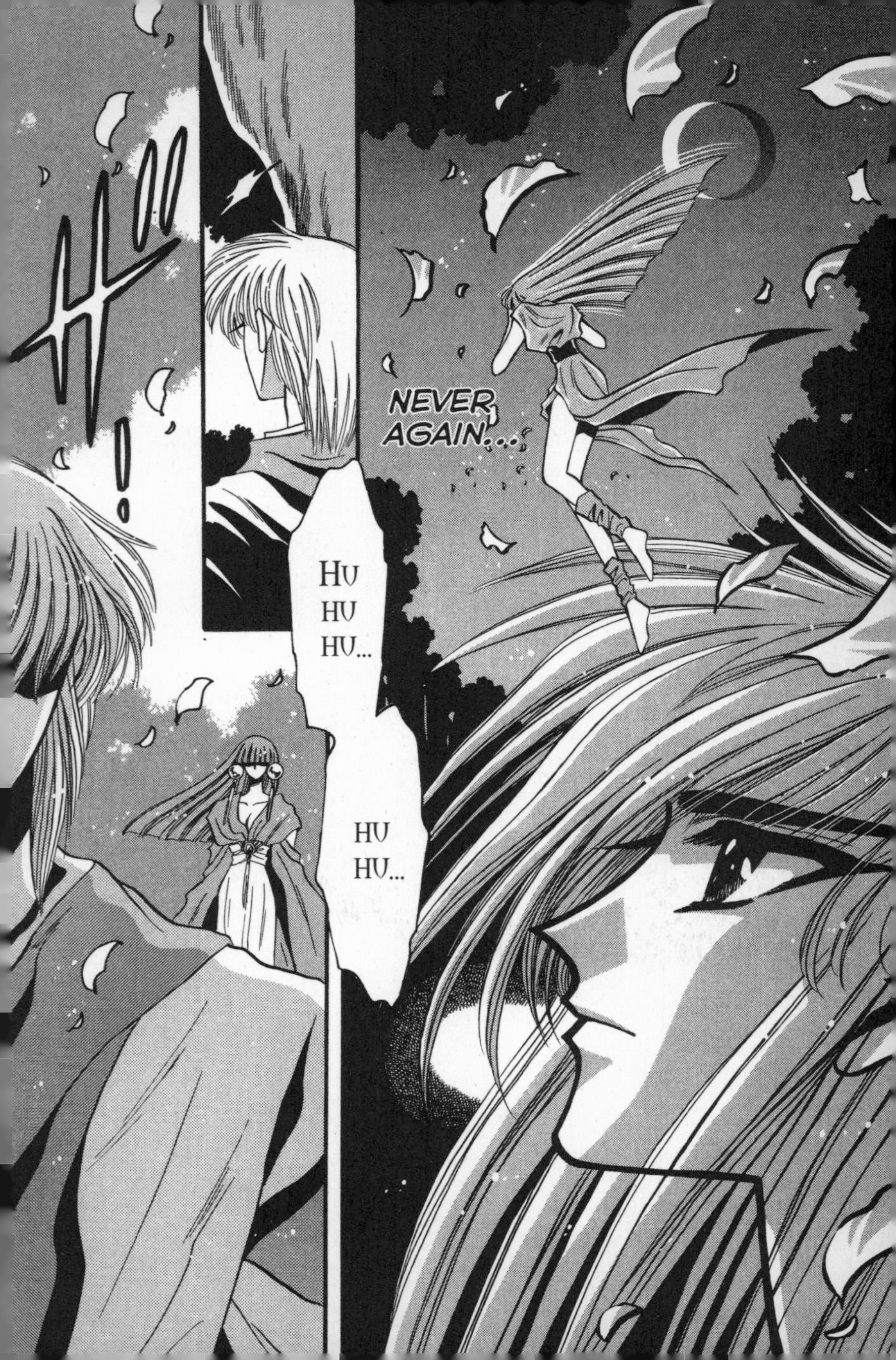
NEVER AGAIN...
HU HU HU...
HU HU...

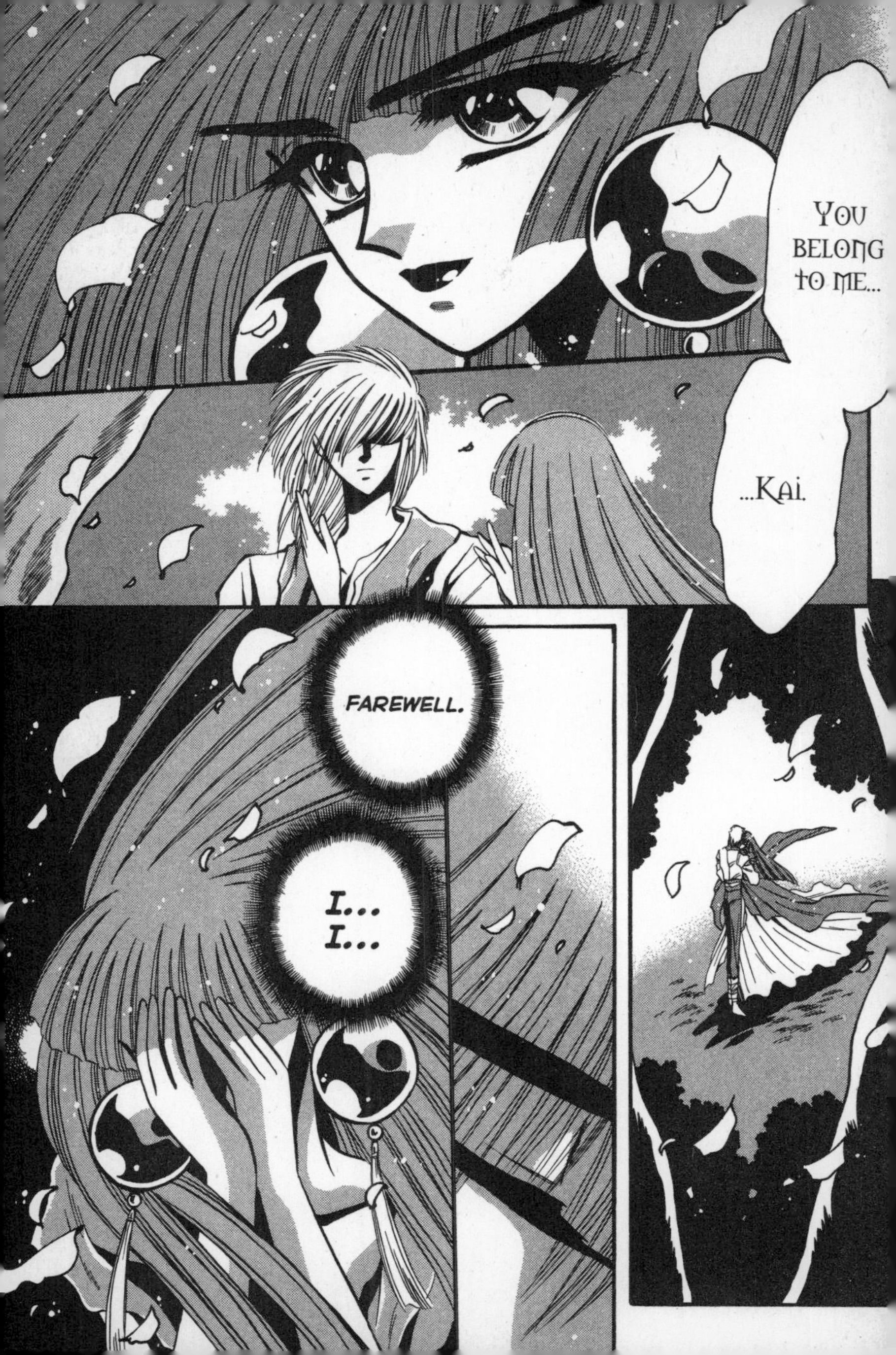
YOU BELONG TO ME...
...KAI.
FAREWELL.
I... I...

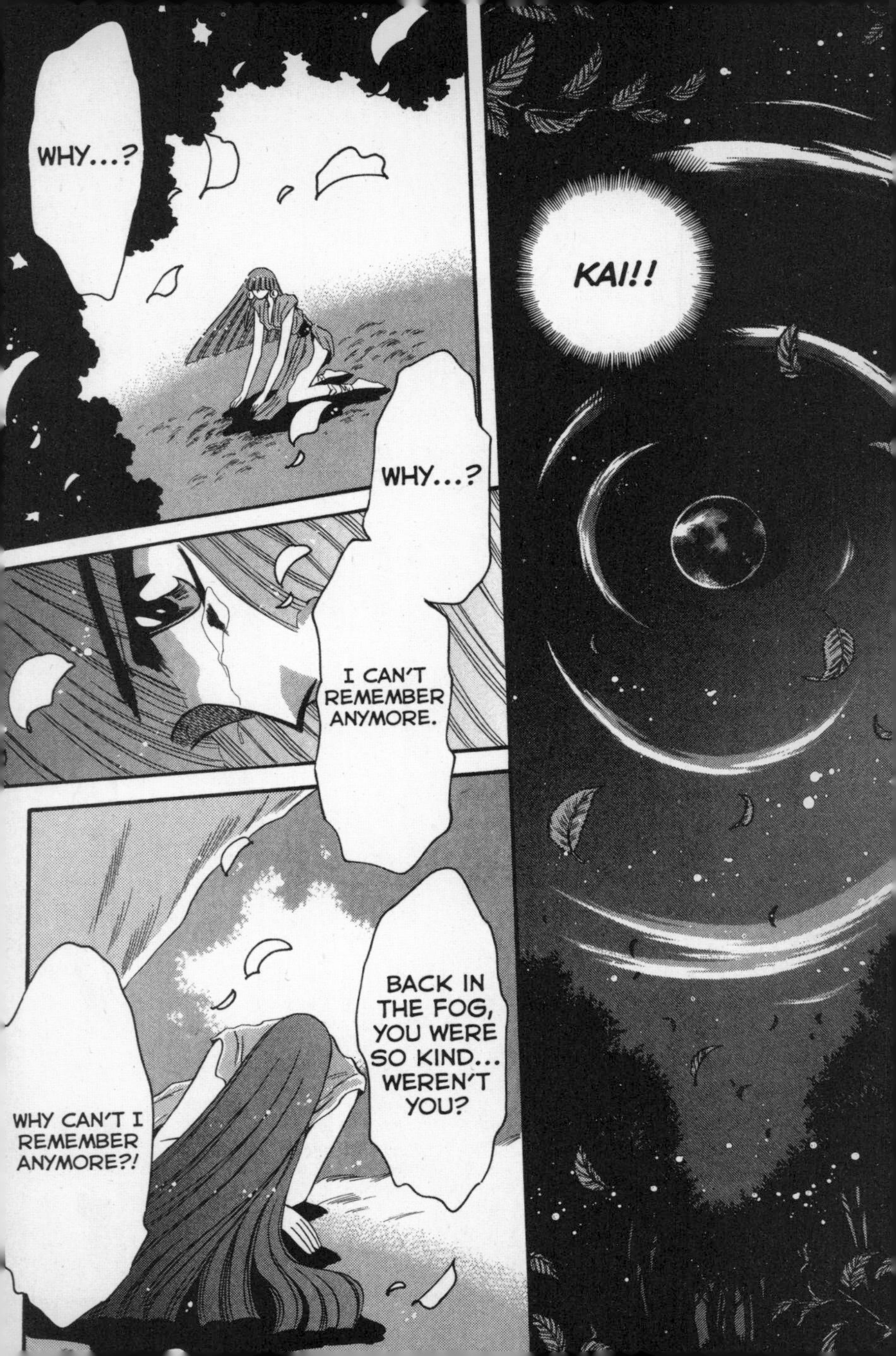
KAI!!
WHY...?
WHY...?
I CAN'T REMEMBER ANYMORE.
BACK IN THE FOG, YOU WERE SO KIND... WEREN'T YOU?
WHY CAN'T I REMEMBER ANYMORE?!

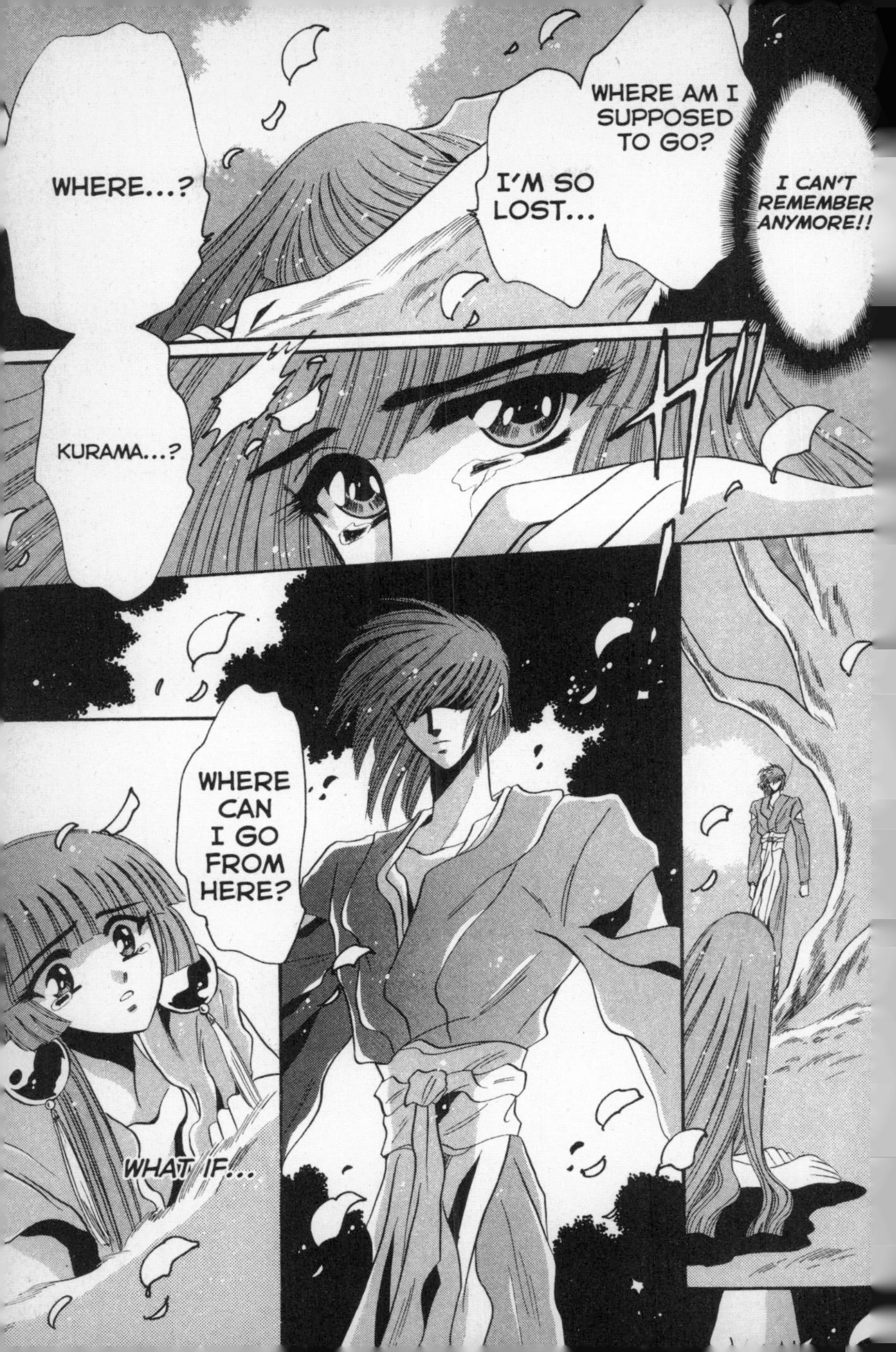
I CAN'T REMEMBER ANYMORE!!
WHERE AM I SUPPOSED TO GO?
I'M SO LOST...
WHERE...?
KURAMA...?
WHERE CAN I GO FROM HERE?
WHAT IF...

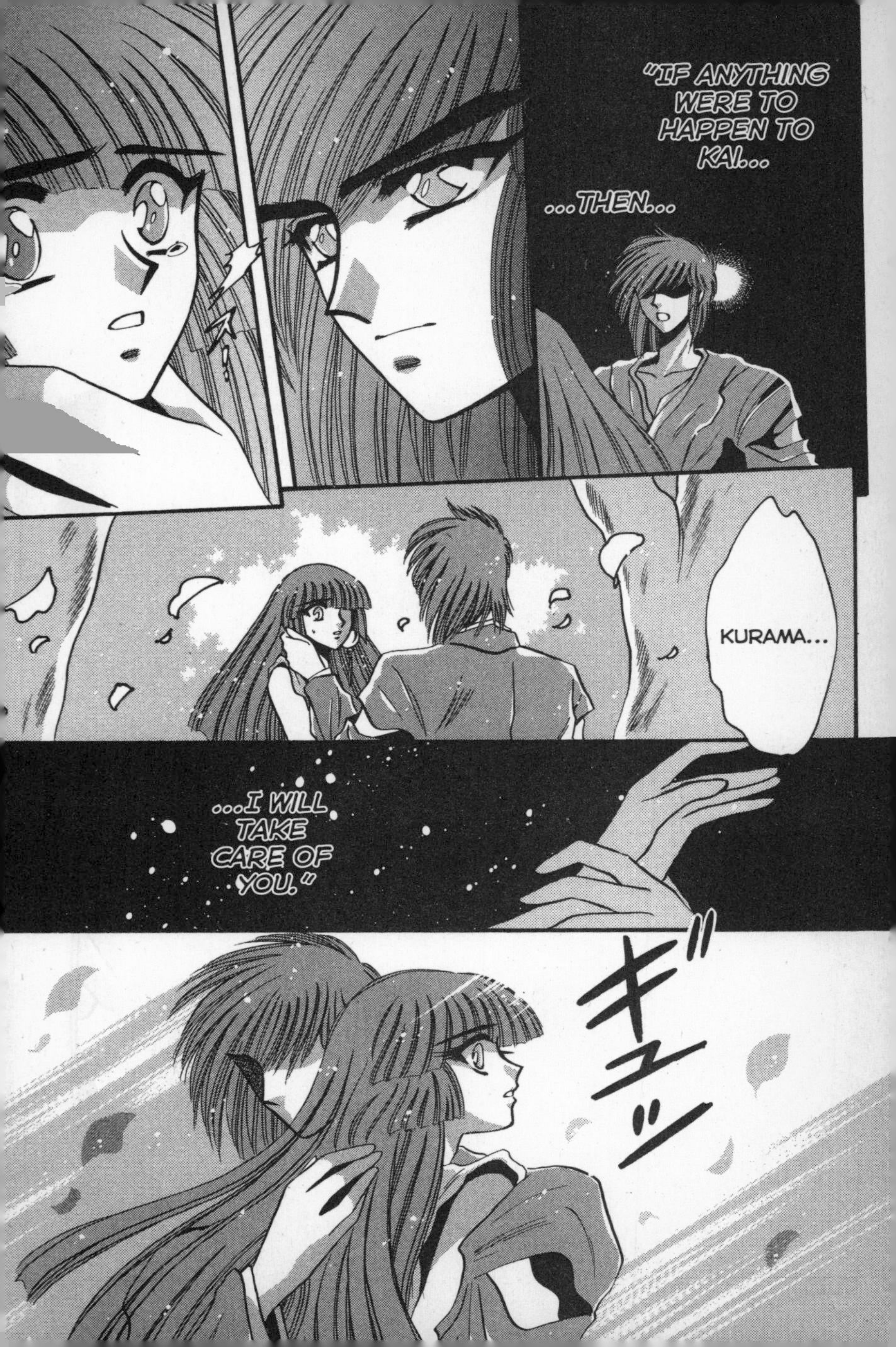
"IF ANYTHING WERE TO HAPPEN TO KAI...
...THEN...
KURAMA...
...I WILL TAKE CARE OF YOU."
ギュッ

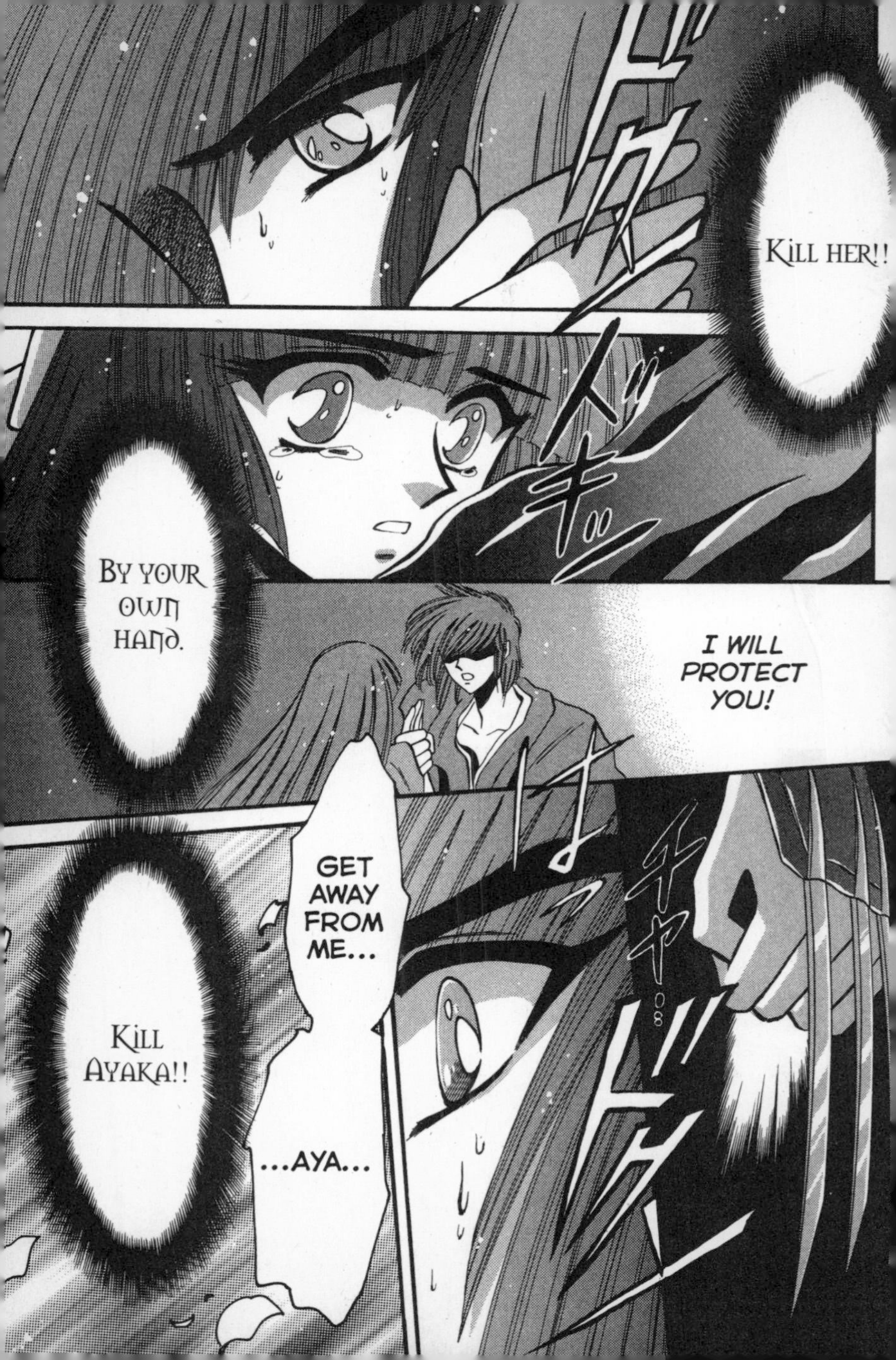
KILL HER!!
BY YOUR OWN HAND.
I WILL PROTECT YOU!
GET AWAY FROM ME...
KILL AYAKA!!
...AYA...

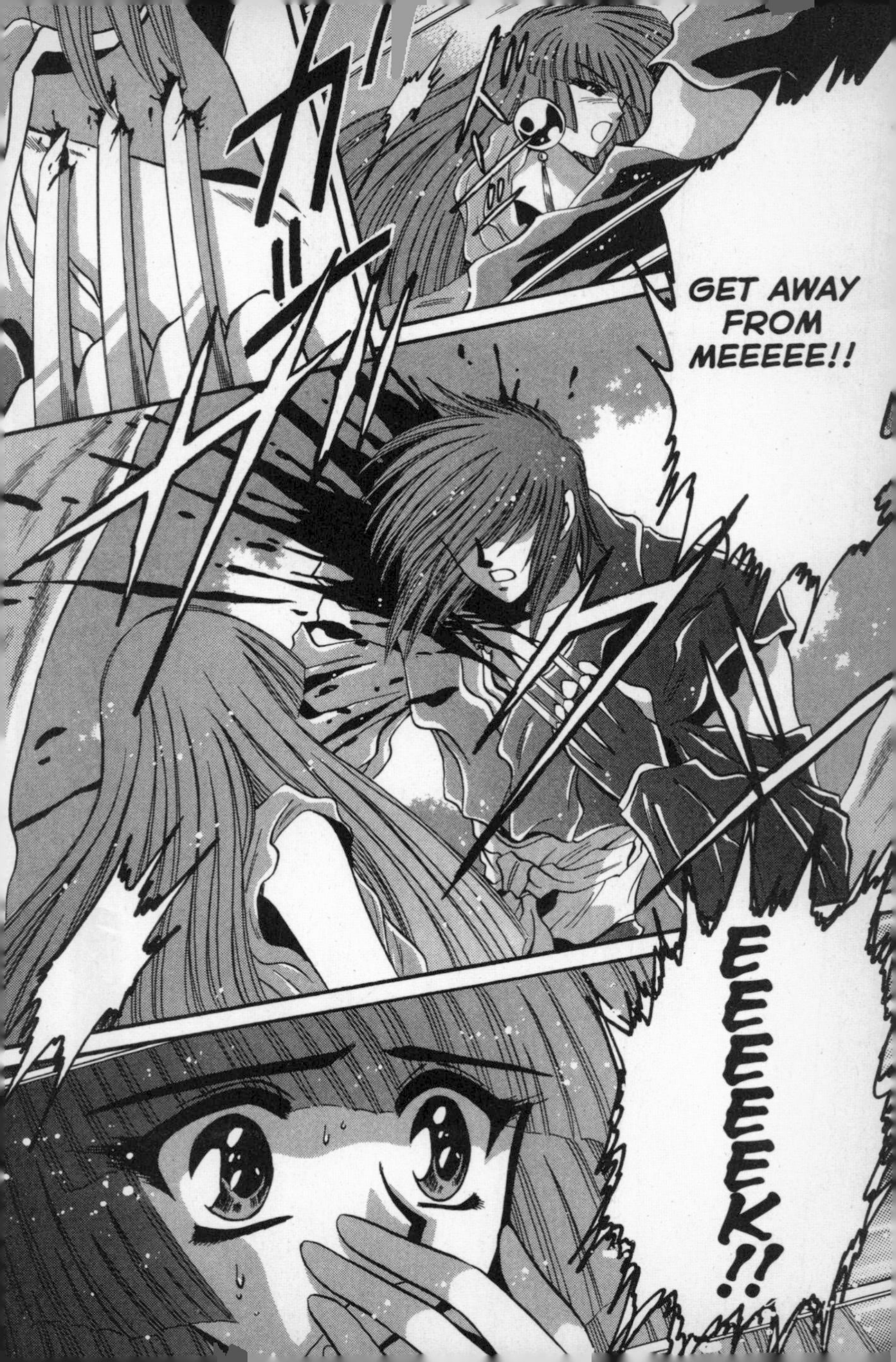
GET AWAY FROM MEEEEEE!!
EEEEEEK!!

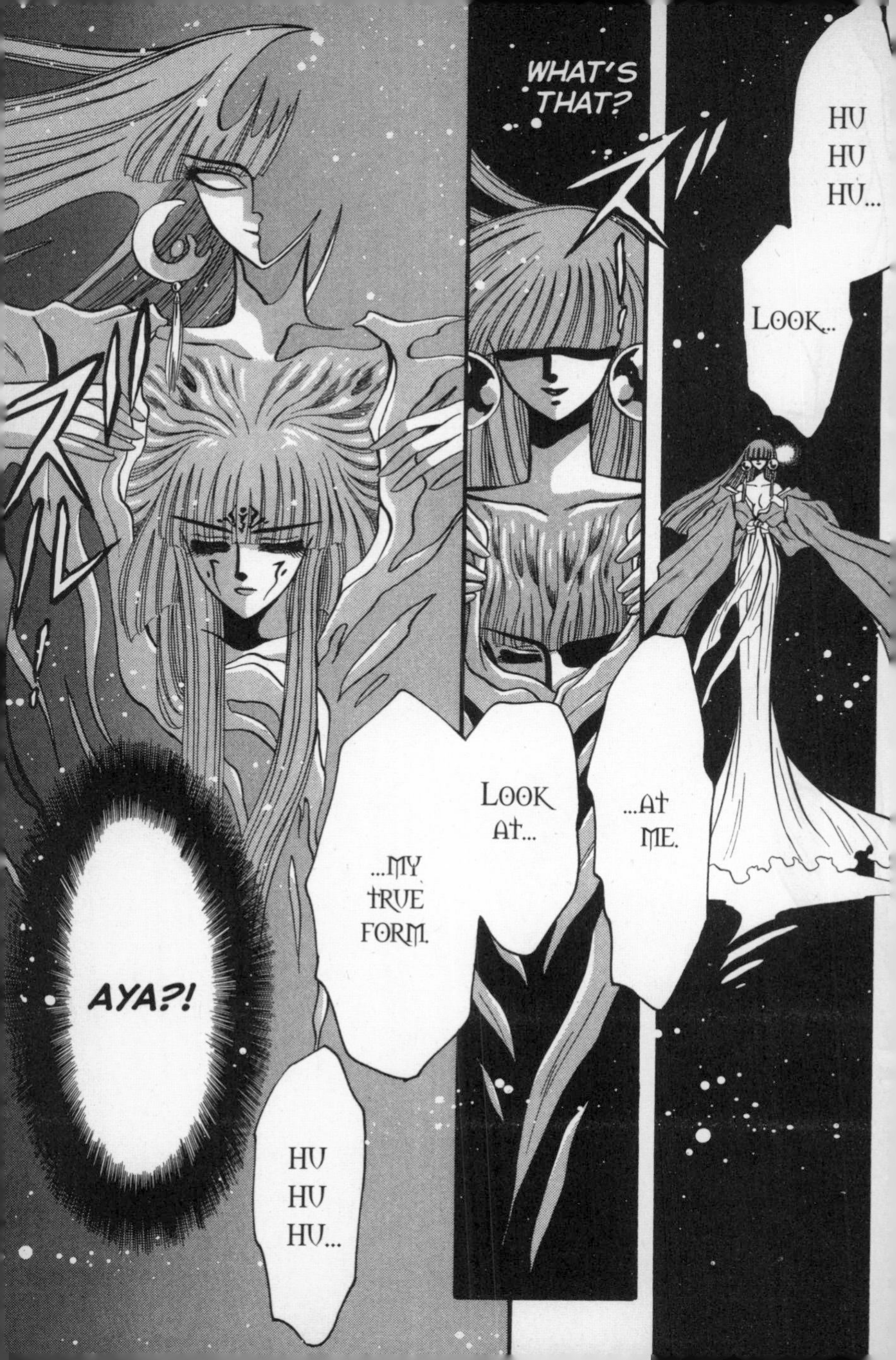
HU HU HU...
LOOK...
WHAT'S THAT?
...AT ME.
LOOK AT...
...MY TRUE FORM.
AYA?!
HU HU HU...

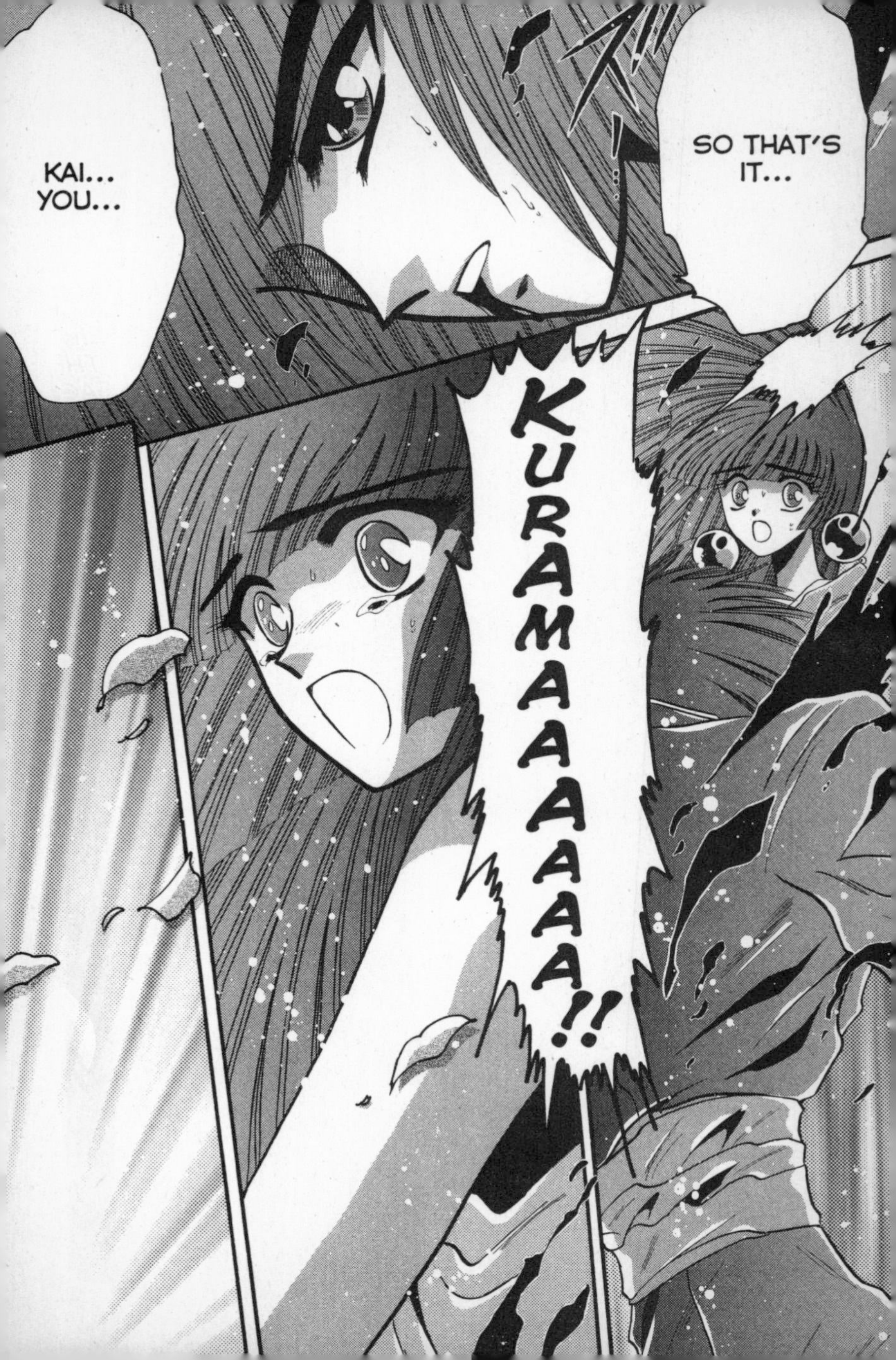
SO THAT'S IT...
KAI... YOU...
KURAMAAAAAA!!

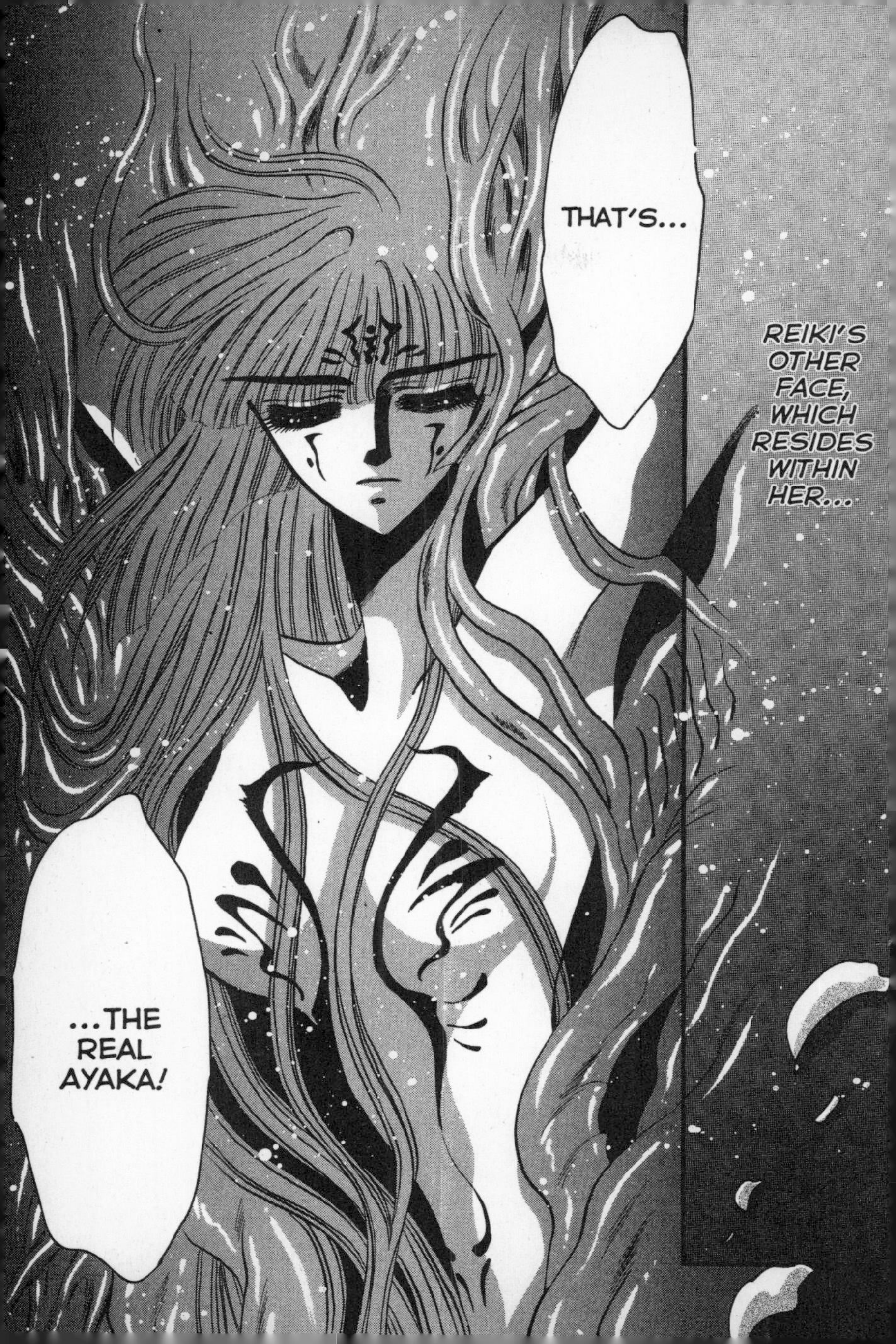
THAT'S...
REIKI'S OTHER FACE, WHICH RESIDES WITHIN HER...
...THE REAL AYAKA!

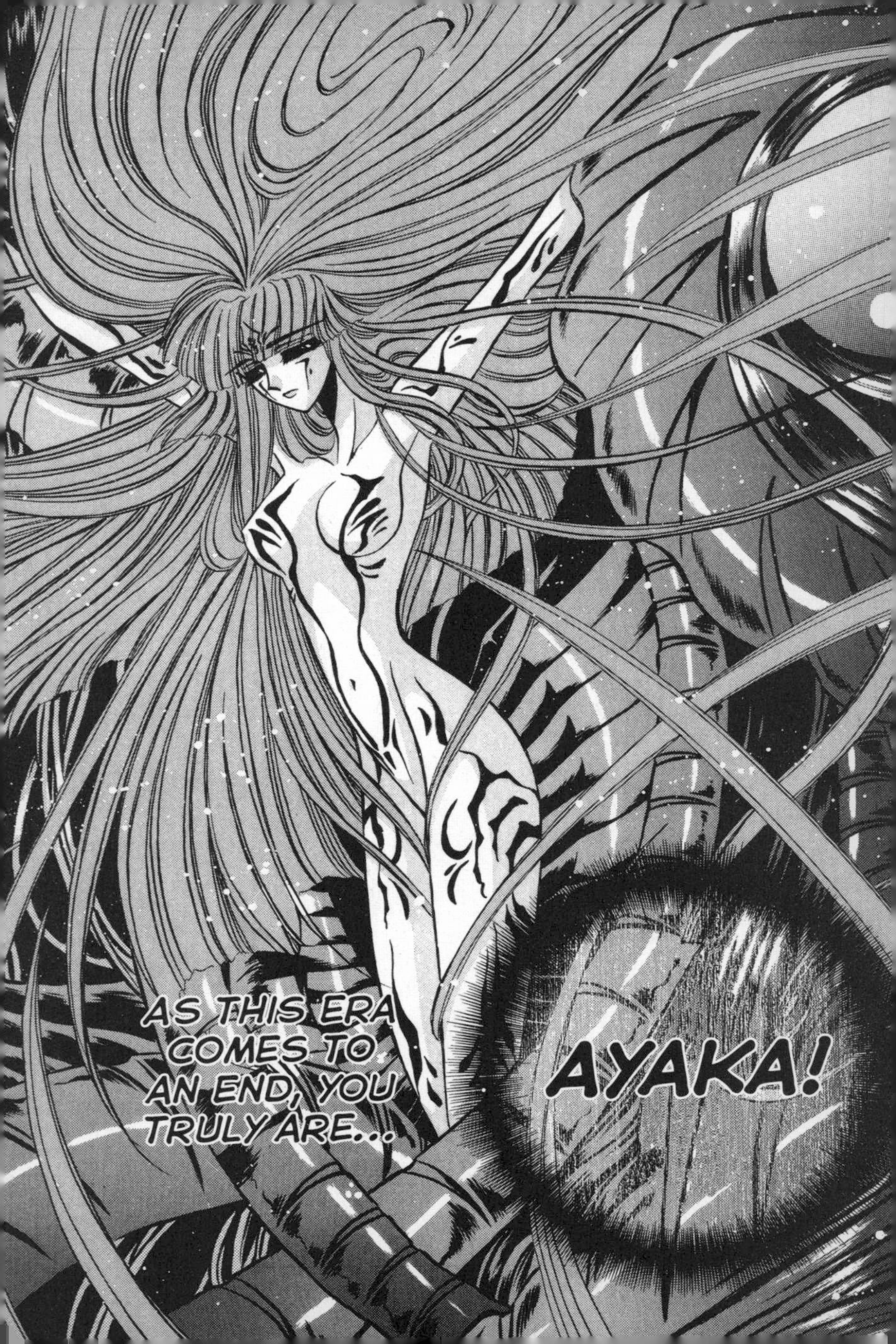
AS THIS ERA COMES TO AN END, YOU TRULY ARE...
AYAKA!

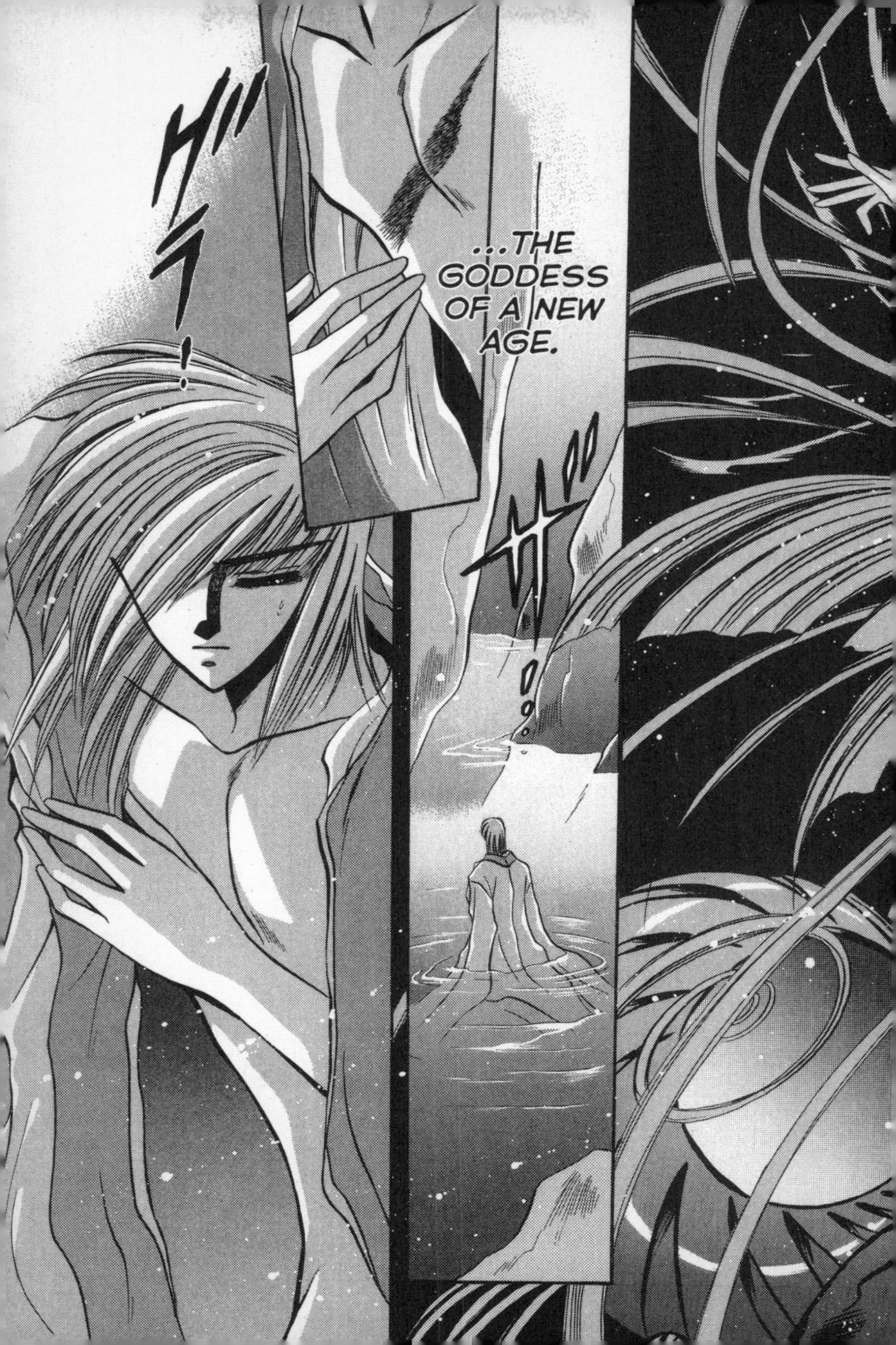
...THE GODDESS OF A NEW AGE.

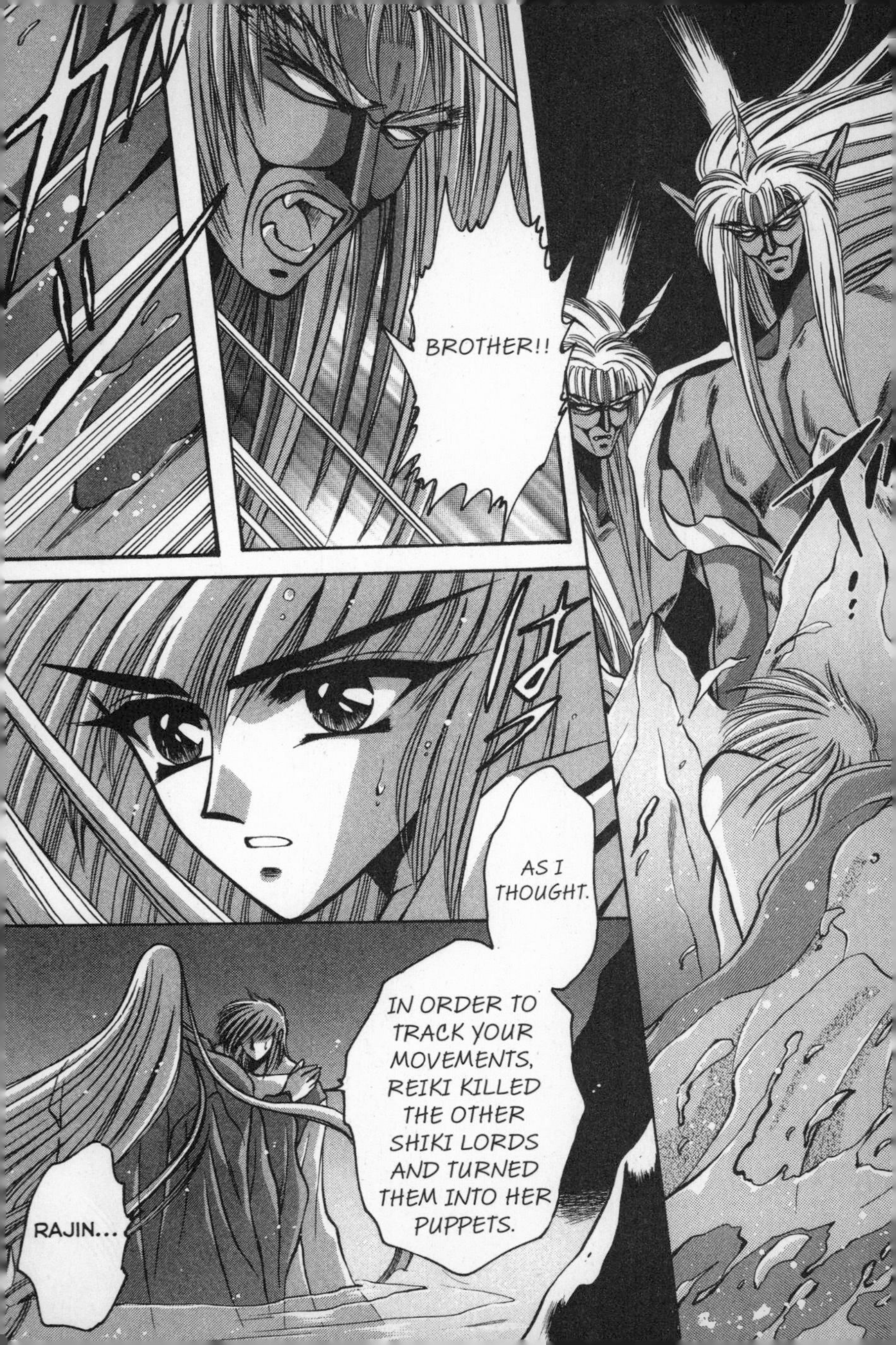
BROTHER!!
AS I THOUGHT.
IN ORDER TO TRACK YOUR MOVEMENTS, REIKI KILLED THE OTHER SHIKI LORDS AND TURNED THEM INTO HER PUPPETS.
RAJIN...

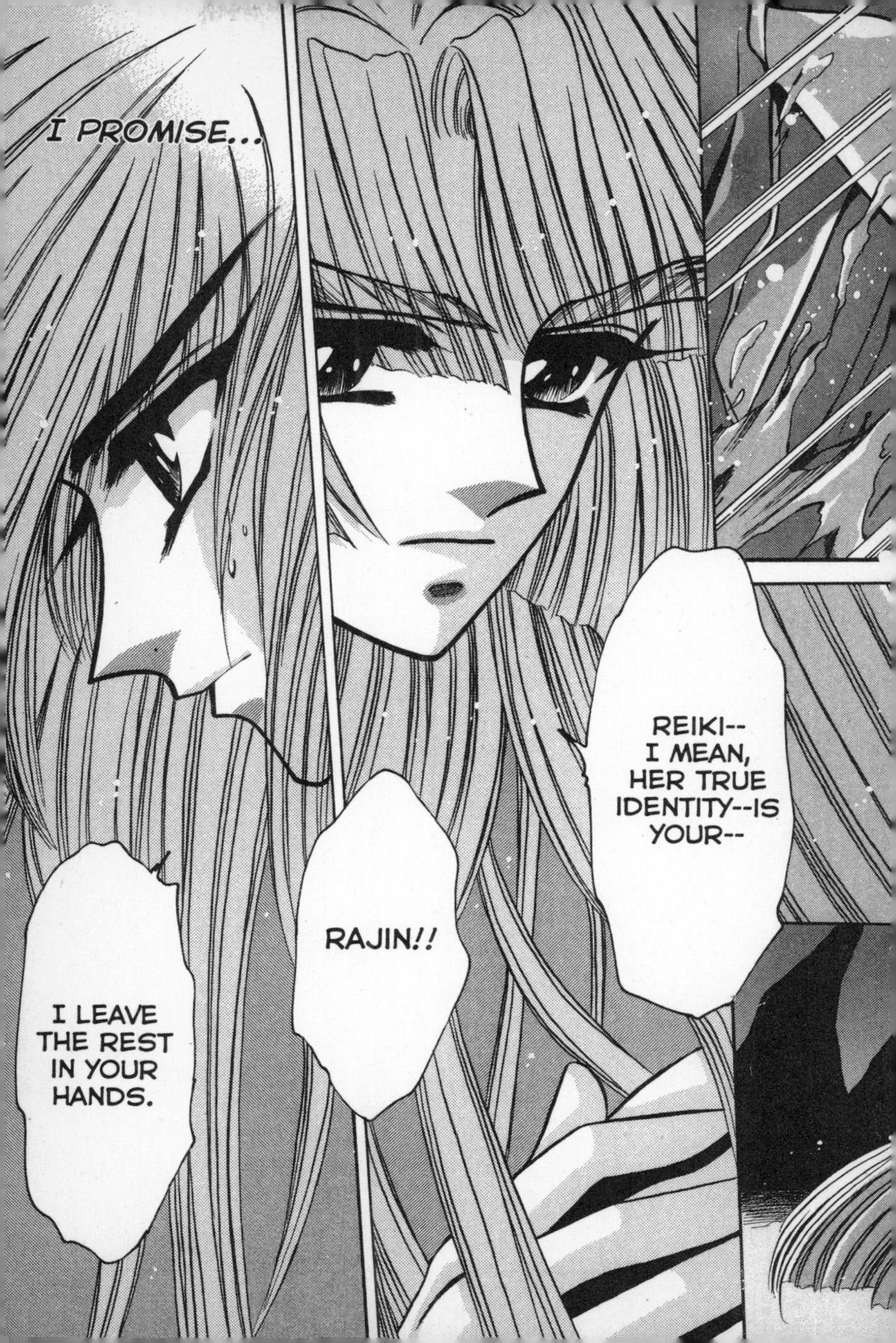
REIKI-- I MEAN, HER TRUE IDENTITY--IS YOUR--
RAJIN!!
I PROMISE...
I LEAVE THE REST IN YOUR HANDS.

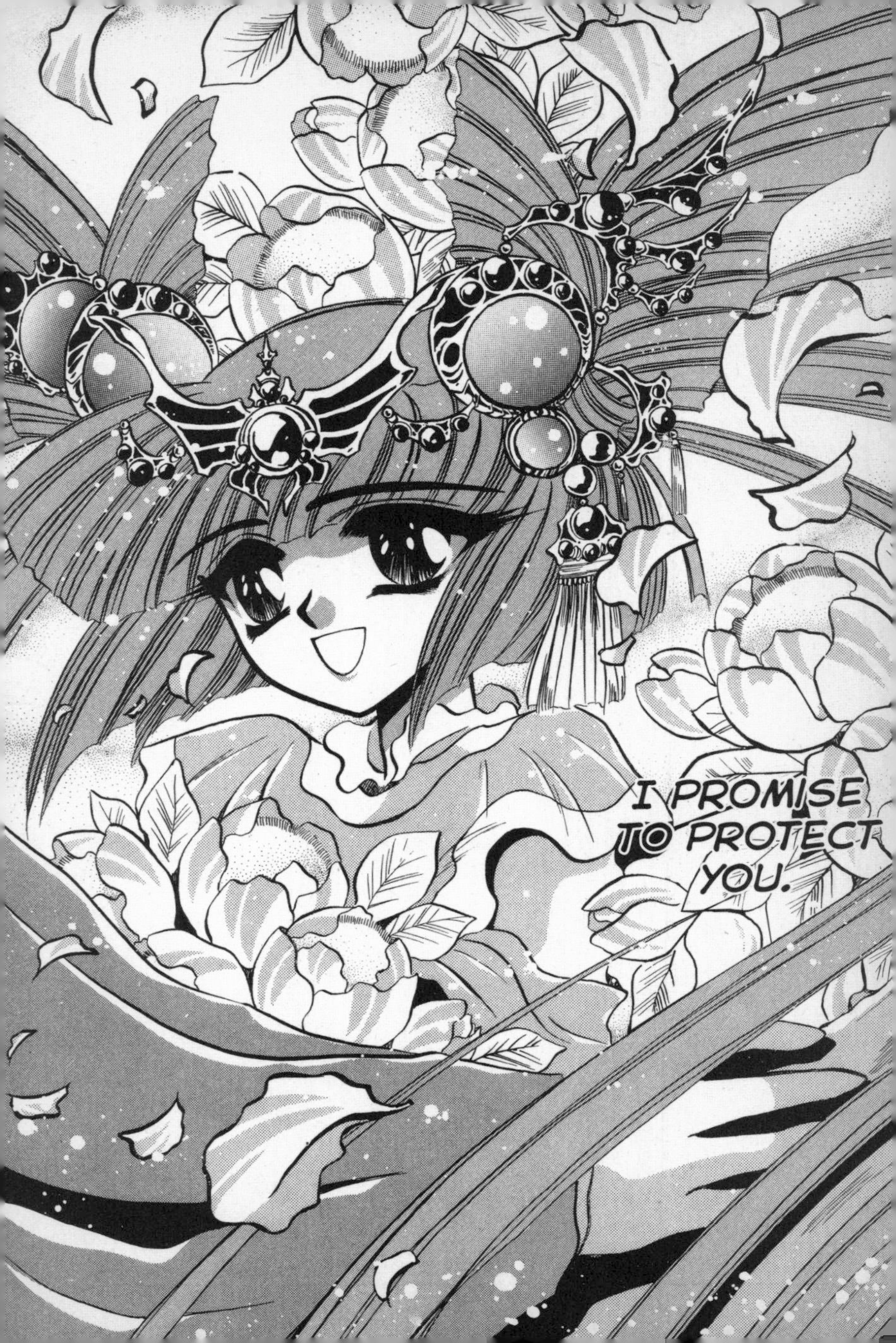
I PROMISE TO PROTECT YOU.

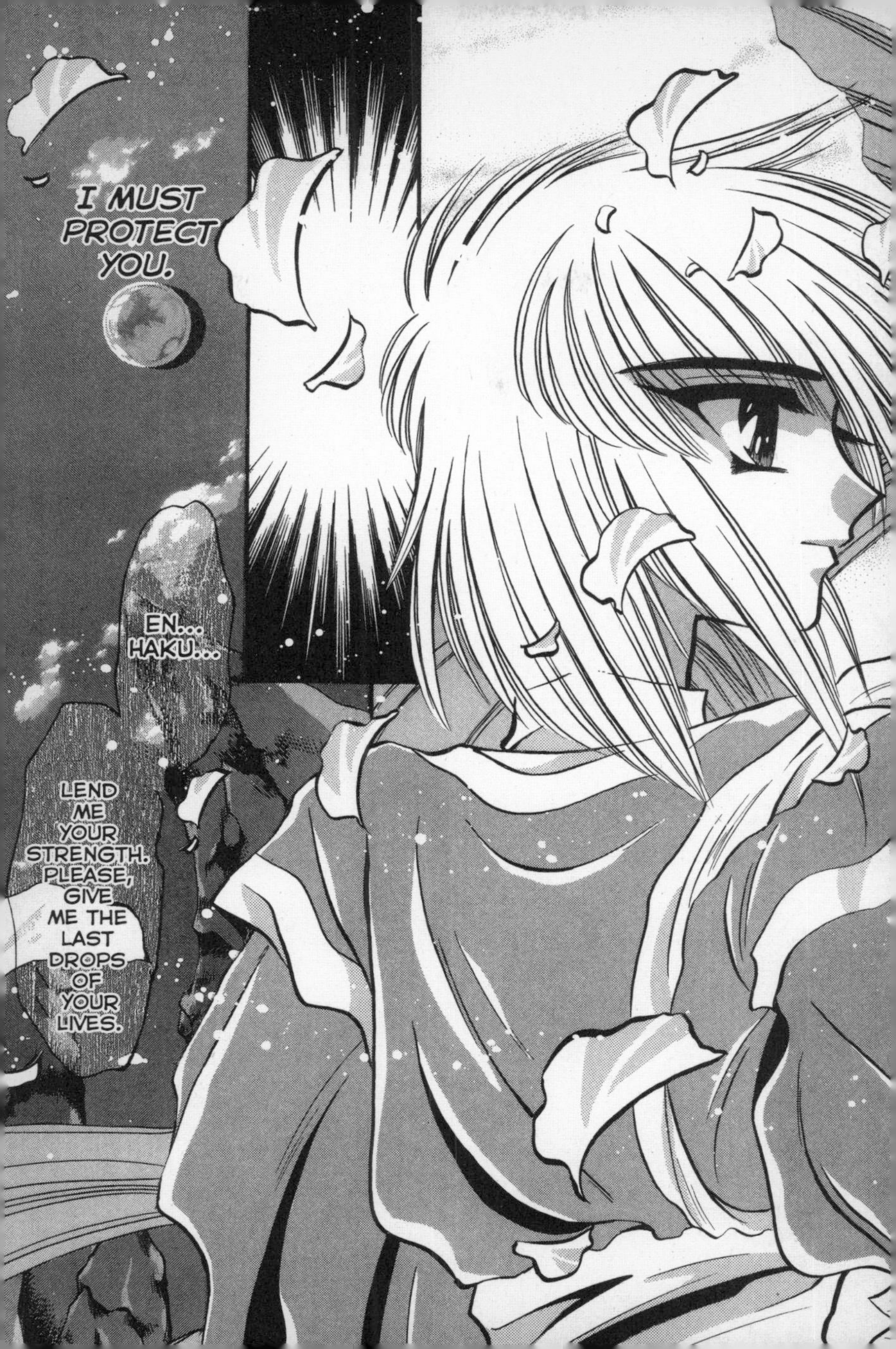
I MUST PROTECT YOU.
EN... HAKU...
LEND ME YOUR STRENGTH. PLEASE, GIVE ME THE LAST DROPS OF YOUR LIVES.

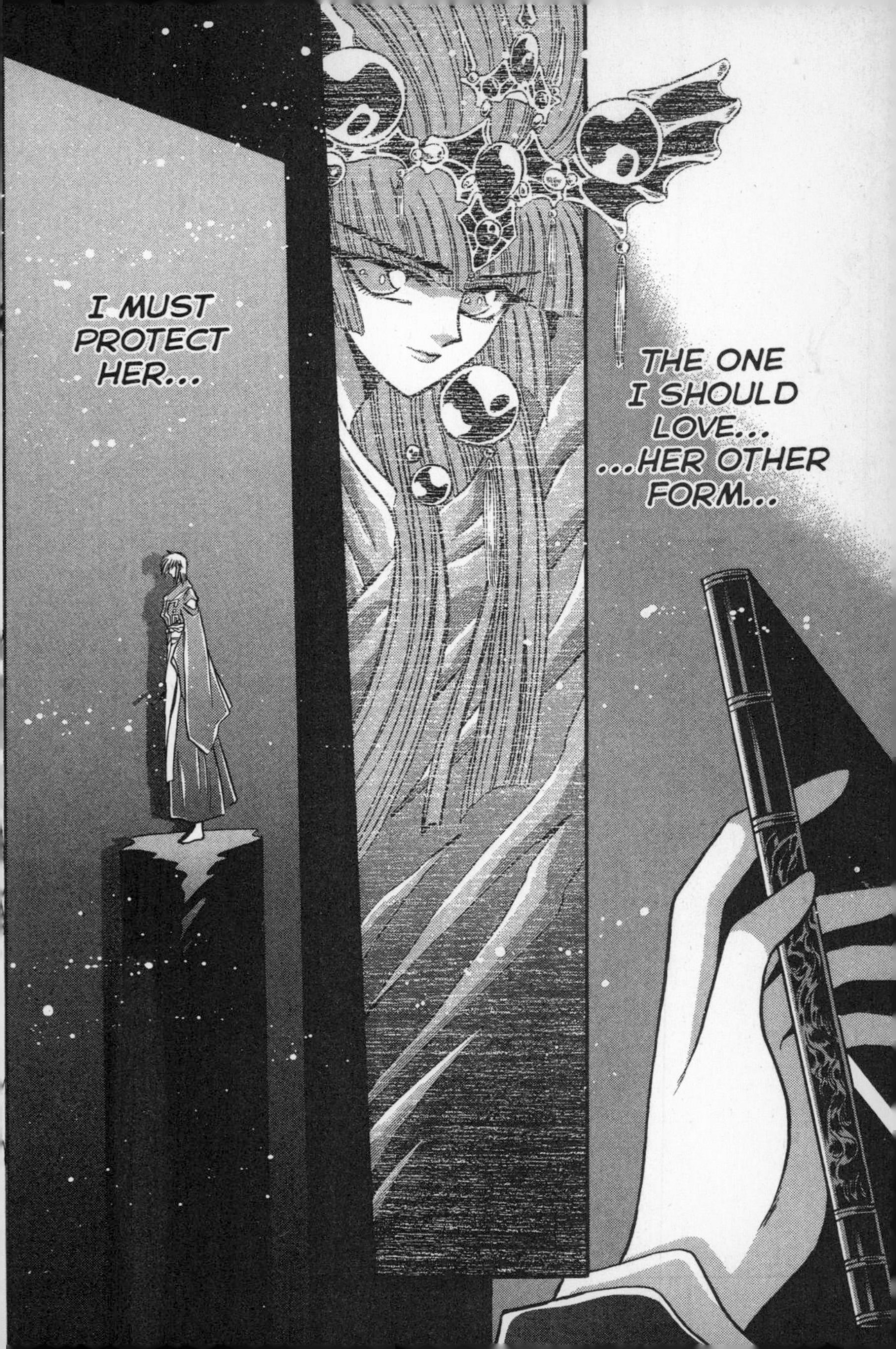
THE ONE I SHOULD LOVE... ...HER OTHER FORM...
I MUST PROTECT HER...

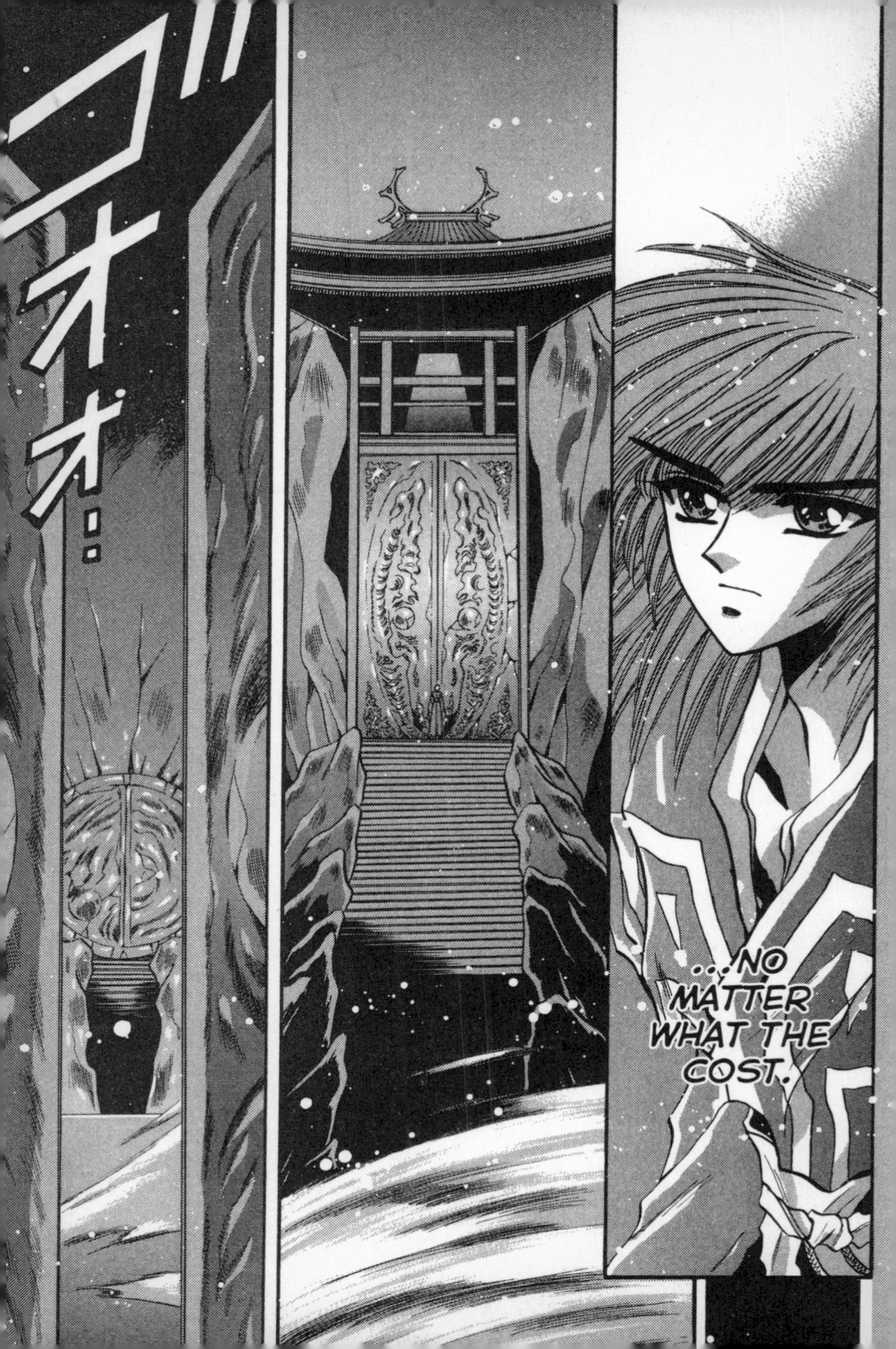
...NO MATTER WHAT THE COST.
ゴオオ!!

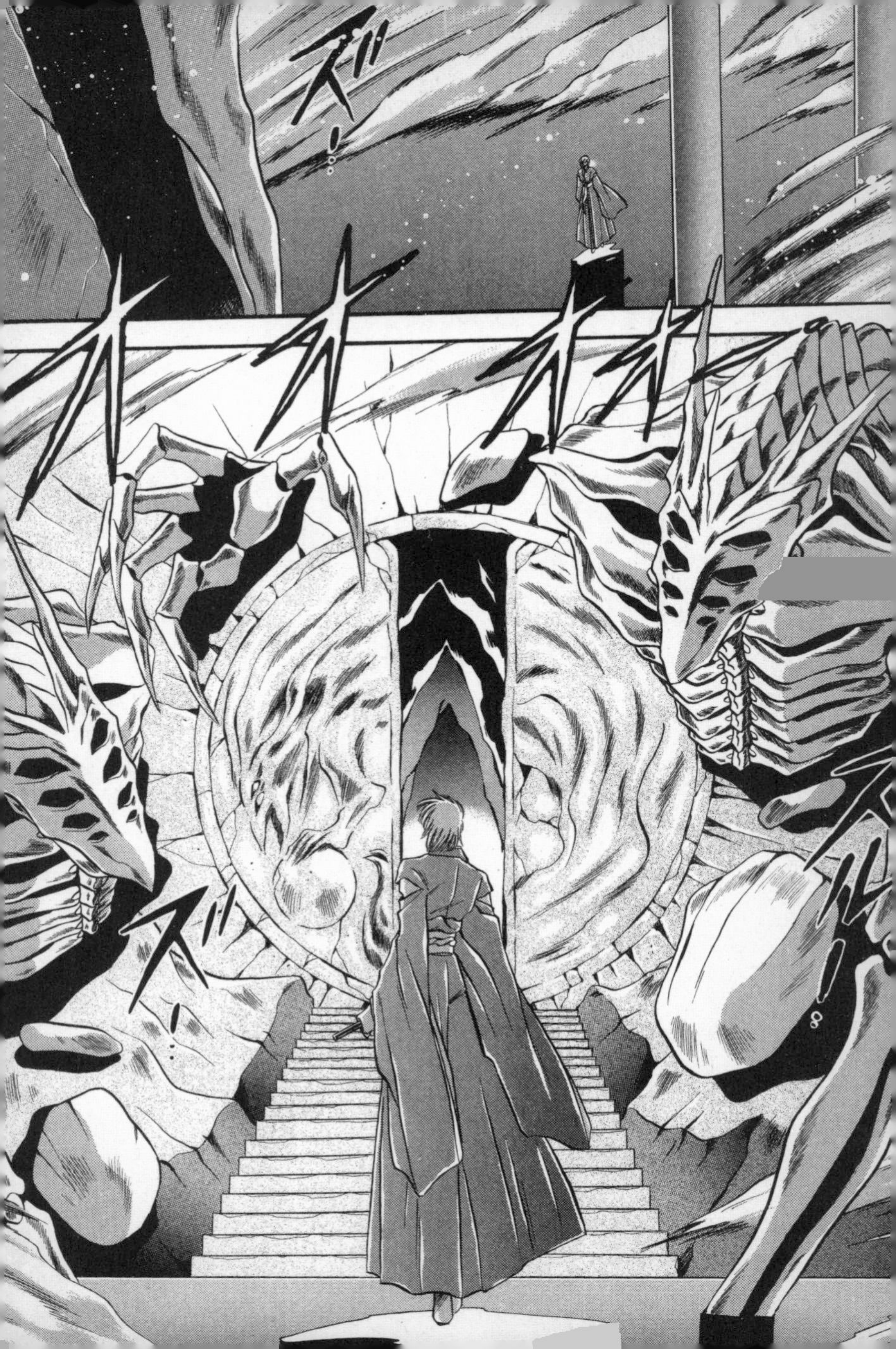
ズ!
オオオオ
ズ!

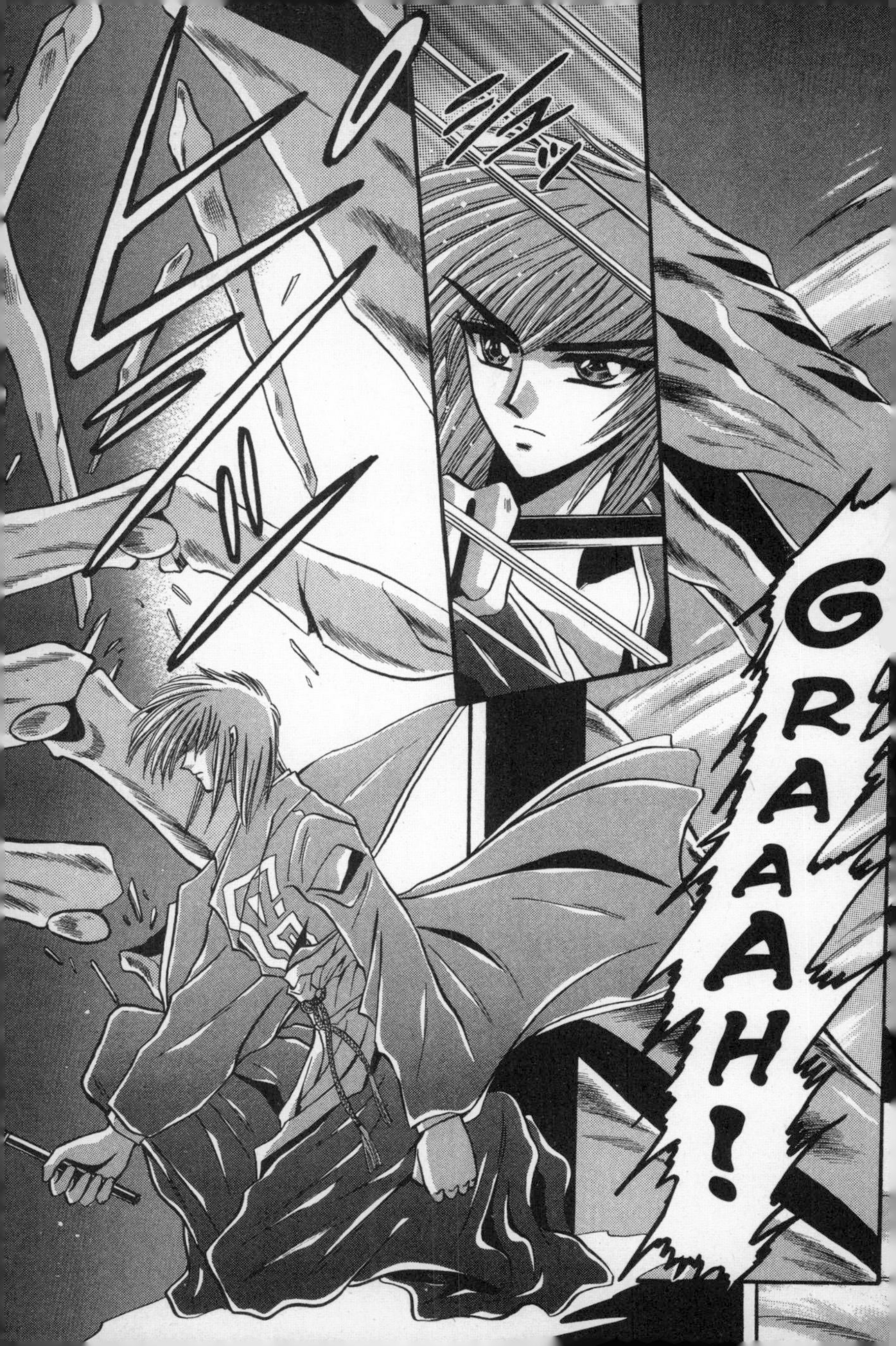
GRAAAH!

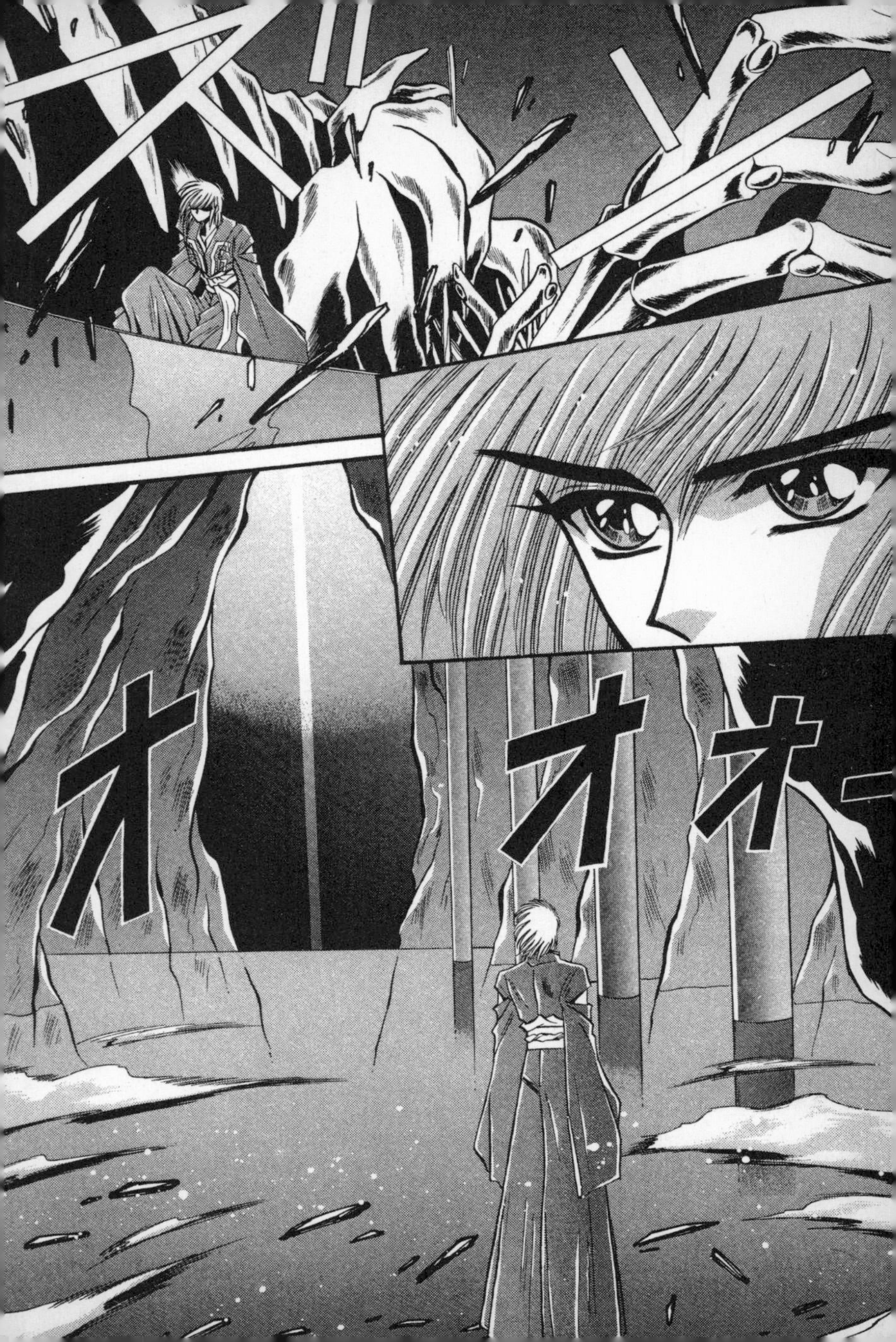
オオオー

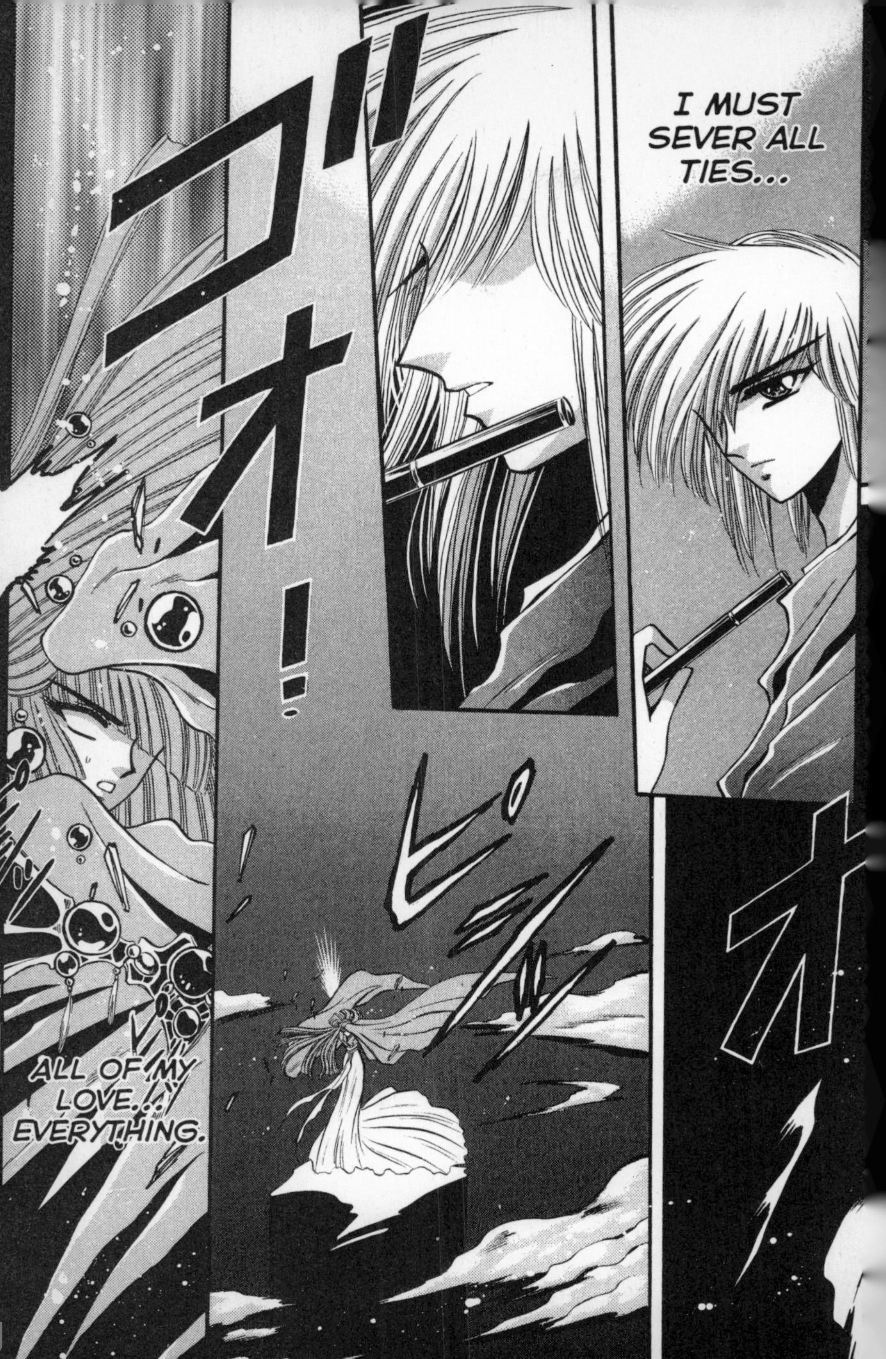
I MUST SEVER ALL TIES...
ALL OF MY LOVE... EVERYTHING.

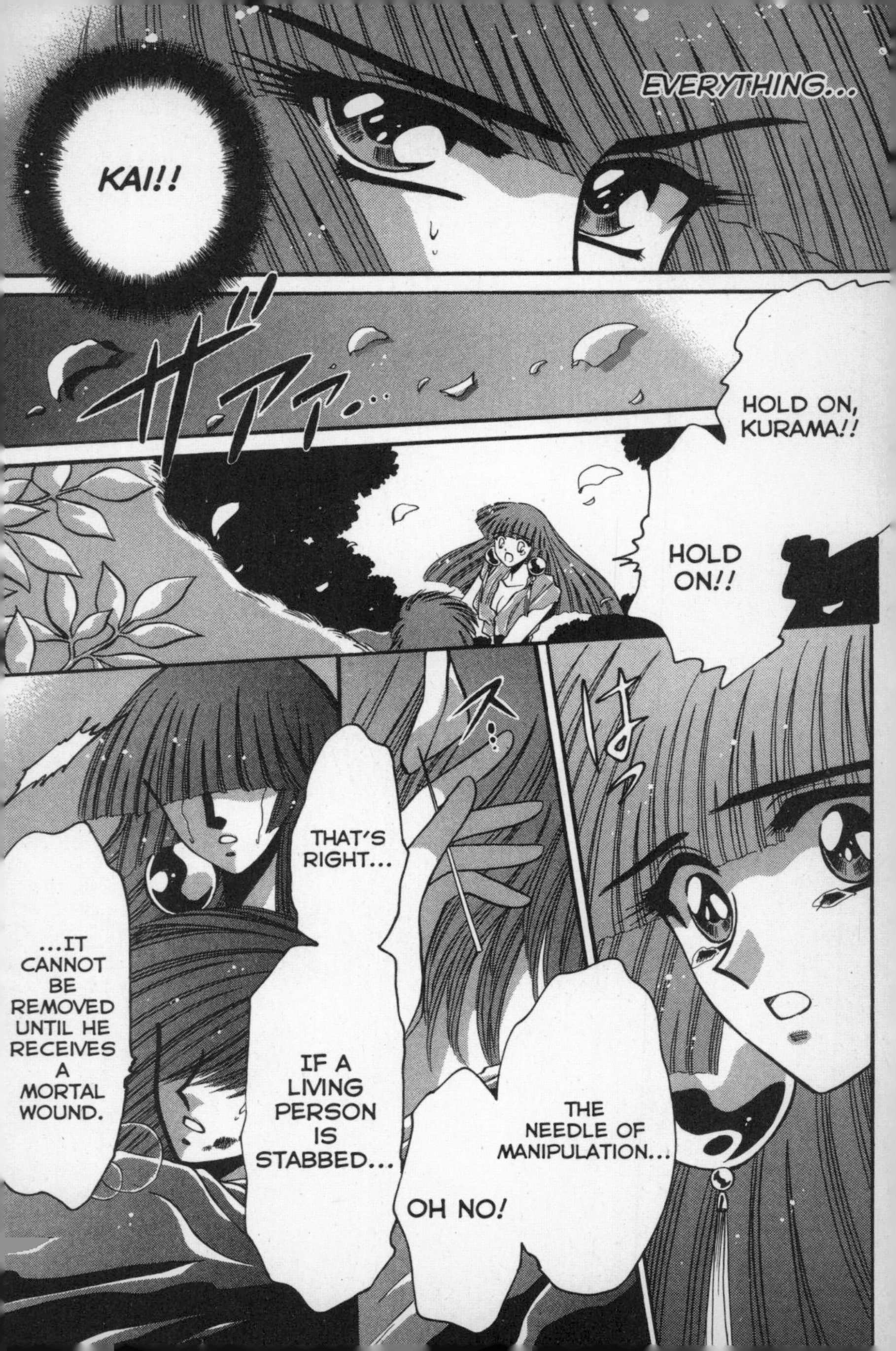
EVERYTHING...
KAI!!
ザアア…
HOLD ON, KURAMA!!
HOLD ON!!
はっ
ス…
THAT'S RIGHT...
THE NEEDLE OF MANIPULATION...
IF A LIVING PERSON IS STABBED...
...IT CANNOT BE REMOVED UNTIL HE RECEIVES A MORTAL WOUND.
OH NO!

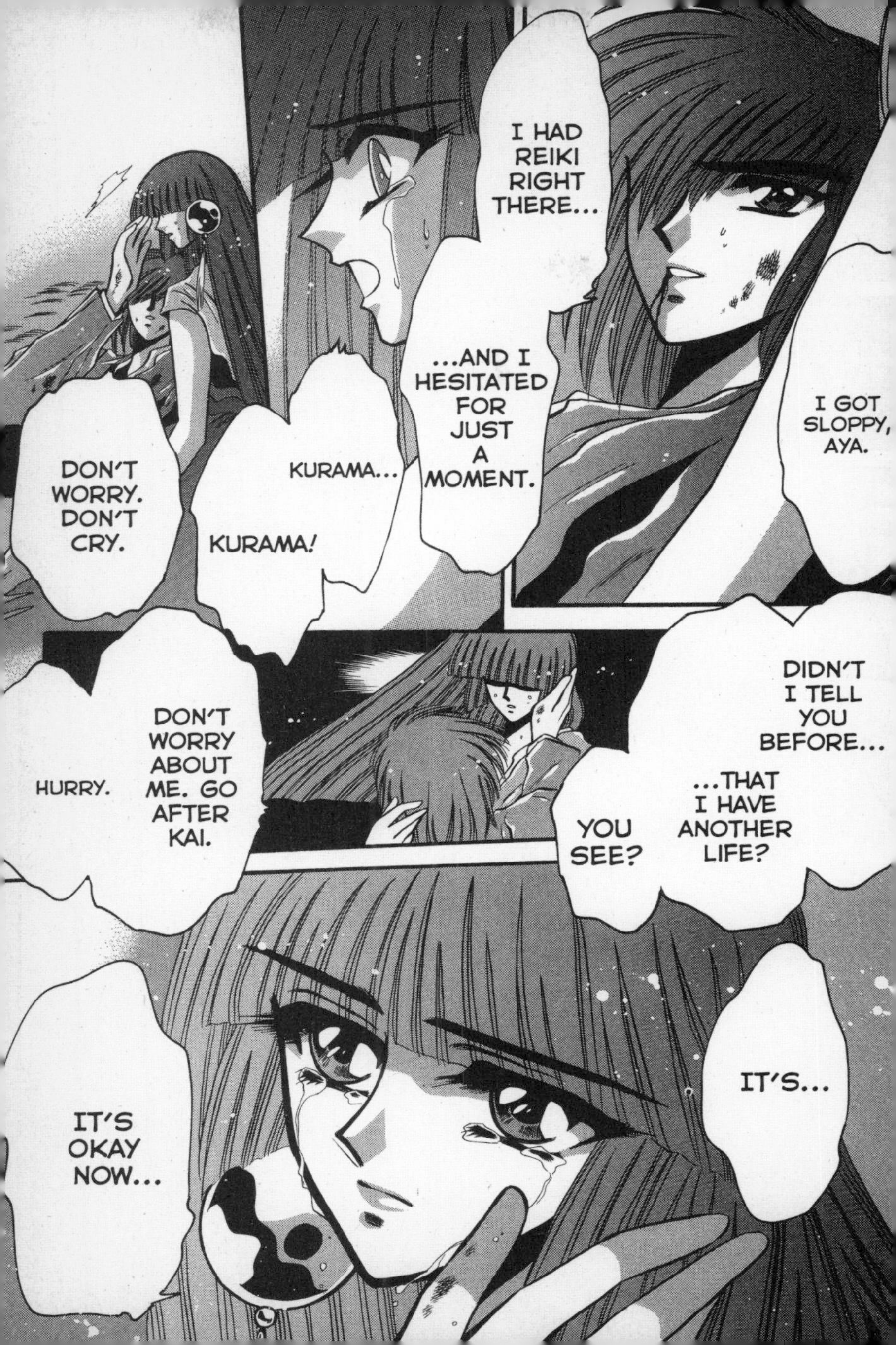

I GOT SLOPPY, AYA.
I HAD REIKI RIGHT THERE...
...AND I HESITATED FOR JUST A MOMENT.
KURAMA...
KURAMA!
DON'T WORRY. DON'T CRY.
DIDN'T I TELL YOU BEFORE...
...THAT I HAVE ANOTHER LIFE?
YOU SEE?
DON'T WORRY ABOUT ME. GO AFTER KAI.
HURRY.
IT'S...
IT'S OKAY NOW...

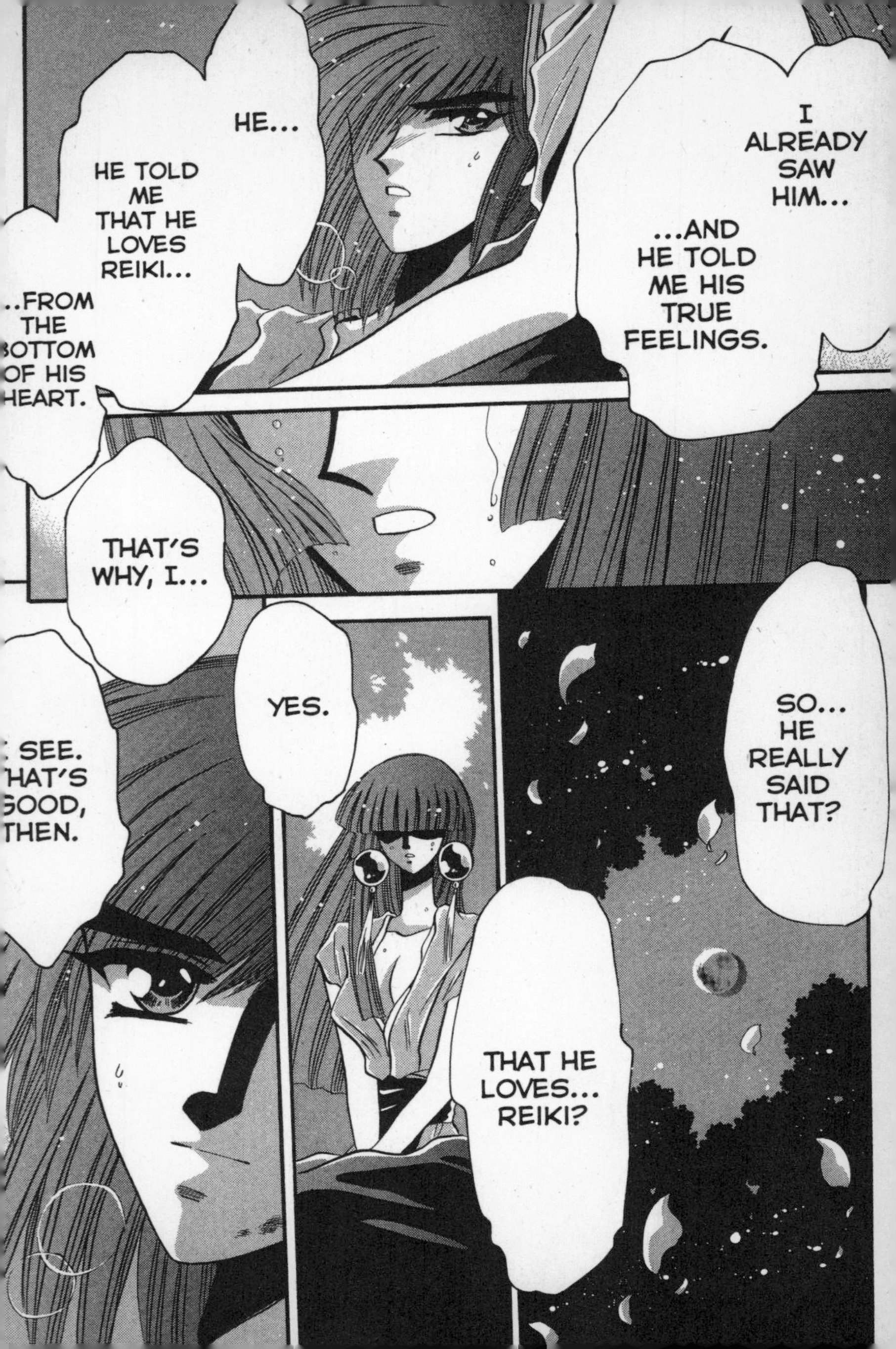

I ALREADY SAW HIM...
...AND HE TOLD ME HIS TRUE FEELINGS.
HE...
HE TOLD ME THAT HE LOVES REIKI...
..FROM THE BOTTOM OF HIS HEART.
THAT'S WHY, I...
SO... HE REALLY SAID THAT?
THAT HE LOVES... REIKI?
YES.
SEE. THAT'S GOOD, THEN.

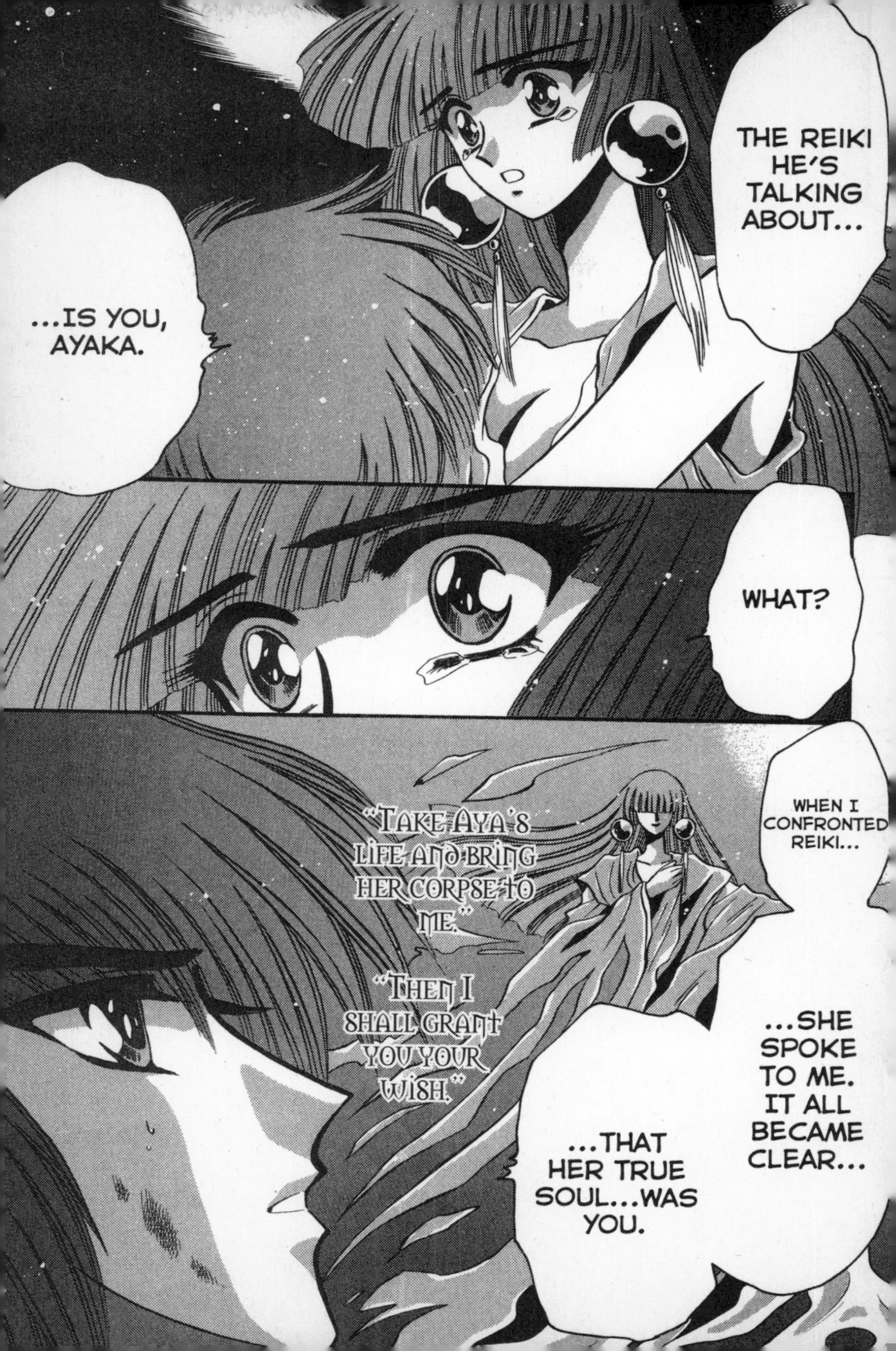
THE REIKI HE'S TALKING ABOUT...
...IS YOU, AYAKA.
WHAT?
WHEN I CONFRONTED REIKI...
"Take Aya's life and bring her corpse to me."
"Then I shall grant you your wish."
...SHE SPOKE TO ME. IT ALL BECAME CLEAR...
...THAT HER TRUE SOUL...WAS YOU.

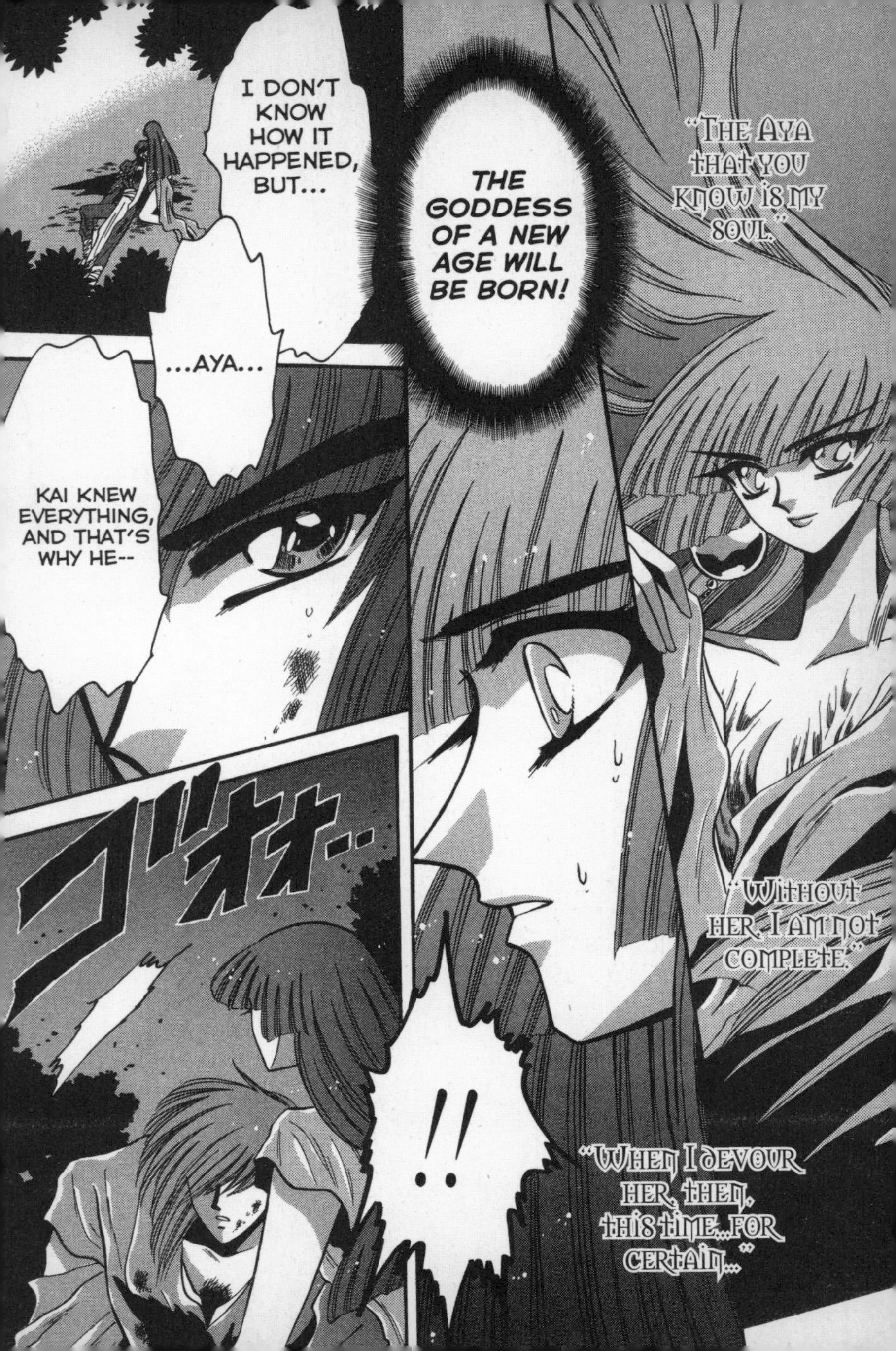
"The Aya that you know is my soul."
THE GODDESS OF A NEW AGE WILL BE BORN!
"Without her, I am not complete."
"When I devour her, then, this time...for certain..."
I DON'T KNOW HOW IT HAPPENED, BUT...
...AYA...
KAI KNEW EVERYTHING, AND THAT'S WHY HE--
ゴオオー‥
!!

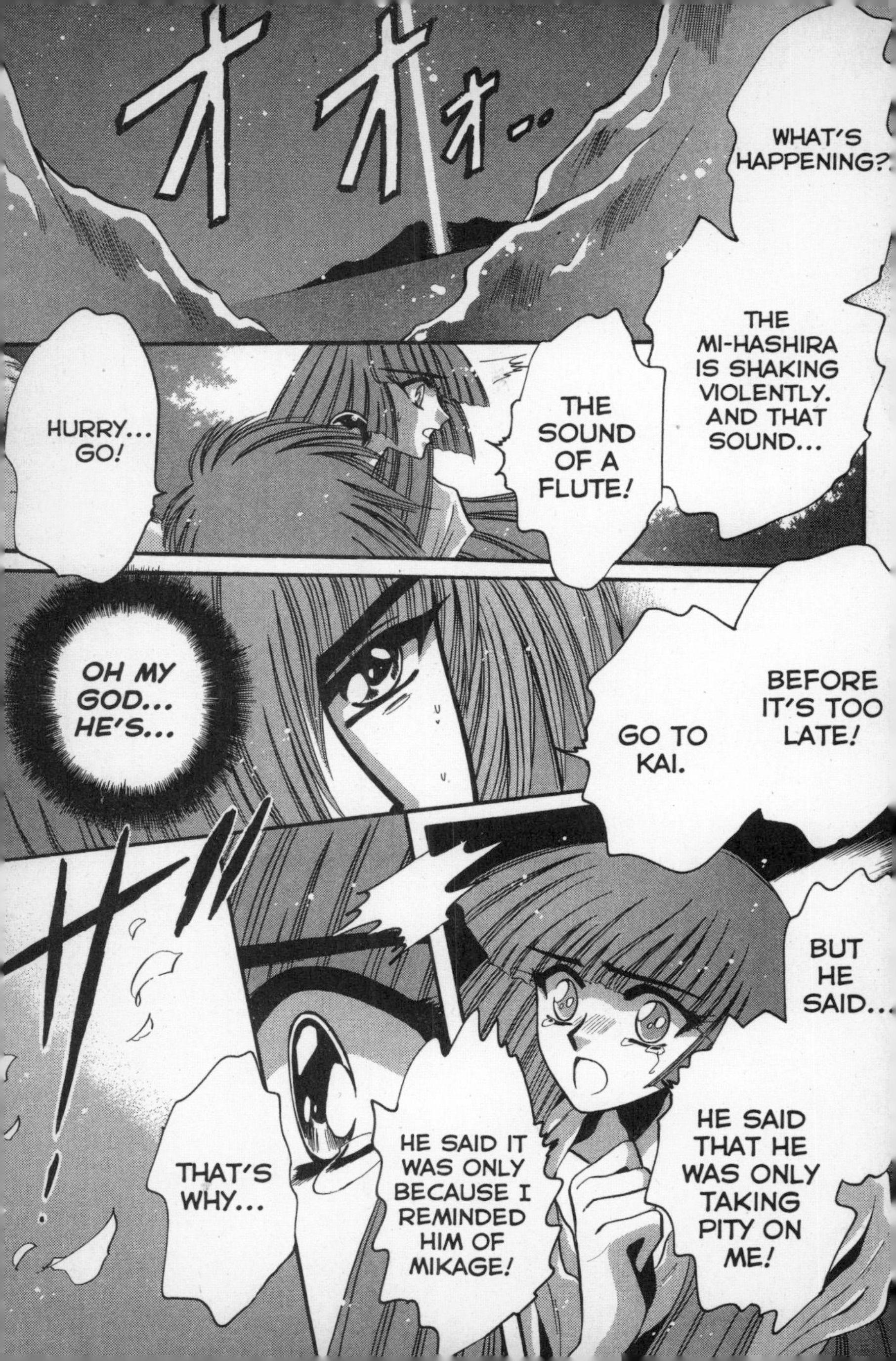

WHAT'S HAPPENING?
オオォー‥
THE MI-HASHIRA IS SHAKING VIOLENTLY. AND THAT SOUND...
THE SOUND OF A FLUTE!
HURRY... GO!
BEFORE IT'S TOO LATE!
GO TO KAI.
OH MY GOD... HE'S...
BUT HE SAID...
HE SAID THAT HE WAS ONLY TAKING PITY ON ME!
HE SAID IT WAS ONLY BECAUSE I REMINDED HIM OF MIKAGE!
THAT'S WHY...
ザ

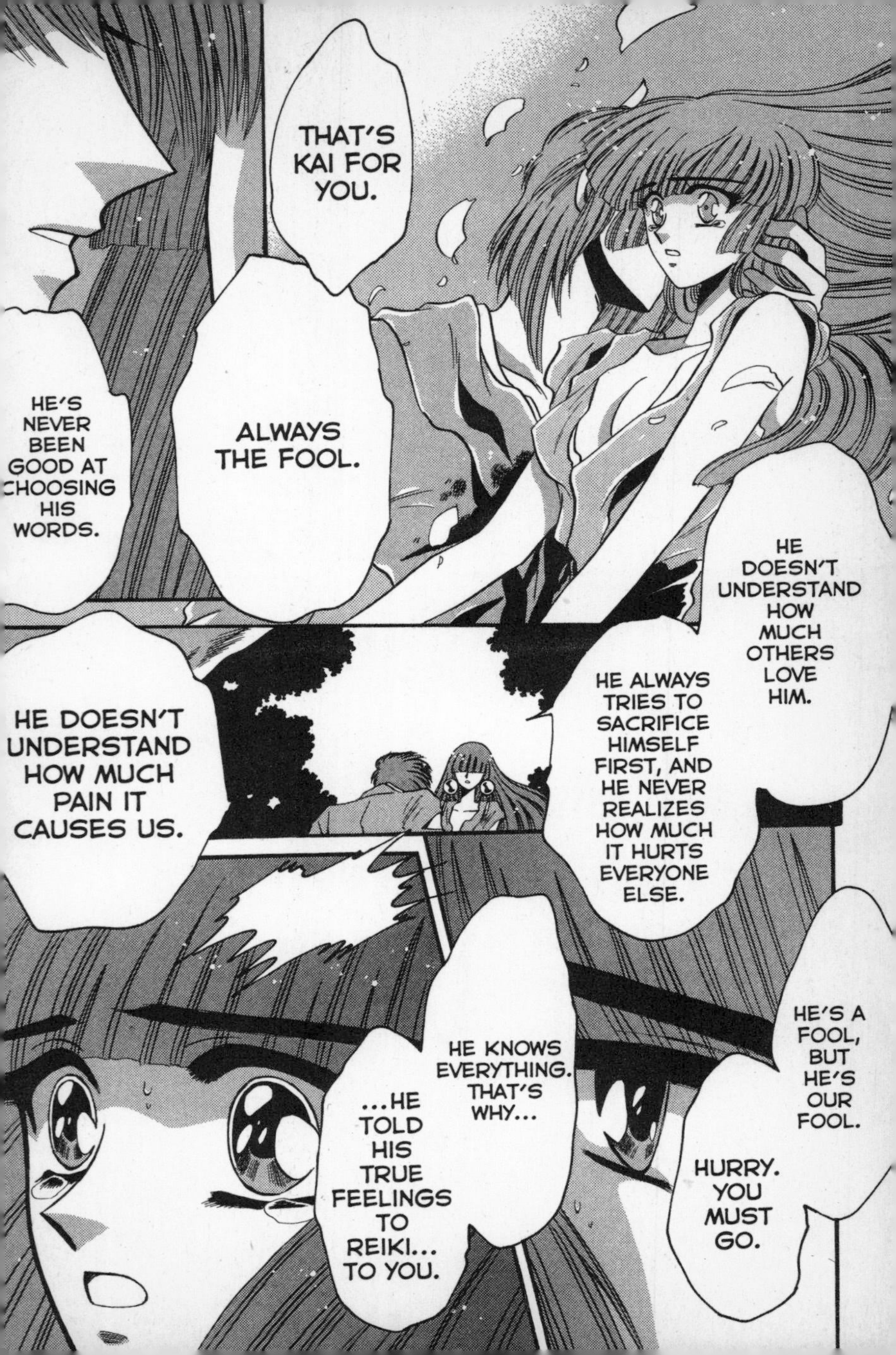
THAT'S KAI FOR YOU.
ALWAYS THE FOOL.
HE'S NEVER BEEN GOOD AT CHOOSING HIS WORDS.
HE DOESN'T UNDERSTAND HOW MUCH OTHERS LOVE HIM.
HE ALWAYS TRIES TO SACRIFICE HIMSELF FIRST, AND HE NEVER REALIZES HOW MUCH IT HURTS EVERYONE ELSE.
HE DOESN'T UNDERSTAND HOW MUCH PAIN IT CAUSES US.
HE'S A FOOL, BUT HE'S OUR FOOL.
HURRY. YOU MUST GO.
HE KNOWS EVERYTHING. THAT'S WHY...
...HE TOLD HIS TRUE FEELINGS TO REIKI... TO YOU.

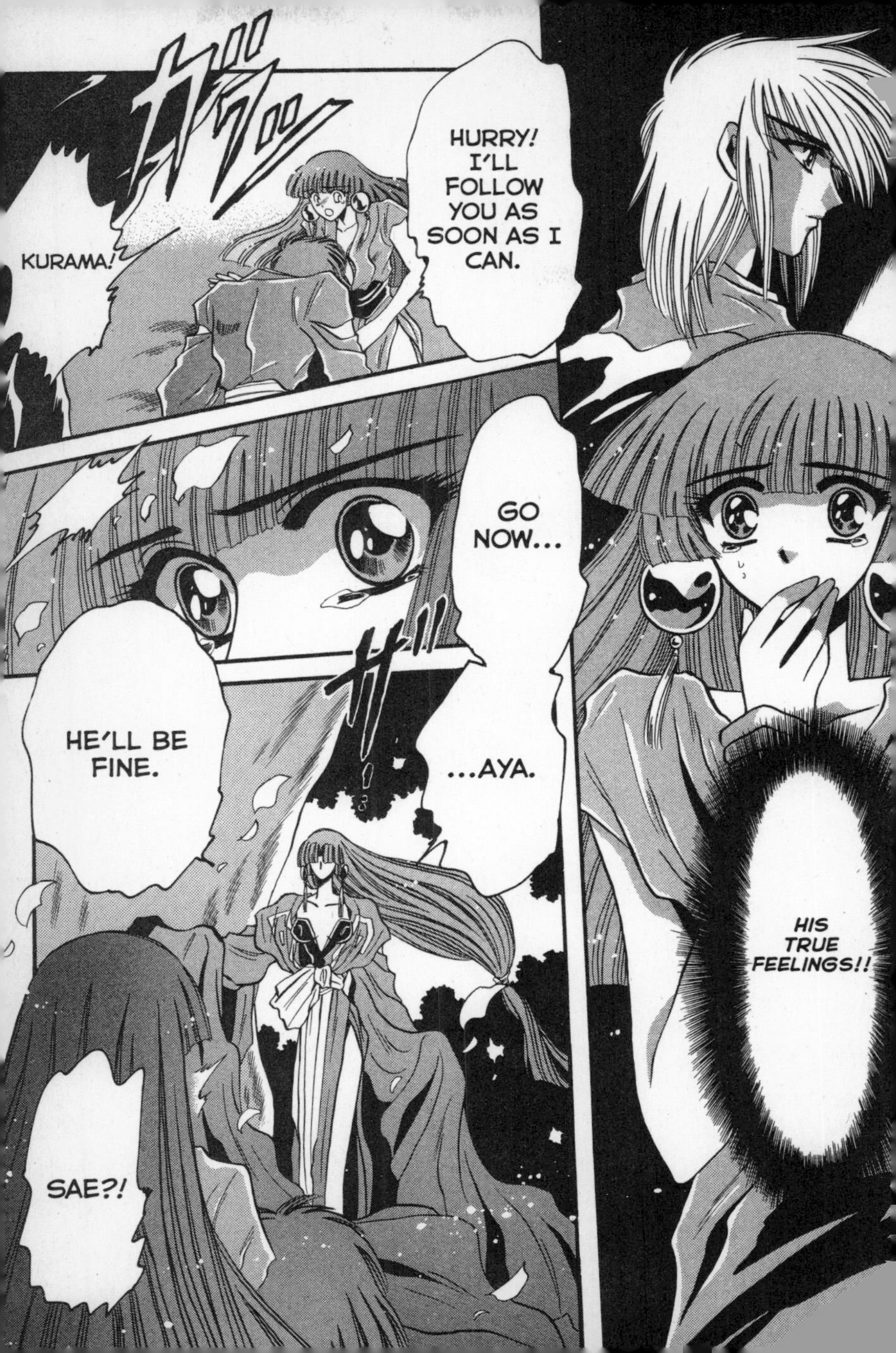
HIS TRUE FEELINGS!!
HURRY! I'LL FOLLOW YOU AS SOON AS I CAN.
KURAMA!
GO NOW...
...AYA.
HE'LL BE FINE.
SAE?!

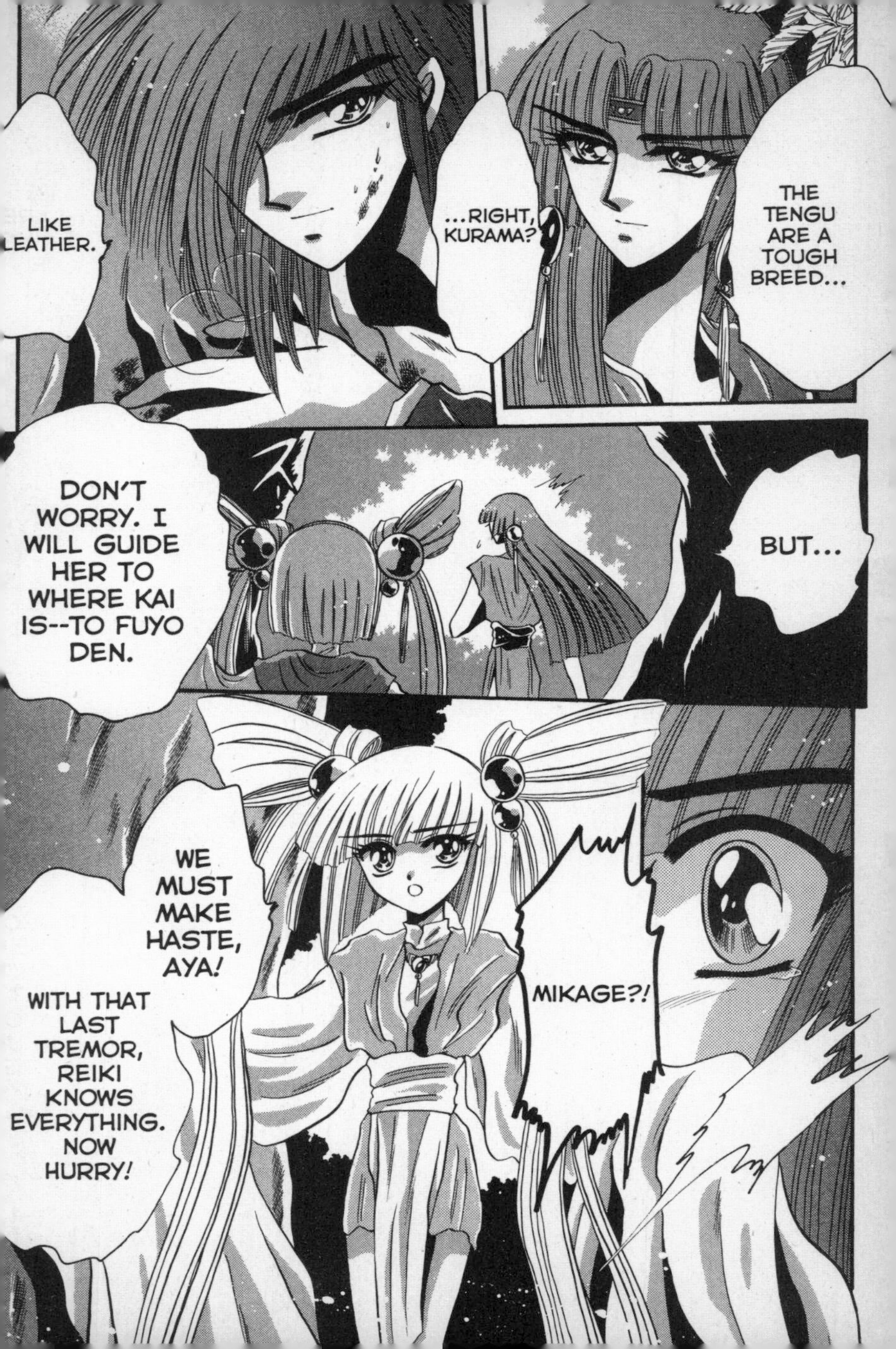
THE TENGU ARE A TOUGH BREED...
...RIGHT, KURAMA?
LIKE LEATHER.
BUT...
DON'T WORRY. I WILL GUIDE HER TO WHERE KAI IS--TO FUYO DEN.
MIKAGE?!
WE MUST MAKE HASTE, AYA!
WITH THAT LAST TREMOR, REIKI KNOWS EVERYTHING. NOW HURRY!

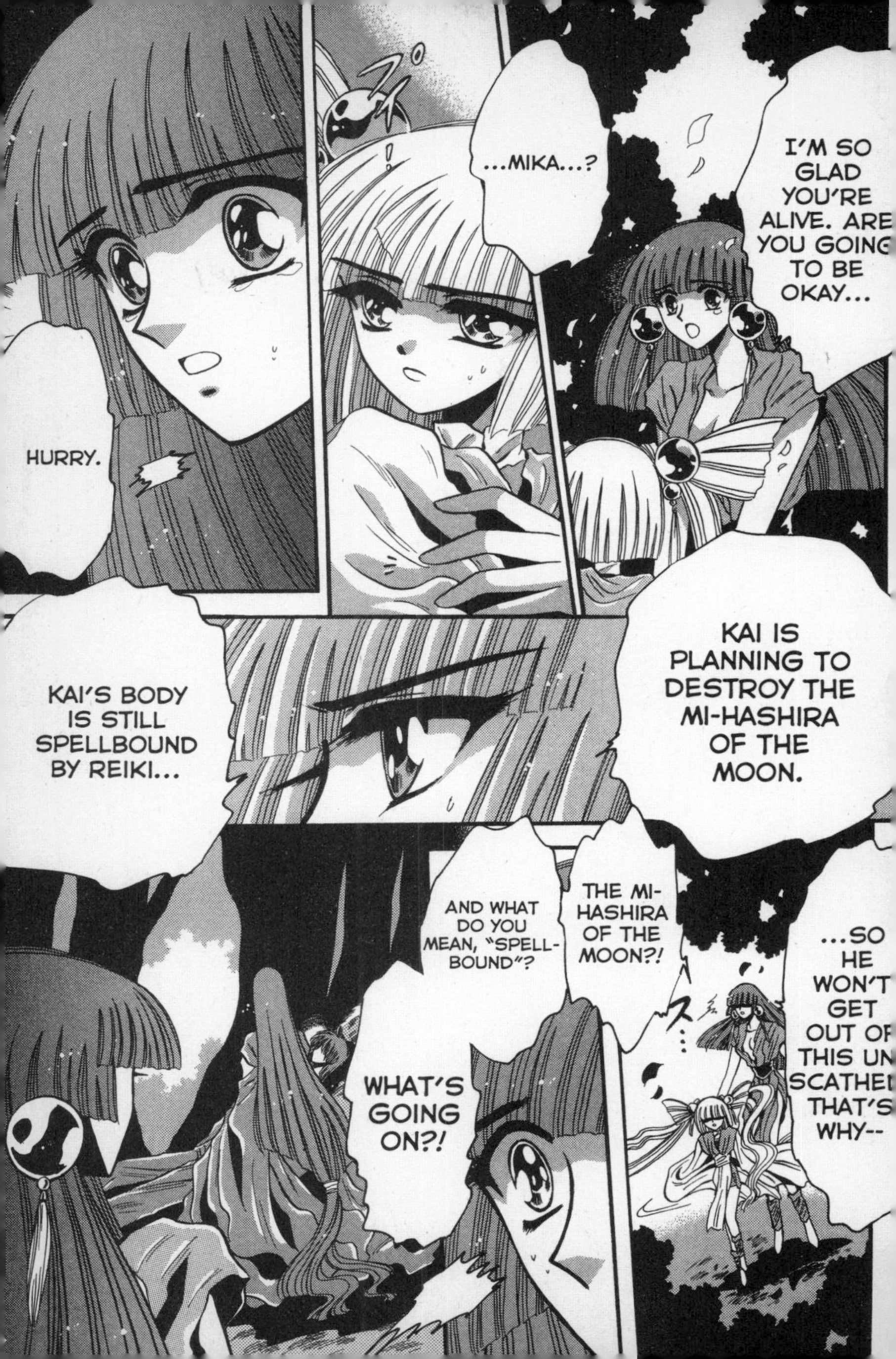
I'M SO GLAD YOU'RE ALIVE. ARE YOU GOING TO BE OKAY...
...MIKA...?
HURRY.
KAI IS PLANNING TO DESTROY THE MI-HASHIRA OF THE MOON.
KAI'S BODY IS STILL SPELLBOUND BY REIKI...
...SO HE WON'T GET OUT OF THIS UNSCATHED THAT'S WHY--
THE MI-HASHIRA OF THE MOON?!
AND WHAT DO YOU MEAN, "SPELLBOUND"?
WHAT'S GOING ON?!

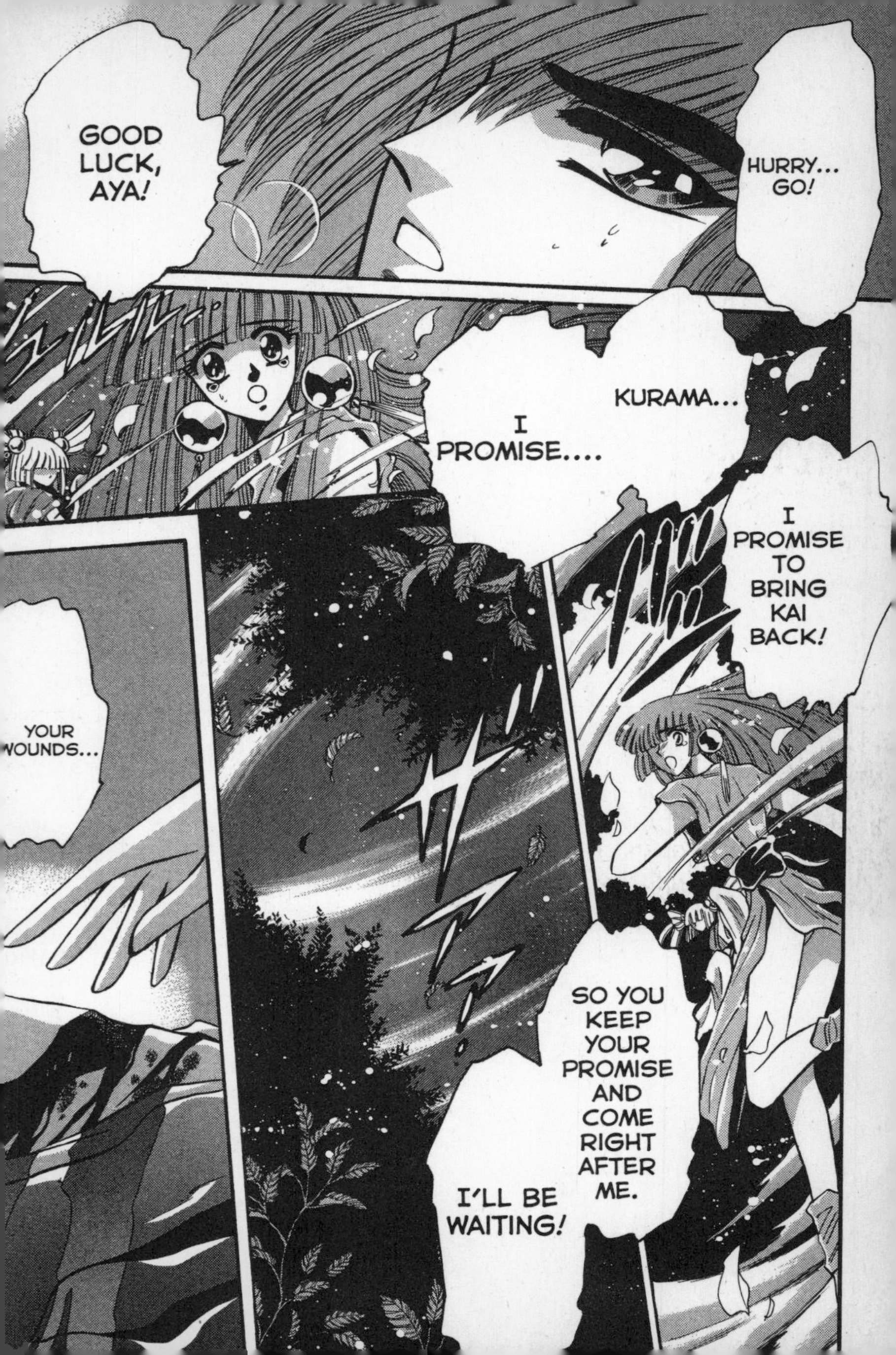
HURRY... GO!
GOOD LUCK, AYA!
KURAMA...
I PROMISE....
I PROMISE TO BRING KAI BACK!
SO YOU KEEP YOUR PROMISE AND COME RIGHT AFTER ME.
I'LL BE WAITING!
YOUR WOUNDS...

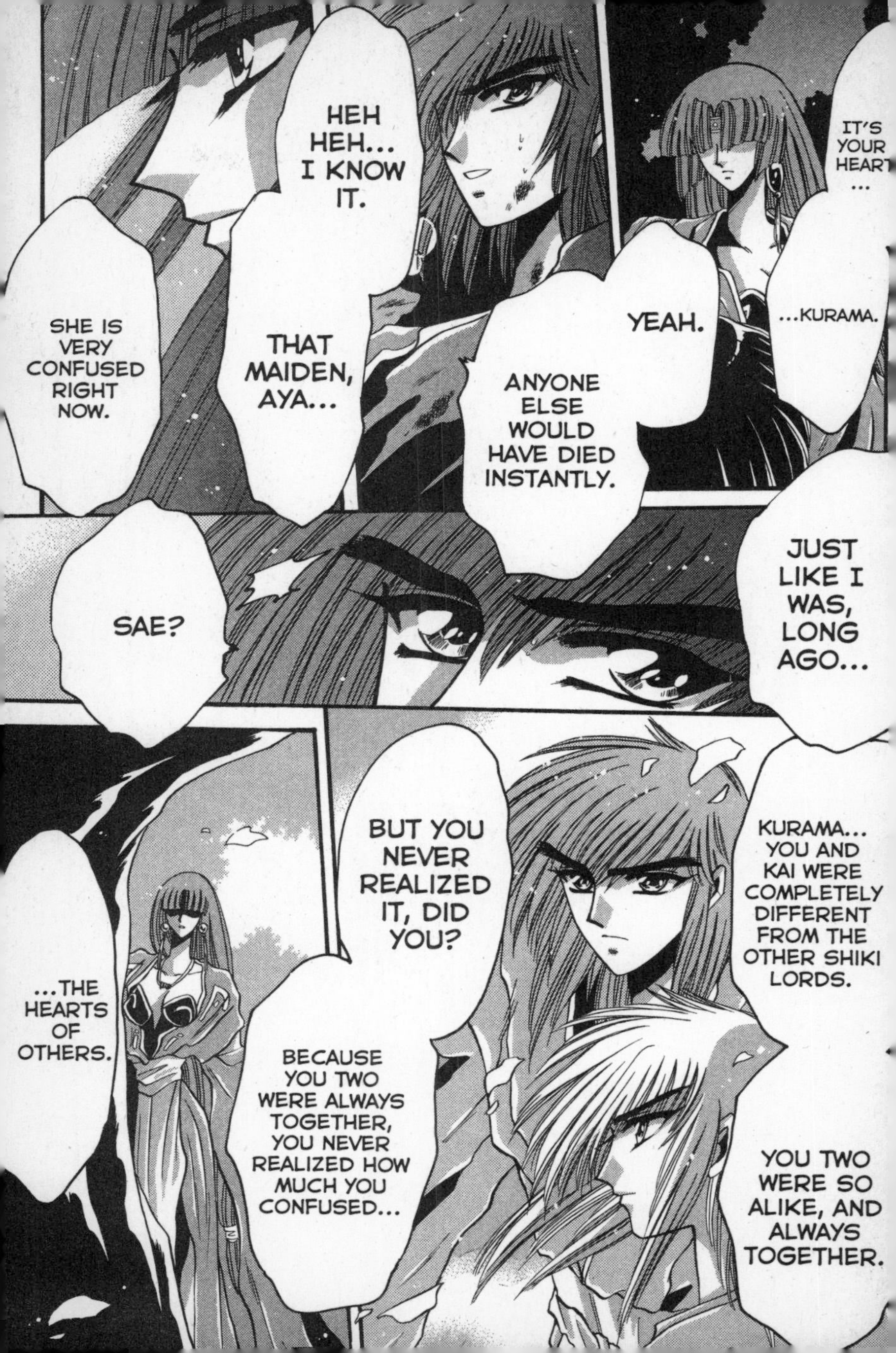
IT'S YOUR HEART...
...KURAMA.
HEH HEH... I KNOW IT.
YEAH.
ANYONE ELSE WOULD HAVE DIED INSTANTLY.
THAT MAIDEN, AYA...
SHE IS VERY CONFUSED RIGHT NOW.
JUST LIKE I WAS, LONG AGO...
SAE?
KURAMA... YOU AND KAI WERE COMPLETELY DIFFERENT FROM THE OTHER SHIKI LORDS.
YOU TWO WERE SO ALIKE, AND ALWAYS TOGETHER.
BUT YOU NEVER REALIZED IT, DID YOU?
BECAUSE YOU TWO WERE ALWAYS TOGETHER, YOU NEVER REALIZED HOW MUCH YOU CONFUSED...
...THE HEARTS OF OTHERS.

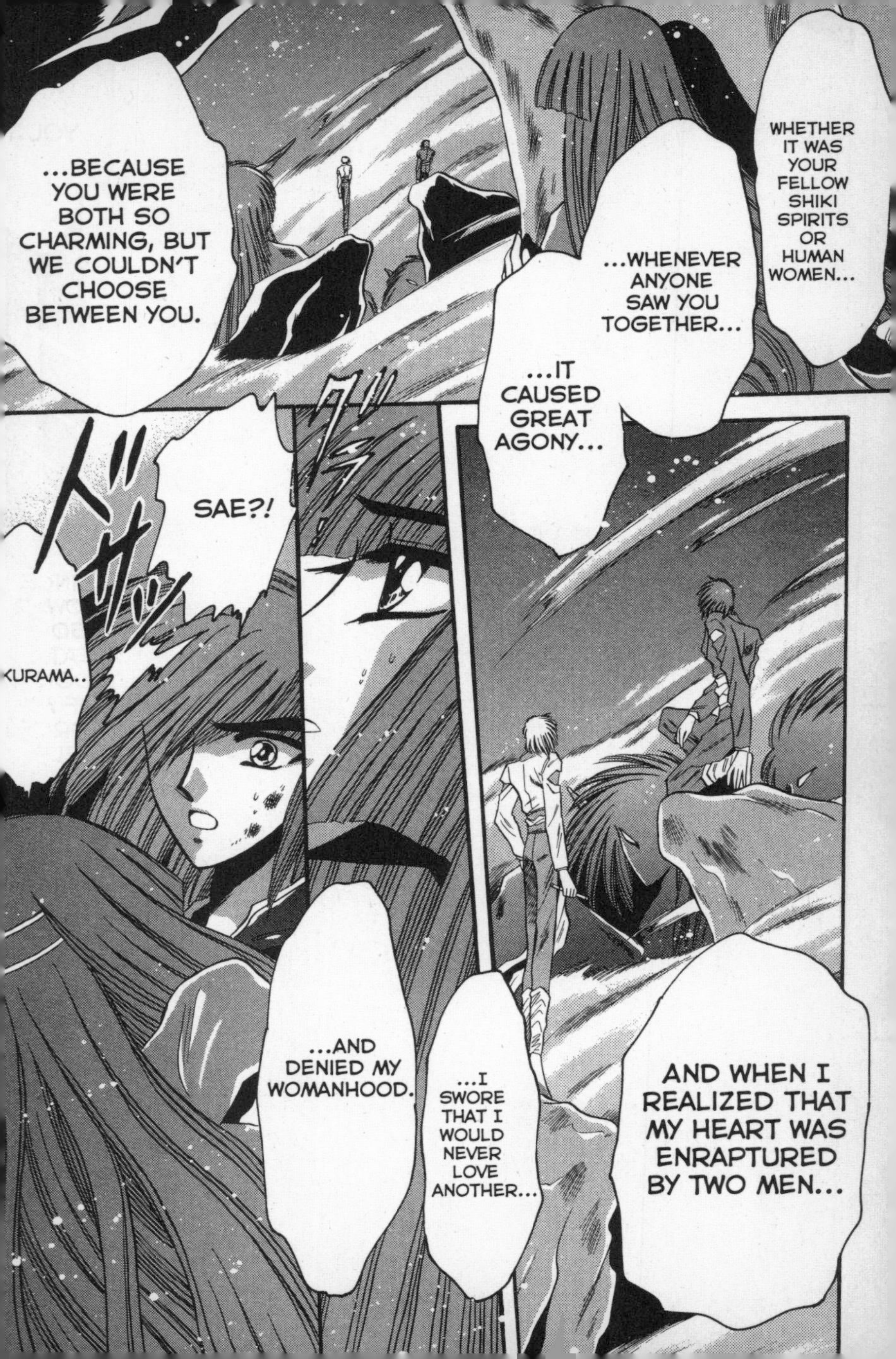
WHETHER IT WAS YOUR FELLOW SHIKI SPIRITS OR HUMAN WOMEN...
...WHENEVER ANYONE SAW YOU TOGETHER...
...IT CAUSED GREAT AGONY...
...BECAUSE YOU WERE BOTH SO CHARMING, BUT WE COULDN'T CHOOSE BETWEEN YOU.
AND WHEN I REALIZED THAT MY HEART WAS ENRAPTURED BY TWO MEN...
...I SWORE THAT I WOULD NEVER LOVE ANOTHER...
...AND DENIED MY WOMANHOOD.
SAE?!
KURAMA..

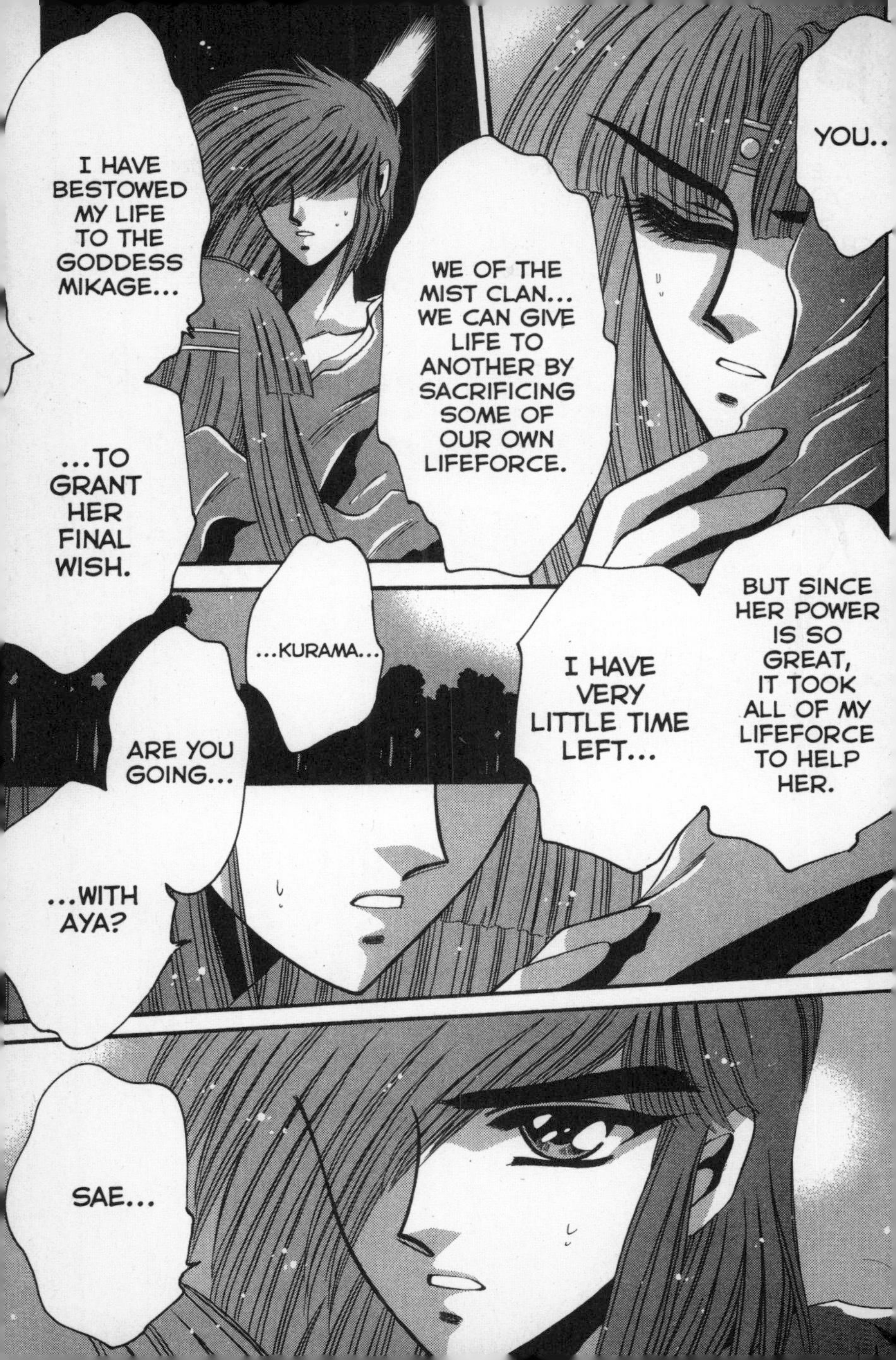
YOU..
WE OF THE MIST CLAN... WE CAN GIVE LIFE TO ANOTHER BY SACRIFICING SOME OF OUR OWN LIFEFORCE.
I HAVE BESTOWED MY LIFE TO THE GODDESS MIKAGE...
...TO GRANT HER FINAL WISH.
BUT SINCE HER POWER IS SO GREAT, IT TOOK ALL OF MY LIFEFORCE TO HELP HER.
I HAVE VERY LITTLE TIME LEFT...
...KURAMA...
ARE YOU GOING...
...WITH AYA?
SAE...

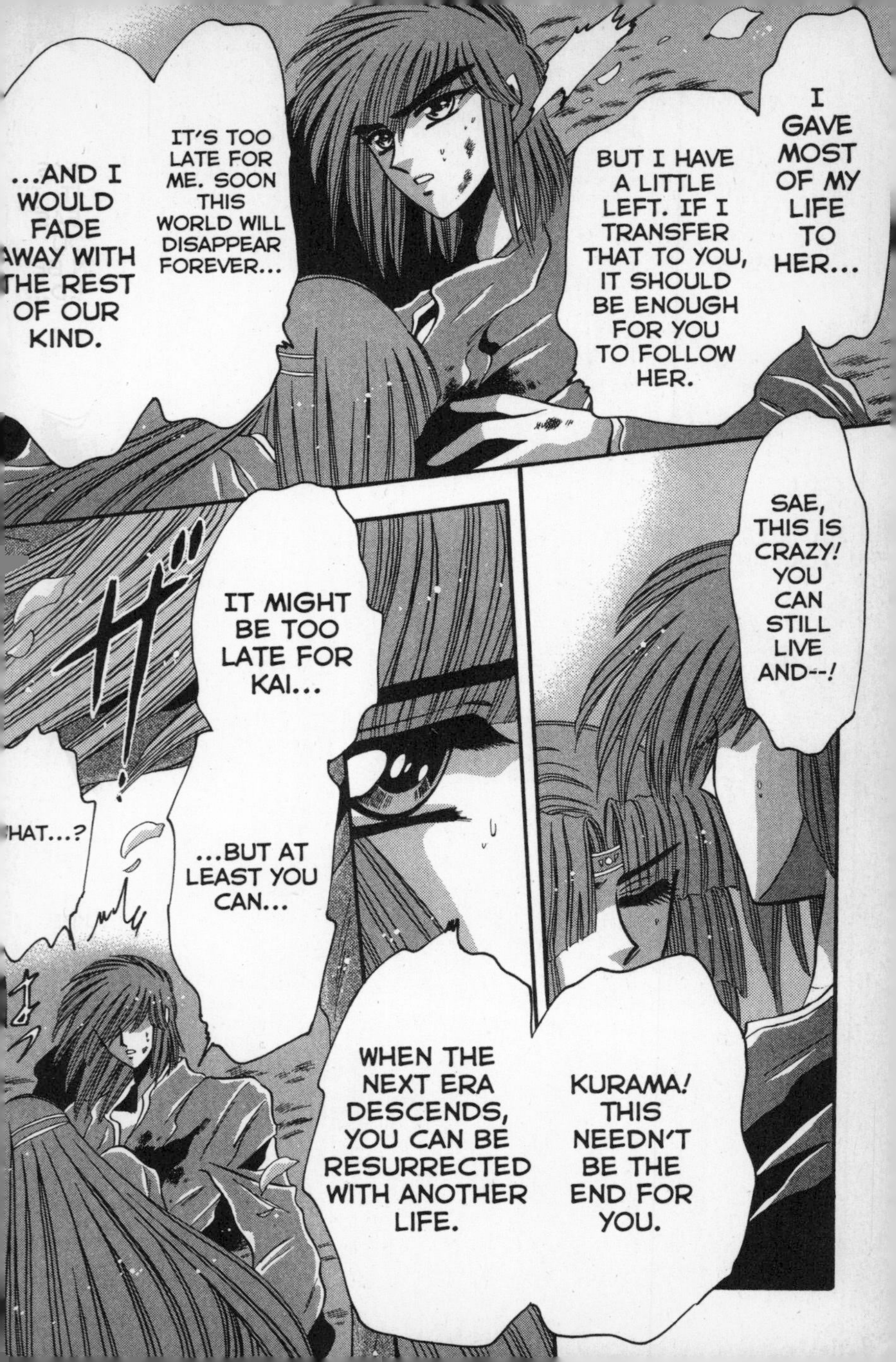
I GAVE MOST OF MY LIFE TO HER...
BUT I HAVE A LITTLE LEFT. IF I TRANSFER THAT TO YOU, IT SHOULD BE ENOUGH FOR YOU TO FOLLOW HER.
IT'S TOO LATE FOR ME. SOON THIS WORLD WILL DISAPPEAR FOREVER...
...AND I WOULD FADE AWAY WITH THE REST OF OUR KIND.
SAE, THIS IS CRAZY! YOU CAN STILL LIVE AND--!
KURAMA! THIS NEEDN'T BE THE END FOR YOU.
IT MIGHT BE TOO LATE FOR KAI...
...BUT AT LEAST YOU CAN...
WHEN THE NEXT ERA DESCENDS, YOU CAN BE RESURRECTED WITH ANOTHER LIFE.
HAT...?

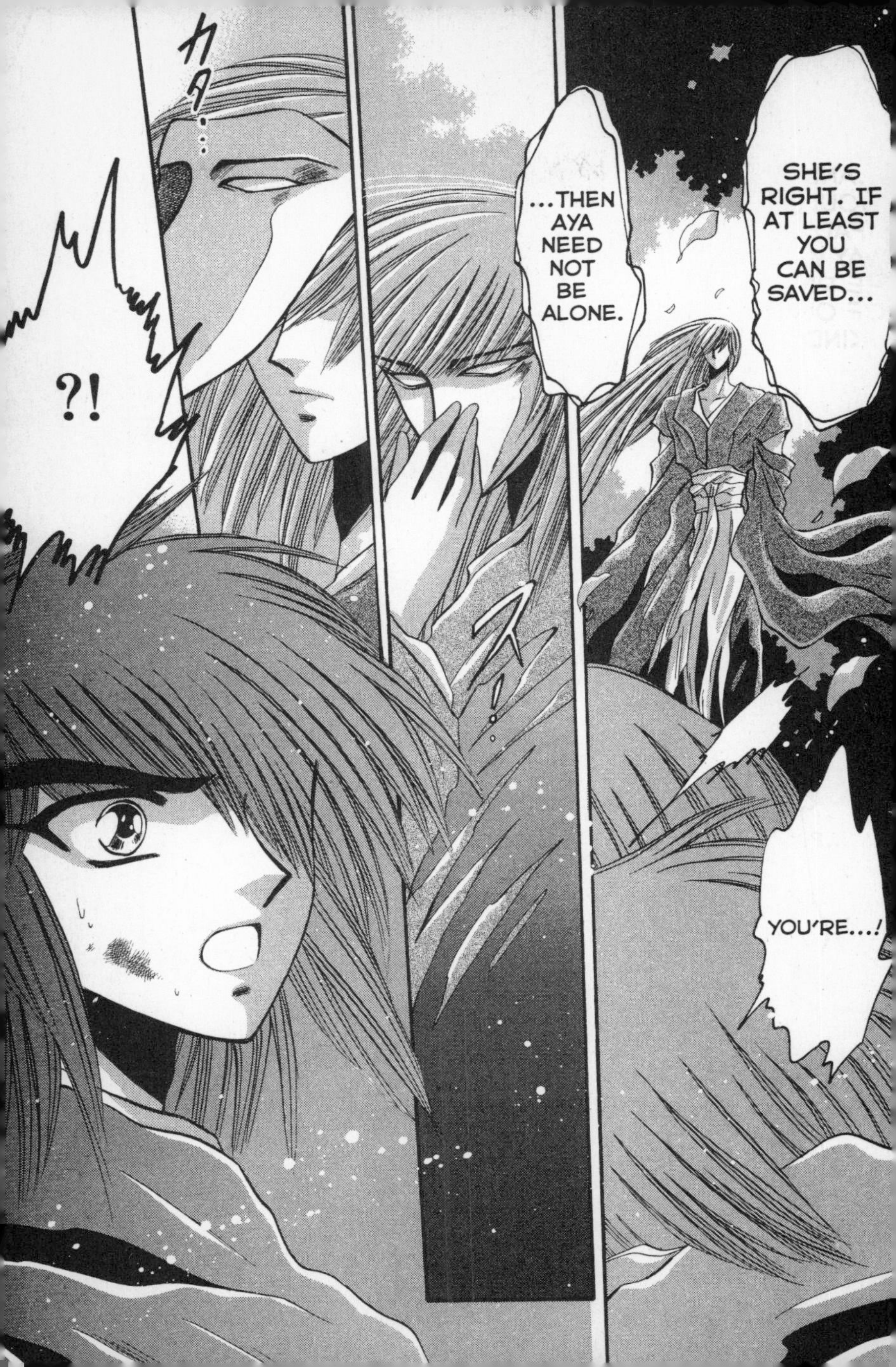
SHE'S RIGHT. IF AT LEAST YOU CAN BE SAVED...
...THEN AYA NEED NOT BE ALONE.
YOU'RE...!
?!

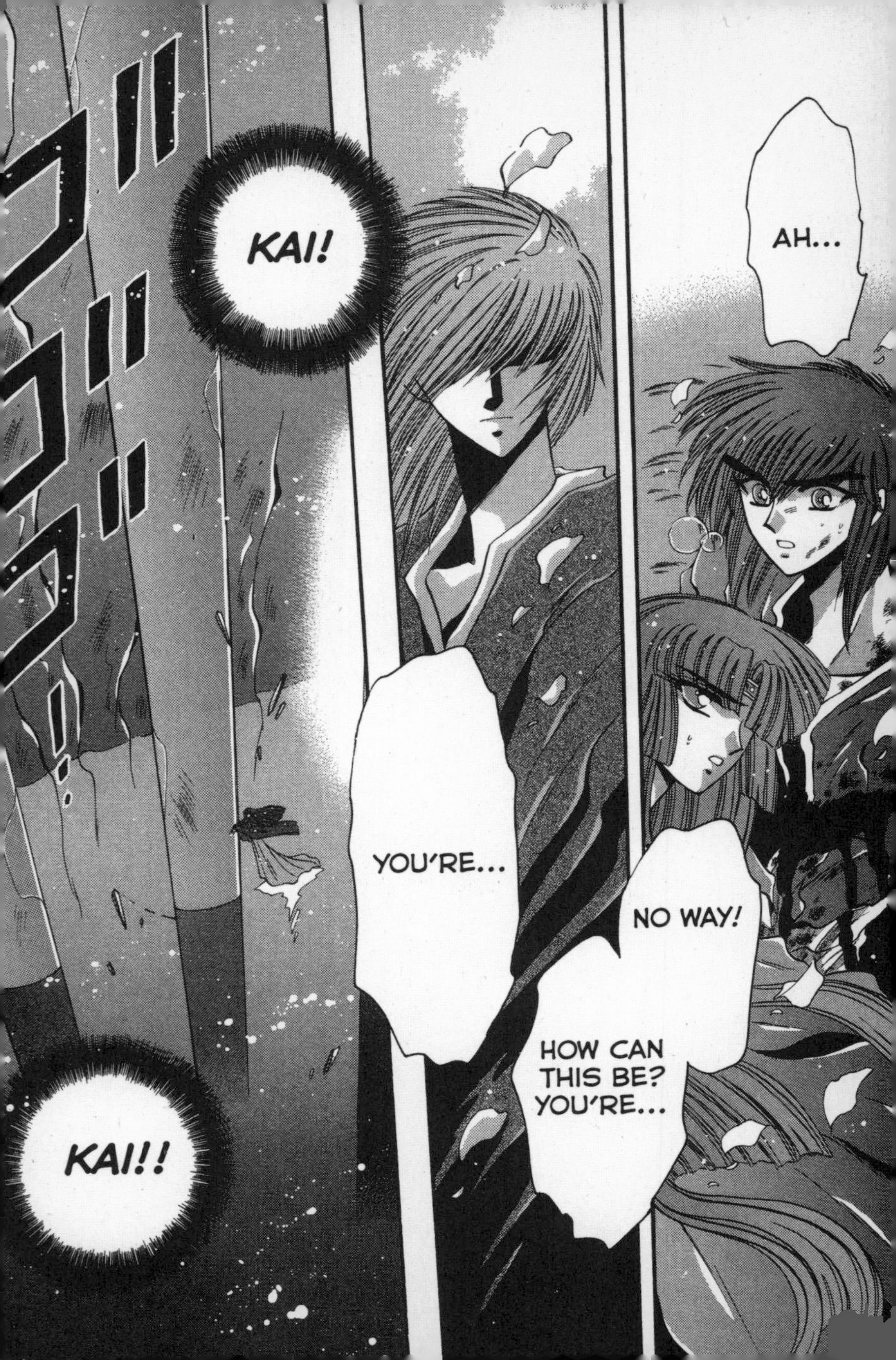
AH...
NO WAY!
HOW CAN THIS BE? YOU'RE...
YOU'RE...
KAI!
KAI!!

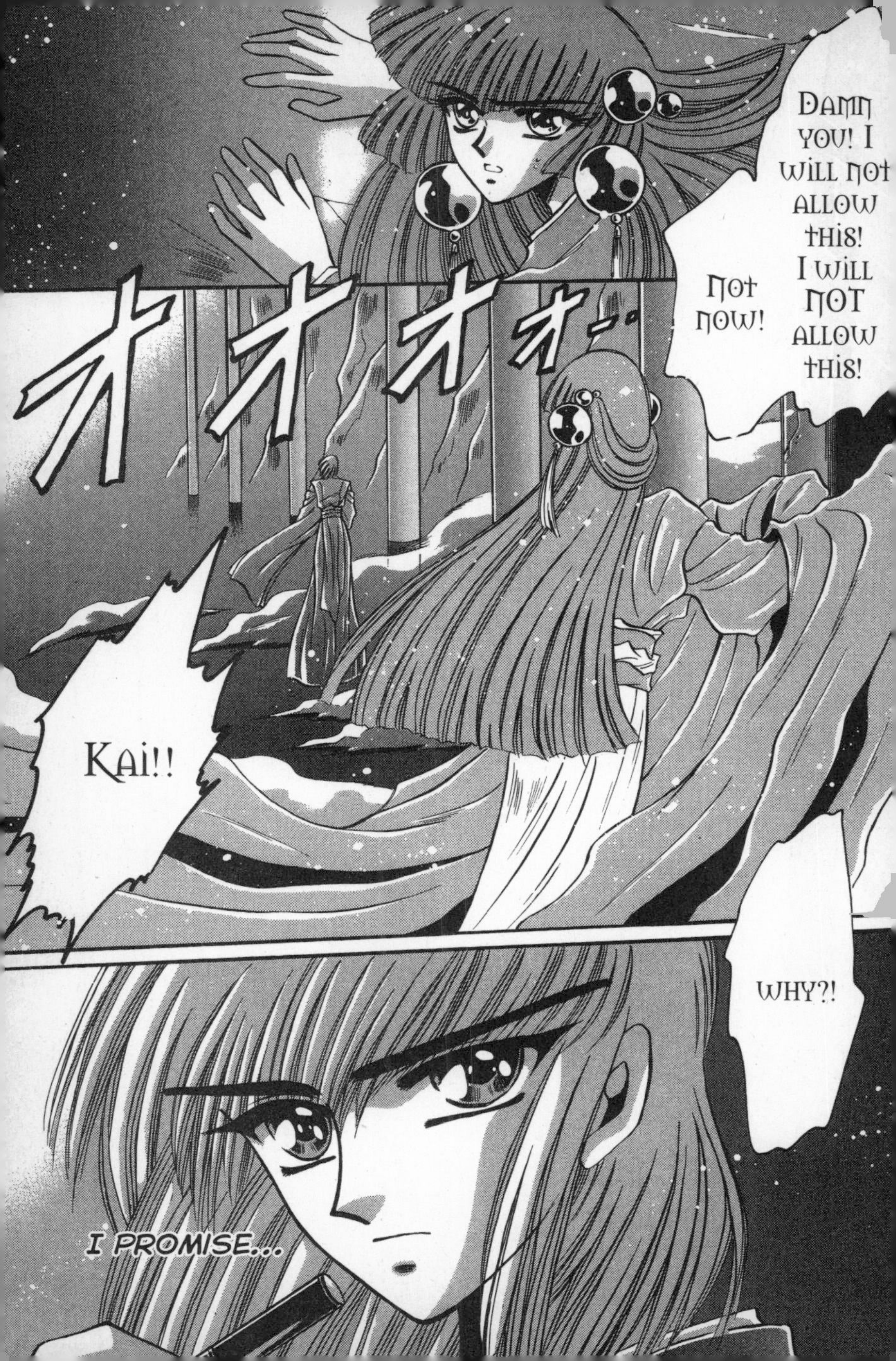
DAMN YOU! I WILL NOT ALLOW THIS! I WILL NOT ALLOW THIS!
NOT NOW!
オオオオー
KAI!!
WHY?!
I PROMISE...

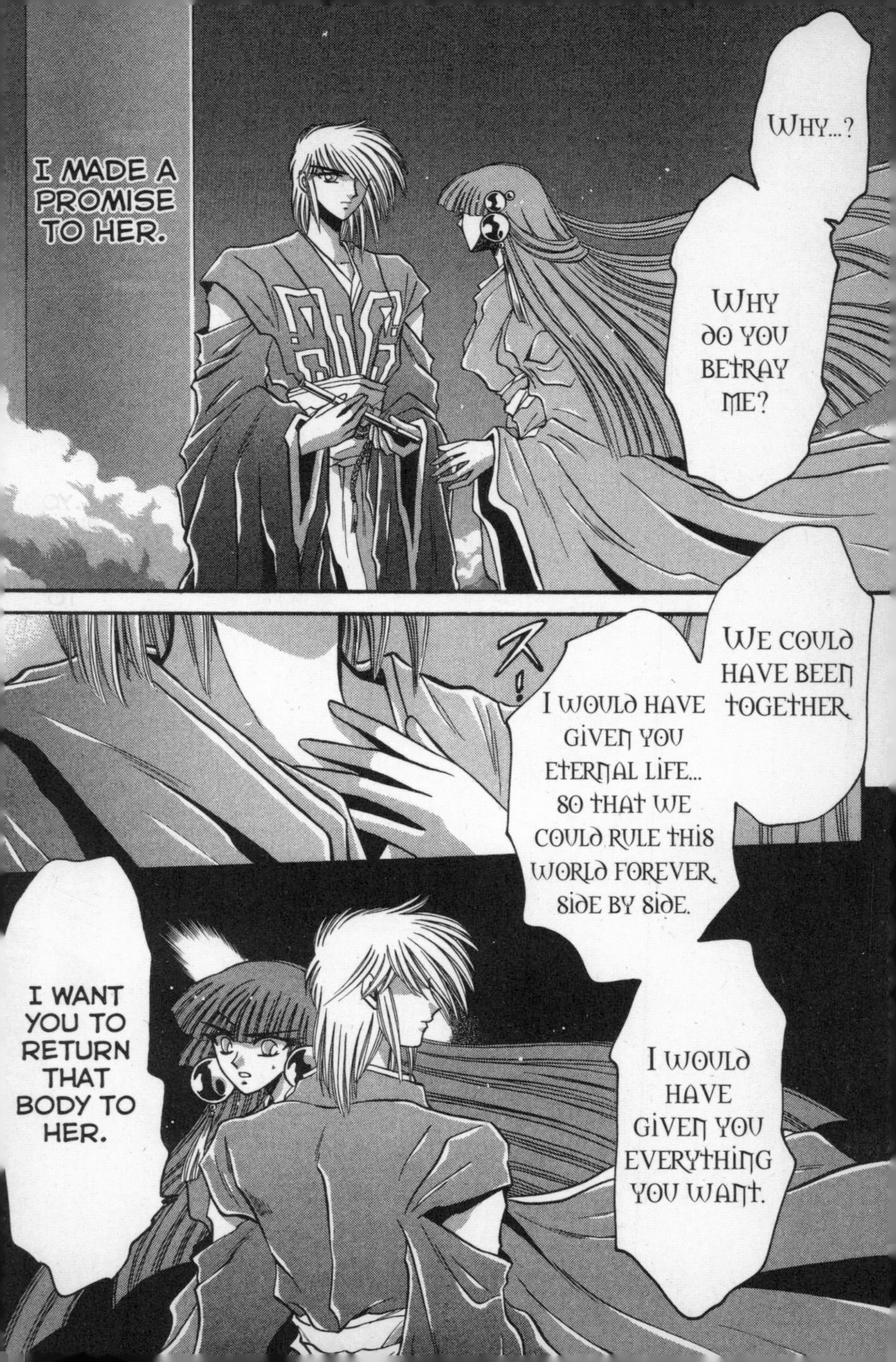
WHY...?
WHY DO YOU BETRAY ME?
I MADE A PROMISE TO HER.
WE COULD HAVE BEEN TOGETHER.
ス
I WOULD HAVE GIVEN YOU ETERNAL LIFE... SO THAT WE COULD RULE THIS WORLD FOREVER, SIDE BY SIDE.
I WOULD HAVE GIVEN YOU EVERYTHING YOU WANT.
I WANT YOU TO RETURN THAT BODY TO HER.

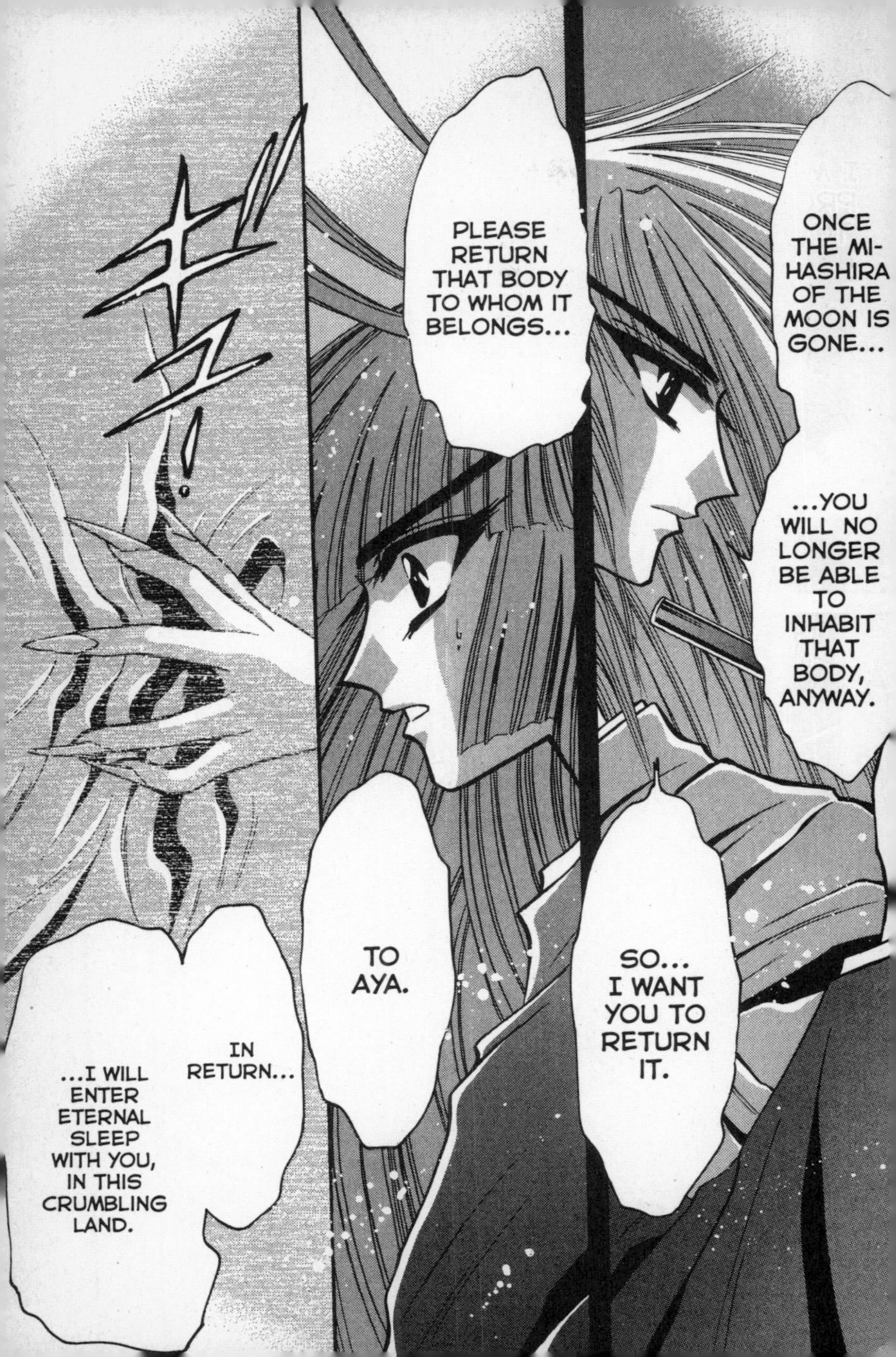
ONCE THE MI-HASHIRA OF THE MOON IS GONE...
...YOU WILL NO LONGER BE ABLE TO INHABIT THAT BODY, ANYWAY.
SO... I WANT YOU TO RETURN IT.
PLEASE RETURN THAT BODY TO WHOM IT BELONGS...
TO AYA.
IN RETURN...
...I WILL ENTER ETERNAL SLEEP WITH YOU, IN THIS CRUMBLING LAND.

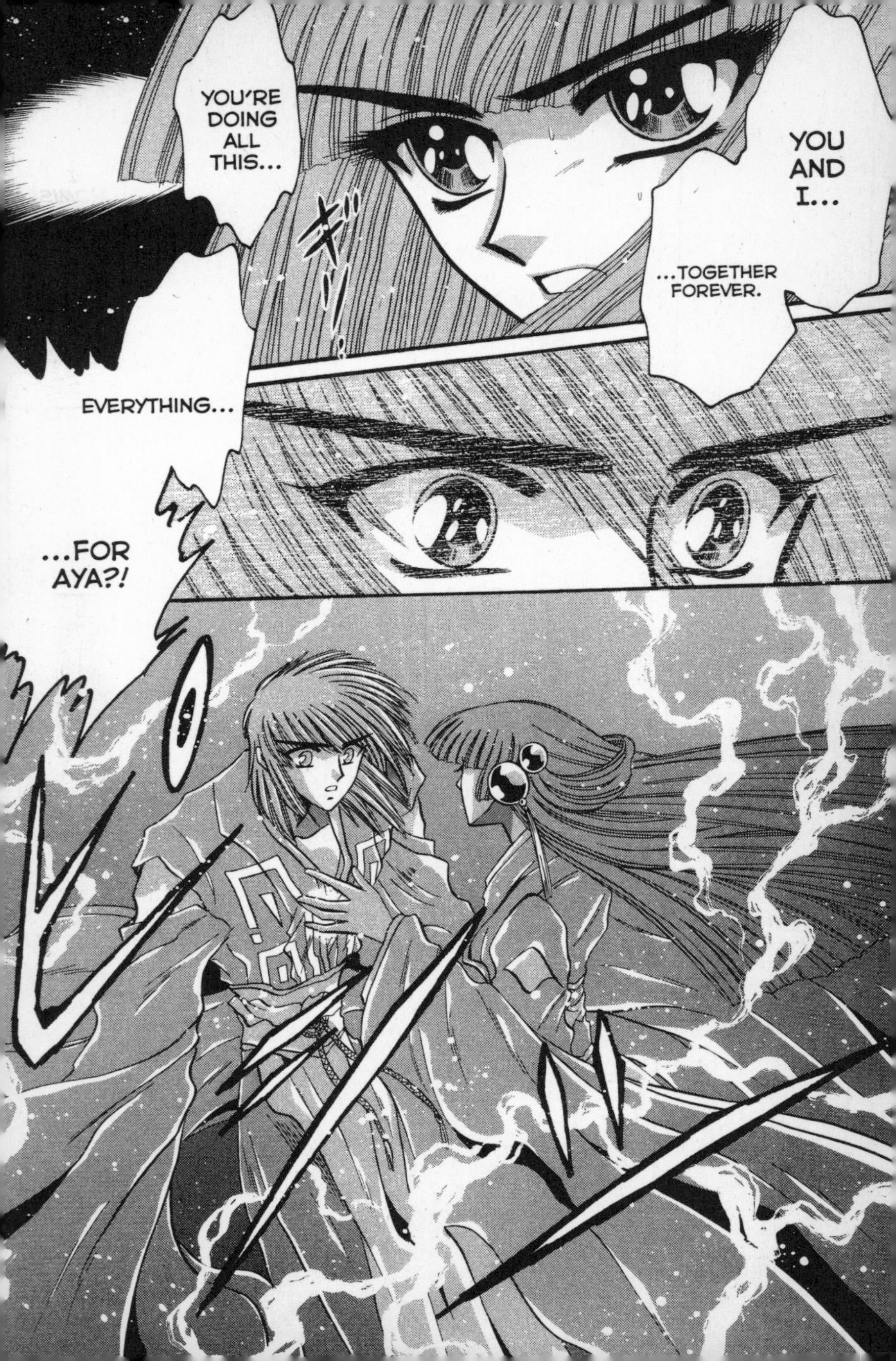
YOU AND I...
...TOGETHER FOREVER.
YOU'RE DOING ALL THIS...
EVERYTHING...
...FOR AYA?!

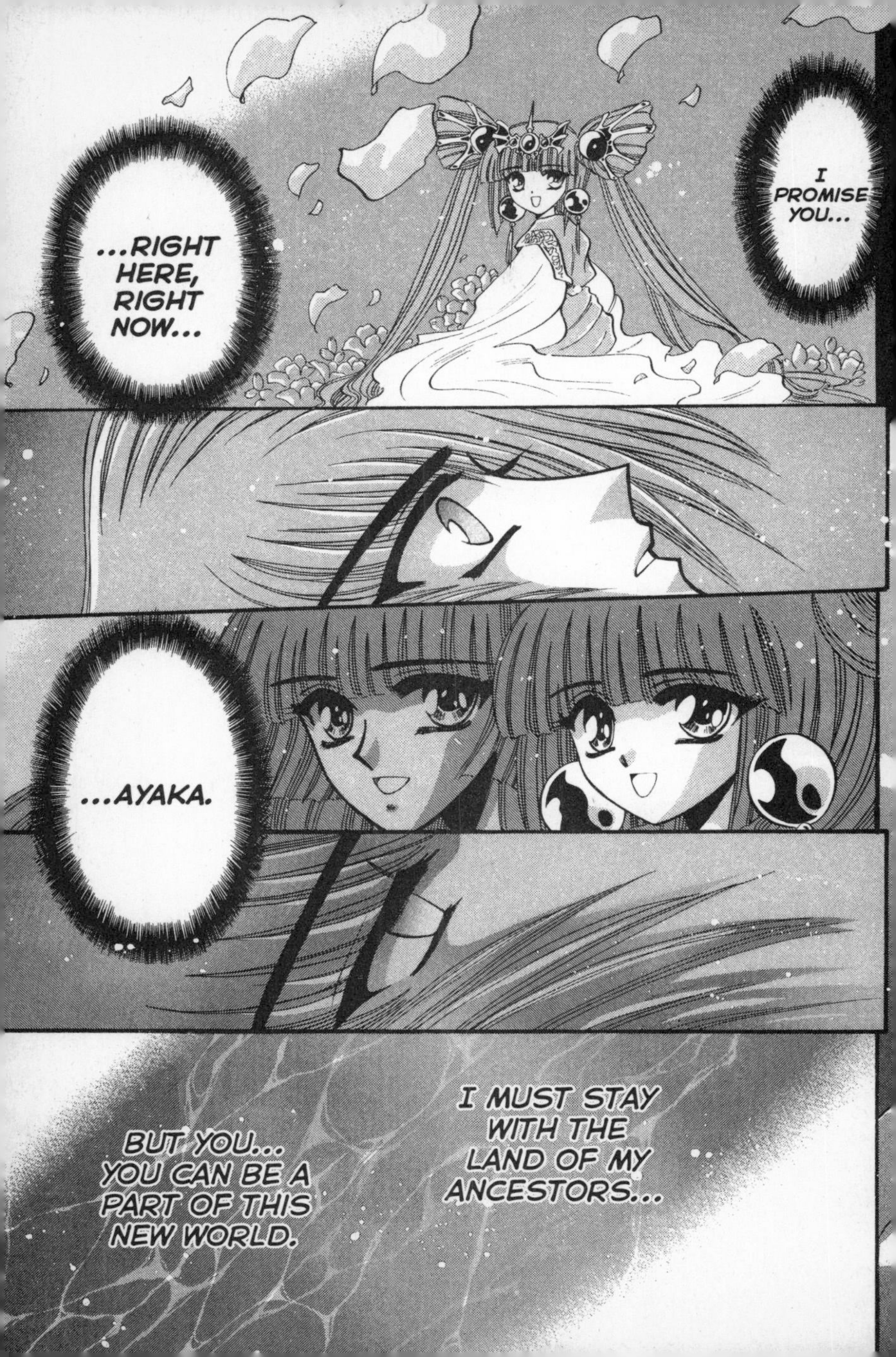
I PROMISE YOU...
...RIGHT HERE, RIGHT NOW...
...AYAKA.
I MUST STAY WITH THE LAND OF MY ANCESTORS...
BUT YOU... YOU CAN BE A PART OF THIS NEW WORLD.

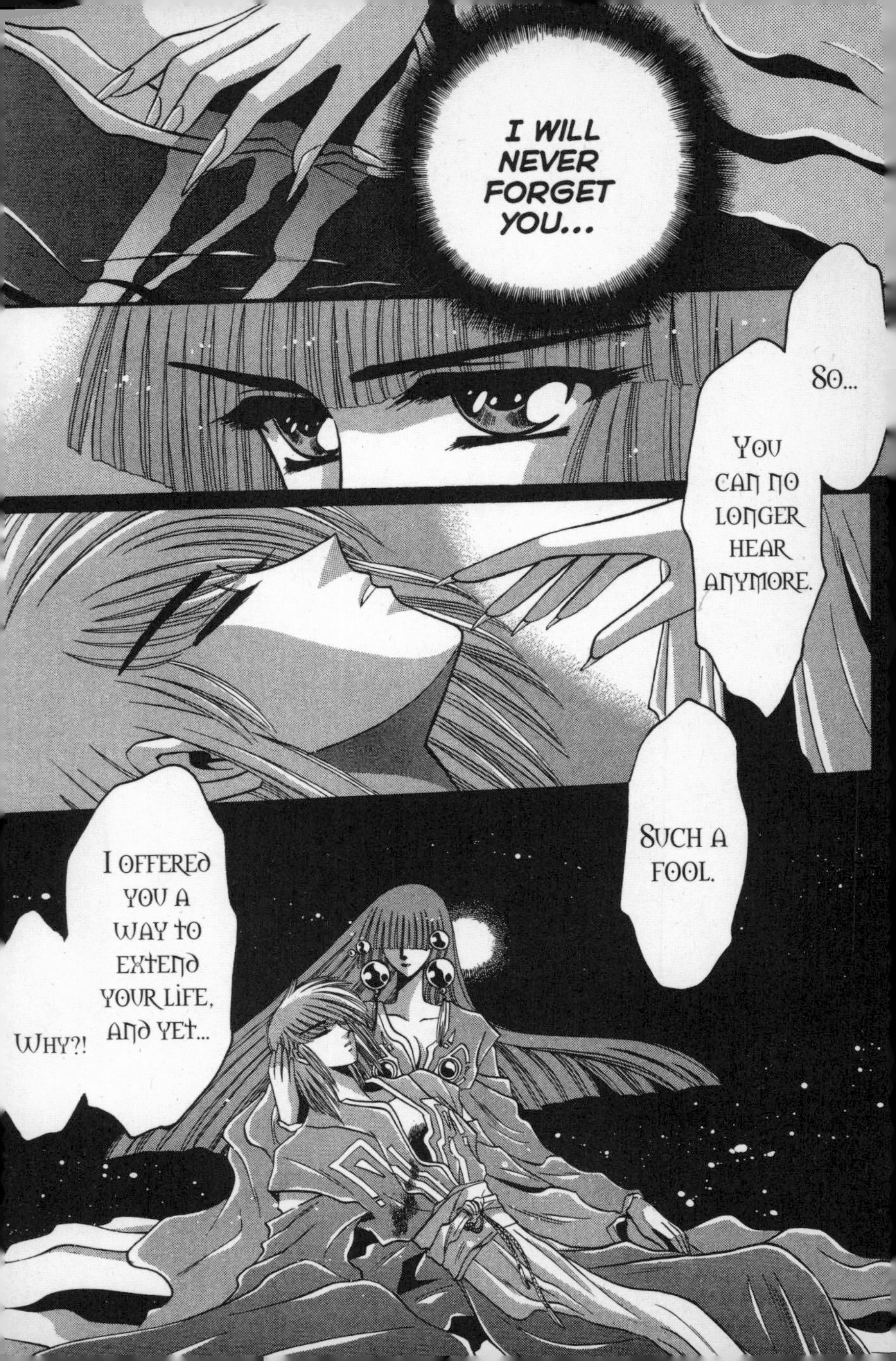
I WILL NEVER FORGET YOU...
SO...
YOU CAN NO LONGER HEAR ANYMORE.
SUCH A FOOL.
I OFFERED YOU A WAY TO EXTEND YOUR LIFE, AND YET...
WHY?!

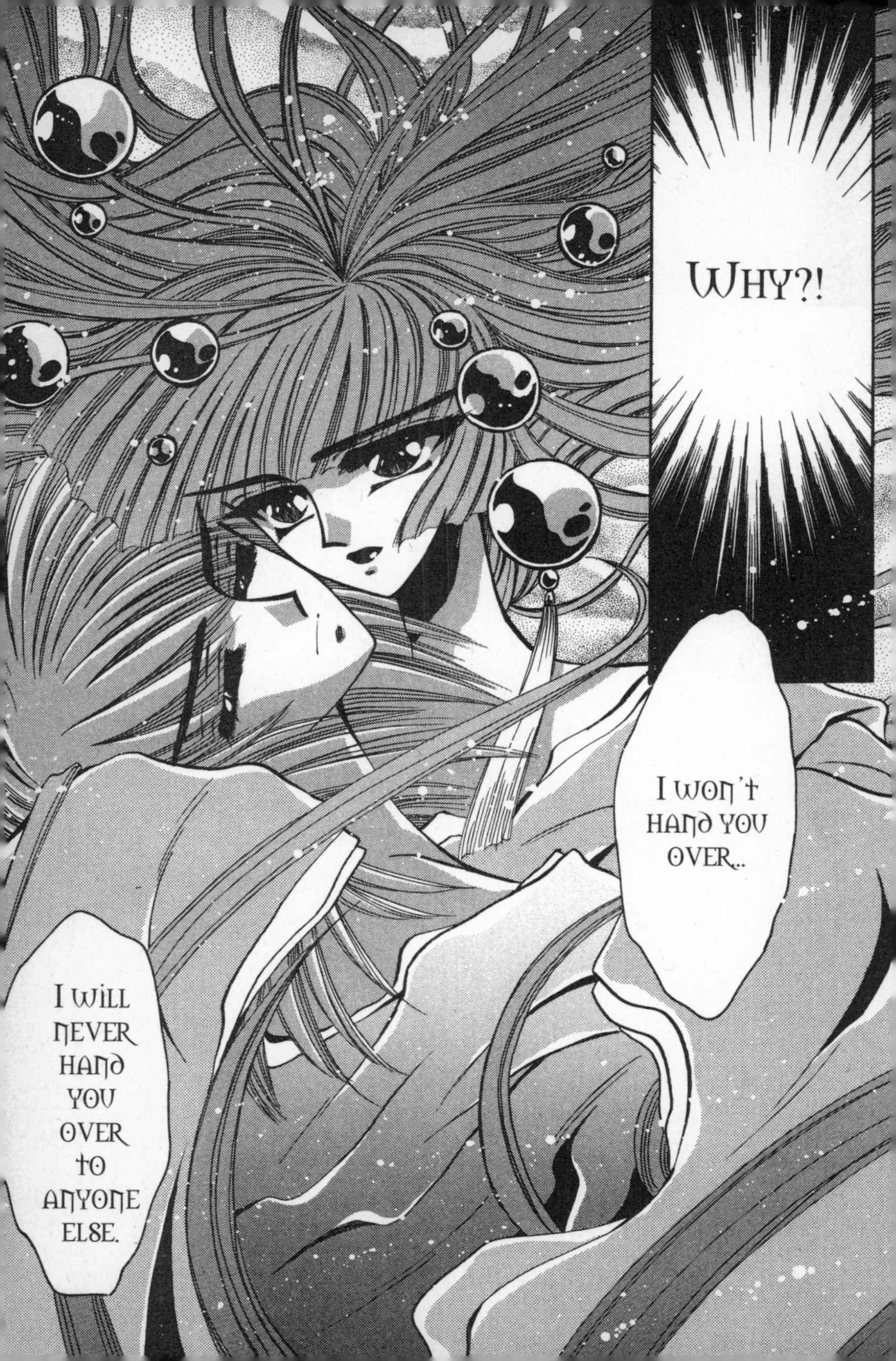
WHY?!
I WON'T HAND YOU OVER...
I WILL NEVER HAND YOU OVER TO ANYONE ELSE.

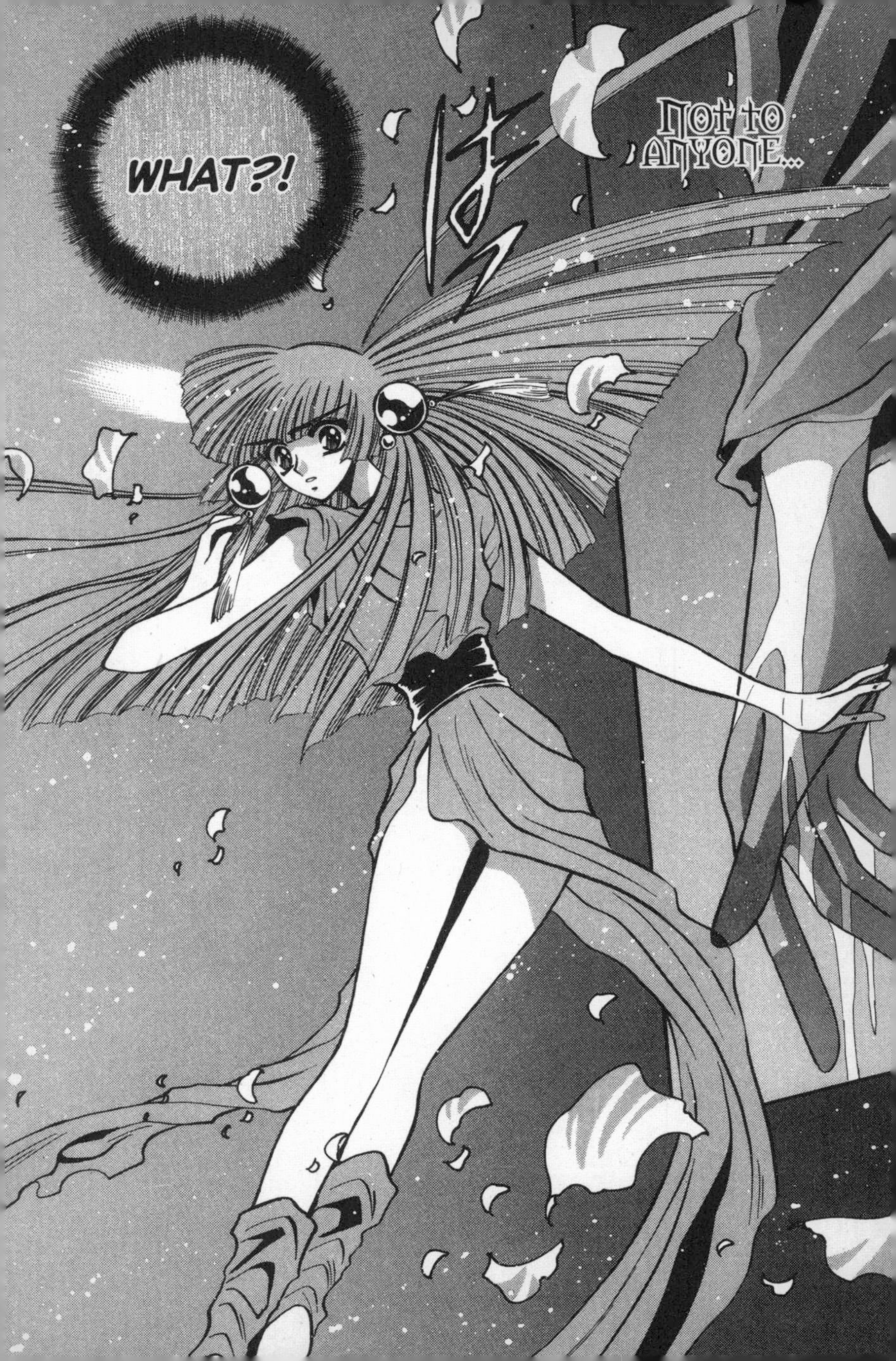
Not to anyone...
は
WHAT?!

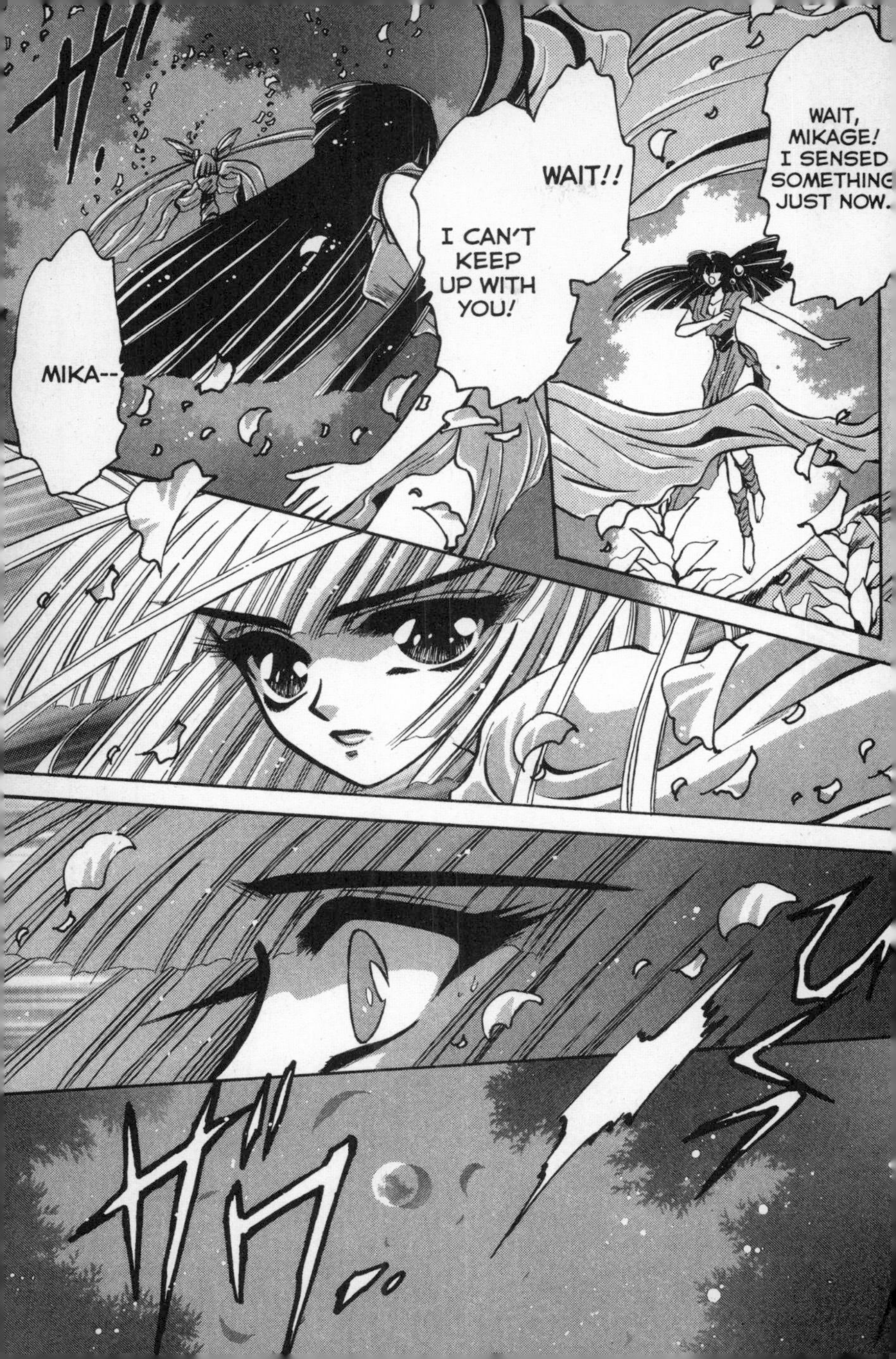
WAIT, MIKAGE! I SENSED SOMETHING JUST NOW.
WAIT!!
I CAN'T KEEP UP WITH YOU!
MIKA--

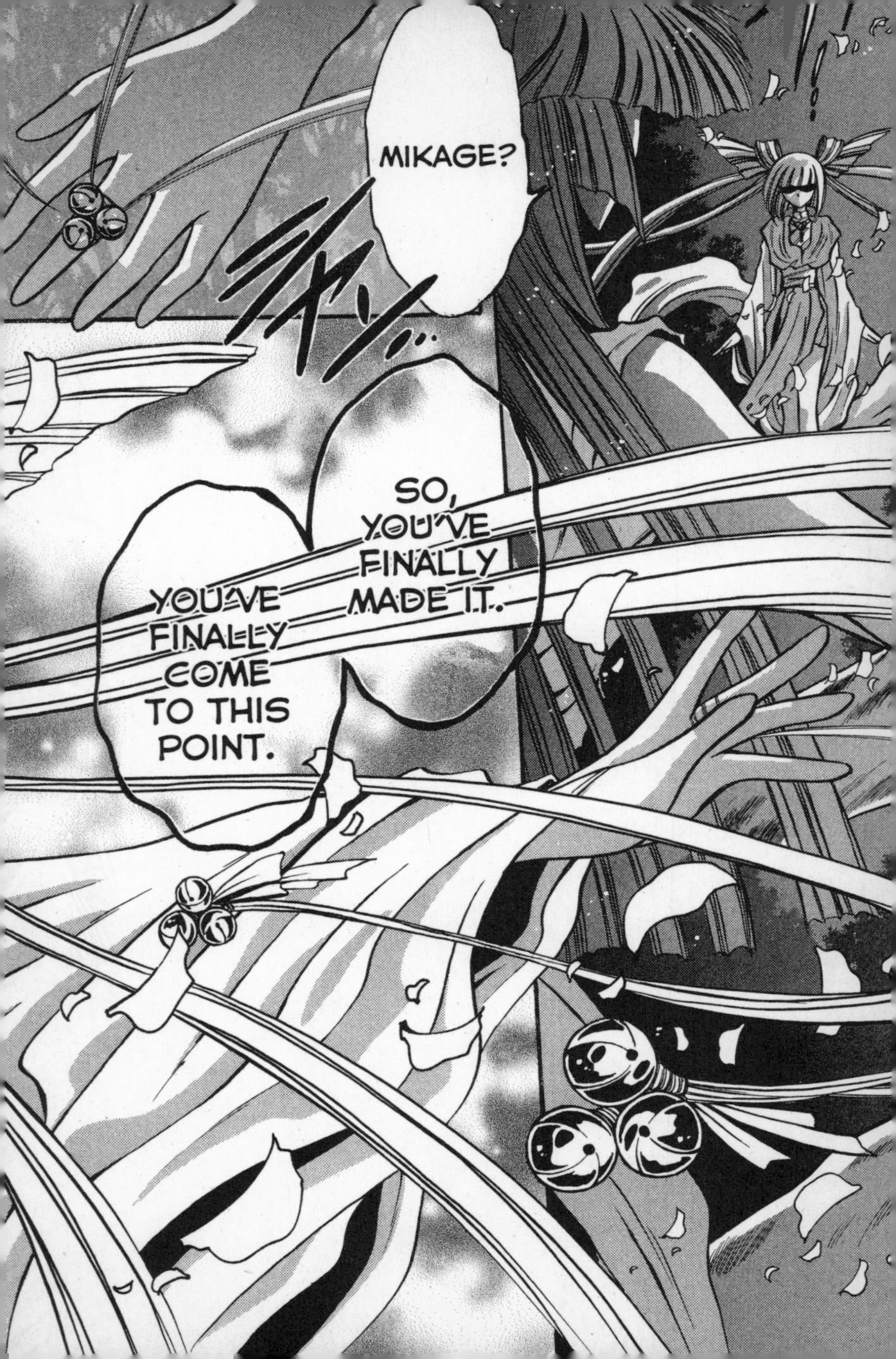
MIKAGE?
SO, YOU'VE FINALLY MADE IT.
YOU'VE FINALLY COME TO THIS POINT.

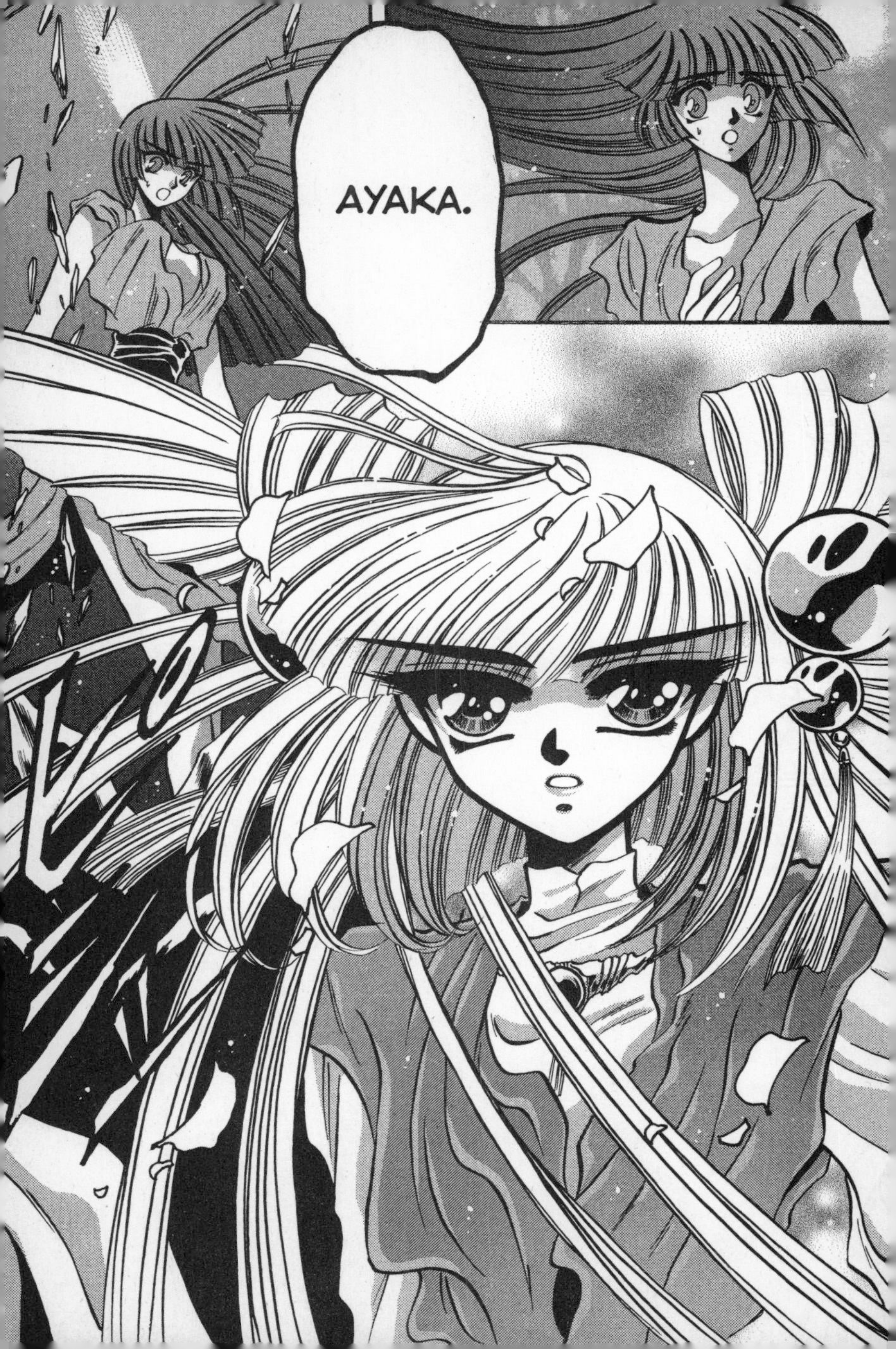
AYAKA.

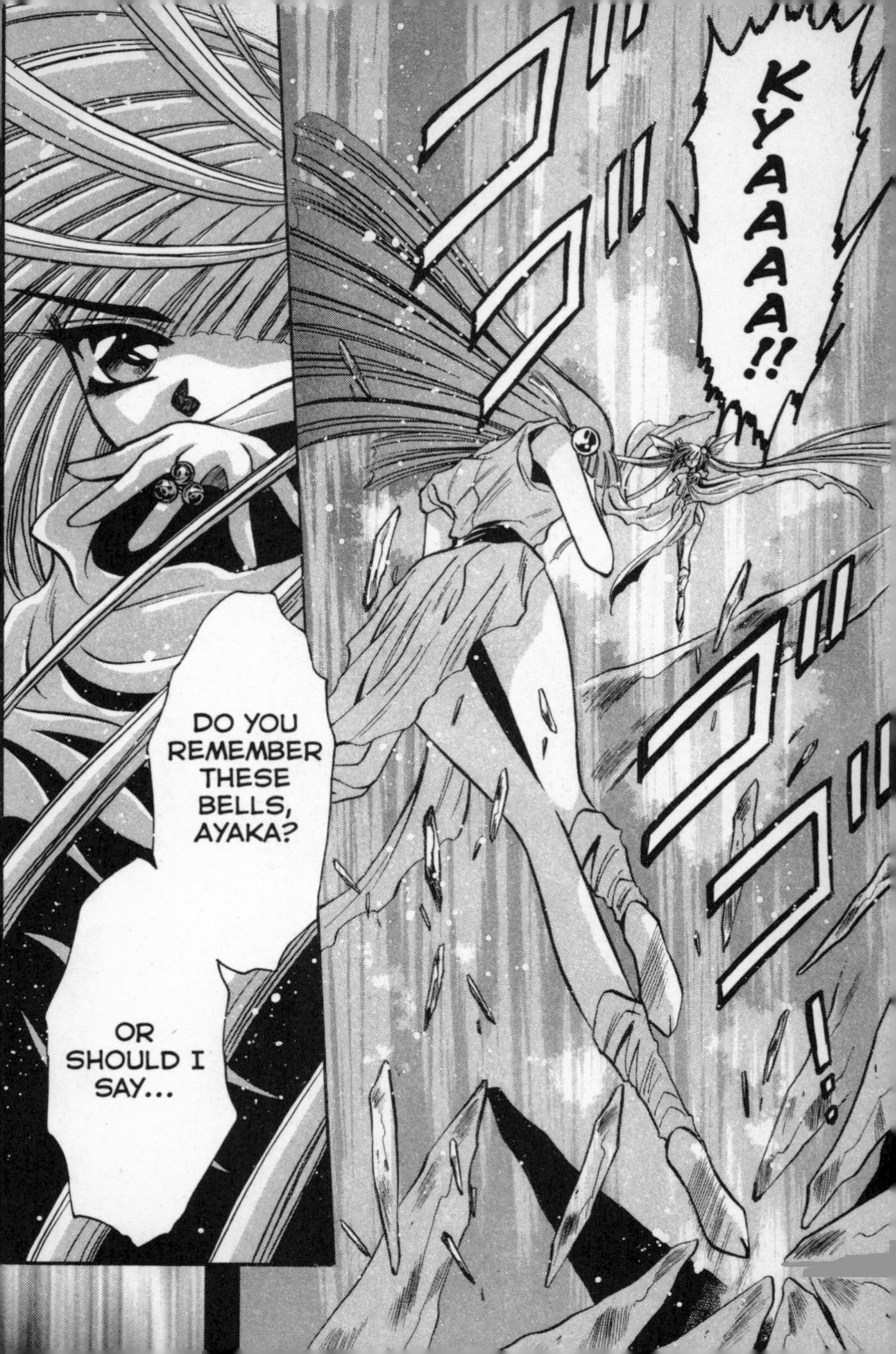
KYAAAA!!
DO YOU REMEMBER THESE BELLS, AYAKA?
OR SHOULD I SAY...

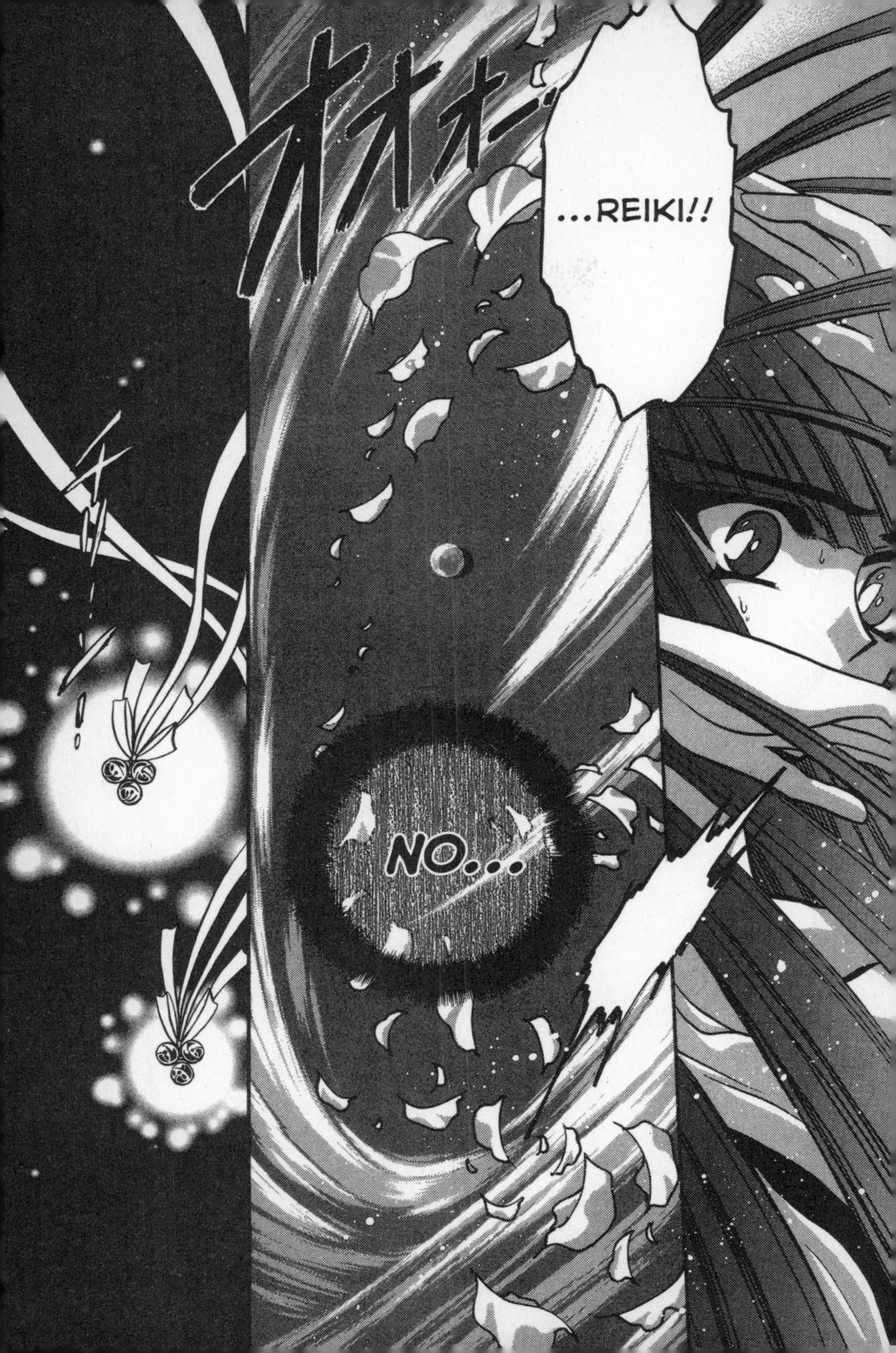
...REIKI!!
オオオー
NO...

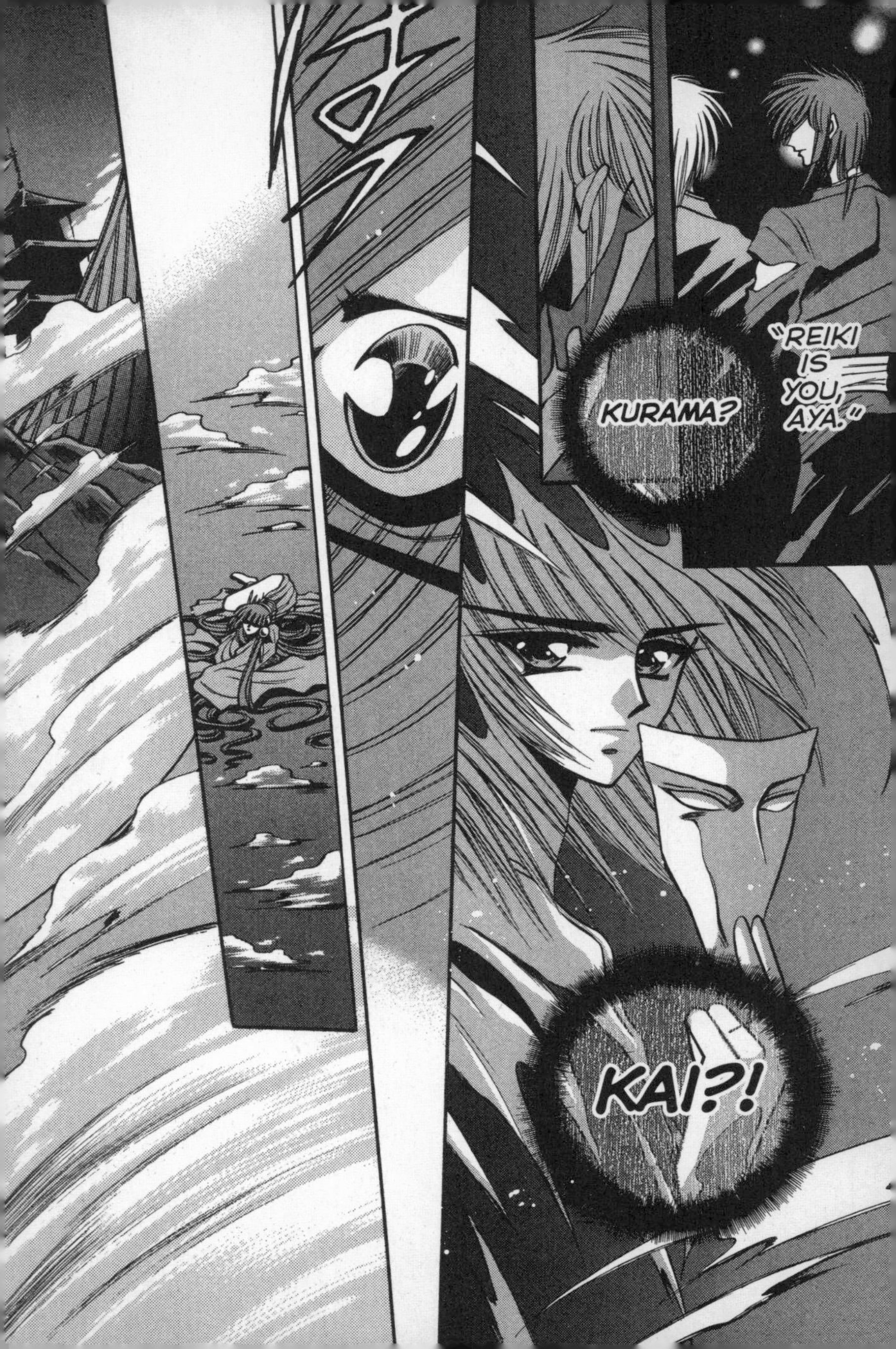
"REIKI IS YOU, AYA."
KURAMA?
KAI?!

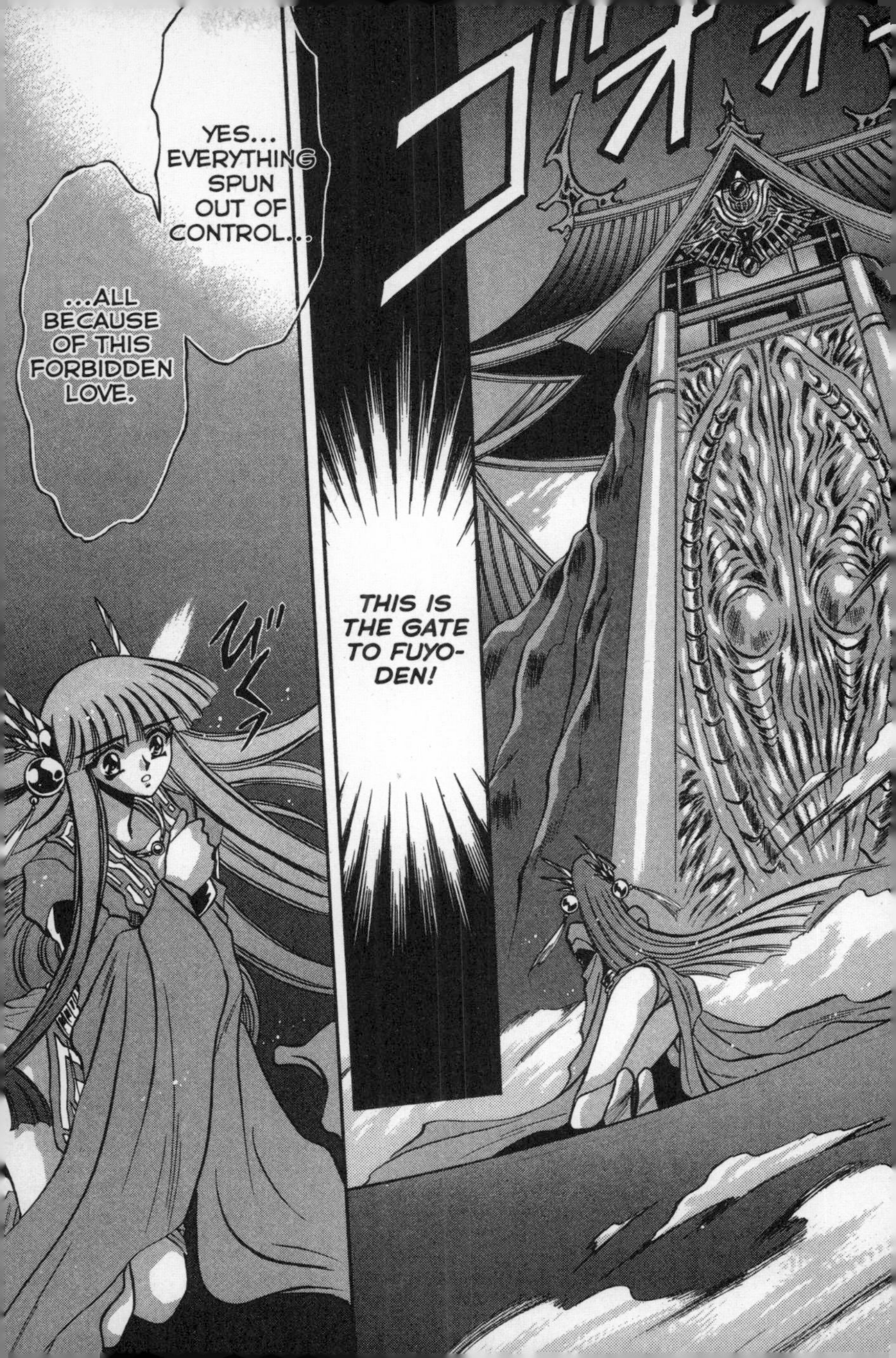
THIS IS THE GATE TO FUYO-DEN!
YES... EVERYTHING SPUN OUT OF CONTROL...
...ALL BECAUSE OF THIS FORBIDDEN LOVE.

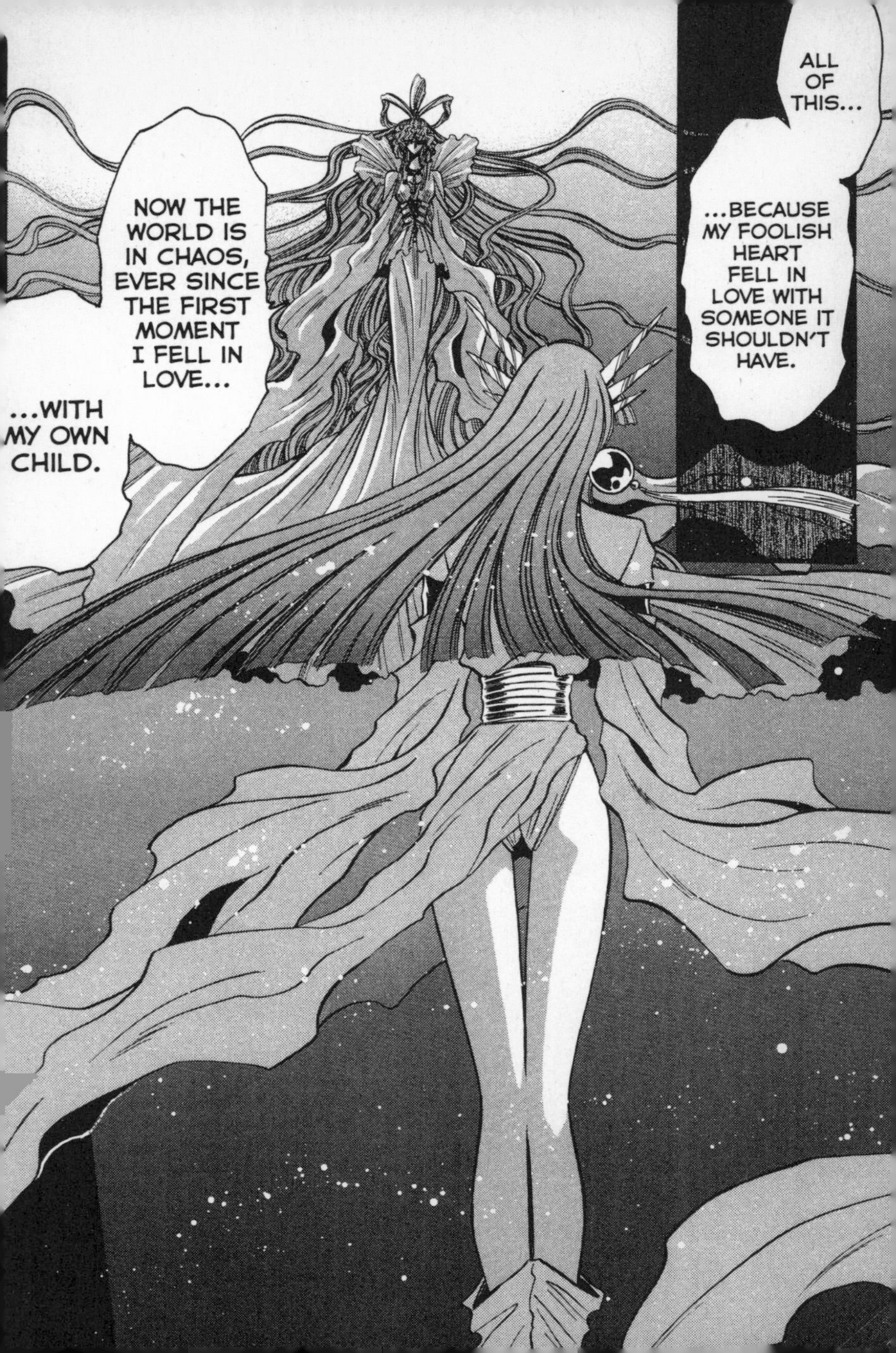
ALL OF THIS...
...BECAUSE MY FOOLISH HEART FELL IN LOVE WITH SOMEONE IT SHOULDN'T HAVE.
NOW THE WORLD IS IN CHAOS, EVER SINCE THE FIRST MOMENT I FELL IN LOVE...
...WITH MY OWN CHILD.

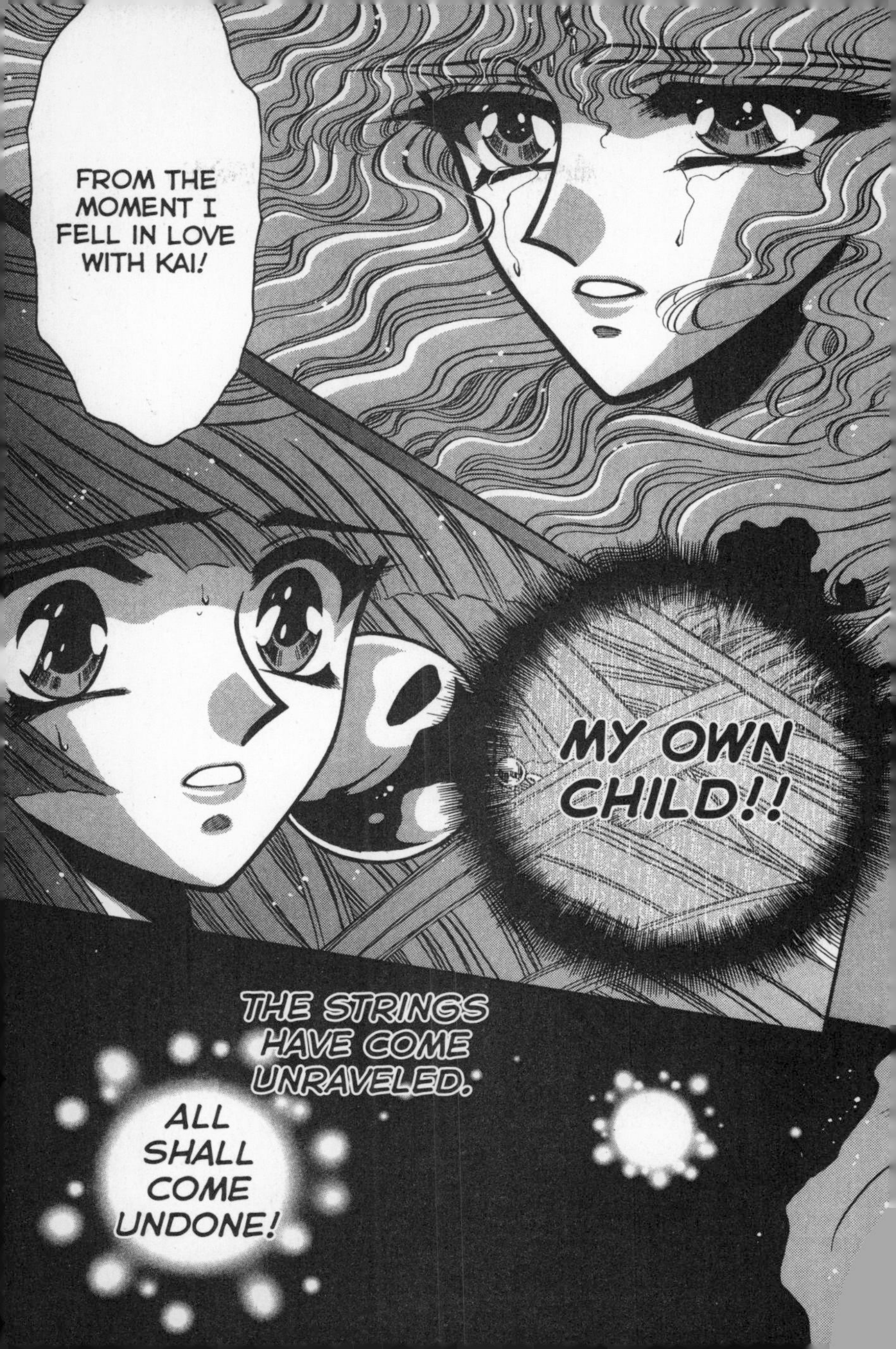
FROM THE MOMENT I FELL IN LOVE WITH KAI!
MY OWN CHILD!!
THE STRINGS HAVE COME UNRAVELED.
ALL SHALL COME UNDONE!

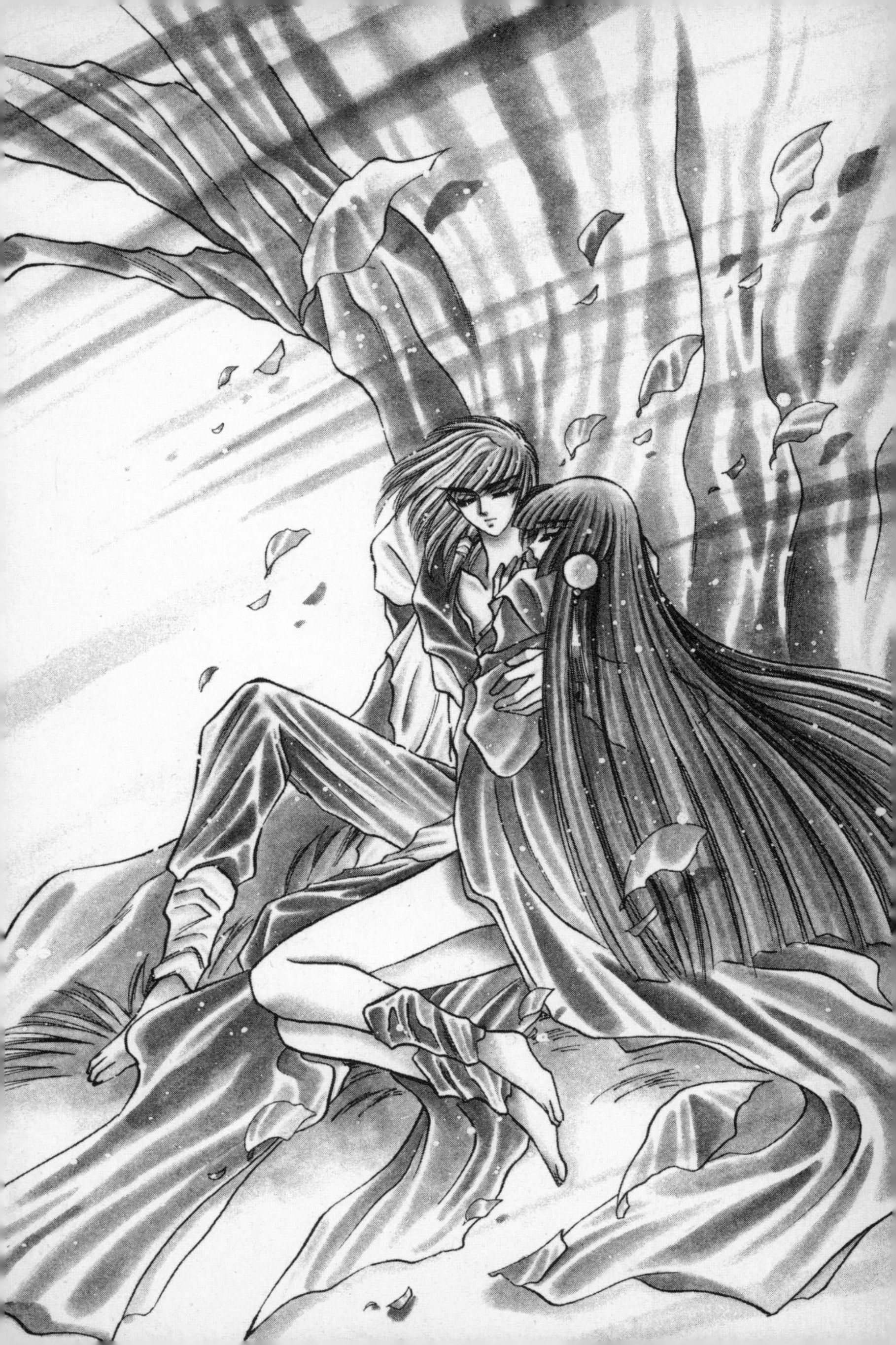

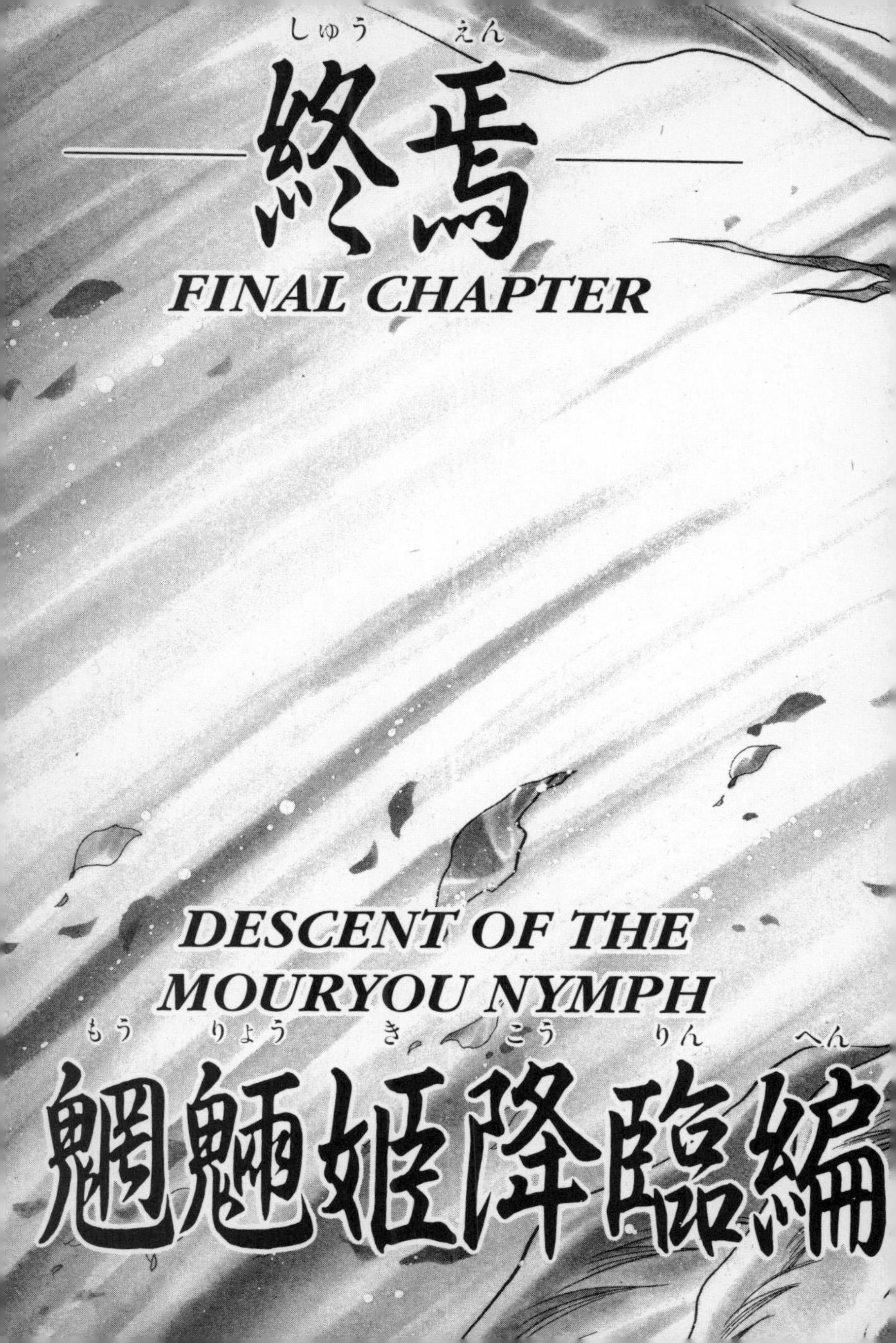

しゅう　えん
—終焉—
FINAL CHAPTER
DESCENT OF THE MOURYOU NYMPH
もう　りょう　き　こう　りん　へん
魍魎姫降臨編

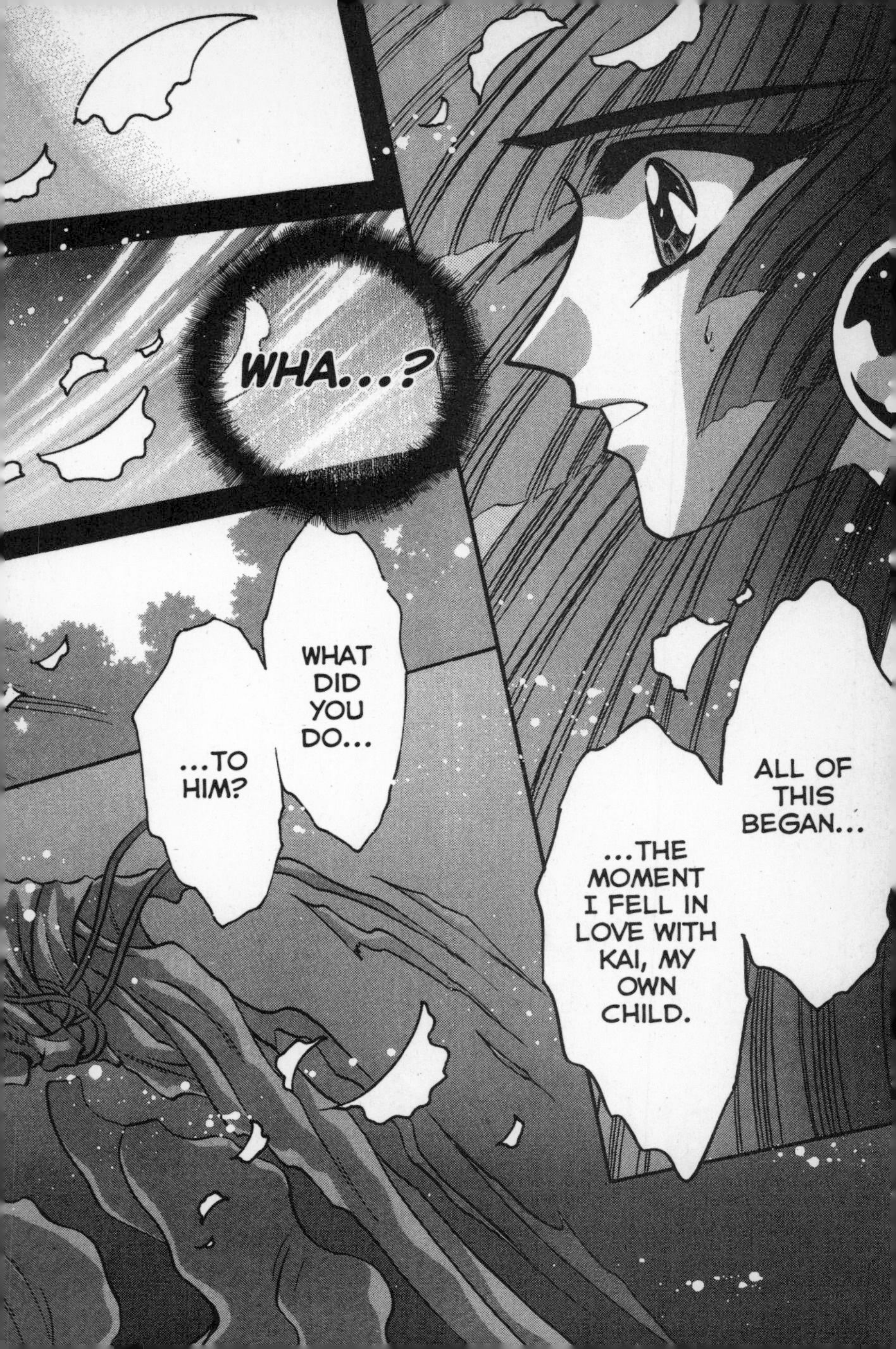
WHA...?
WHAT DID YOU DO...
...TO HIM?
ALL OF THIS BEGAN...
...THE MOMENT I FELL IN LOVE WITH KAI, MY OWN CHILD.

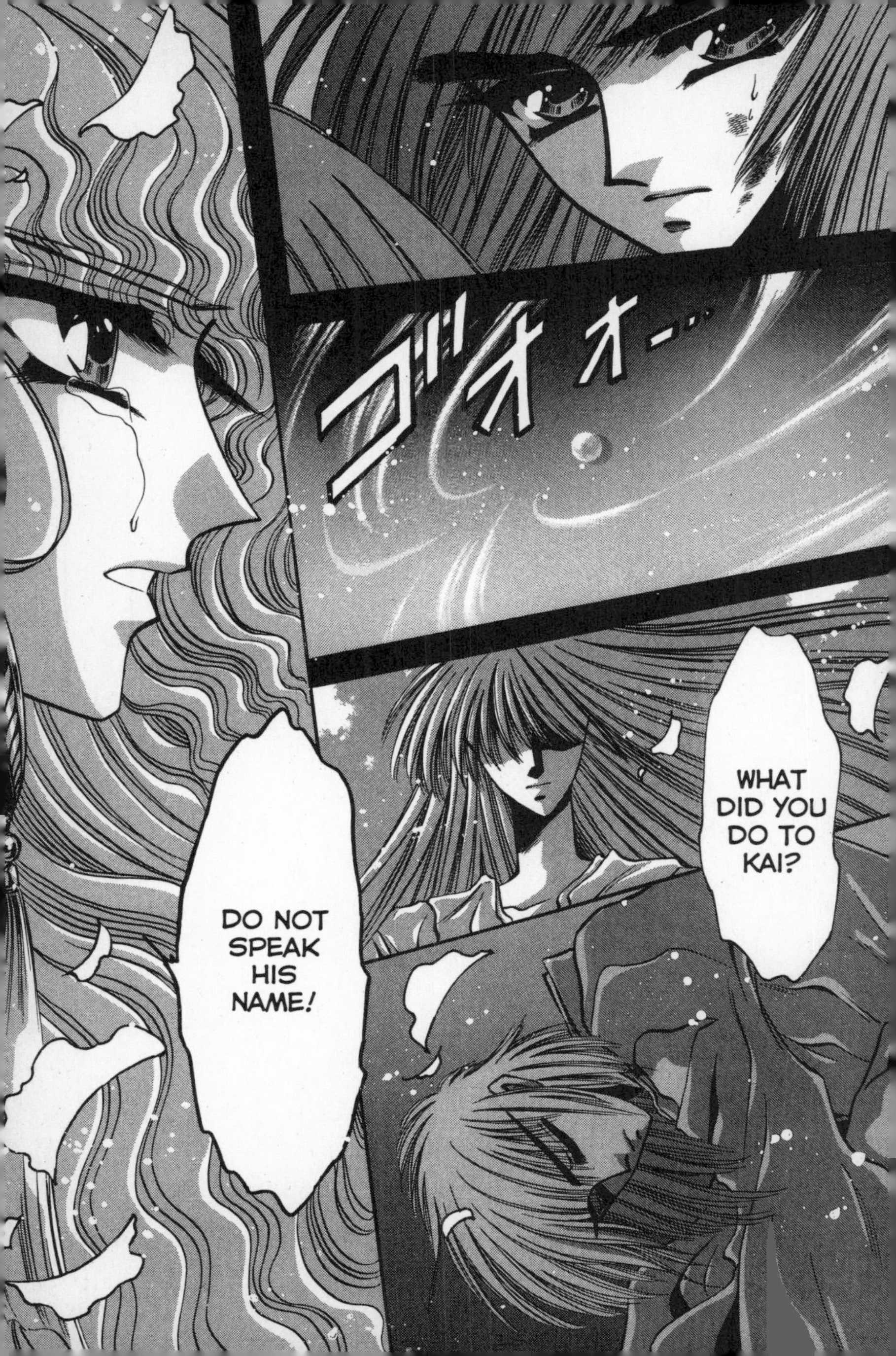
ゴオオー…
WHAT DID YOU DO TO KAI?
DO NOT SPEAK HIS NAME!

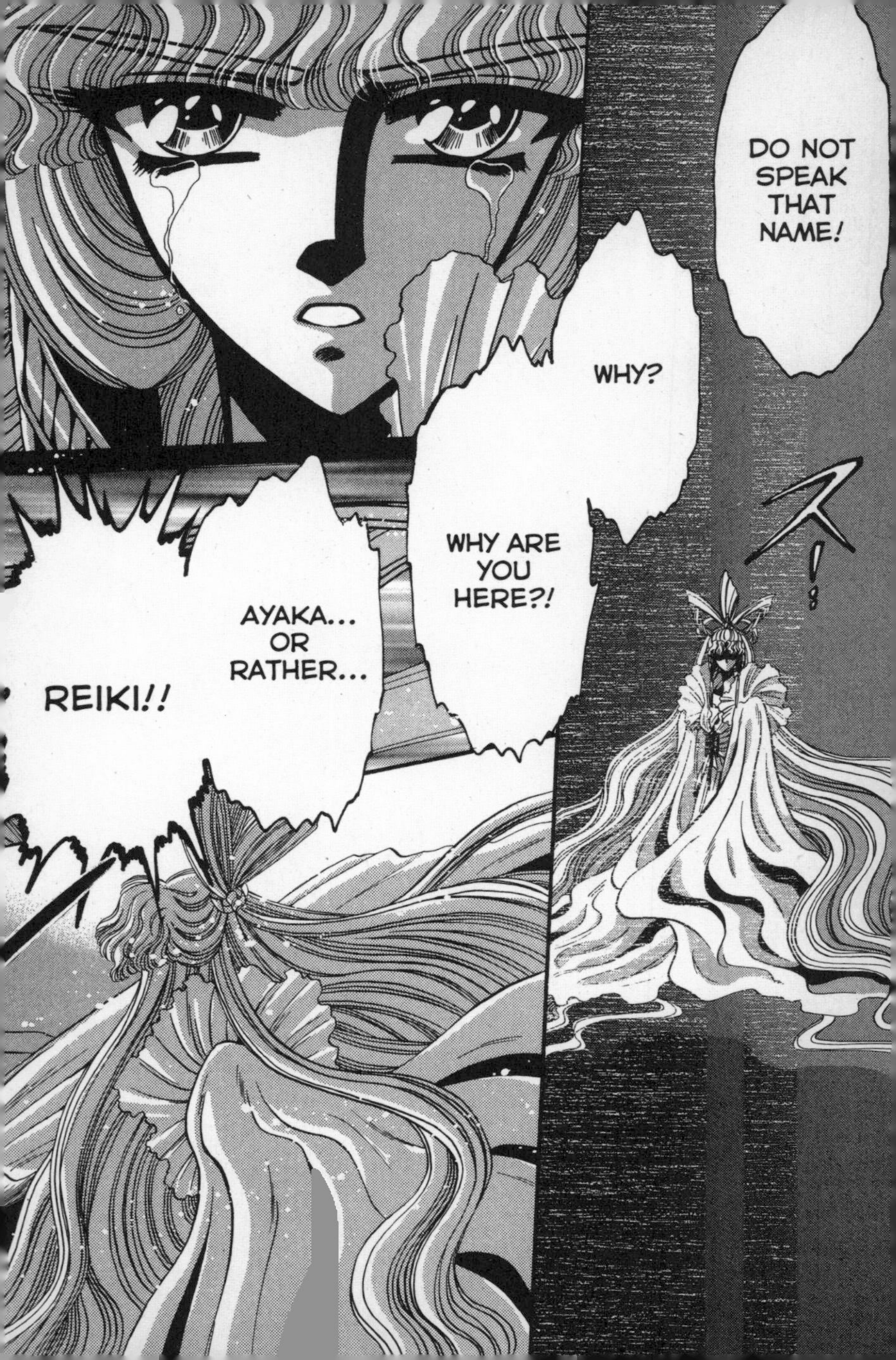
DO NOT SPEAK THAT NAME!
ス!
WHY?
WHY ARE YOU HERE?!
AYAKA... OR RATHER...
REIKI!!

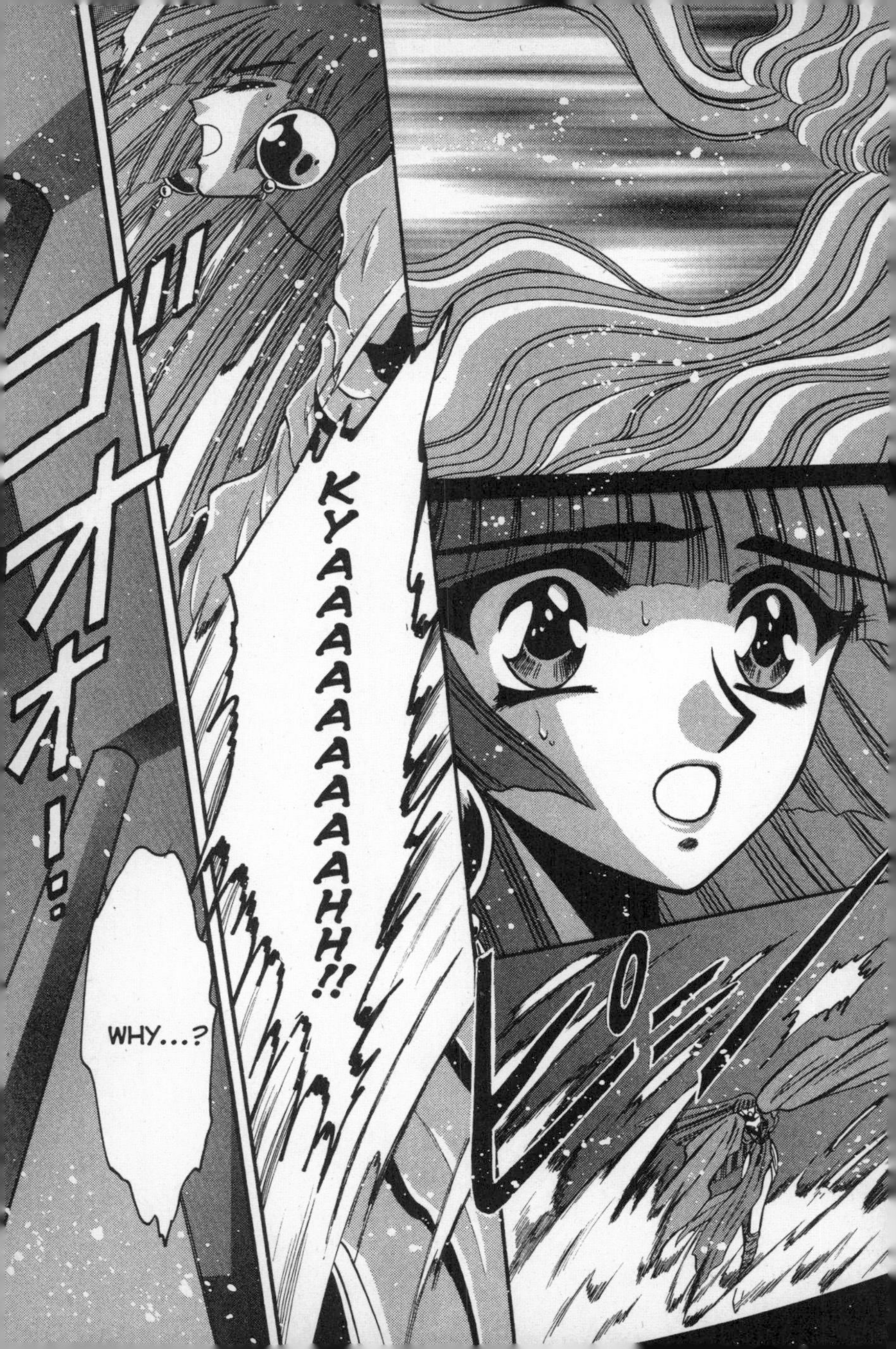
KYAAAAAAAAAHH!!
WHY...?

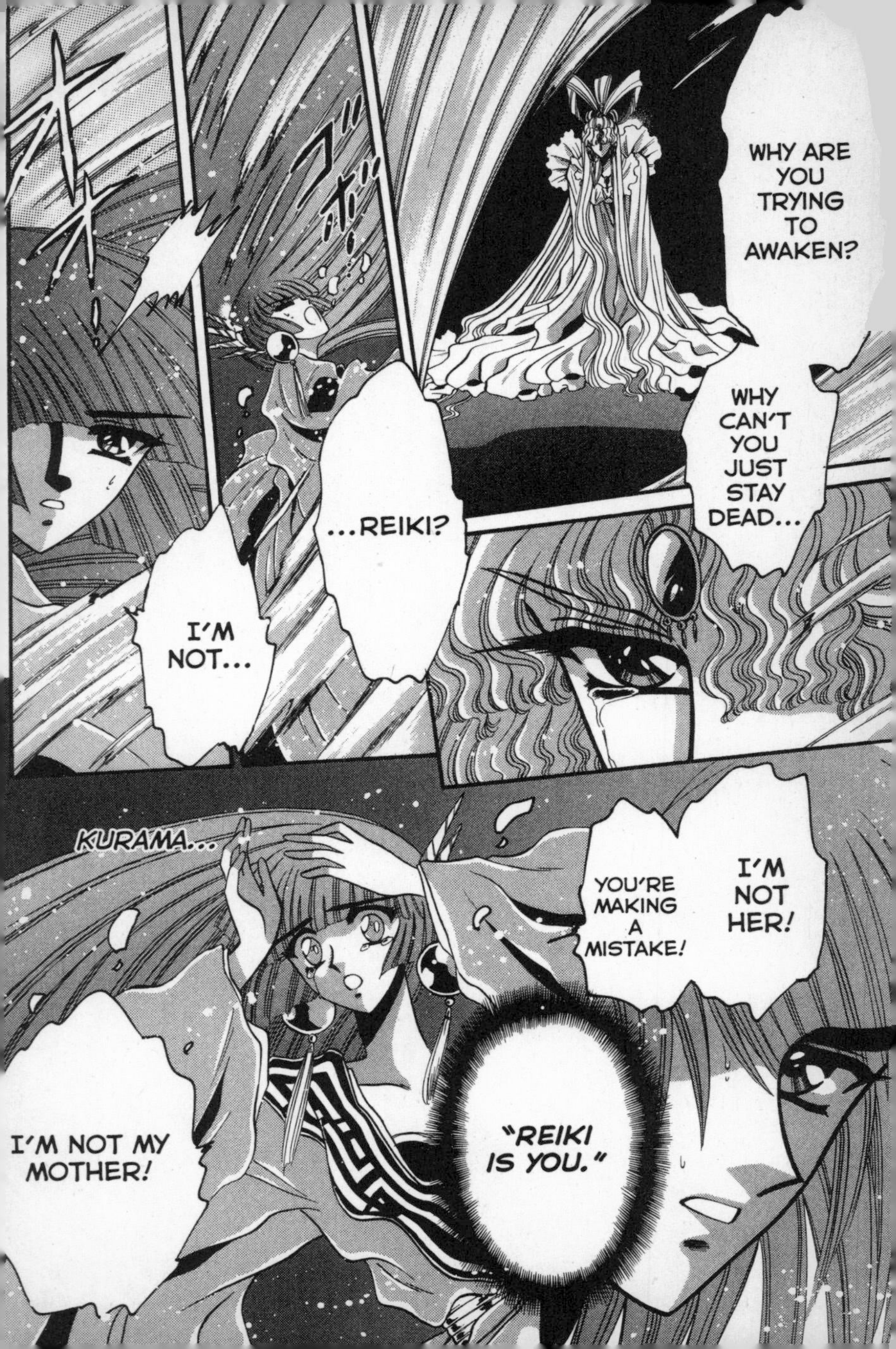
WHY ARE YOU TRYING TO AWAKEN?
WHY CAN'T YOU JUST STAY DEAD...
...REIKI?
I'M NOT...
I'M NOT HER!
YOU'RE MAKING A MISTAKE!
KURAMA...
"REIKI IS YOU."
I'M NOT MY MOTHER!

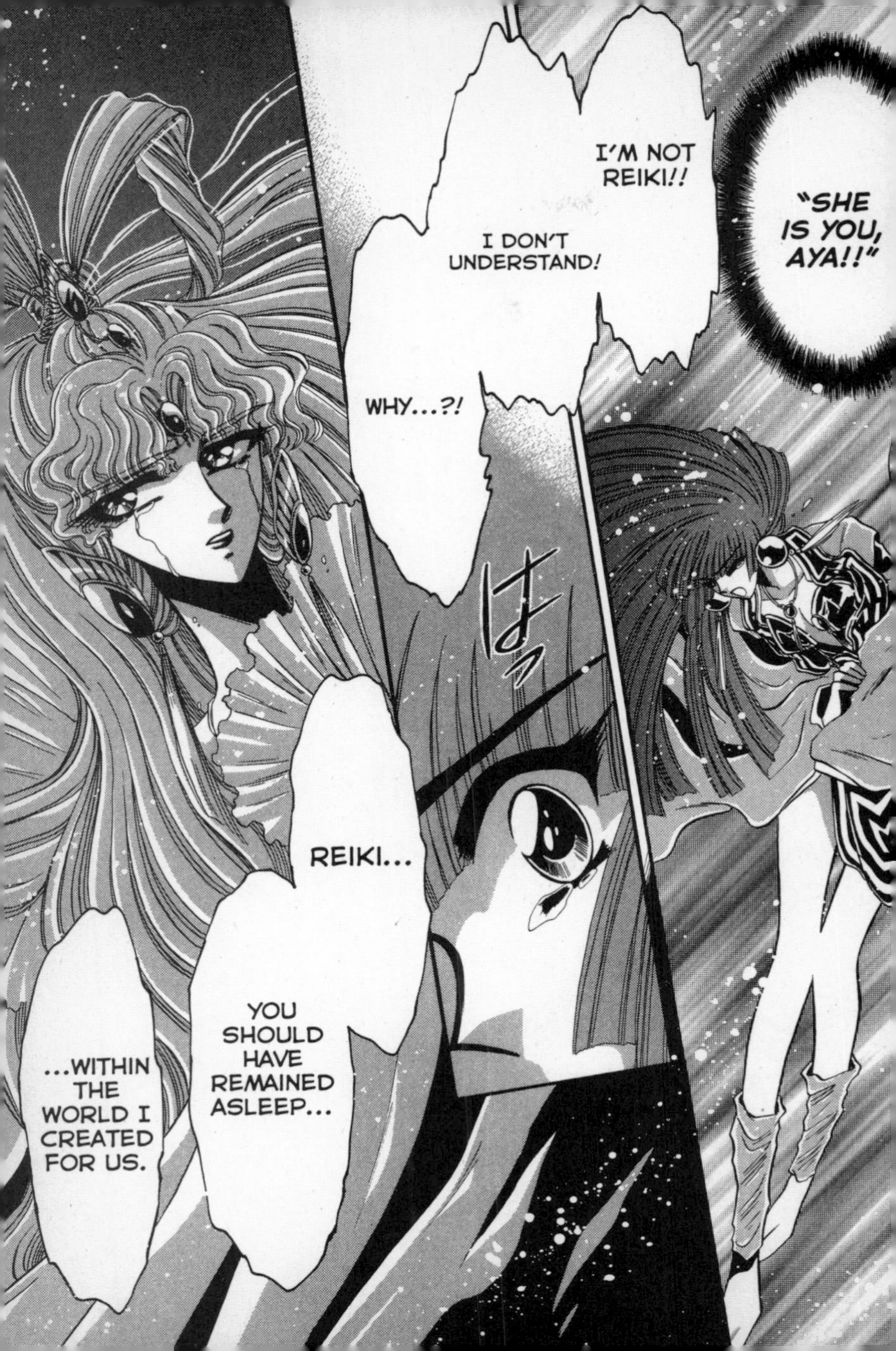
"SHE IS YOU, AYA!!"
I'M NOT REIKI!!
I DON'T UNDERSTAND!
WHY...?!
はっ
REIKI...
YOU SHOULD HAVE REMAINED ASLEEP...
...WITHIN THE WORLD I CREATED FOR US.

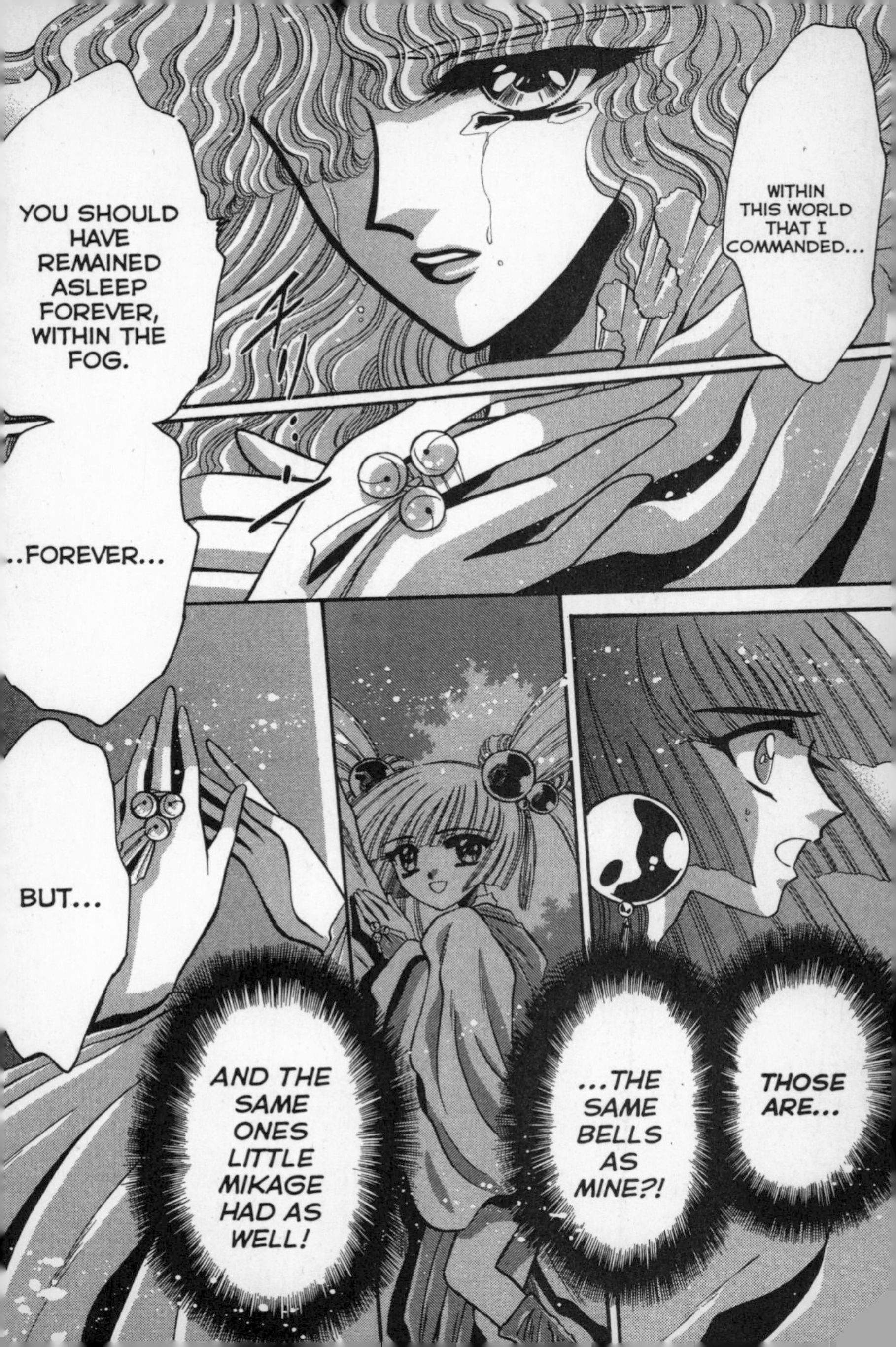
WITHIN THIS WORLD THAT I COMMANDED...
YOU SHOULD HAVE REMAINED ASLEEP FOREVER, WITHIN THE FOG.
..FOREVER...
BUT...
THOSE ARE...
...THE SAME BELLS AS MINE?!
AND THE SAME ONES LITTLE MIKAGE HAD AS WELL!

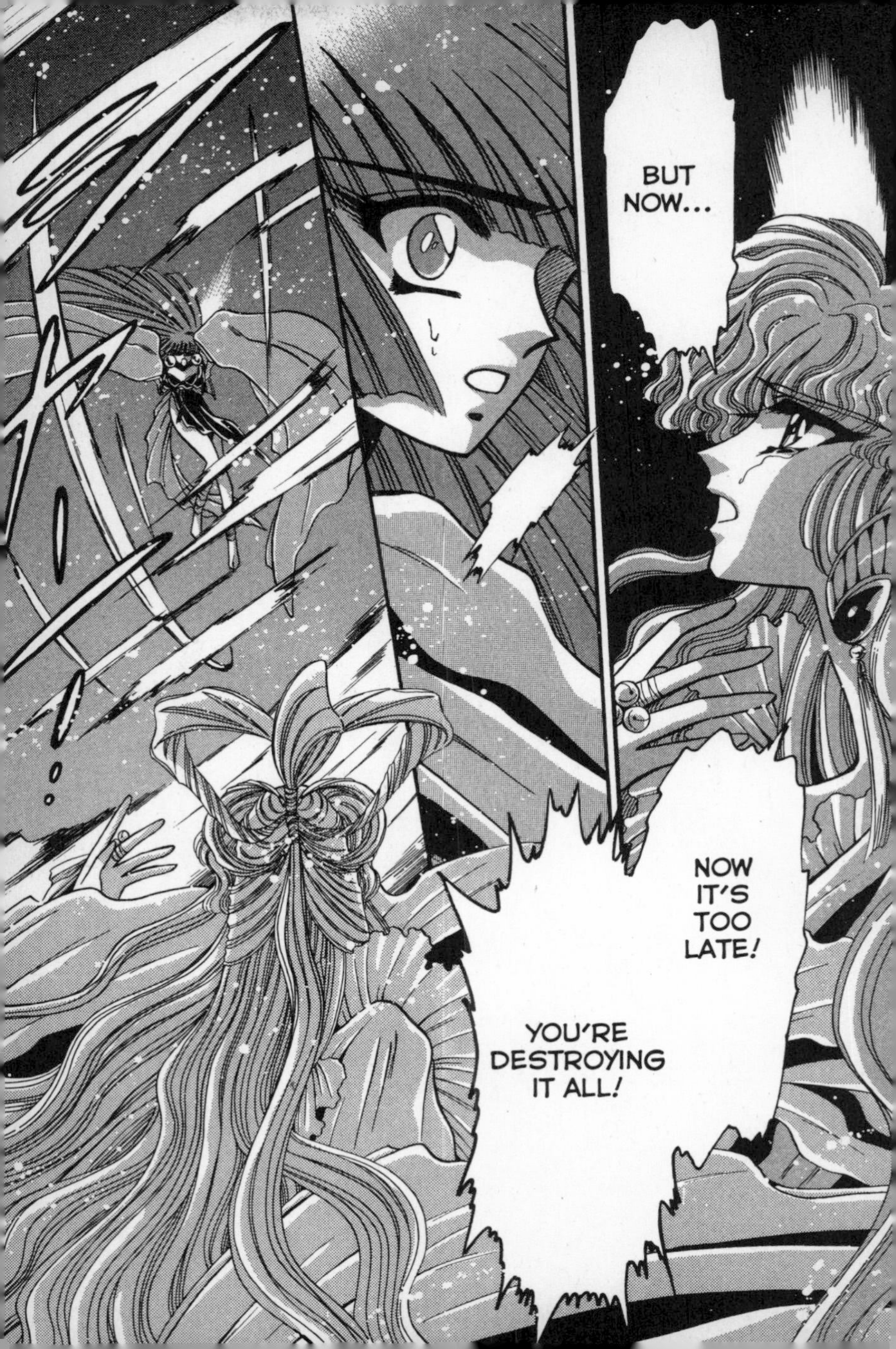
BUT NOW...
NOW IT'S TOO LATE!
YOU'RE DESTROYING IT ALL!

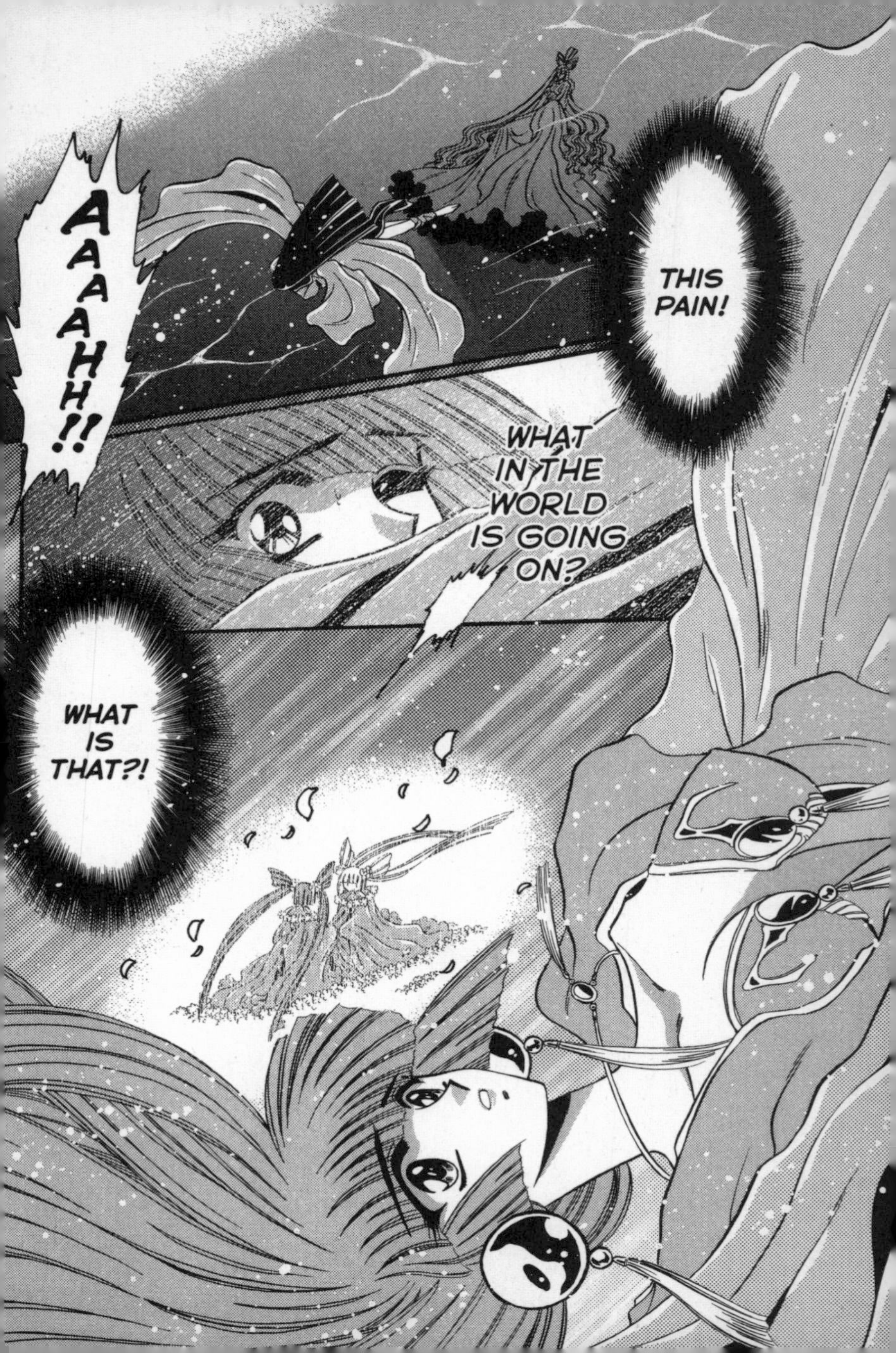
THIS PAIN!
AAAAHH!!
WHAT IN THE WORLD IS GOING ON?
WHAT IS THAT?!

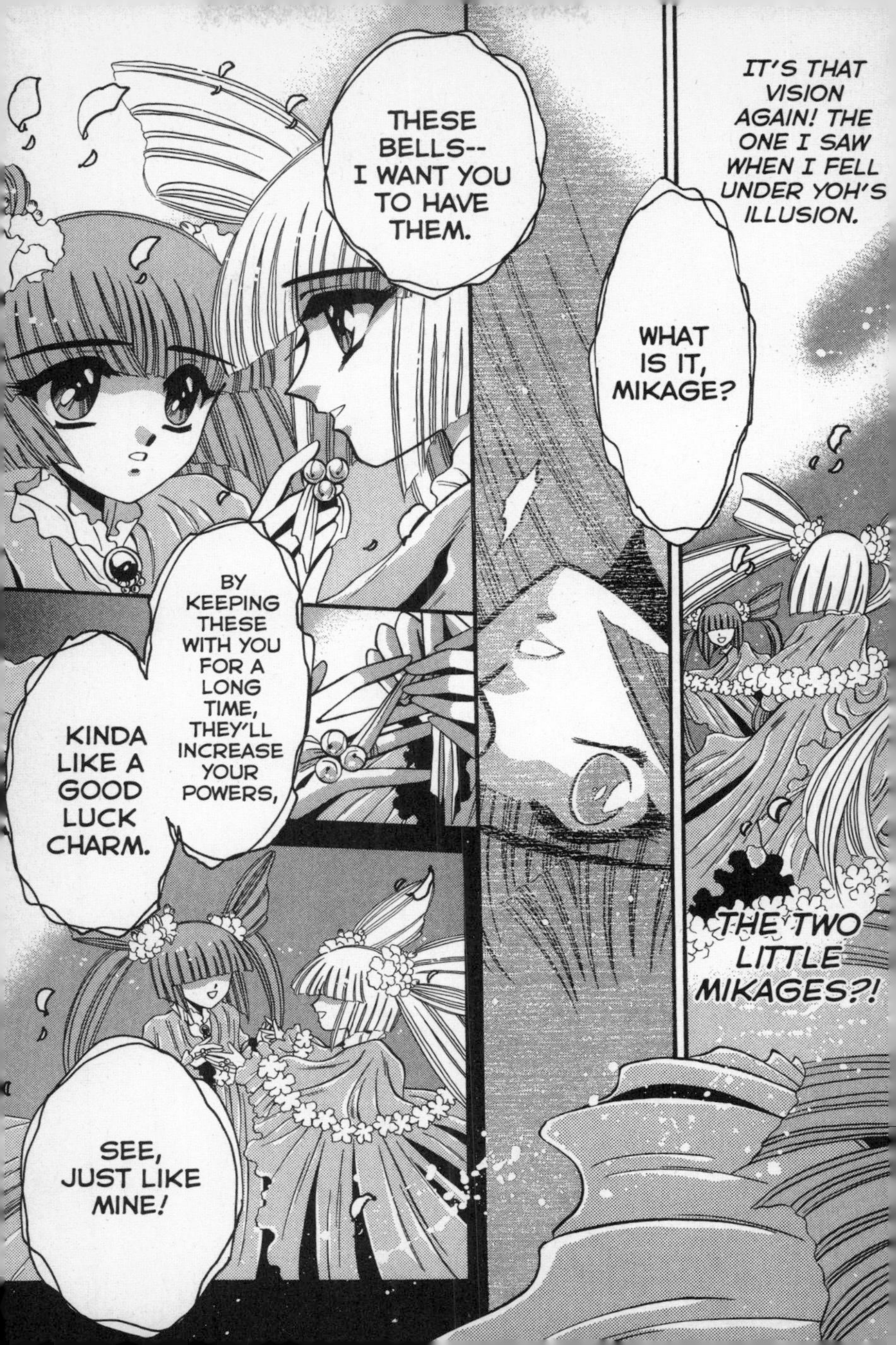
IT'S THAT VISION AGAIN! THE ONE I SAW WHEN I FELL UNDER YOH'S ILLUSION.
WHAT IS IT, MIKAGE?
THE TWO LITTLE MIKAGES?!
THESE BELLS-- I WANT YOU TO HAVE THEM.
BY KEEPING THESE WITH YOU FOR A LONG TIME, THEY'LL INCREASE YOUR POWERS,
KINDA LIKE A GOOD LUCK CHARM.
SEE, JUST LIKE MINE!

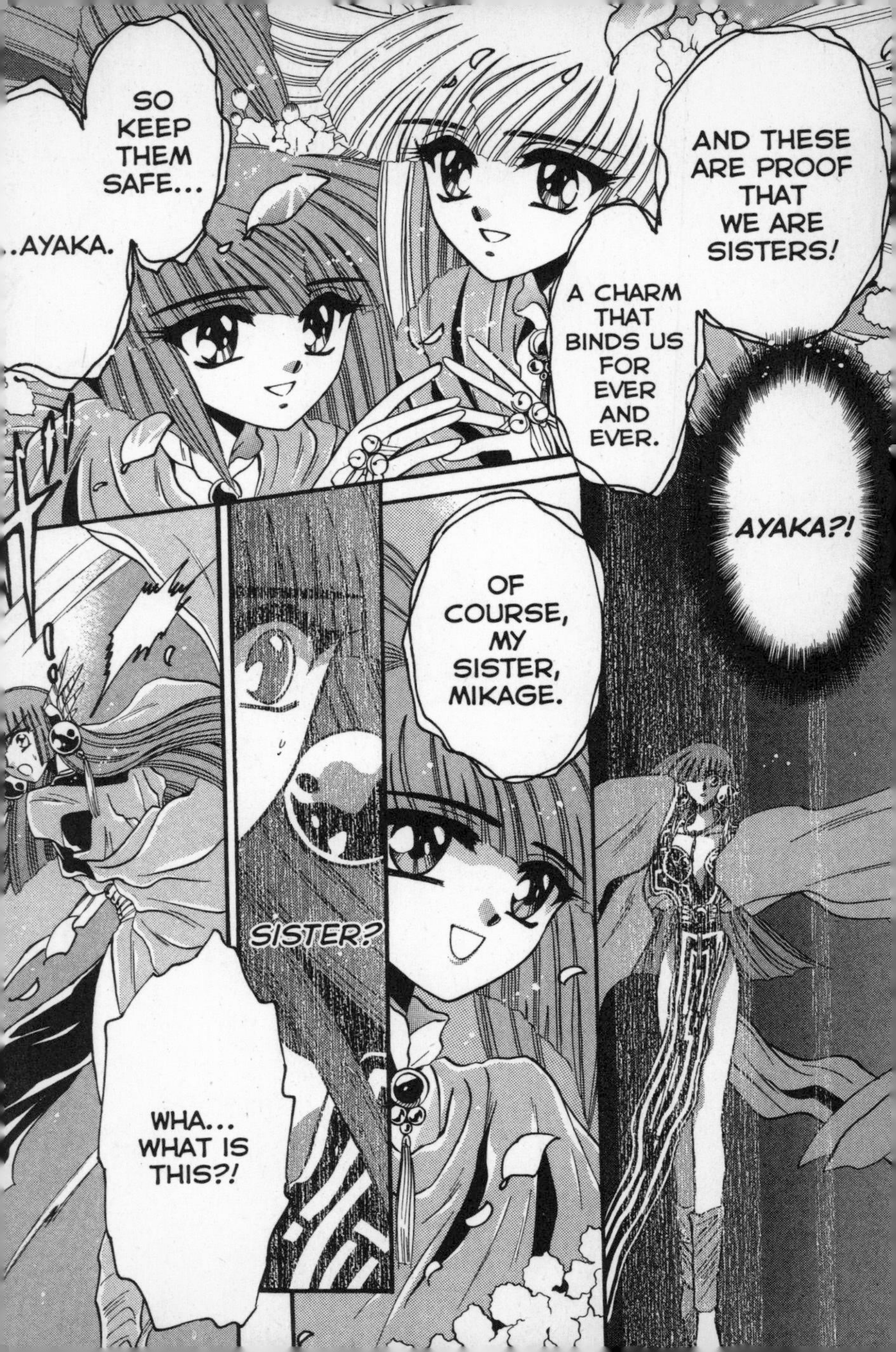
AND THESE ARE PROOF THAT WE ARE SISTERS!
A CHARM THAT BINDS US FOR EVER AND EVER.
SO KEEP THEM SAFE...
.AYAKA.
AYAKA?!
OF COURSE, MY SISTER, MIKAGE.
SISTER?
WHA... WHAT IS THIS?!

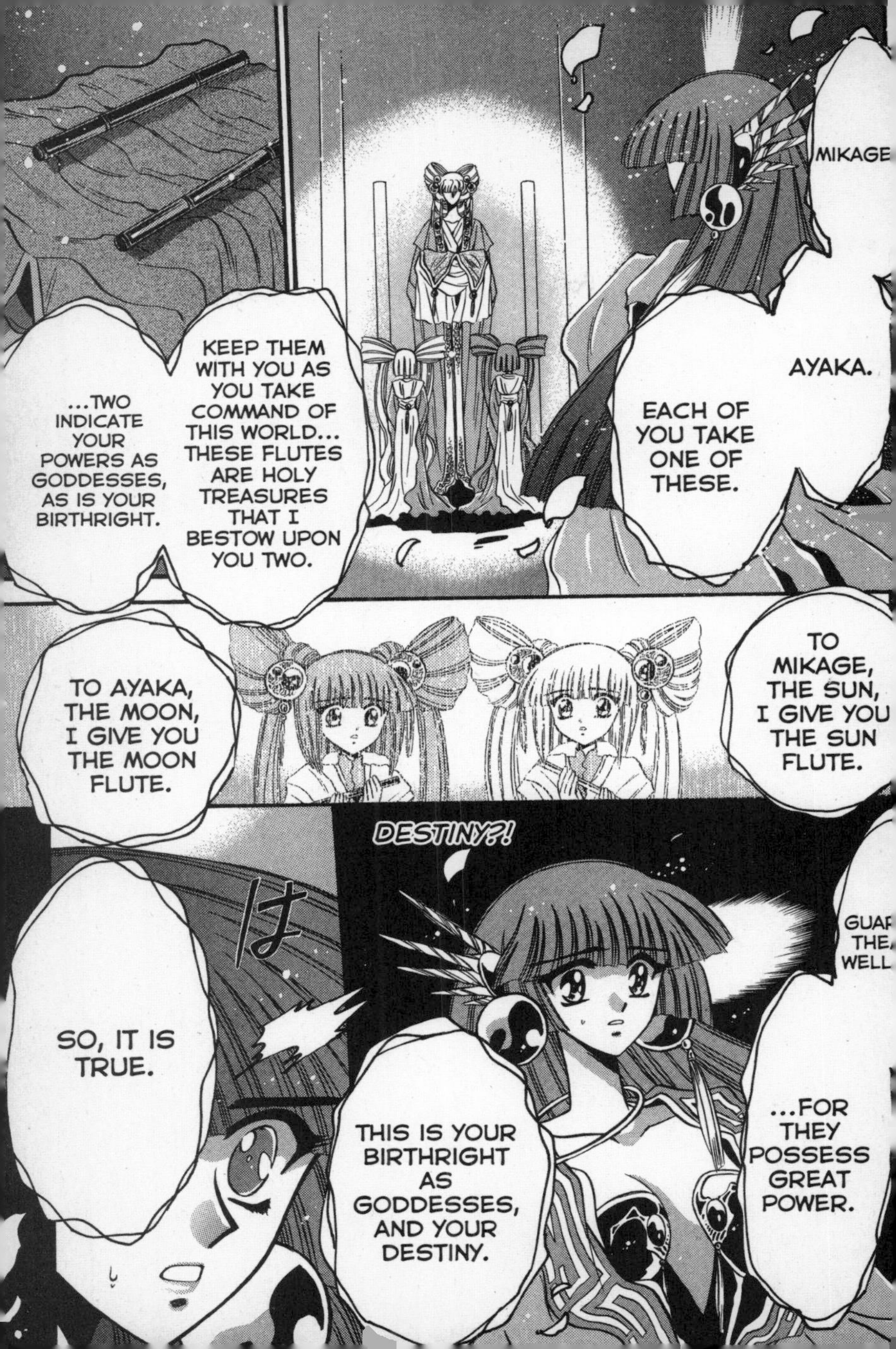
MIKAGE
AYAKA.
EACH OF YOU TAKE ONE OF THESE.
KEEP THEM WITH YOU AS YOU TAKE COMMAND OF THIS WORLD... THESE FLUTES ARE HOLY TREASURES THAT I BESTOW UPON YOU TWO.
...TWO INDICATE YOUR POWERS AS GODDESSES, AS IS YOUR BIRTHRIGHT.
TO MIKAGE, THE SUN, I GIVE YOU THE SUN FLUTE.
TO AYAKA, THE MOON, I GIVE YOU THE MOON FLUTE.
...FOR THEY POSSESS GREAT POWER.
THIS IS YOUR BIRTHRIGHT AS GODDESSES, AND YOUR DESTINY.
DESTINY?!
は
SO, IT IS TRUE.

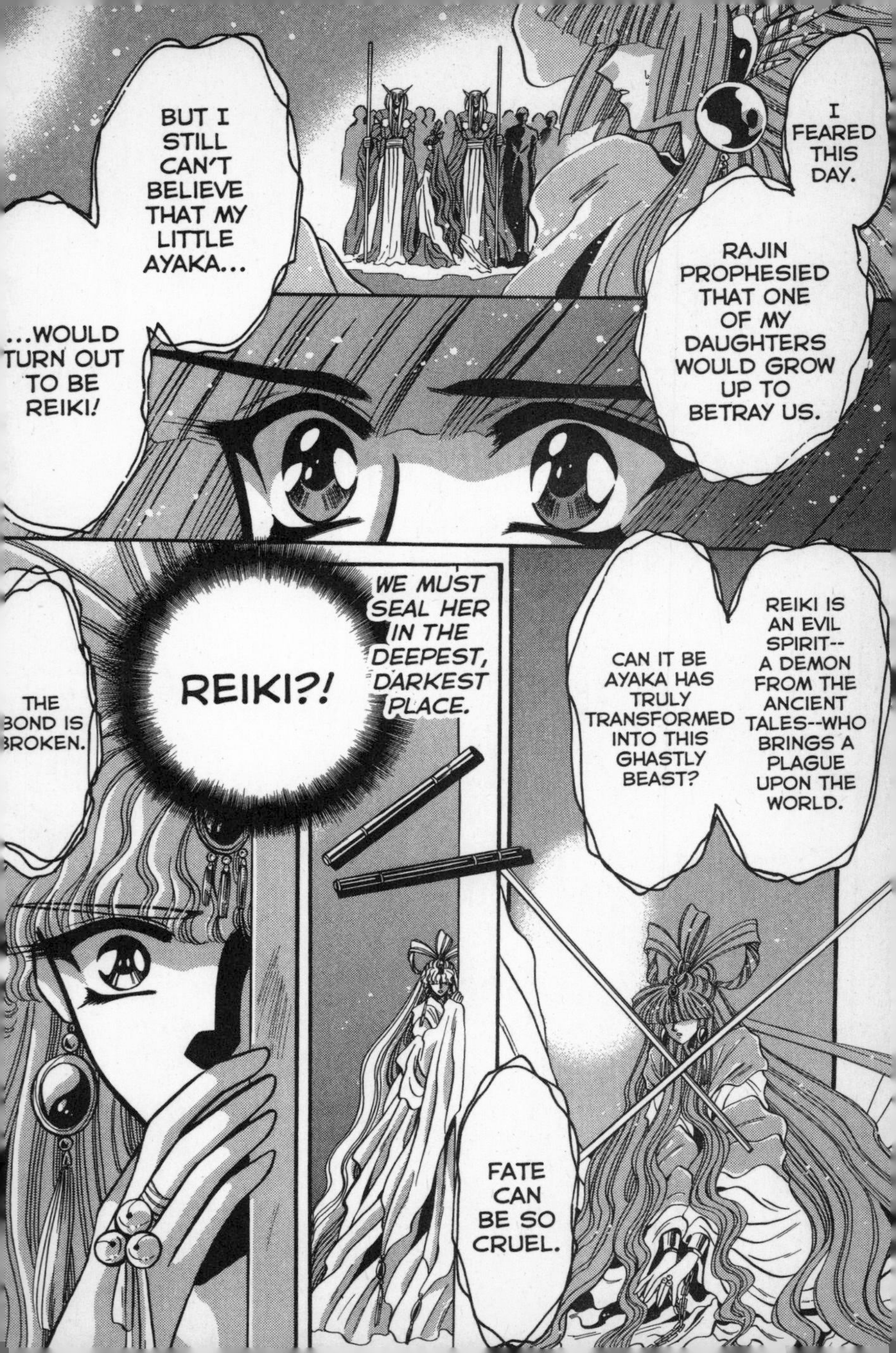

I FEARED THIS DAY.
RAJIN PROPHESIED THAT ONE OF MY DAUGHTERS WOULD GROW UP TO BETRAY US.
BUT I STILL CAN'T BELIEVE THAT MY LITTLE AYAKA...
...WOULD TURN OUT TO BE REIKI!
REIKI IS AN EVIL SPIRIT-- A DEMON FROM THE ANCIENT TALES--WHO BRINGS A PLAGUE UPON THE WORLD.
CAN IT BE AYAKA HAS TRULY TRANSFORMED INTO THIS GHASTLY BEAST?
FATE CAN BE SO CRUEL.
WE MUST SEAL HER IN THE DEEPEST, DARKEST PLACE.
REIKI?!
THE BOND IS BROKEN.

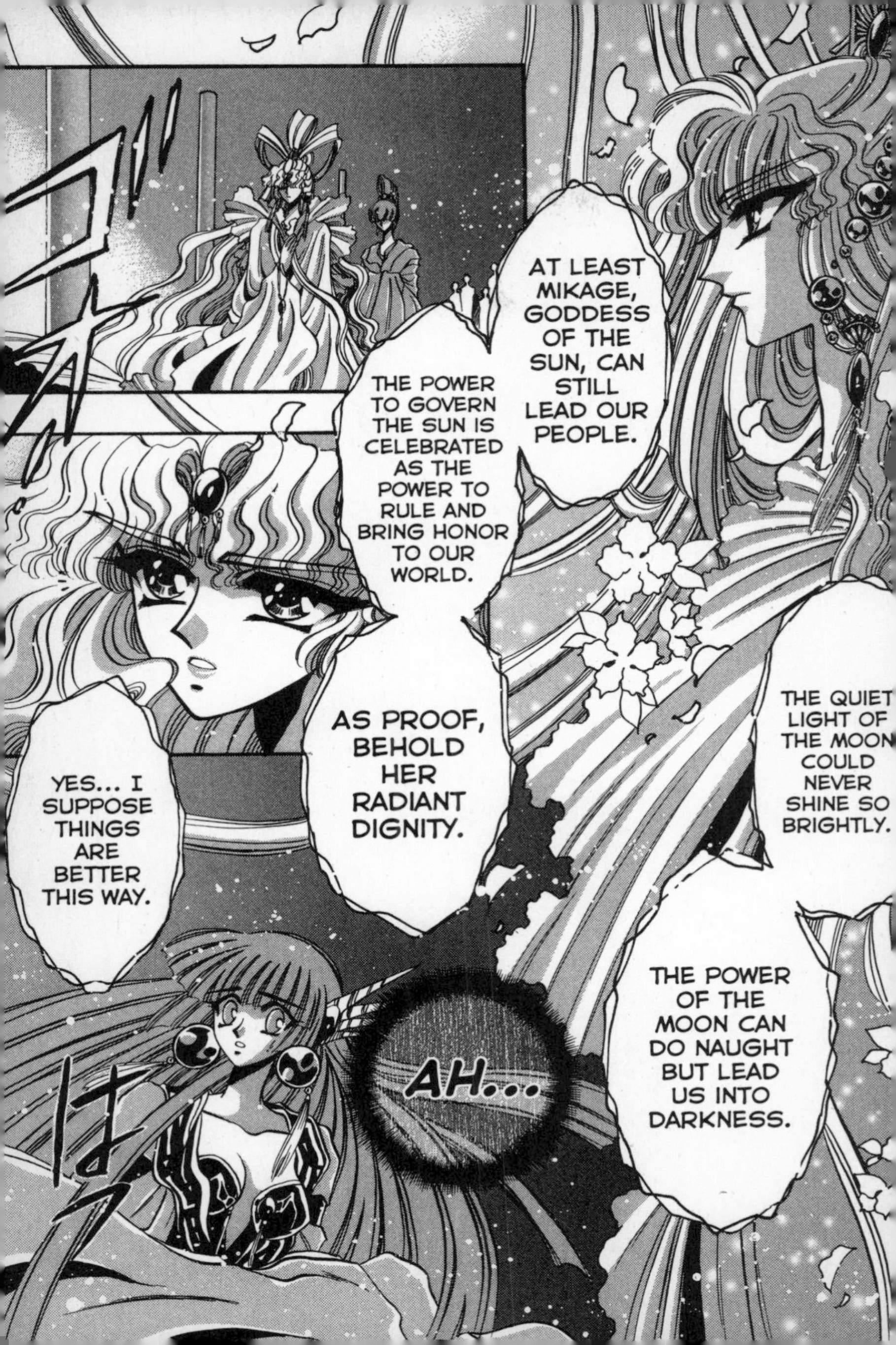
AT LEAST MIKAGE, GODDESS OF THE SUN, CAN STILL LEAD OUR PEOPLE.
THE POWER TO GOVERN THE SUN IS CELEBRATED AS THE POWER TO RULE AND BRING HONOR TO OUR WORLD.
AS PROOF, BEHOLD HER RADIANT DIGNITY.
THE QUIET LIGHT OF THE MOON COULD NEVER SHINE SO BRIGHTLY.
THE POWER OF THE MOON CAN DO NAUGHT BUT LEAD US INTO DARKNESS.
YES... I SUPPOSE THINGS ARE BETTER THIS WAY.
AH...

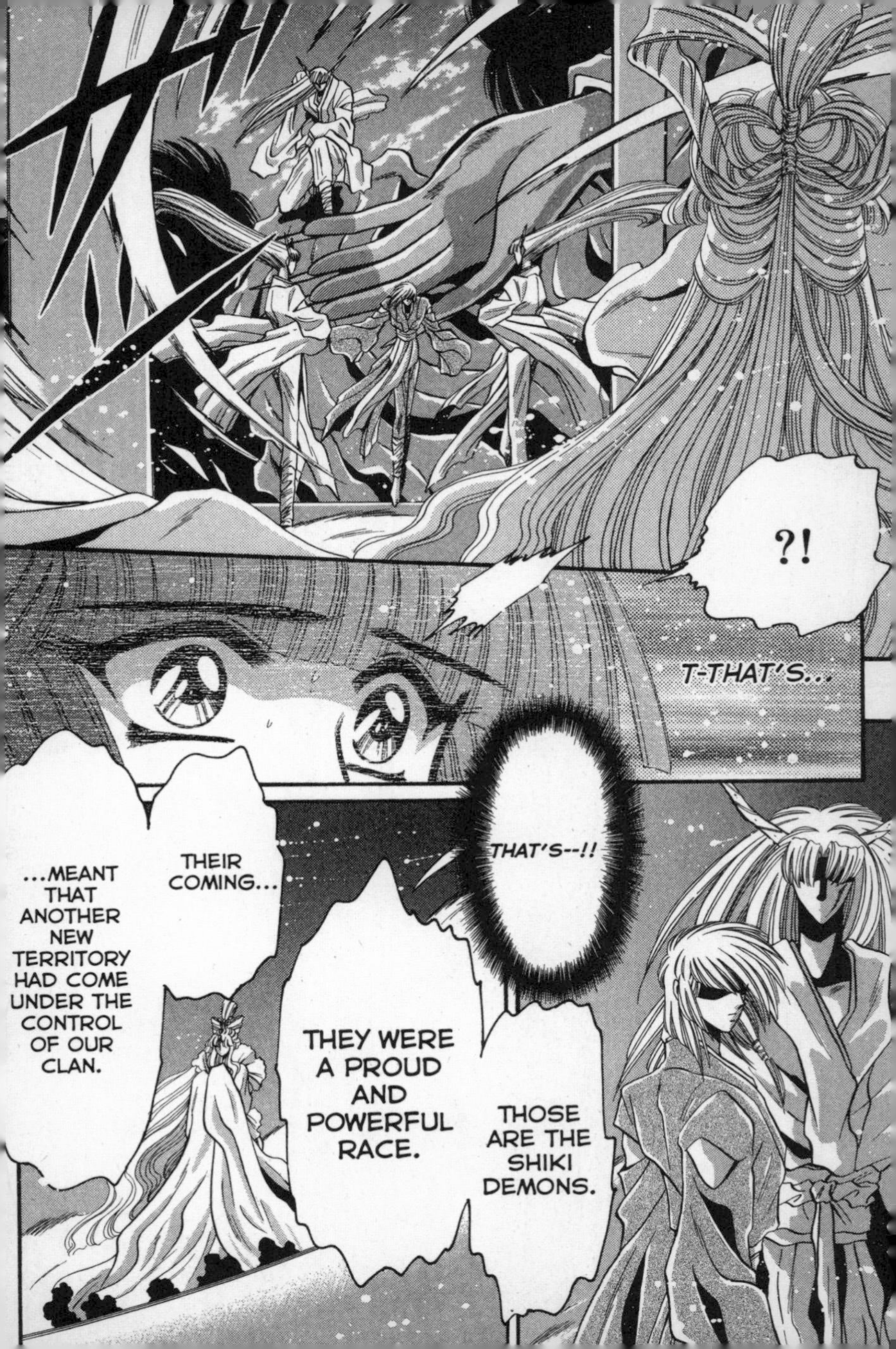
?!
T-THAT'S...
THAT'S--!!
THOSE ARE THE SHIKI DEMONS.
THEY WERE A PROUD AND POWERFUL RACE.
THEIR COMING...
...MEANT THAT ANOTHER NEW TERRITORY HAD COME UNDER THE CONTROL OF OUR CLAN.

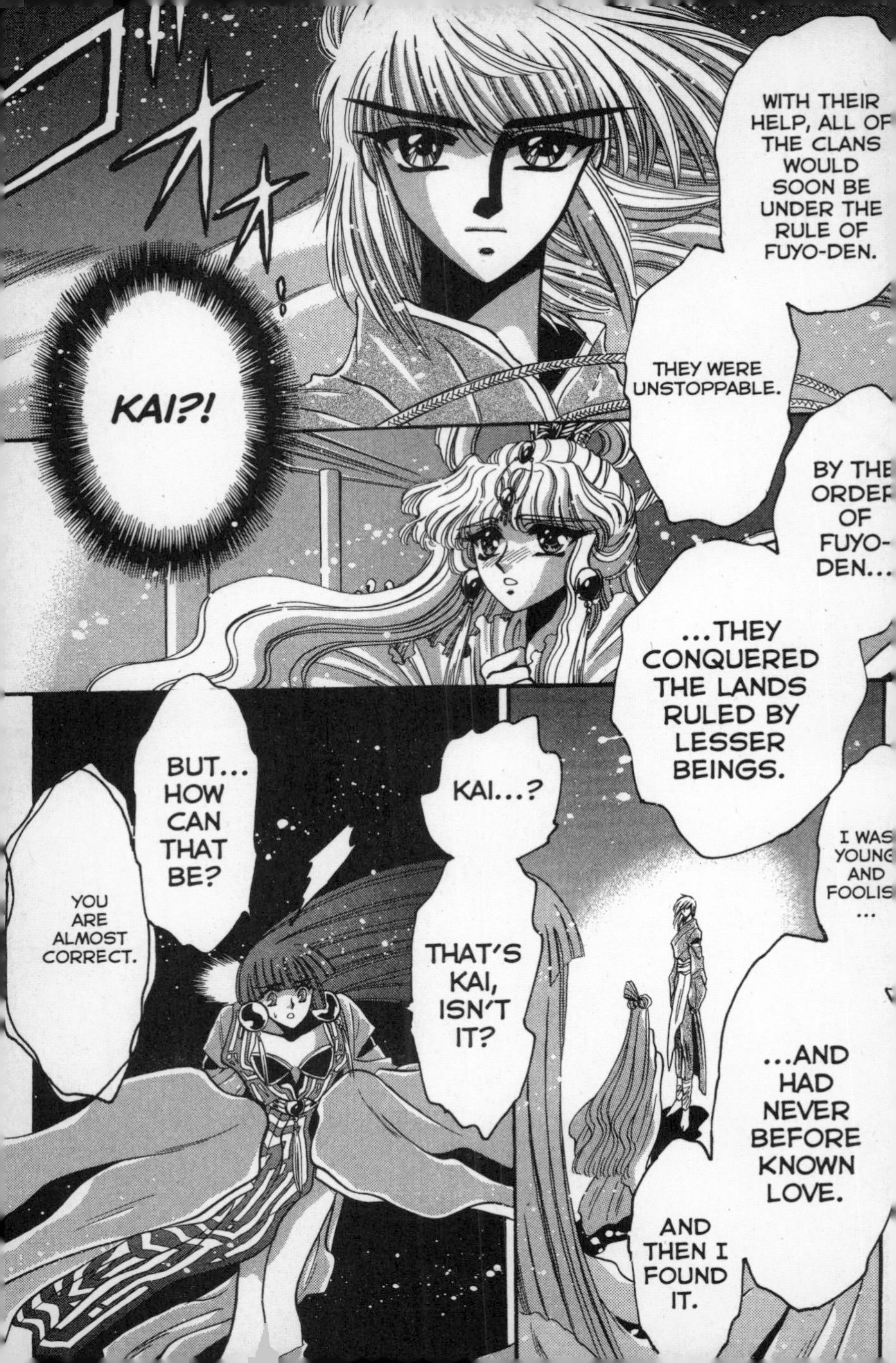
WITH THEIR HELP, ALL OF THE CLANS WOULD SOON BE UNDER THE RULE OF FUYO-DEN.
THEY WERE UNSTOPPABLE.
KAI?!
BY THE ORDER OF FUYO-DEN...
...THEY CONQUERED THE LANDS RULED BY LESSER BEINGS.
I WAS YOUNG AND FOOLIS ...
...AND HAD NEVER BEFORE KNOWN LOVE.
AND THEN I FOUND IT.
KAI...?
THAT'S KAI, ISN'T IT?
BUT... HOW CAN THAT BE?
YOU ARE ALMOST CORRECT.

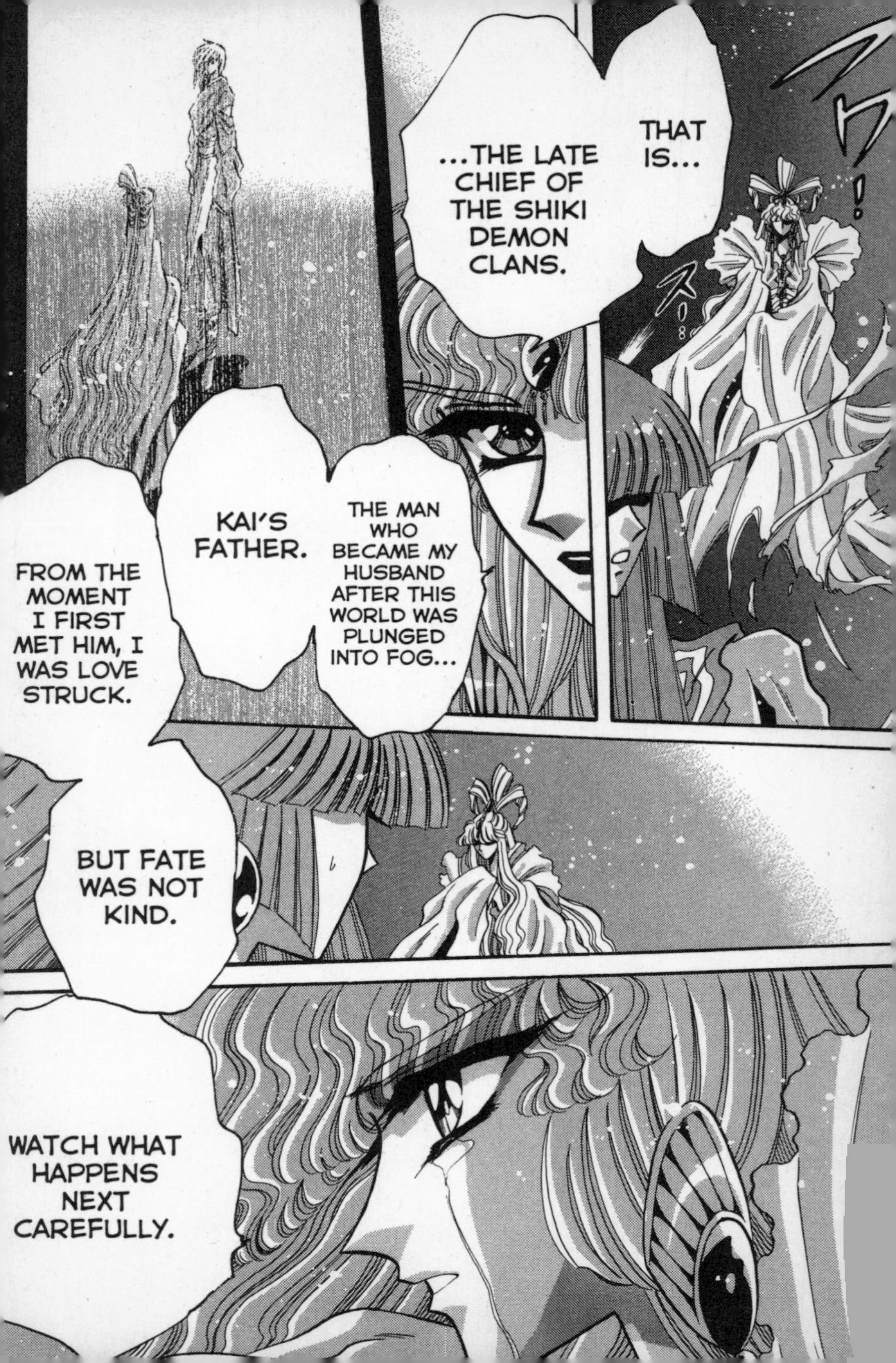
THAT IS...
...THE LATE CHIEF OF THE SHIKI DEMON CLANS.
THE MAN WHO BECAME MY HUSBAND AFTER THIS WORLD WAS PLUNGED INTO FOG...
KAI'S FATHER.
FROM THE MOMENT I FIRST MET HIM, I WAS LOVE STRUCK.
BUT FATE WAS NOT KIND.
WATCH WHAT HAPPENS NEXT CAREFULLY.

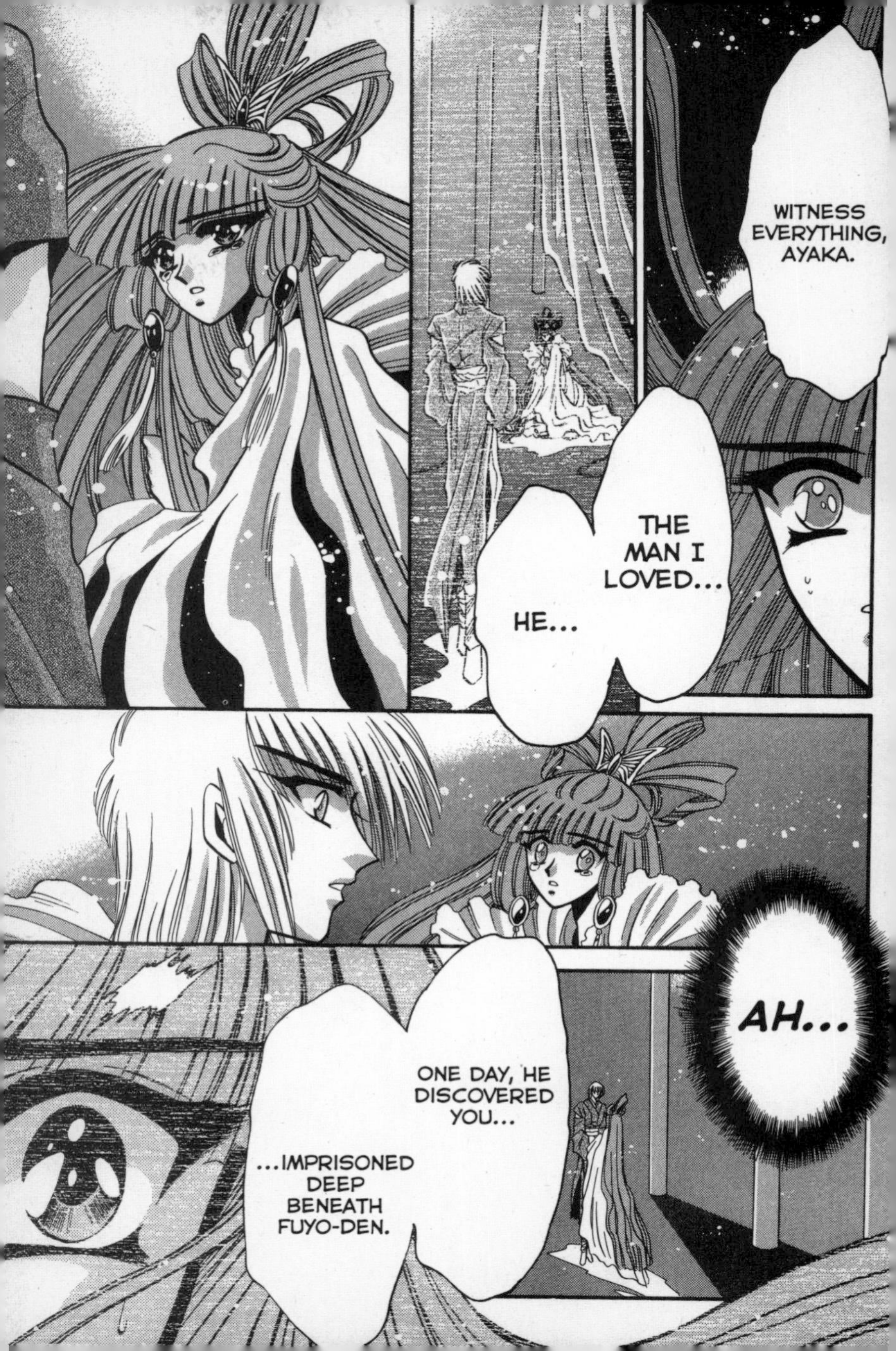

WITNESS EVERYTHING, AYAKA.
THE MAN I LOVED... HE...
AH...
ONE DAY, HE DISCOVERED YOU...
...IMPRISONED DEEP BENEATH FUYO-DEN.

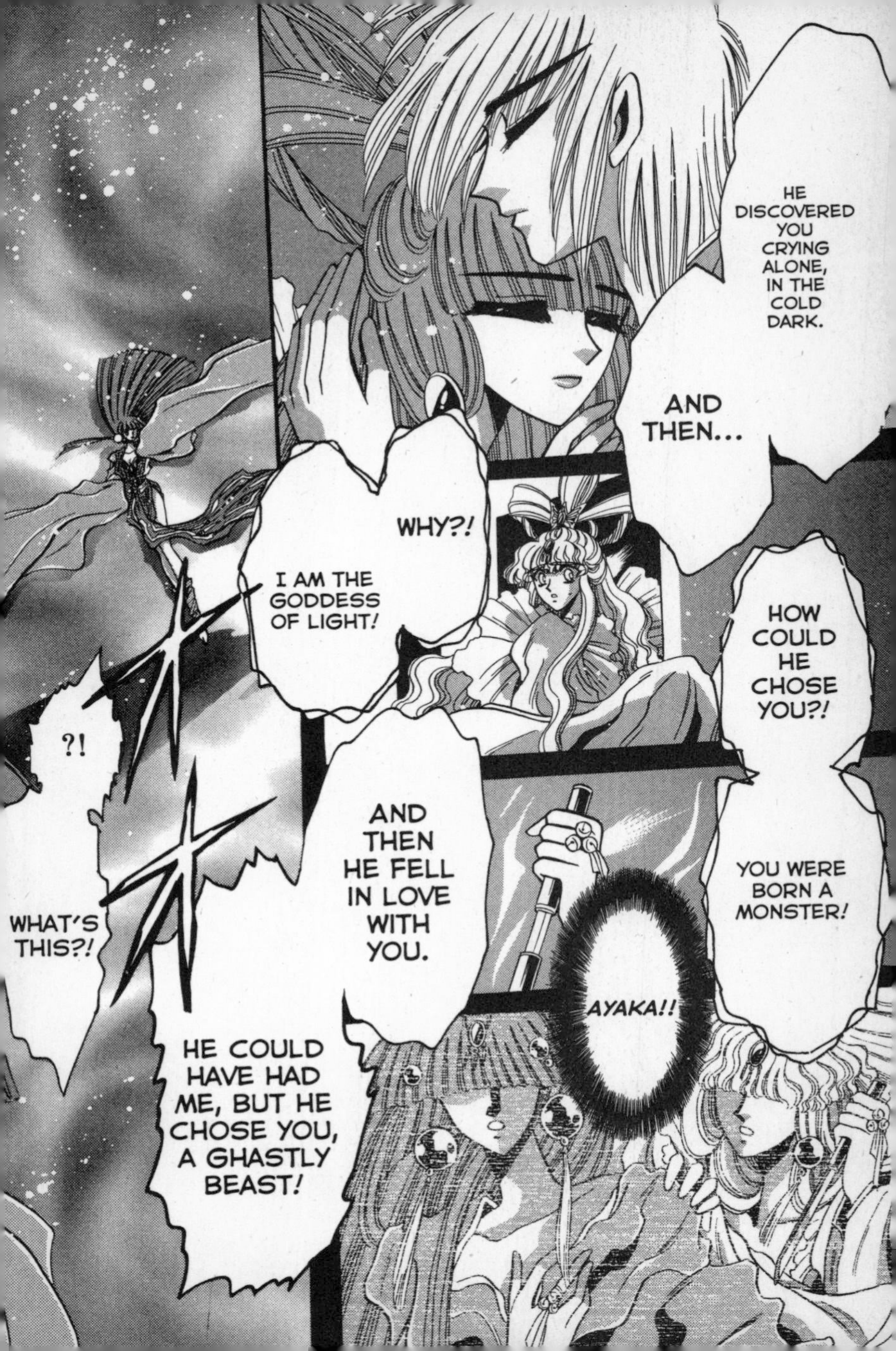
HE DISCOVERED YOU CRYING ALONE, IN THE COLD DARK.
AND THEN...
HOW COULD HE CHOSE YOU?!
WHY?!
I AM THE GODDESS OF LIGHT!
YOU WERE BORN A MONSTER!
AND THEN HE FELL IN LOVE WITH YOU.
HE COULD HAVE HAD ME, BUT HE CHOSE YOU, A GHASTLY BEAST!
AYAKA!!
?!
WHAT'S THIS?!

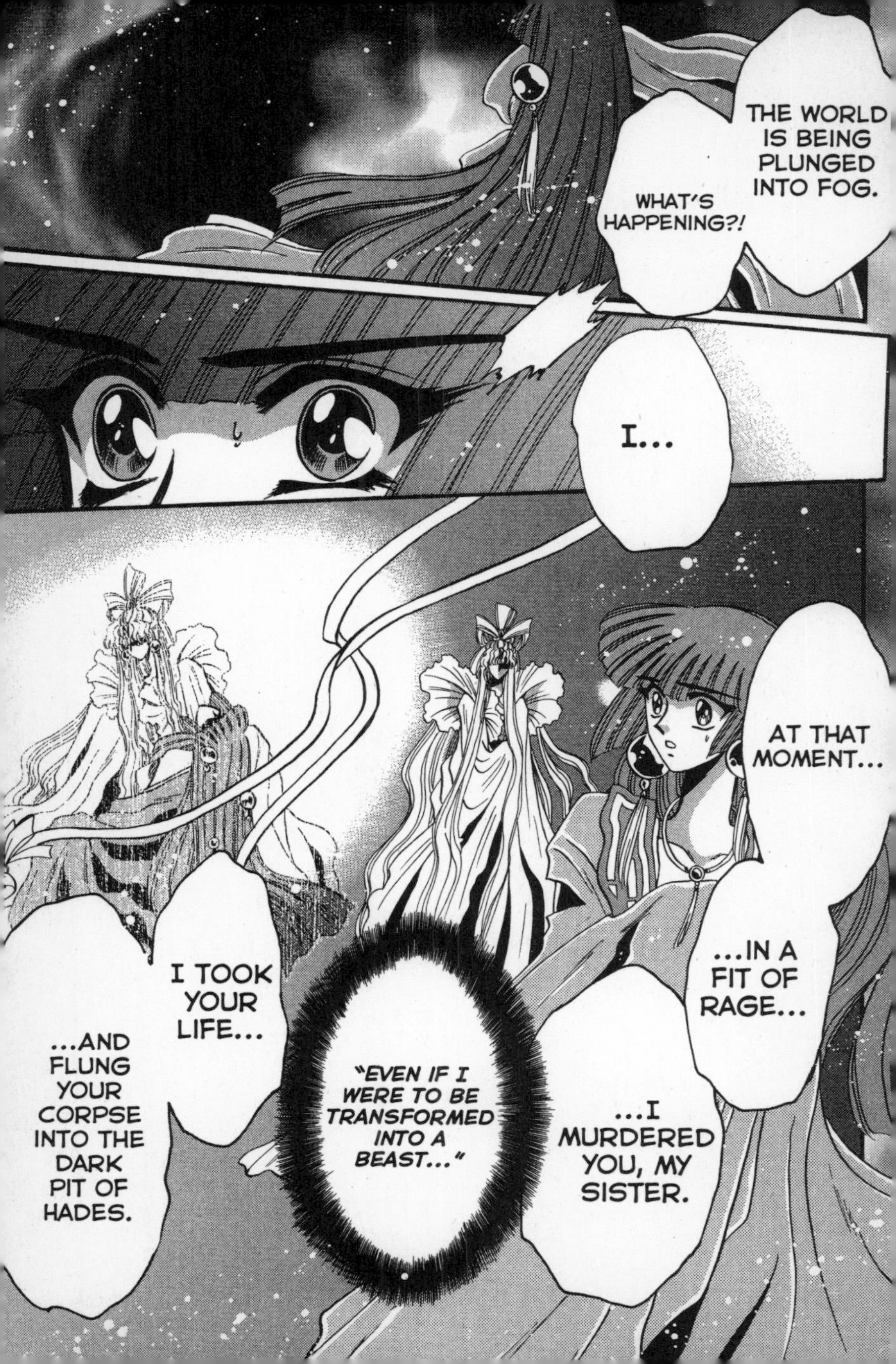
THE WORLD IS BEING PLUNGED INTO FOG.
WHAT'S HAPPENING?!
I...
AT THAT MOMENT...
...IN A FIT OF RAGE...
...I MURDERED YOU, MY SISTER.
"EVEN IF I WERE TO BE TRANSFORMED INTO A BEAST..."
I TOOK YOUR LIFE...
...AND FLUNG YOUR CORPSE INTO THE DARK PIT OF HADES.

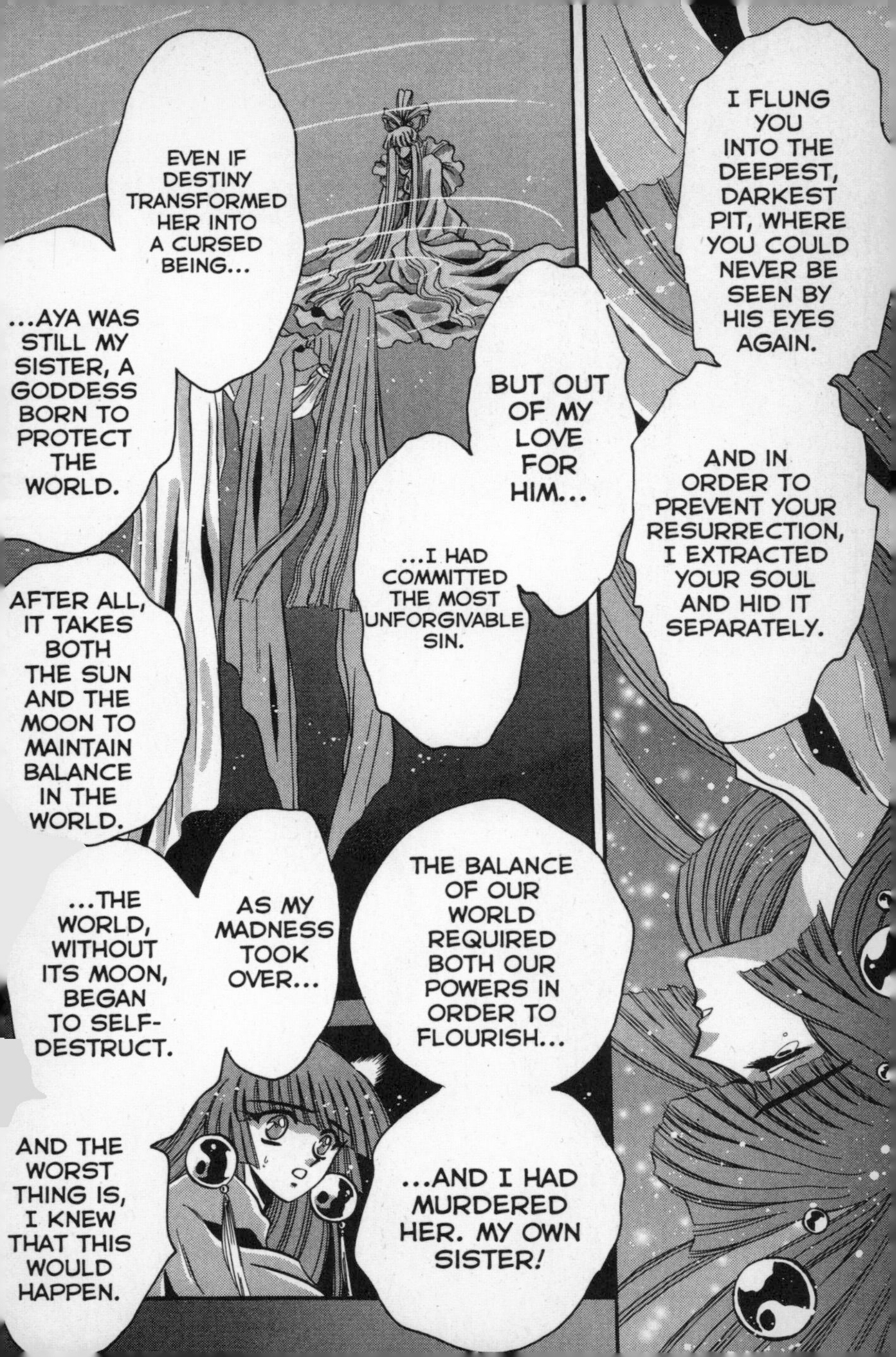
I FLUNG YOU INTO THE DEEPEST, DARKEST PIT, WHERE YOU COULD NEVER BE SEEN BY HIS EYES AGAIN.
AND IN ORDER TO PREVENT YOUR RESURRECTION, I EXTRACTED YOUR SOUL AND HID IT SEPARATELY.
EVEN IF DESTINY TRANSFORMED HER INTO A CURSED BEING...
BUT OUT OF MY LOVE FOR HIM...
...AYA WAS STILL MY SISTER, A GODDESS BORN TO PROTECT THE WORLD.
...I HAD COMMITTED THE MOST UNFORGIVABLE SIN.
AFTER ALL, IT TAKES BOTH THE SUN AND THE MOON TO MAINTAIN BALANCE IN THE WORLD.
THE BALANCE OF OUR WORLD REQUIRED BOTH OUR POWERS IN ORDER TO FLOURISH...
AS MY MADNESS TOOK OVER...
...THE WORLD, WITHOUT ITS MOON, BEGAN TO SELF-DESTRUCT.
...AND I HAD MURDERED HER. MY OWN SISTER!
AND THE WORST THING IS, I KNEW THAT THIS WOULD HAPPEN.

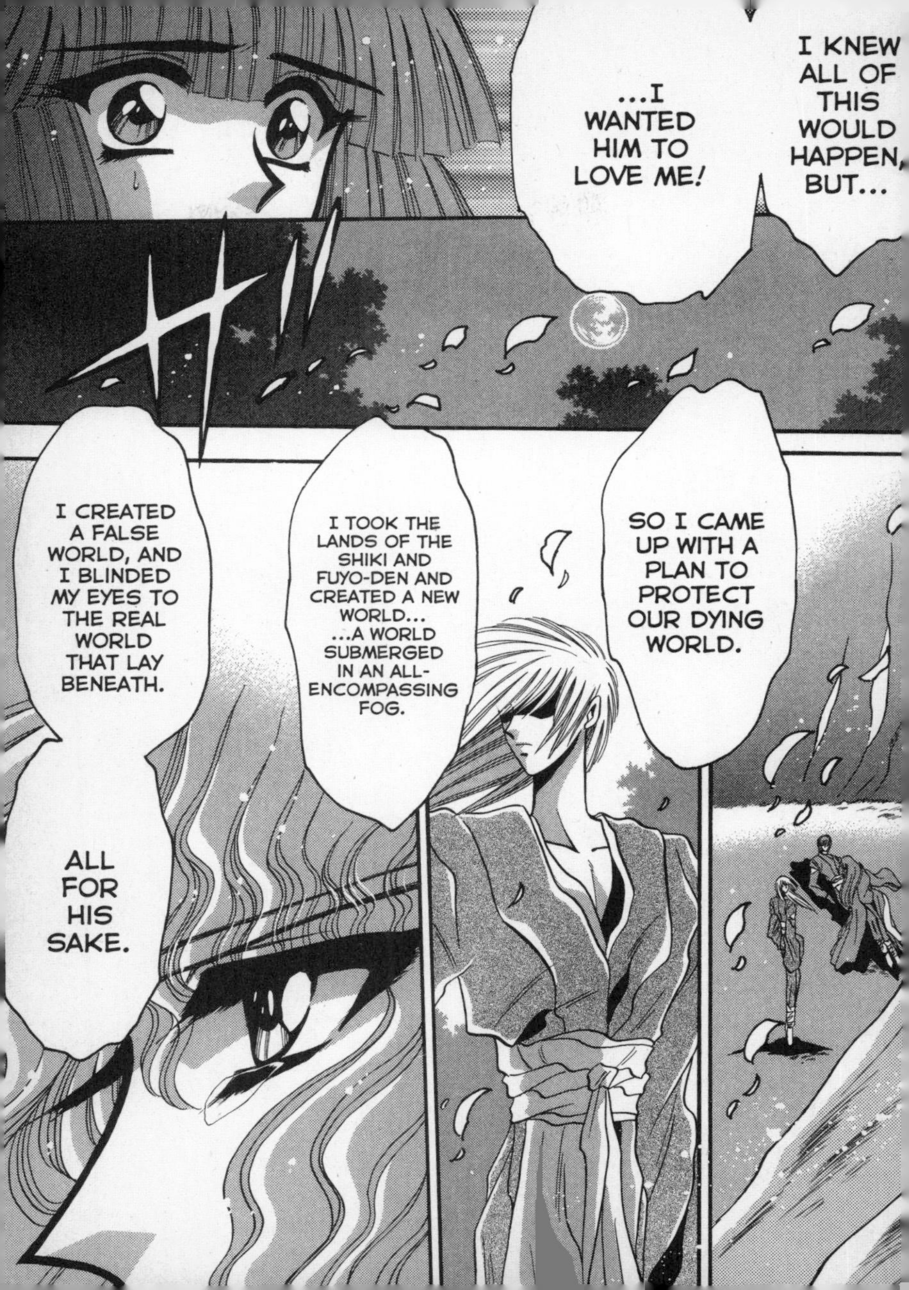
I KNEW ALL OF THIS WOULD HAPPEN, BUT...
...I WANTED HIM TO LOVE ME!
SO I CAME UP WITH A PLAN TO PROTECT OUR DYING WORLD.
I TOOK THE LANDS OF THE SHIKI AND FUYO-DEN AND CREATED A NEW WORLD... ...A WORLD SUBMERGED IN AN ALL-ENCOMPASSING FOG.
I CREATED A FALSE WORLD, AND I BLINDED MY EYES TO THE REAL WORLD THAT LAY BENEATH.
ALL FOR HIS SAKE.

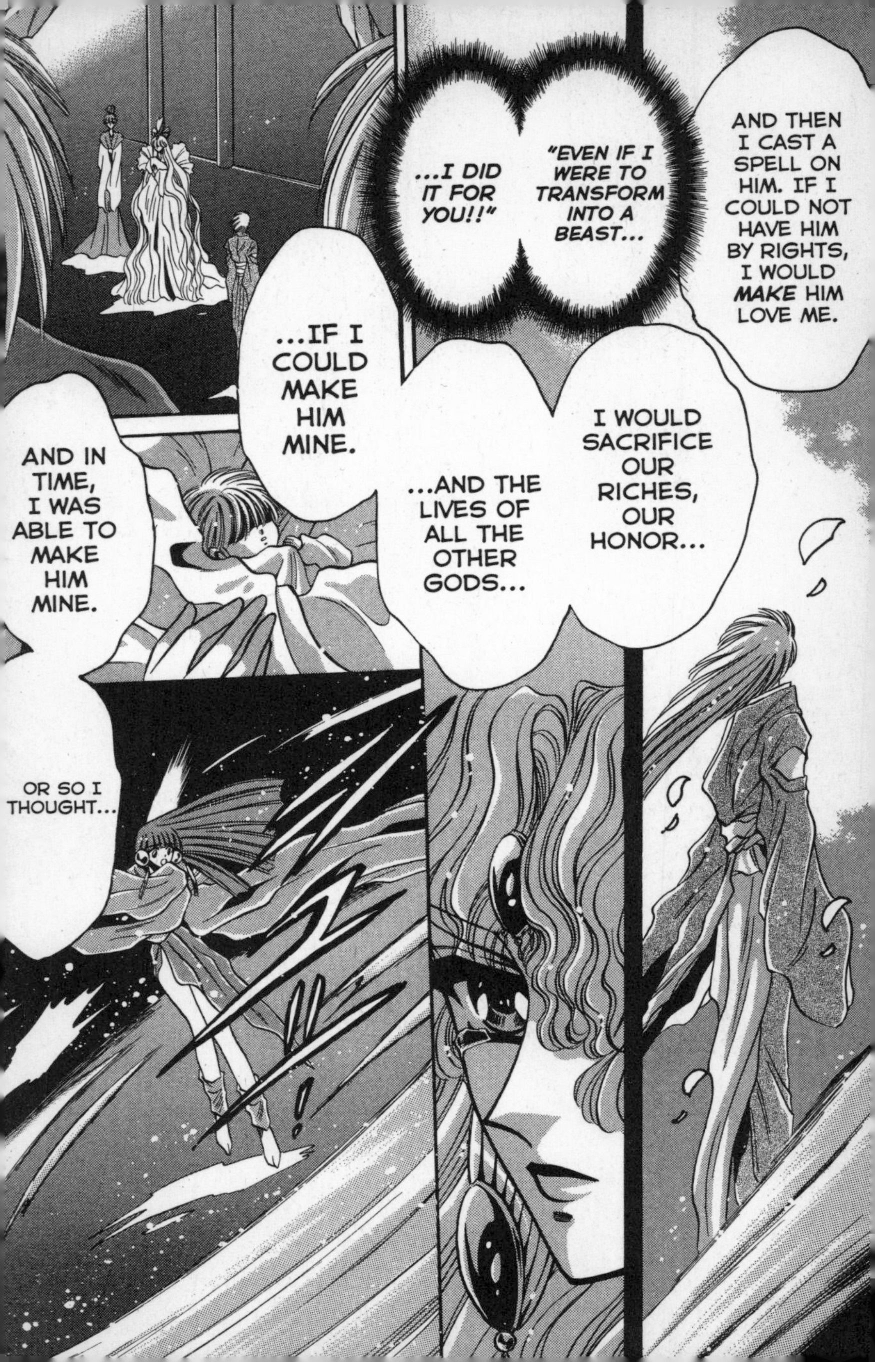

"EVEN IF I WERE TO TRANSFORM INTO A BEAST...
...I DID IT FOR YOU!!"
AND THEN I CAST A SPELL ON HIM. IF I COULD NOT HAVE HIM BY RIGHTS, I WOULD *MAKE* HIM LOVE ME.
I WOULD SACRIFICE OUR RICHES, OUR HONOR...
...AND THE LIVES OF ALL THE OTHER GODS...
...IF I COULD MAKE HIM MINE.
AND IN TIME, I WAS ABLE TO MAKE HIM MINE.
OR SO I THOUGHT...

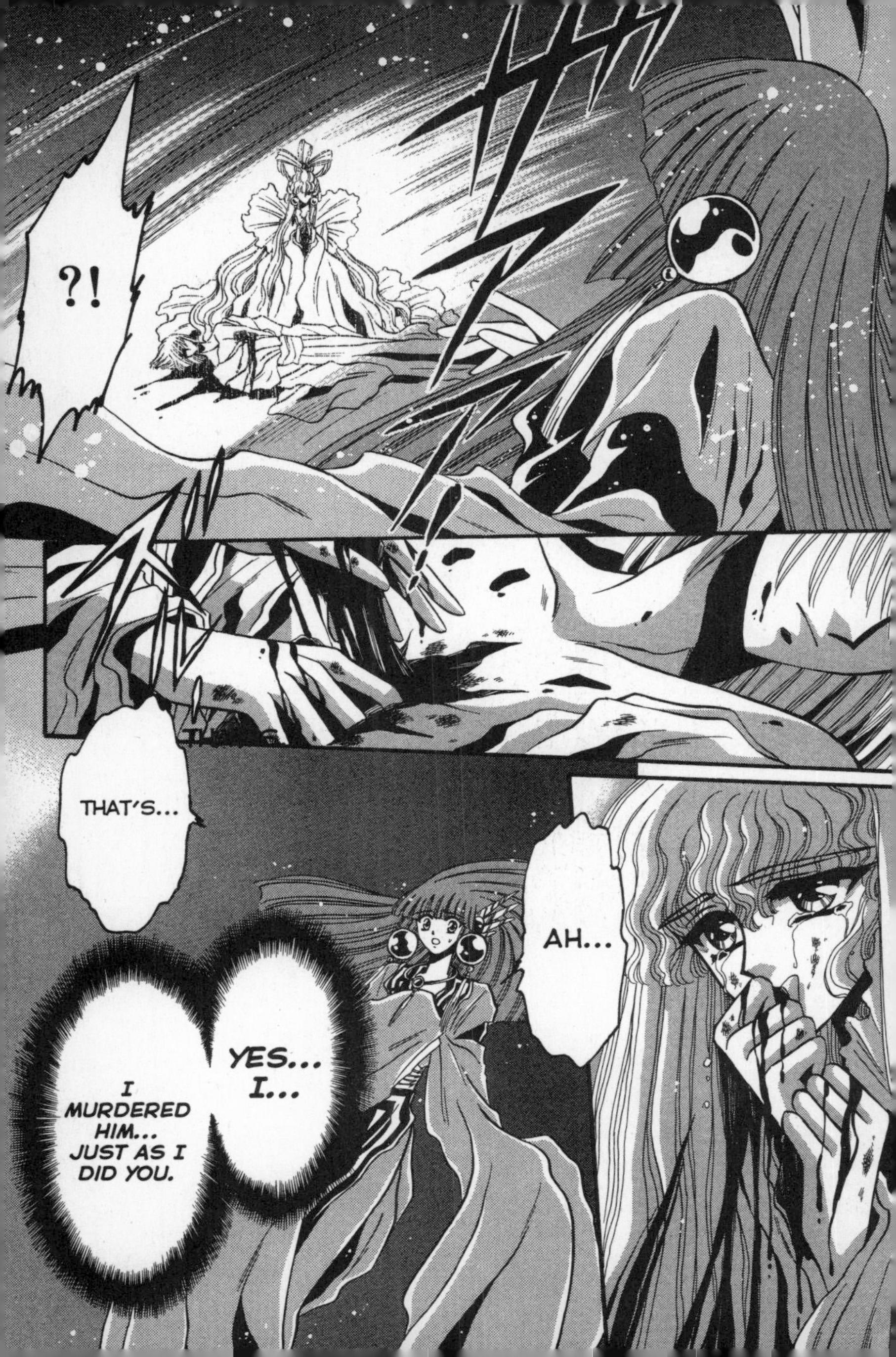
?!
THAT'S...
AH...
YES... I...
I MURDERED HIM... JUST AS I DID YOU.

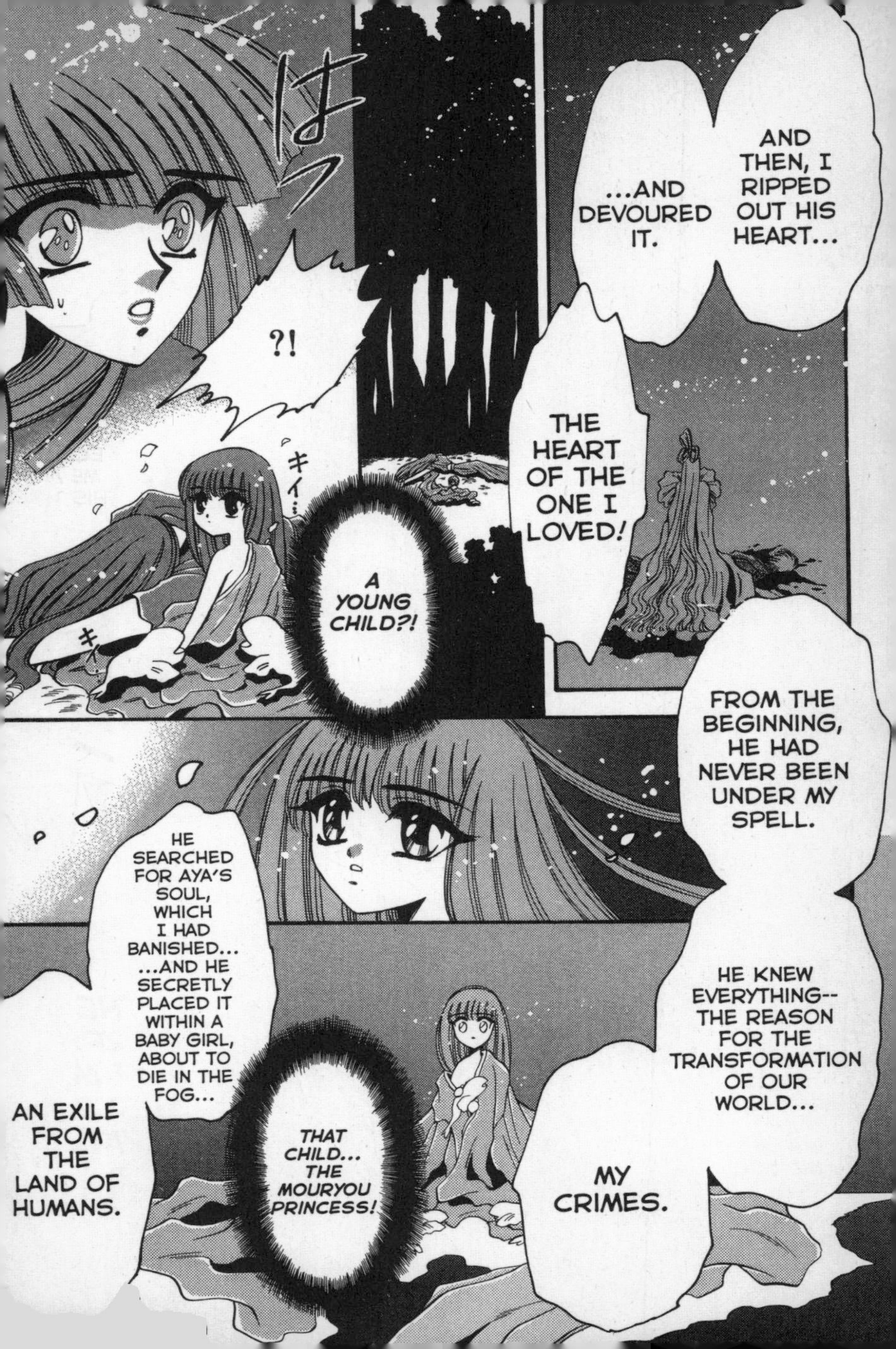
AND THEN, I RIPPED OUT HIS HEART...
...AND DEVOURED IT.
THE HEART OF THE ONE I LOVED!
はっ
?!
キイ…
キイ
A YOUNG CHILD?!
FROM THE BEGINNING, HE HAD NEVER BEEN UNDER MY SPELL.
HE SEARCHED FOR AYA'S SOUL, WHICH I HAD BANISHED... ...AND HE SECRETLY PLACED IT WITHIN A BABY GIRL, ABOUT TO DIE IN THE FOG...
HE KNEW EVERYTHING-- THE REASON FOR THE TRANSFORMATION OF OUR WORLD...
MY CRIMES.
THAT CHILD... THE MOURYOU PRINCESS!
AN EXILE FROM THE LAND OF HUMANS.

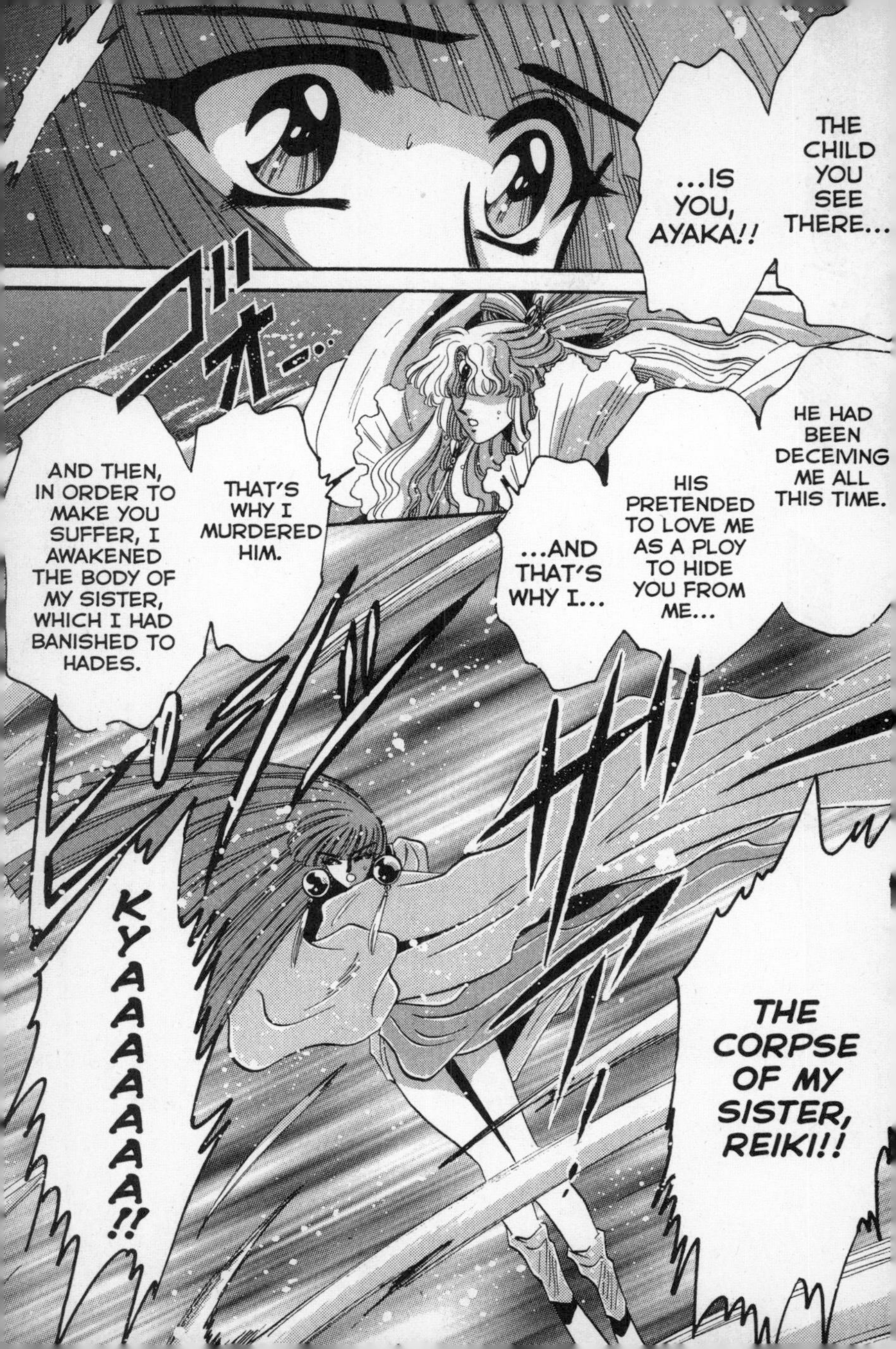
THE CHILD YOU SEE THERE...
...IS YOU, AYAKA!!
HE HAD BEEN DECEIVING ME ALL THIS TIME.
HIS PRETENDED TO LOVE ME AS A PLOY TO HIDE YOU FROM ME...
...AND THAT'S WHY I...
THAT'S WHY I MURDERED HIM.
AND THEN, IN ORDER TO MAKE YOU SUFFER, I AWAKENED THE BODY OF MY SISTER, WHICH I HAD BANISHED TO HADES.
THE CORPSE OF MY SISTER, REIKI!!
KYAAAAAAAAA!!

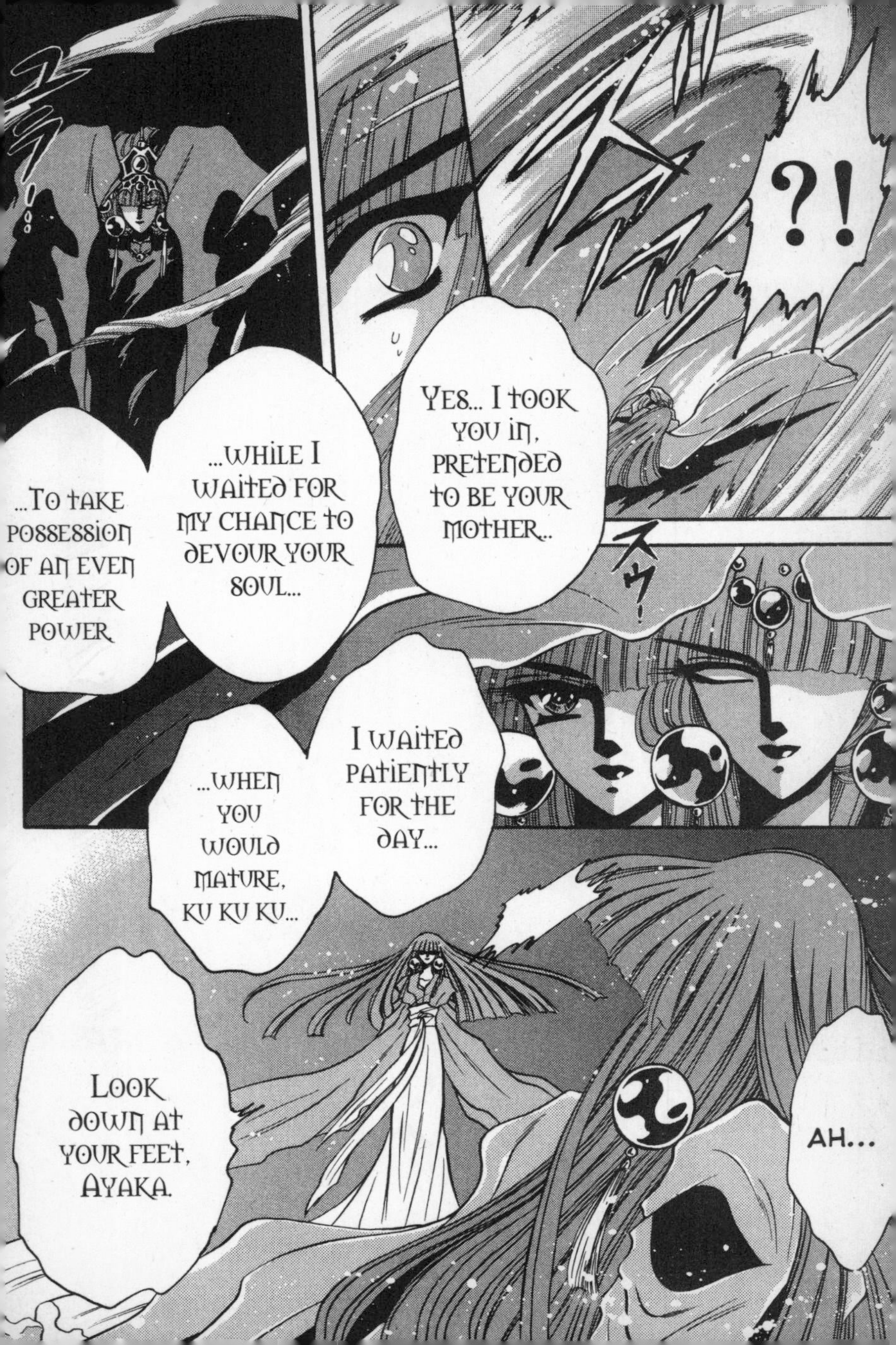
?!
YES... I TOOK YOU IN, PRETENDED TO BE YOUR MOTHER...
...WHILE I WAITED FOR MY CHANCE TO DEVOUR YOUR SOUL...
...TO TAKE POSSESSION OF AN EVEN GREATER POWER.
I WAITED PATIENTLY FOR THE DAY...
...WHEN YOU WOULD MATURE, KU KU KU...
AH...
LOOK DOWN AT YOUR FEET, AYAKA.

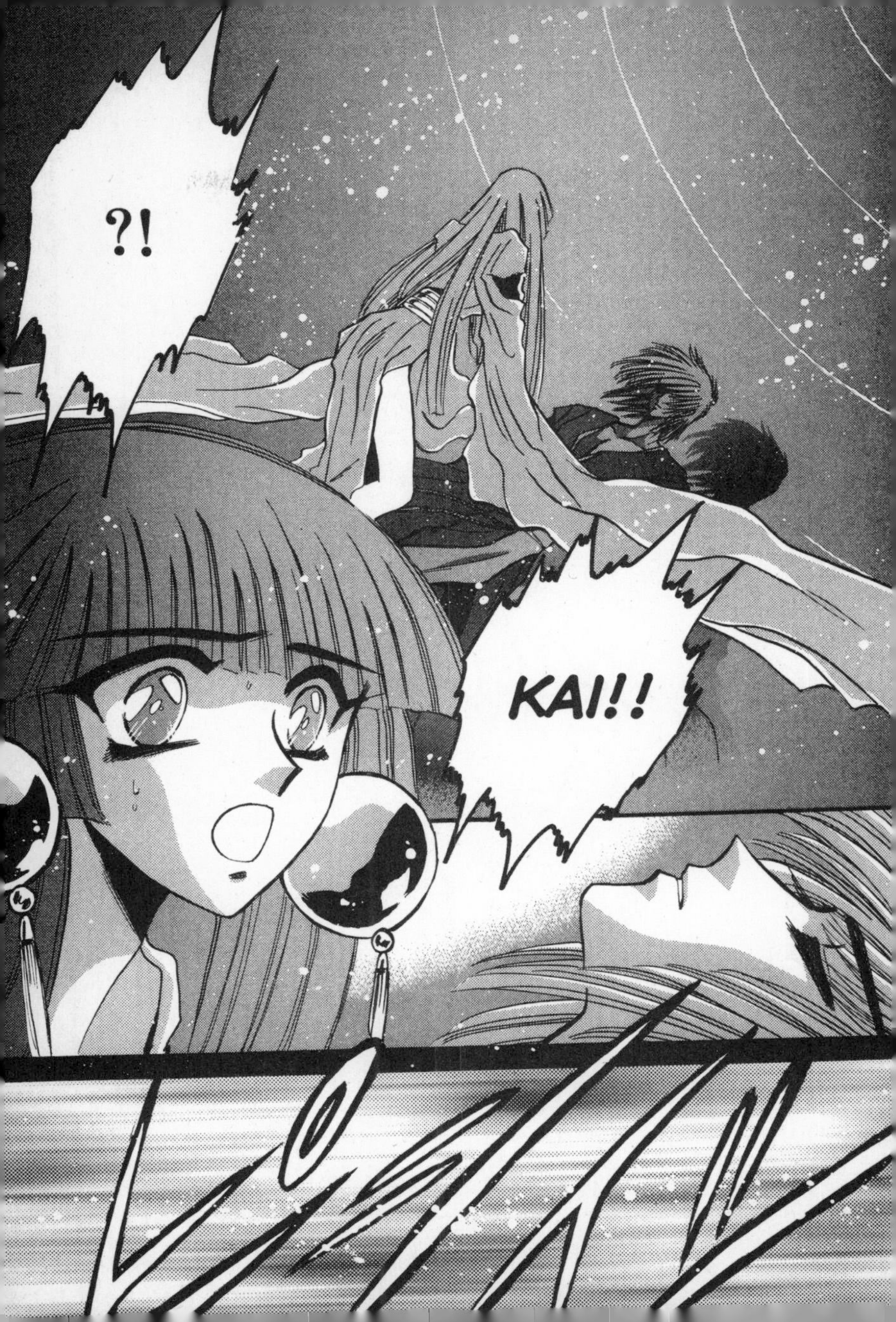
?!
KAI!!

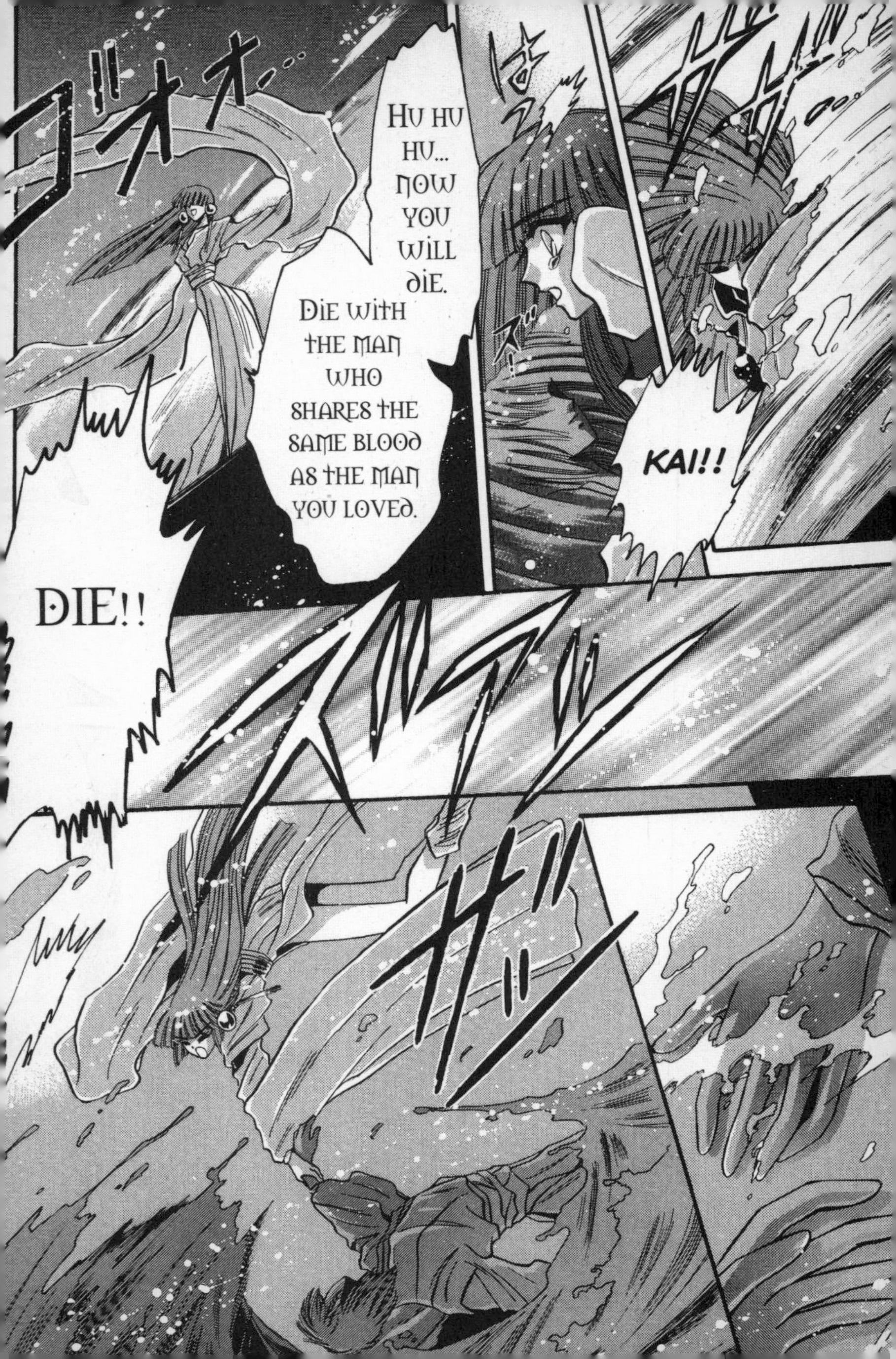
KAI!!
Hu hu hu... now you will die.
Die with the man who shares the same blood as the man you loved.
DIE!!

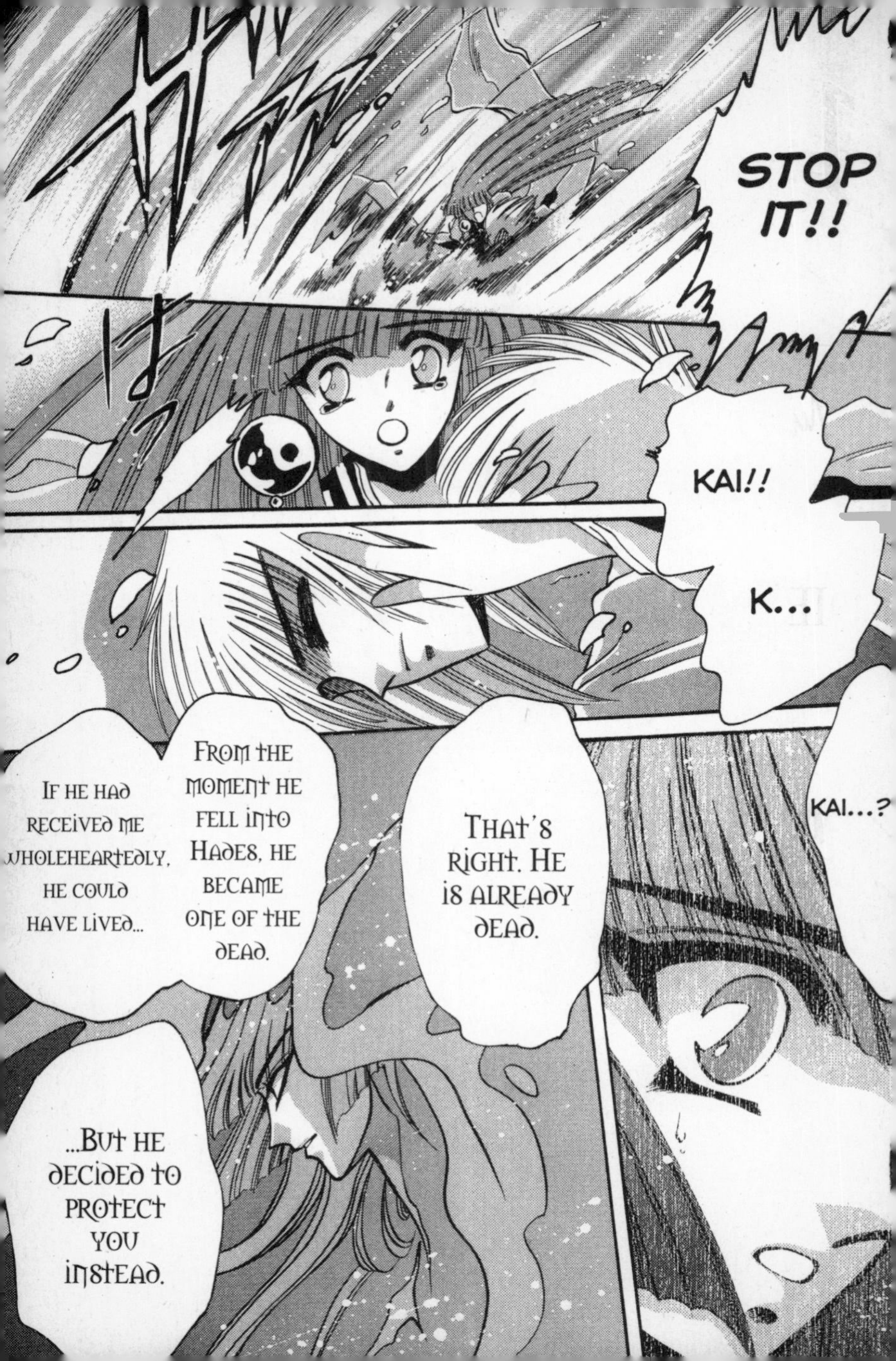
STOP IT!!
KAI!!
K...
KAI...?
THAT'S RIGHT. HE IS ALREADY DEAD.
FROM THE MOMENT HE FELL INTO HADES, HE BECAME ONE OF THE DEAD.
IF HE HAD RECEIVED ME WHOLEHEARTEDLY, HE COULD HAVE LIVED...
...BUT HE DECIDED TO PROTECT YOU INSTEAD.

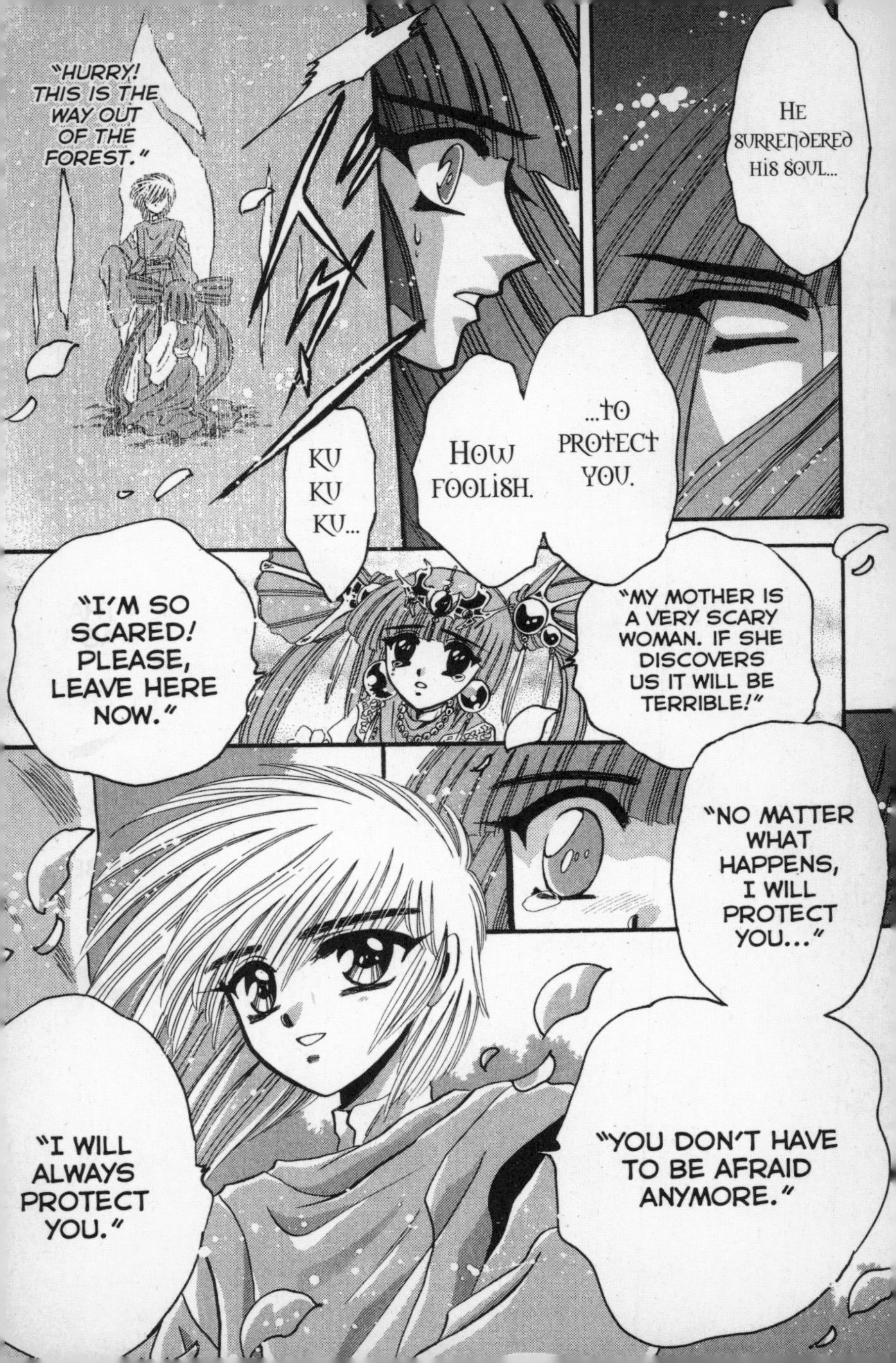
HE SURRENDERED HIS SOUL...
...TO PROTECT YOU.
HOW FOOLISH.
KU KU KU...
"HURRY! THIS IS THE WAY OUT OF THE FOREST."
"MY MOTHER IS A VERY SCARY WOMAN. IF SHE DISCOVERS US IT WILL BE TERRIBLE!"
"I'M SO SCARED! PLEASE, LEAVE HERE NOW."
"NO MATTER WHAT HAPPENS, I WILL PROTECT YOU..."
"YOU DON'T HAVE TO BE AFRAID ANYMORE."
"I WILL ALWAYS PROTECT YOU."

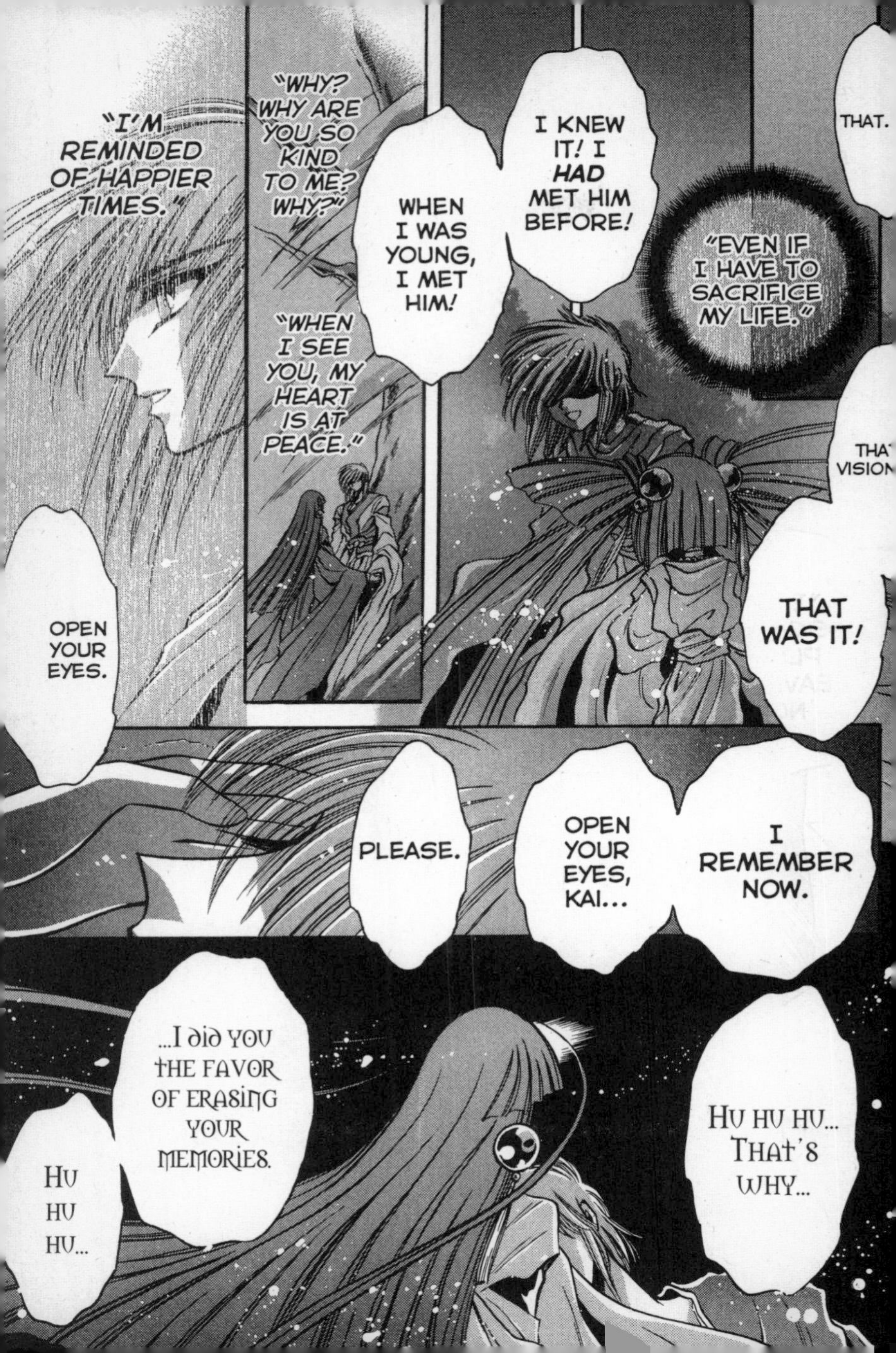
THAT.
THAT VISION
THAT WAS IT!
"EVEN IF I HAVE TO SACRIFICE MY LIFE."
I KNEW IT! I *HAD* MET HIM BEFORE!
WHEN I WAS YOUNG, I MET HIM!
"WHY? WHY ARE YOU SO KIND TO ME? WHY?"
"WHEN I SEE YOU, MY HEART IS AT PEACE."
"I'M REMINDED OF HAPPIER TIMES."
OPEN YOUR EYES.
I REMEMBER NOW.
OPEN YOUR EYES, KAI...
PLEASE.
Hu hu hu... That's why...
...I did you the favor of erasing your memories.
Hu hu hu...

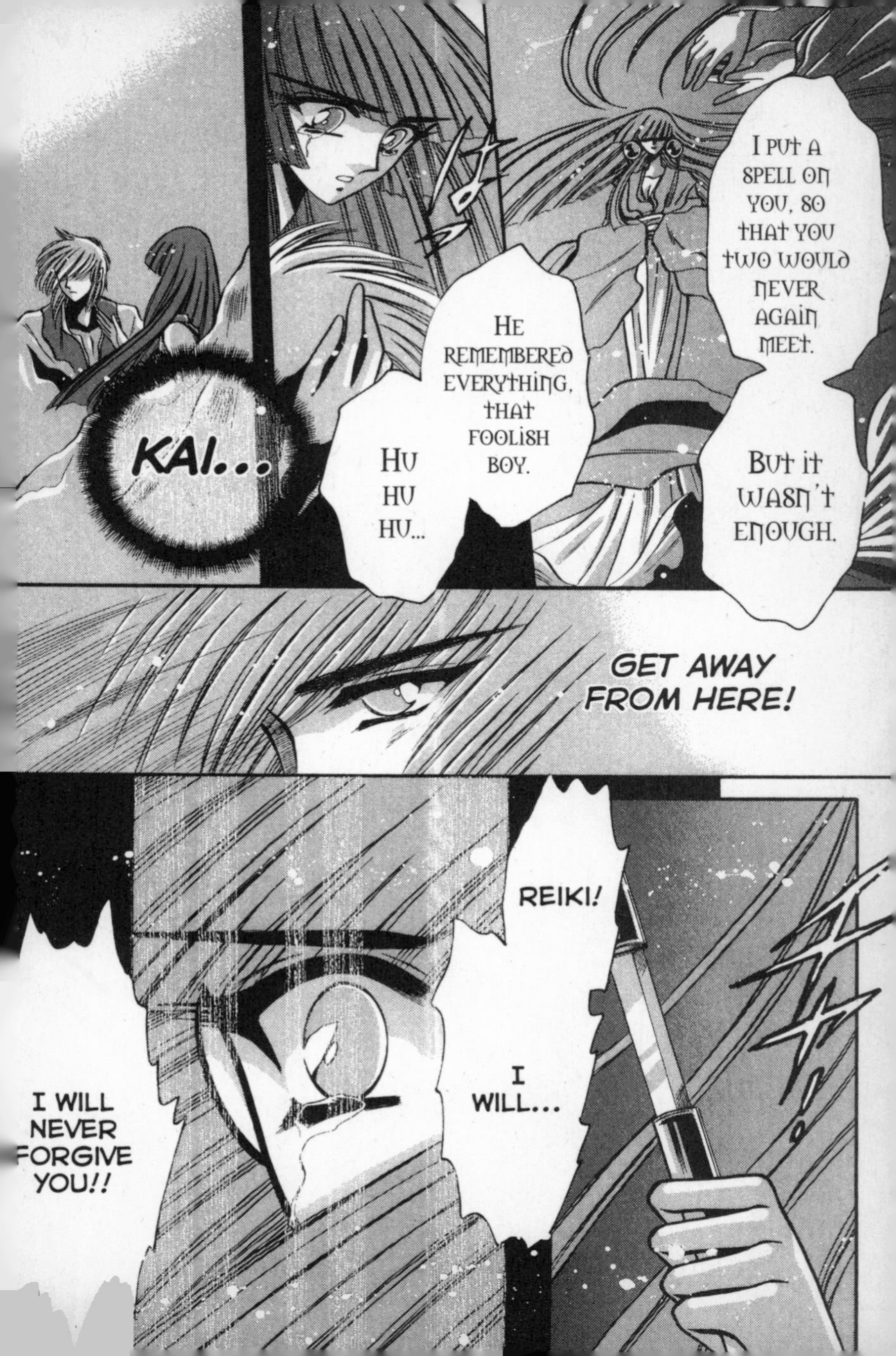
I PUT A SPELL ON YOU, SO THAT YOU TWO WOULD NEVER AGAIN MEET.
BUT IT WASN'T ENOUGH.
HE REMEMBERED EVERYTHING, THAT FOOLISH BOY.
HU HU HU...
KAI...
GET AWAY FROM HERE!
REIKI!
I WILL...
I WILL NEVER FORGIVE YOU!!

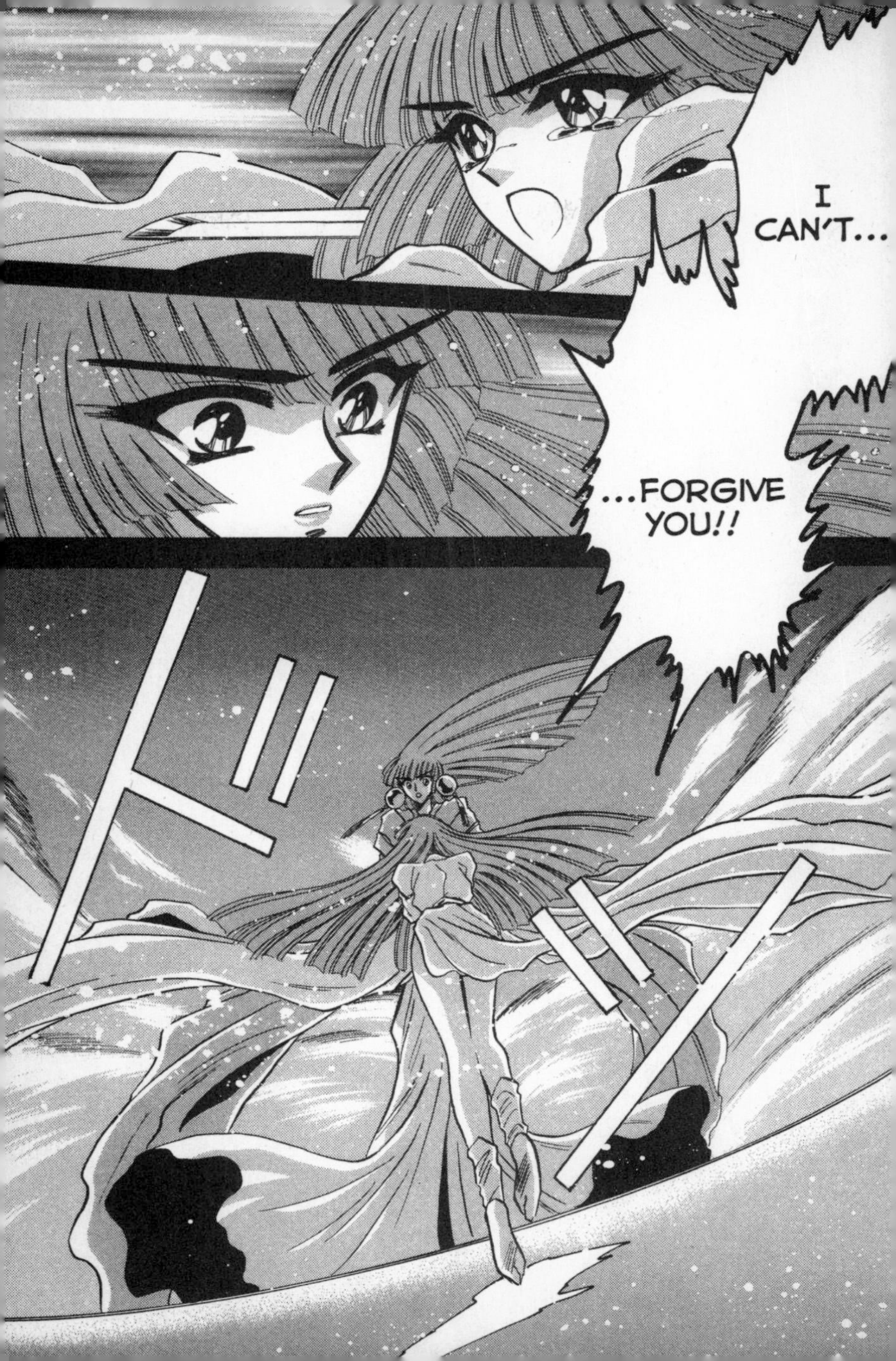
I CAN'T...
...FORGIVE YOU!!

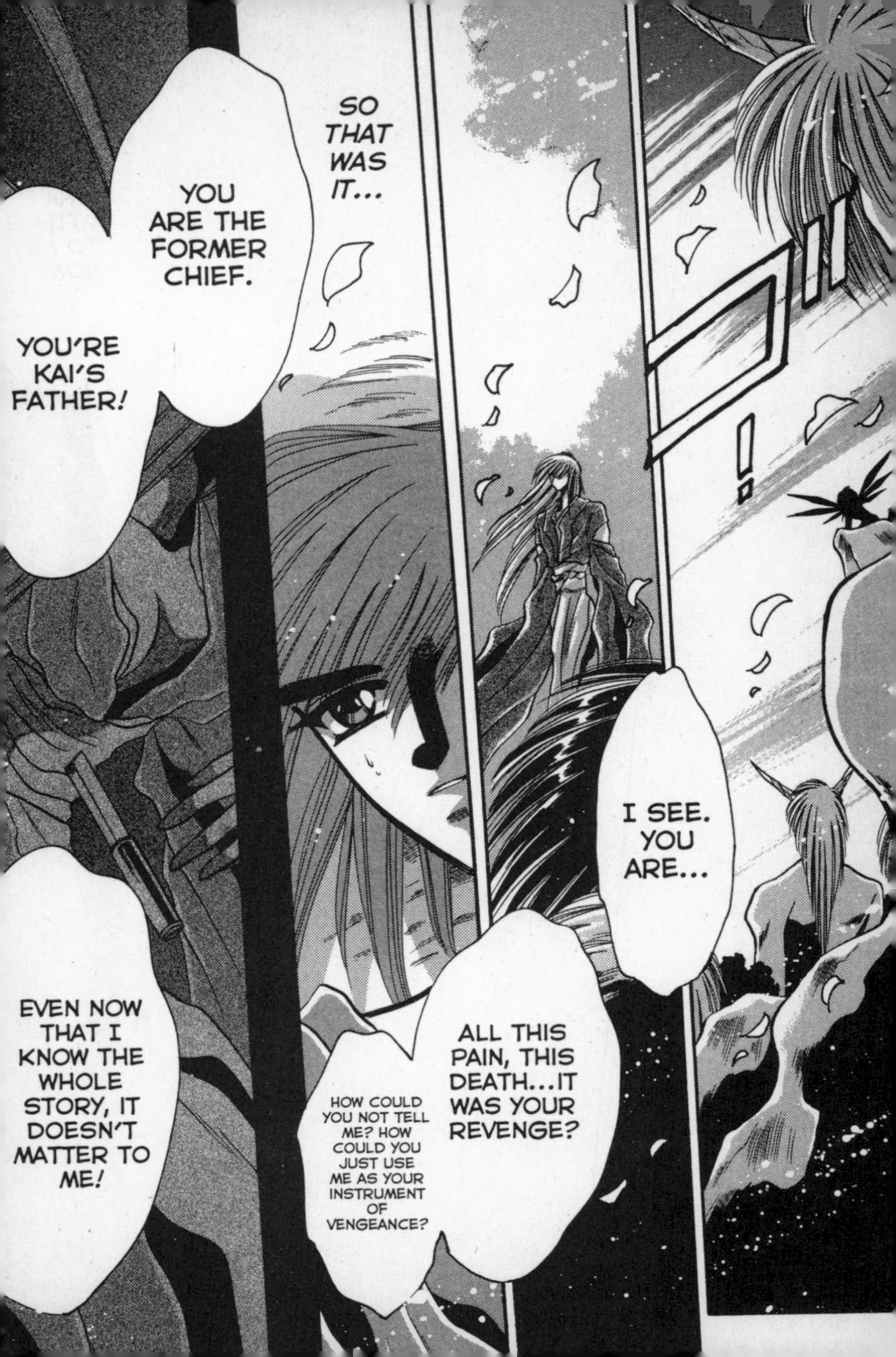

I SEE. YOU ARE...
SO THAT WAS IT...
ALL THIS PAIN, THIS DEATH...IT WAS YOUR REVENGE?
HOW COULD YOU NOT TELL ME? HOW COULD YOU JUST USE ME AS YOUR INSTRUMENT OF VENGEANCE?
YOU ARE THE FORMER CHIEF.
YOU'RE KAI'S FATHER!
EVEN NOW THAT I KNOW THE WHOLE STORY, IT DOESN'T MATTER TO ME!

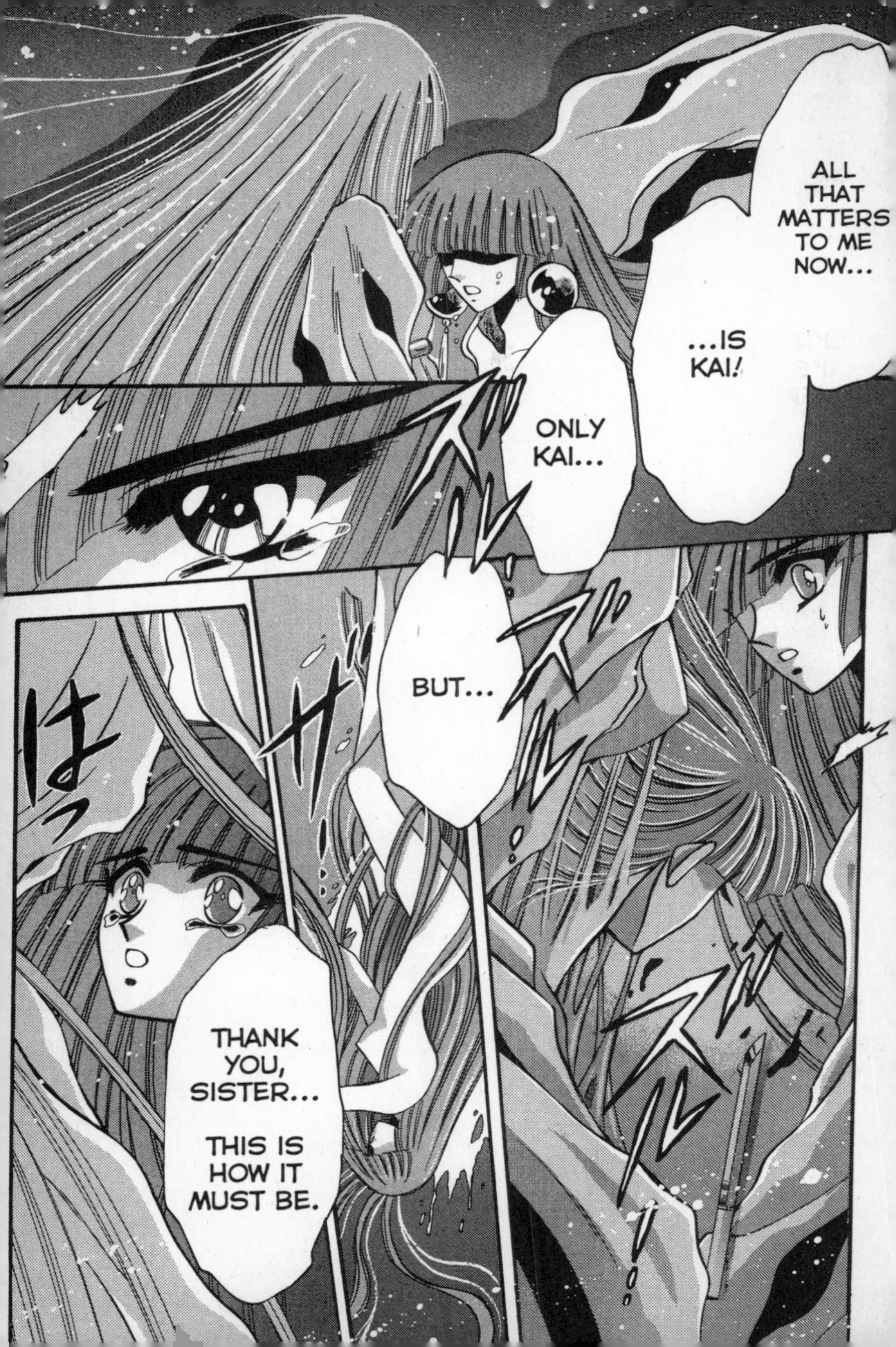
ALL THAT MATTERS TO ME NOW...
...IS KAI!
ONLY KAI...
BUT...
はっ
THANK YOU, SISTER...
THIS IS HOW IT MUST BE.

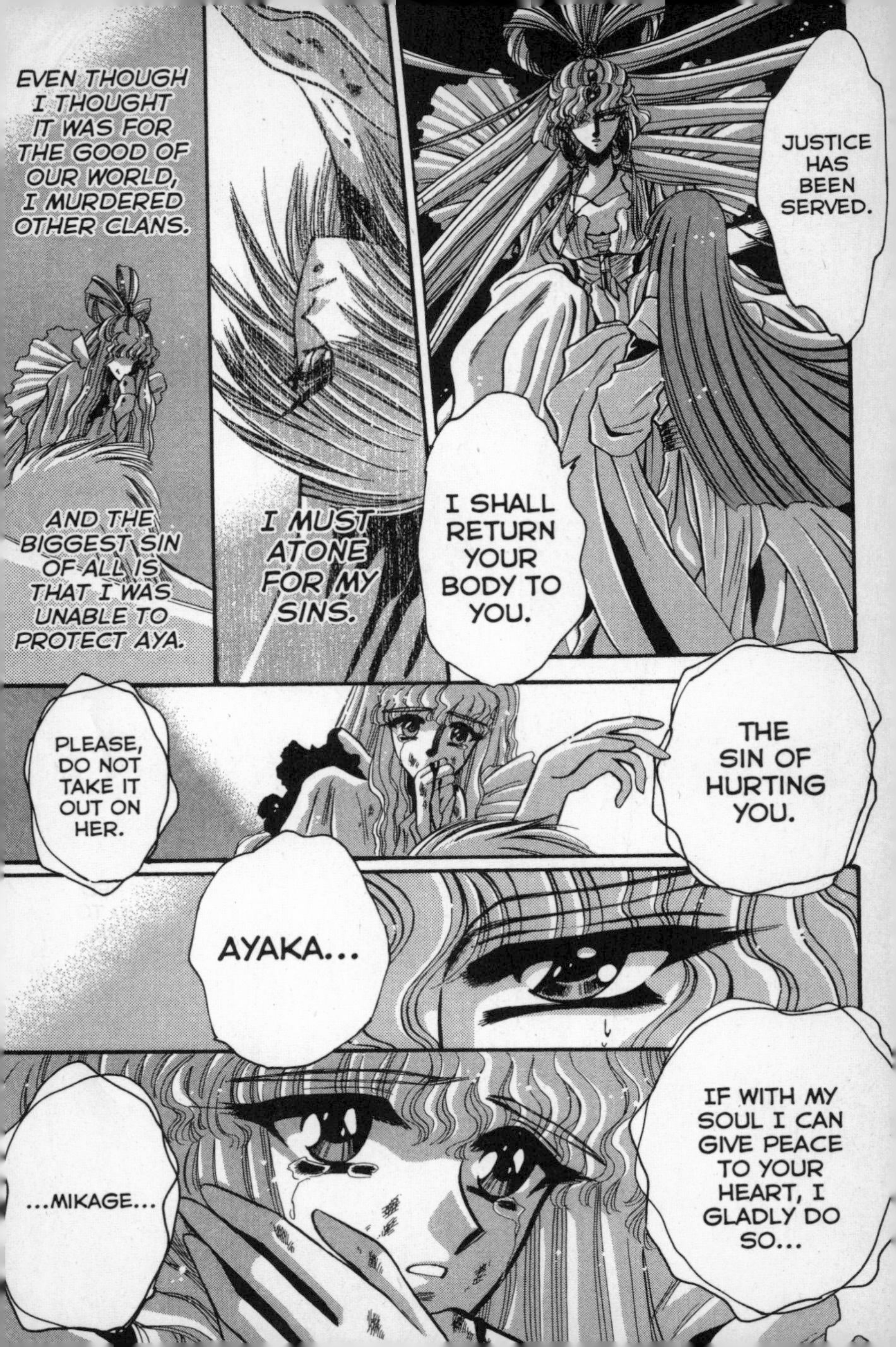
JUSTICE HAS BEEN SERVED.
I SHALL RETURN YOUR BODY TO YOU.
I MUST ATONE FOR MY SINS.
EVEN THOUGH I THOUGHT IT WAS FOR THE GOOD OF OUR WORLD, I MURDERED OTHER CLANS.
AND THE BIGGEST SIN OF ALL IS THAT I WAS UNABLE TO PROTECT AYA.
THE SIN OF HURTING YOU.
PLEASE, DO NOT TAKE IT OUT ON HER.
AYAKA...
IF WITH MY SOUL I CAN GIVE PEACE TO YOUR HEART, I GLADLY DO SO...
...MIKAGE...

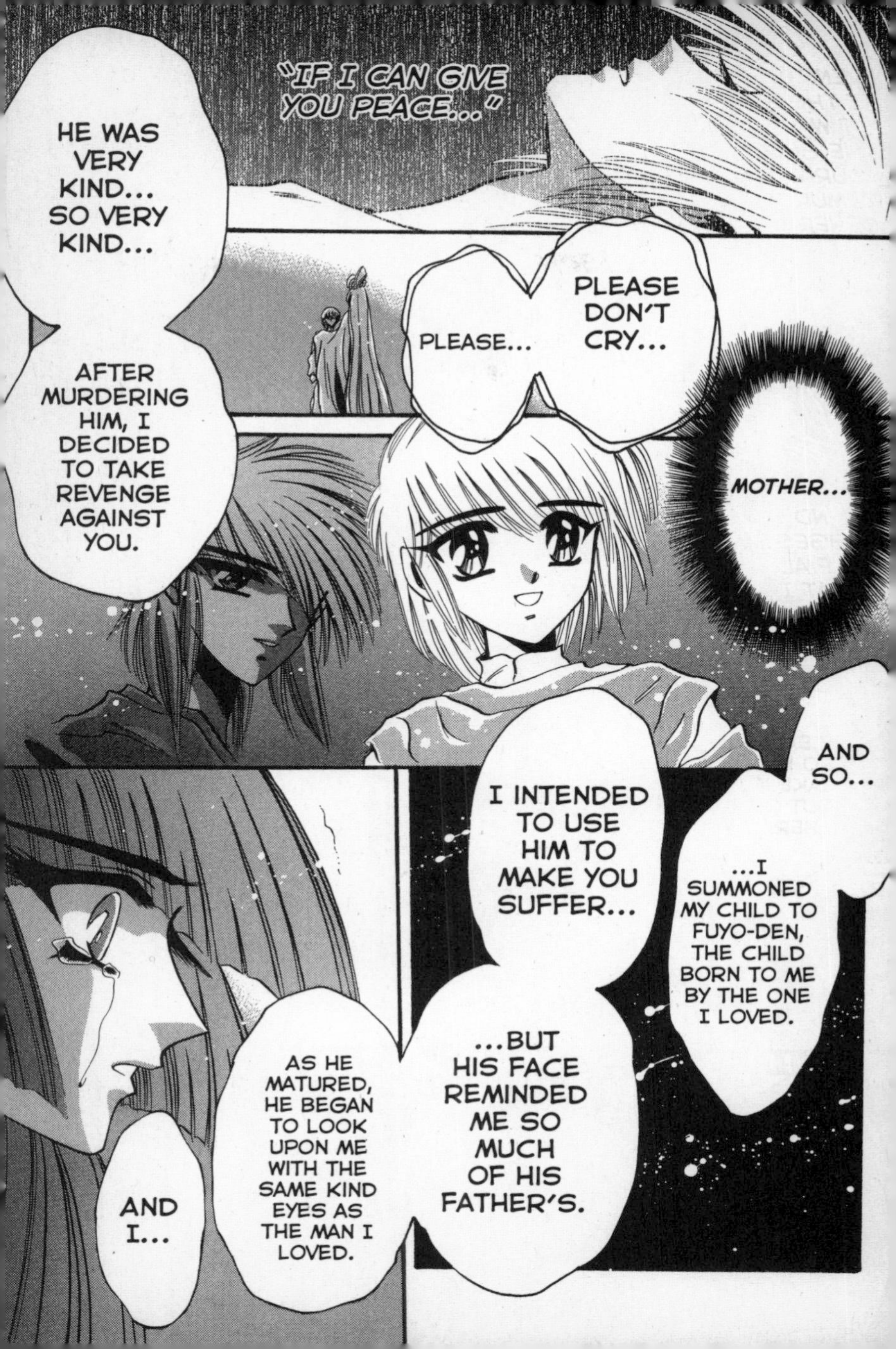
"IF I CAN GIVE YOU PEACE..."
HE WAS VERY KIND... SO VERY KIND...
PLEASE... PLEASE DON'T CRY...
MOTHER...
AFTER MURDERING HIM, I DECIDED TO TAKE REVENGE AGAINST YOU.
AND SO...
...I SUMMONED MY CHILD TO FUYO-DEN, THE CHILD BORN TO ME BY THE ONE I LOVED.
I INTENDED TO USE HIM TO MAKE YOU SUFFER...
...BUT HIS FACE REMINDED ME SO MUCH OF HIS FATHER'S.
AS HE MATURED, HE BEGAN TO LOOK UPON ME WITH THE SAME KIND EYES AS THE MAN I LOVED.
AND I...

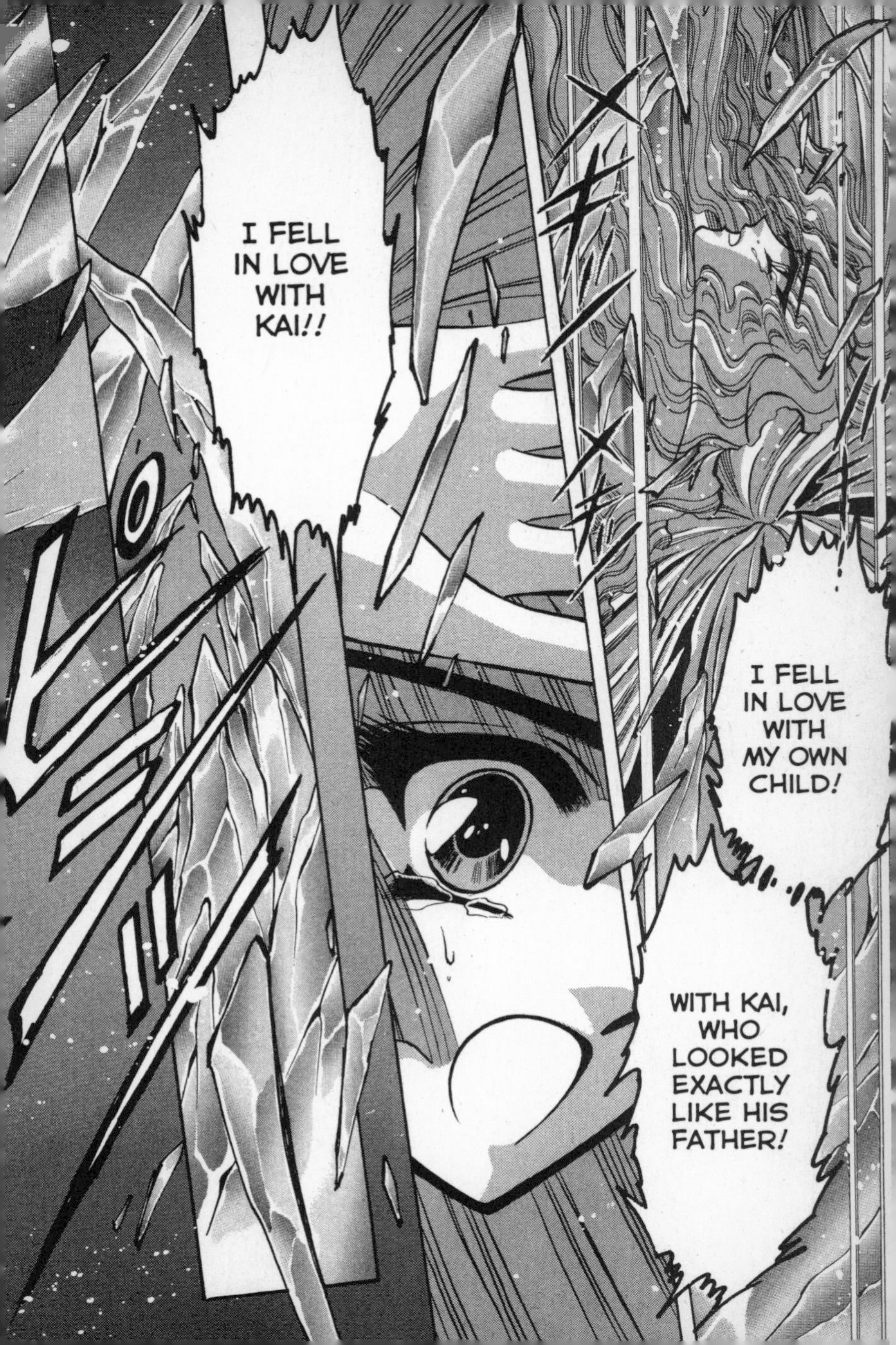
I FELL IN LOVE WITH KAI!!
I FELL IN LOVE WITH MY OWN CHILD!
WITH KAI, WHO LOOKED EXACTLY LIKE HIS FATHER!

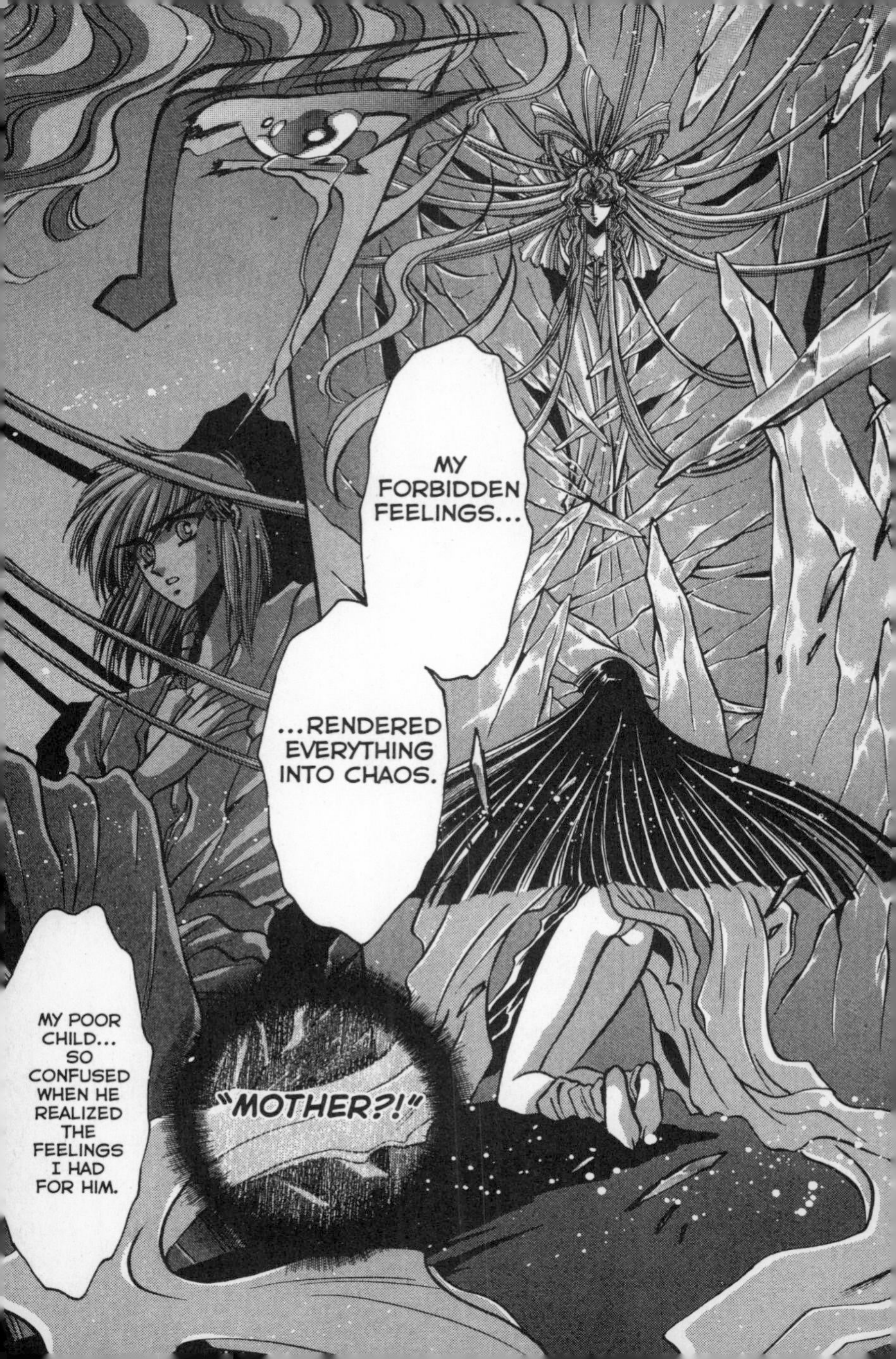
MY FORBIDDEN FEELINGS...
...RENDERED EVERYTHING INTO CHAOS.
"MOTHER?!"
MY POOR CHILD... SO CONFUSED WHEN HE REALIZED THE FEELINGS I HAD FOR HIM.

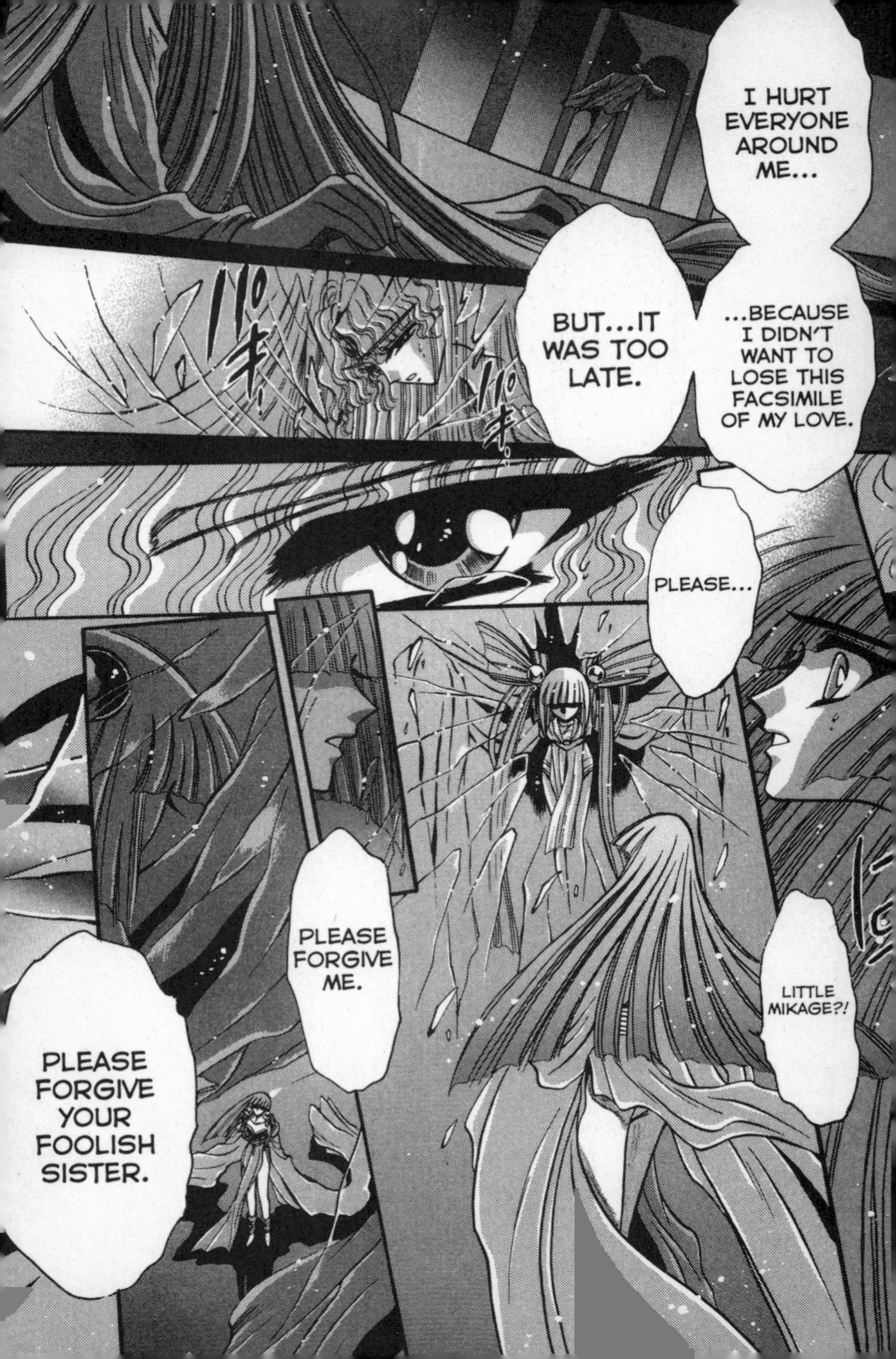
I HURT EVERYONE AROUND ME...
...BECAUSE I DIDN'T WANT TO LOSE THIS FACSIMILE OF MY LOVE.
BUT...IT WAS TOO LATE.
PLEASE...
LITTLE MIKAGE?!
PLEASE FORGIVE ME.
PLEASE FORGIVE YOUR FOOLISH SISTER.

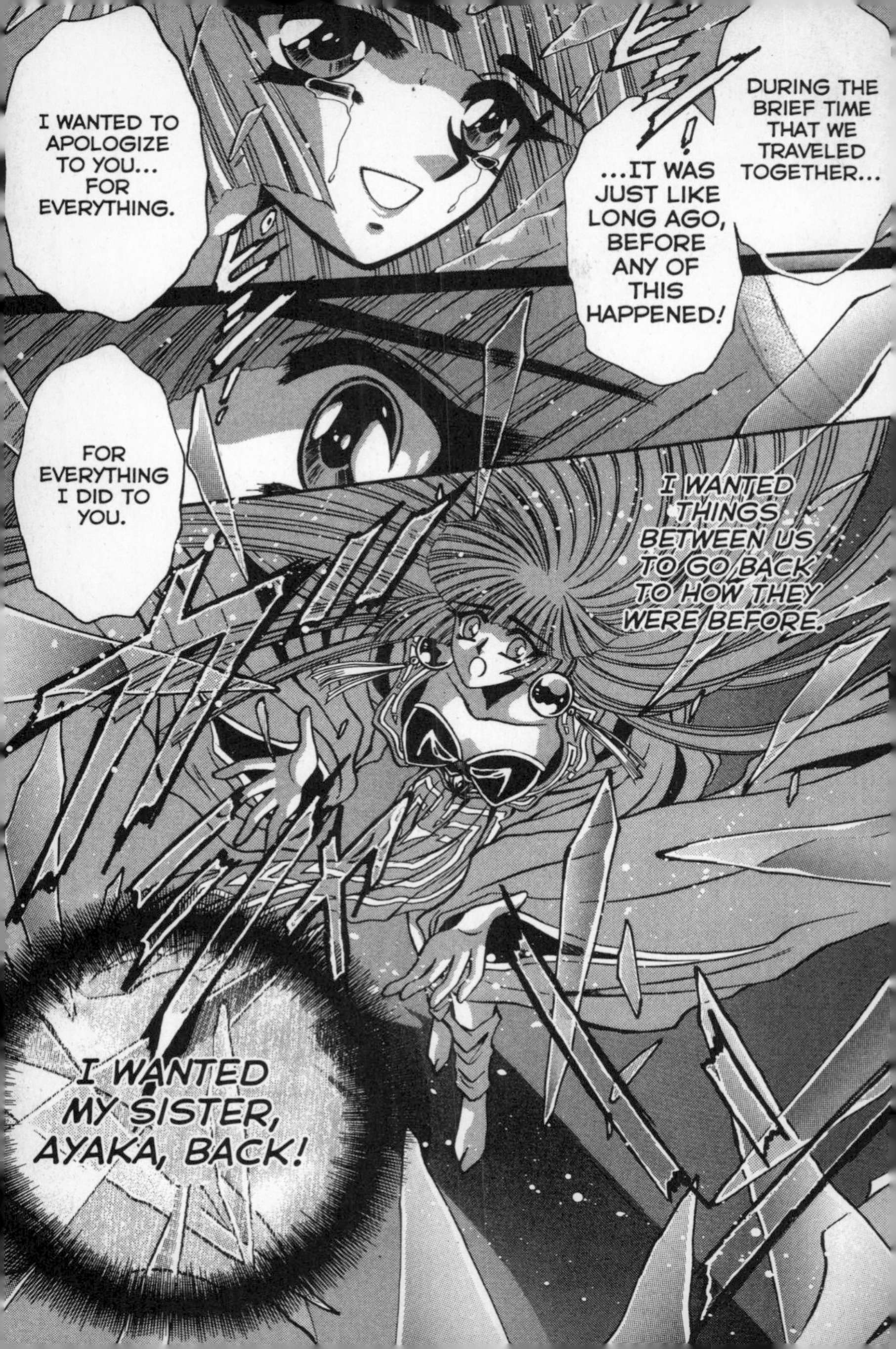
DURING THE BRIEF TIME THAT WE TRAVELED TOGETHER...
...IT WAS JUST LIKE LONG AGO, BEFORE ANY OF THIS HAPPENED!
I WANTED TO APOLOGIZE TO YOU... FOR EVERYTHING.
FOR EVERYTHING I DID TO YOU.
I WANTED THINGS BETWEEN US TO GO BACK TO HOW THEY WERE BEFORE.
I WANTED MY SISTER, AYAKA, BACK!

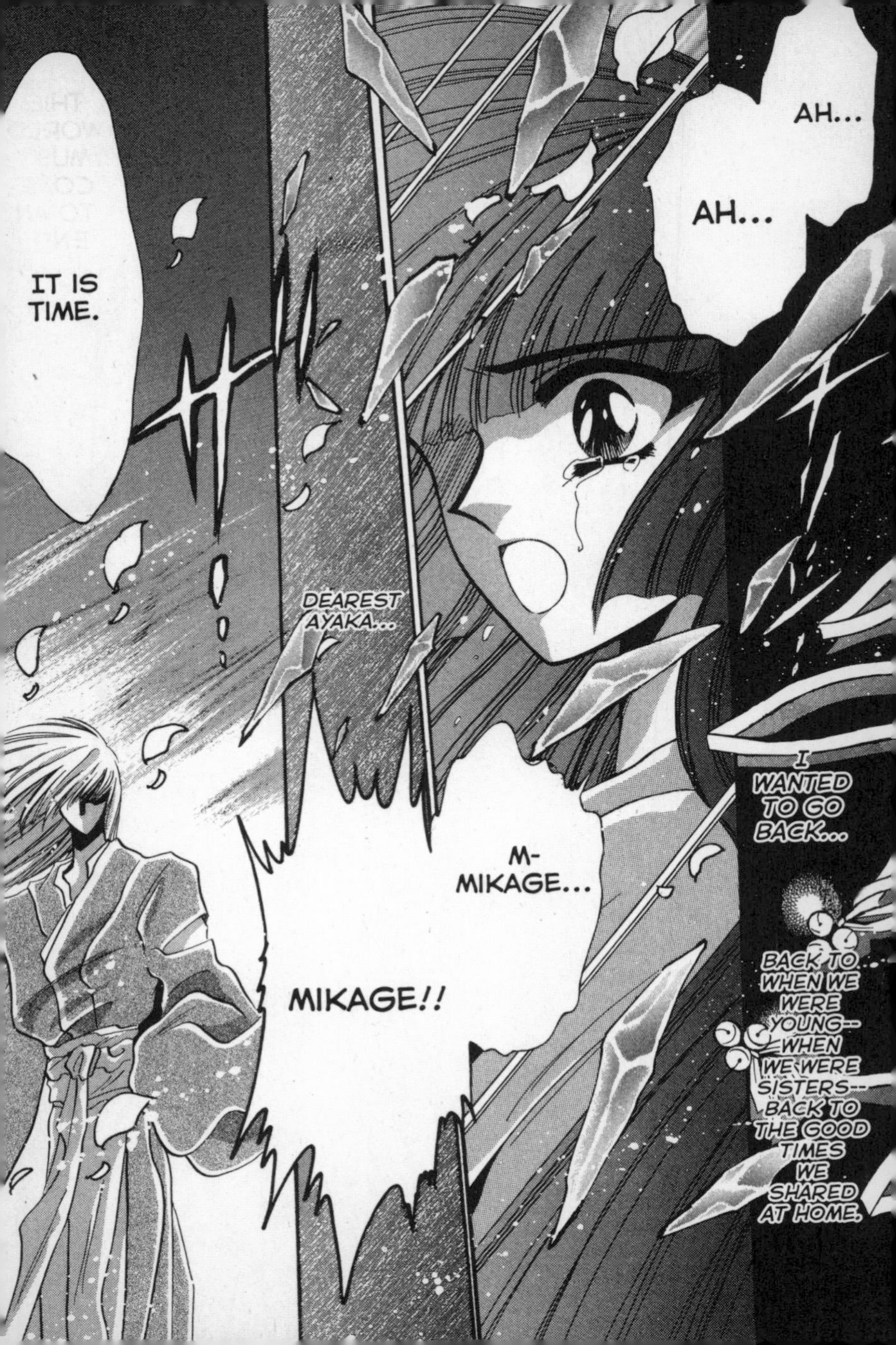
AH...
AH...
IT IS TIME.
DEAREST AYAKA...
I WANTED TO GO BACK...
M- MIKAGE...
BACK TO WHEN WE WERE YOUNG-- WHEN WE WERE SISTERS-- BACK TO THE GOOD TIMES WE SHARED AT HOME.
MIKAGE!!

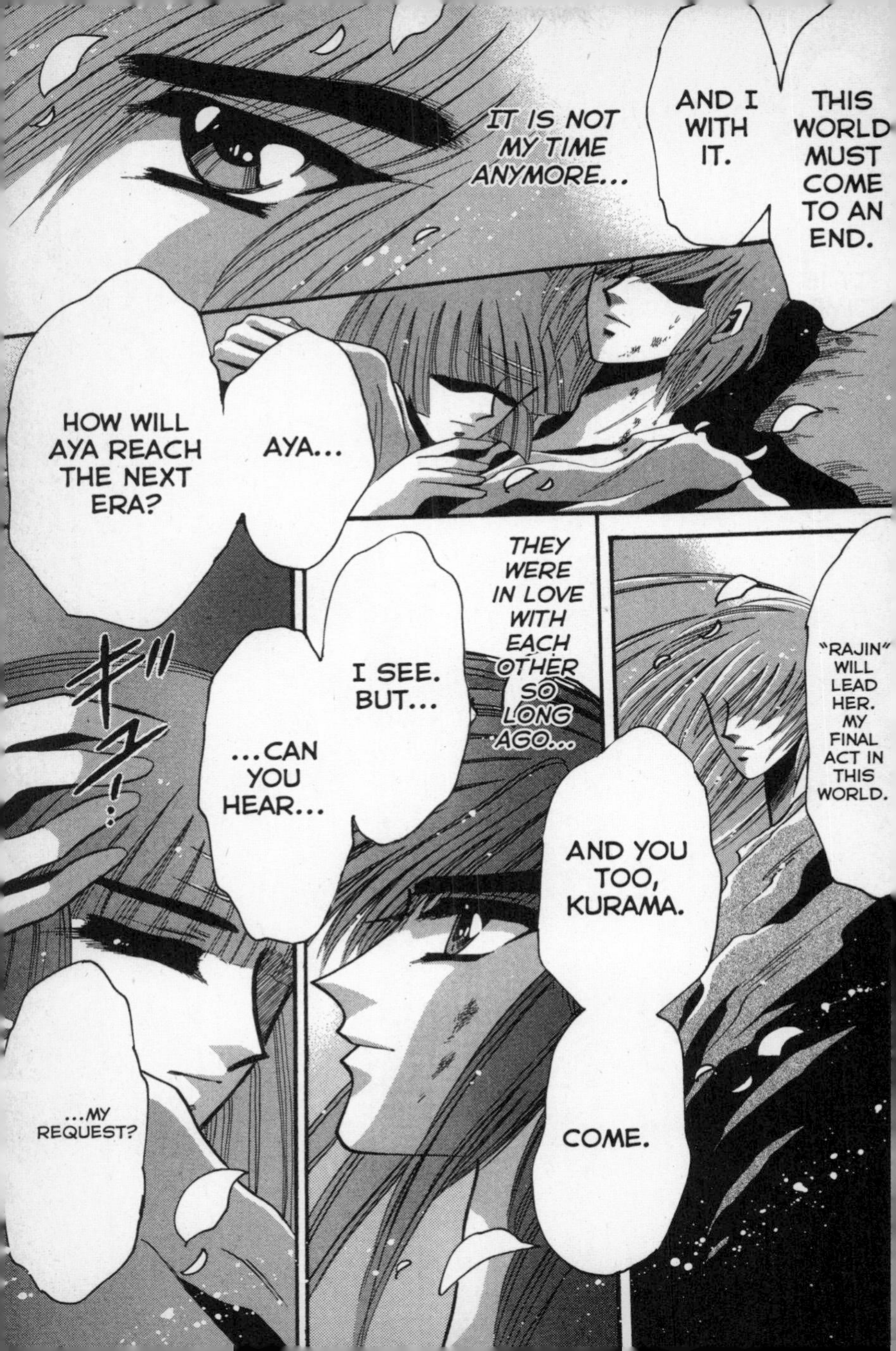
THIS WORLD MUST COME TO AN END.
AND I WITH IT.
IT IS NOT MY TIME ANYMORE...
AYA...
HOW WILL AYA REACH THE NEXT ERA?
"RAJIN" WILL LEAD HER. MY FINAL ACT IN THIS WORLD.
AND YOU TOO, KURAMA.
COME.
THEY WERE IN LOVE WITH EACH OTHER SO LONG AGO...
I SEE. BUT...
...CAN YOU HEAR...
...MY REQUEST?

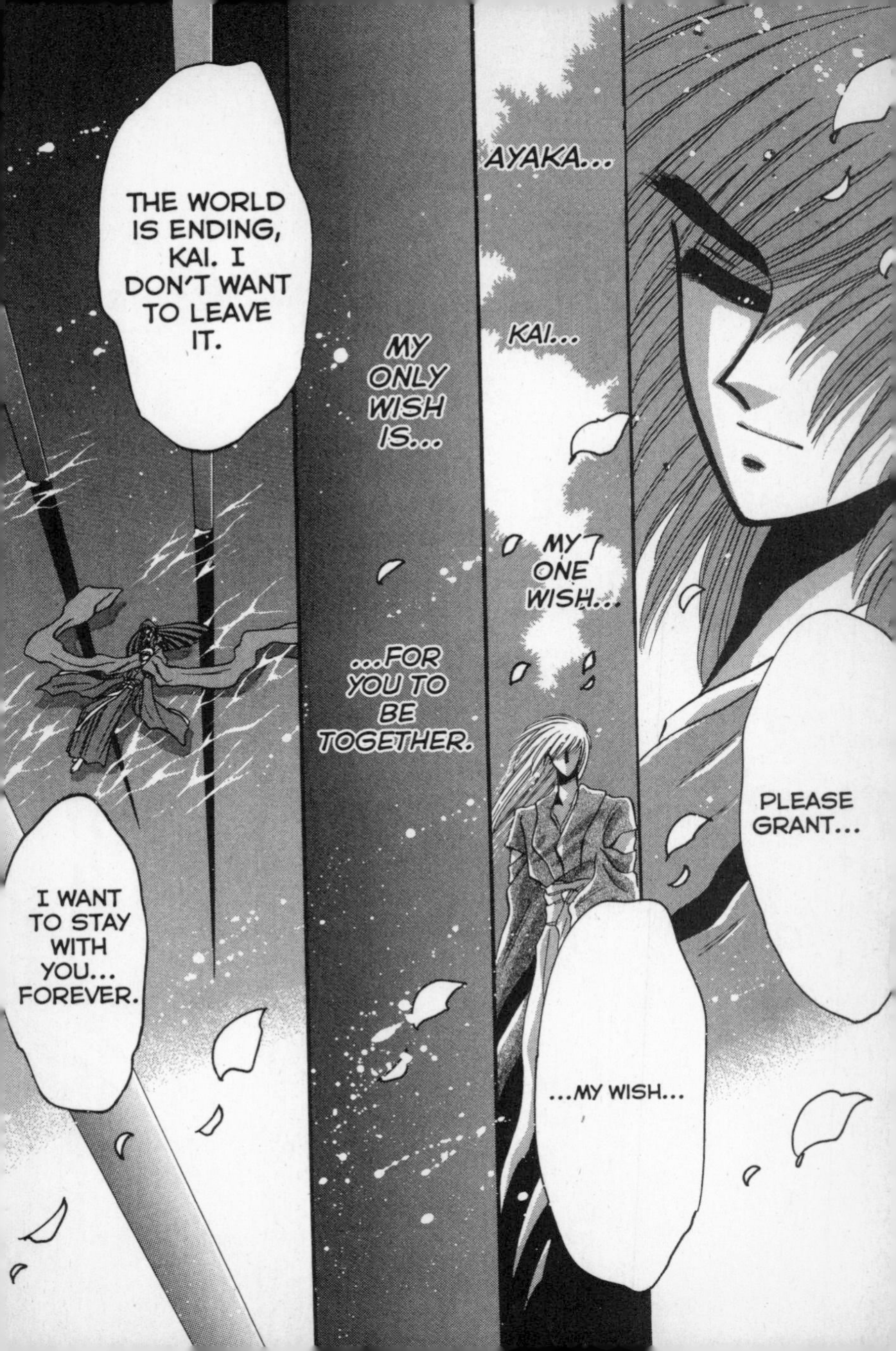

PLEASE GRANT...
...MY WISH...
AYAKA...
KAI...
MY ONE WISH...
MY ONLY WISH IS...
...FOR YOU TO BE TOGETHER.
THE WORLD IS ENDING, KAI. I DON'T WANT TO LEAVE IT.
I WANT TO STAY WITH YOU... FOREVER.

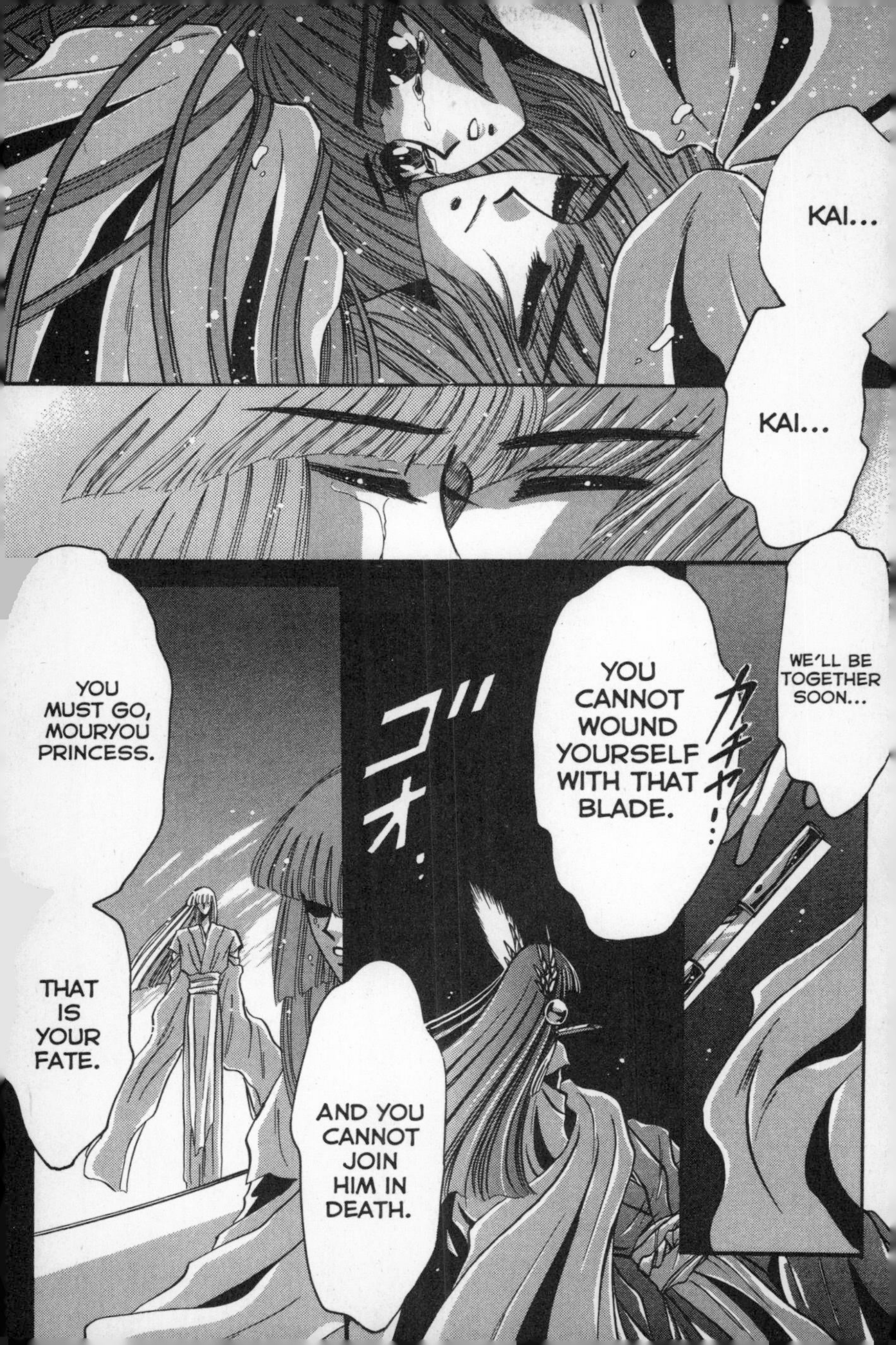
KAI...
KAI...
WE'LL BE TOGETHER SOON...
カチャ…
YOU CANNOT WOUND YOURSELF WITH THAT BLADE.
ゴオ…
AND YOU CANNOT JOIN HIM IN DEATH.
YOU MUST GO, MOURYOU PRINCESS.
THAT IS YOUR FATE.

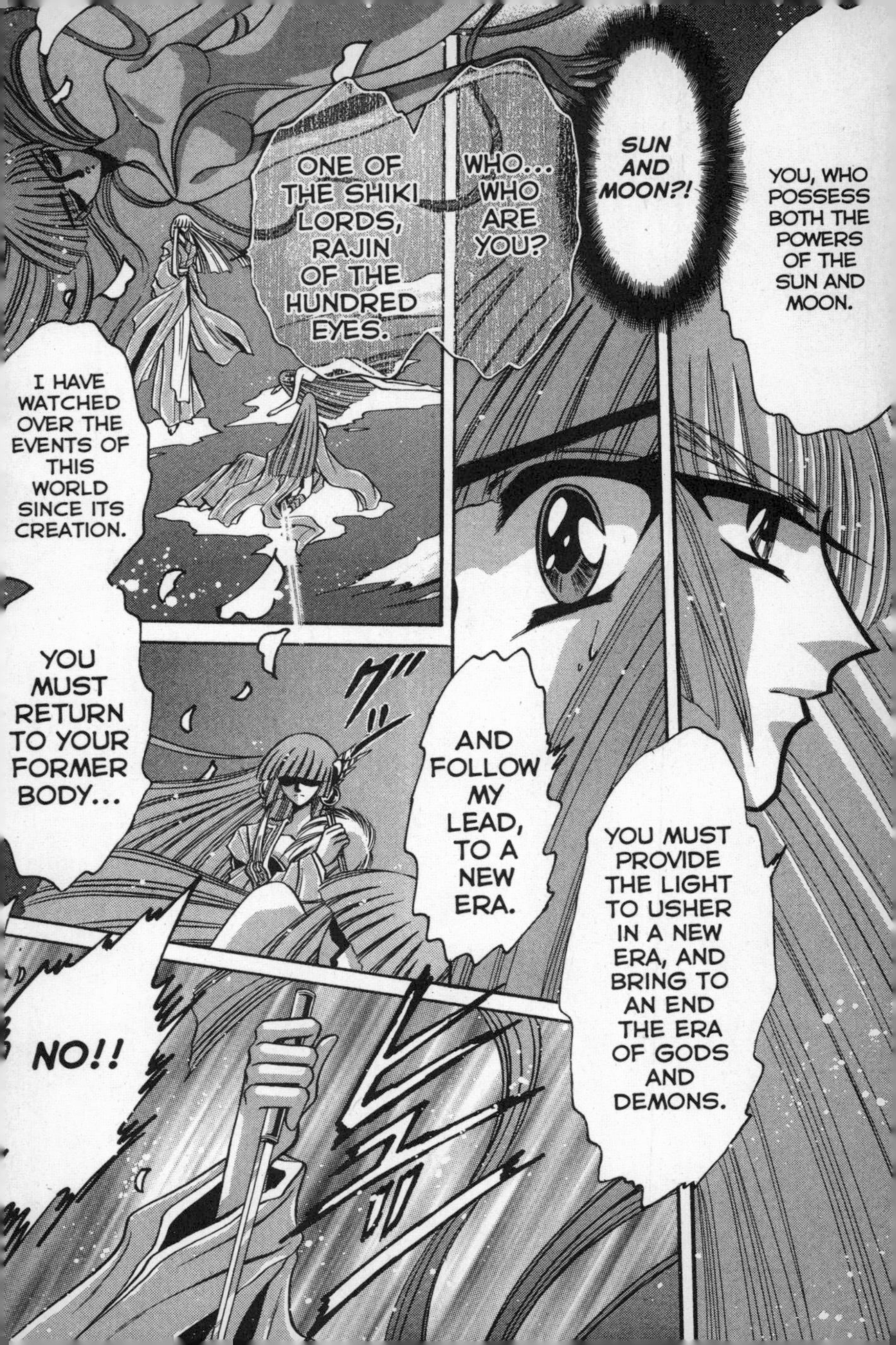
YOU, WHO POSSESS BOTH THE POWERS OF THE SUN AND MOON.
SUN AND MOON?!
WHO... WHO ARE YOU?
ONE OF THE SHIKI LORDS, RAJIN OF THE HUNDRED EYES.
I HAVE WATCHED OVER THE EVENTS OF THIS WORLD SINCE ITS CREATION.
YOU MUST RETURN TO YOUR FORMER BODY...
AND FOLLOW MY LEAD, TO A NEW ERA.
YOU MUST PROVIDE THE LIGHT TO USHER IN A NEW ERA, AND BRING TO AN END THE ERA OF GODS AND DEMONS.
NO!!

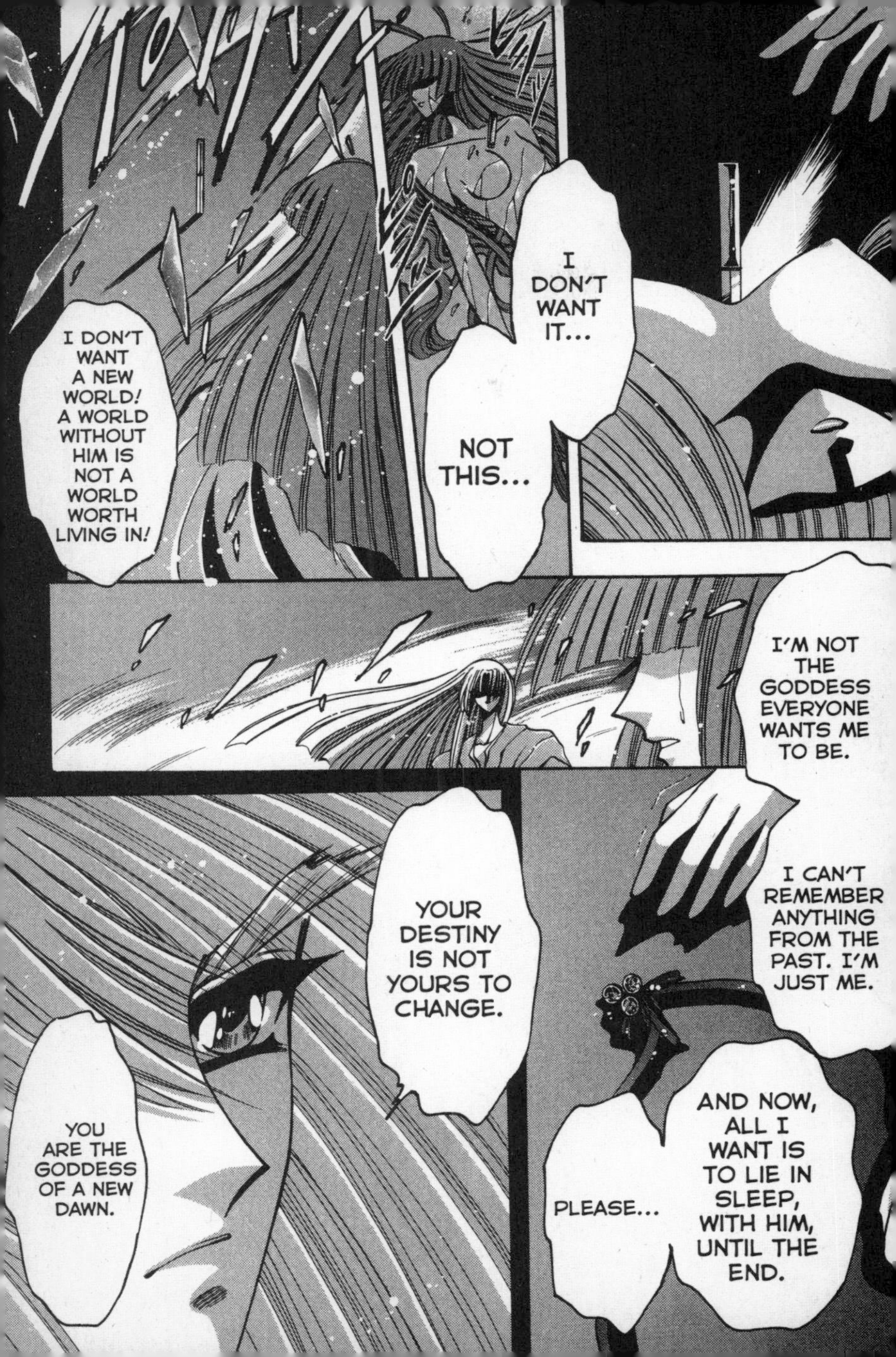
I DON'T WANT IT...
NOT THIS...
I DON'T WANT A NEW WORLD! A WORLD WITHOUT HIM IS NOT A WORLD WORTH LIVING IN!
I'M NOT THE GODDESS EVERYONE WANTS ME TO BE.
I CAN'T REMEMBER ANYTHING FROM THE PAST. I'M JUST ME.
AND NOW, ALL I WANT IS TO LIE IN SLEEP, WITH HIM, UNTIL THE END.
PLEASE...
YOUR DESTINY IS NOT YOURS TO CHANGE.
YOU ARE THE GODDESS OF A NEW DAWN.

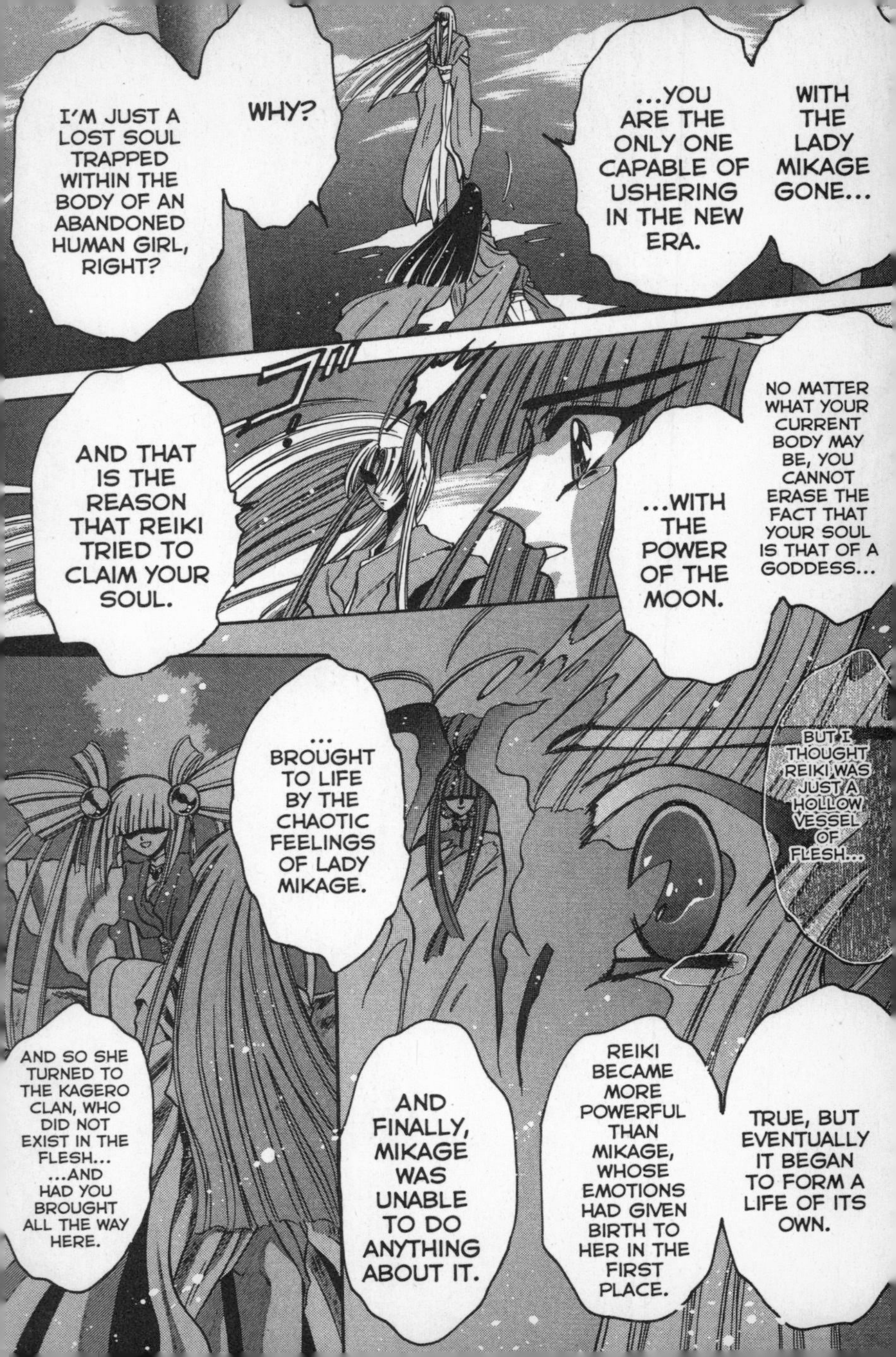
WITH THE LADY MIKAGE GONE...
...YOU ARE THE ONLY ONE CAPABLE OF USHERING IN THE NEW ERA.
WHY?
I'M JUST A LOST SOUL TRAPPED WITHIN THE BODY OF AN ABANDONED HUMAN GIRL, RIGHT?
NO MATTER WHAT YOUR CURRENT BODY MAY BE, YOU CANNOT ERASE THE FACT THAT YOUR SOUL IS THAT OF A GODDESS...
...WITH THE POWER OF THE MOON.
AND THAT IS THE REASON THAT REIKI TRIED TO CLAIM YOUR SOUL.
BUT I THOUGHT REIKI WAS JUST A HOLLOW VESSEL OF FLESH...
... BROUGHT TO LIFE BY THE CHAOTIC FEELINGS OF LADY MIKAGE.
TRUE, BUT EVENTUALLY IT BEGAN TO FORM A LIFE OF ITS OWN.
REIKI BECAME MORE POWERFUL THAN MIKAGE, WHOSE EMOTIONS HAD GIVEN BIRTH TO HER IN THE FIRST PLACE.
AND FINALLY, MIKAGE WAS UNABLE TO DO ANYTHING ABOUT IT.
AND SO SHE TURNED TO THE KAGERO CLAN, WHO DID NOT EXIST IN THE FLESH... ...AND HAD YOU BROUGHT ALL THE WAY HERE.

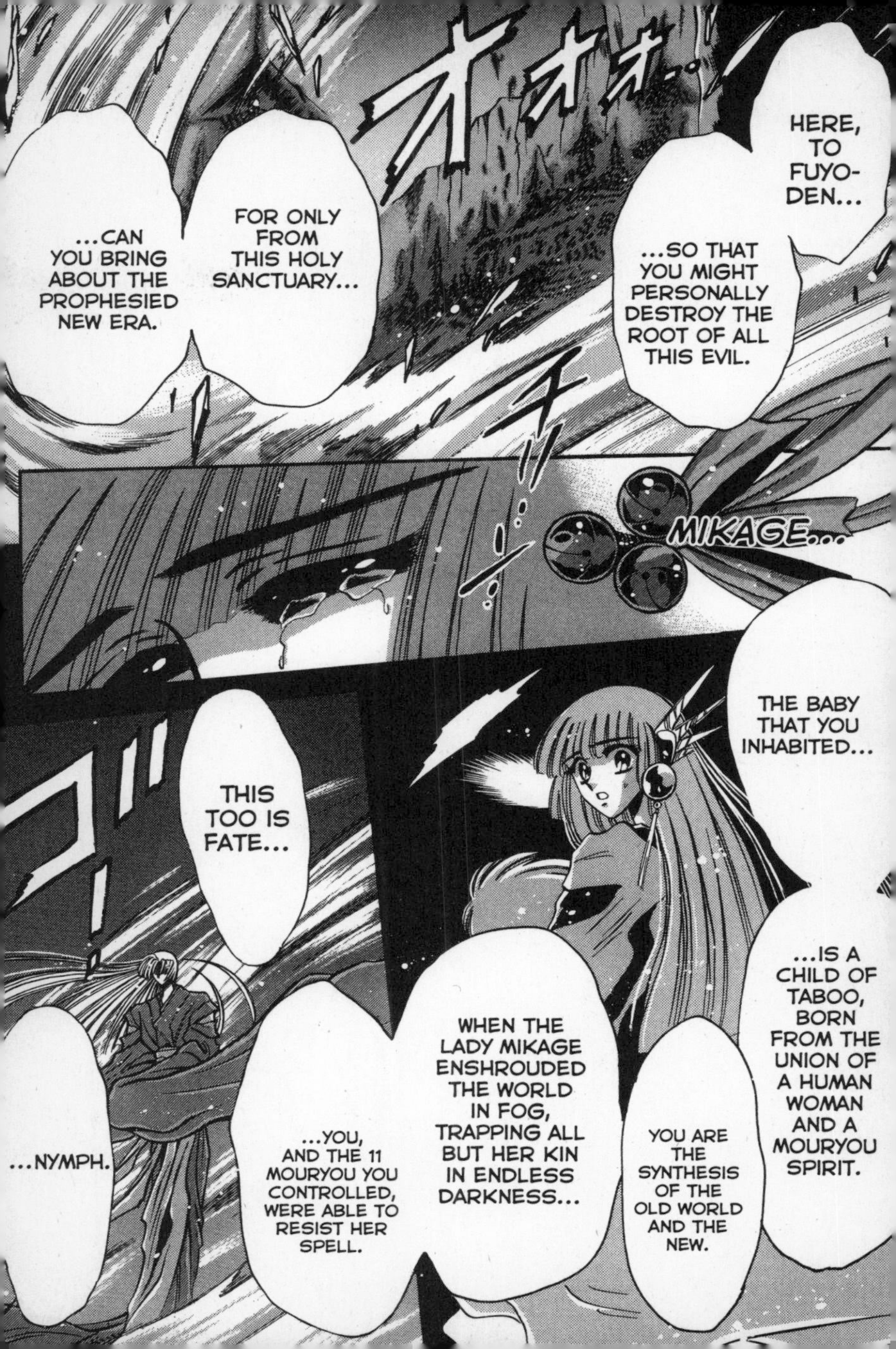

オオオ…
HERE, TO FUYO-DEN...
...SO THAT YOU MIGHT PERSONALLY DESTROY THE ROOT OF ALL THIS EVIL.
FOR ONLY FROM THIS HOLY SANCTUARY...
...CAN YOU BRING ABOUT THE PROPHESIED NEW ERA.
MIKAGE...
THE BABY THAT YOU INHABITED...
...IS A CHILD OF TABOO, BORN FROM THE UNION OF A HUMAN WOMAN AND A MOURYOU SPIRIT.
YOU ARE THE SYNTHESIS OF THE OLD WORLD AND THE NEW.
WHEN THE LADY MIKAGE ENSHROUDED THE WORLD IN FOG, TRAPPING ALL BUT HER KIN IN ENDLESS DARKNESS...
...YOU, AND THE 11 MOURYOU YOU CONTROLLED, WERE ABLE TO RESIST HER SPELL.
THIS TOO IS FATE...
...NYMPH.

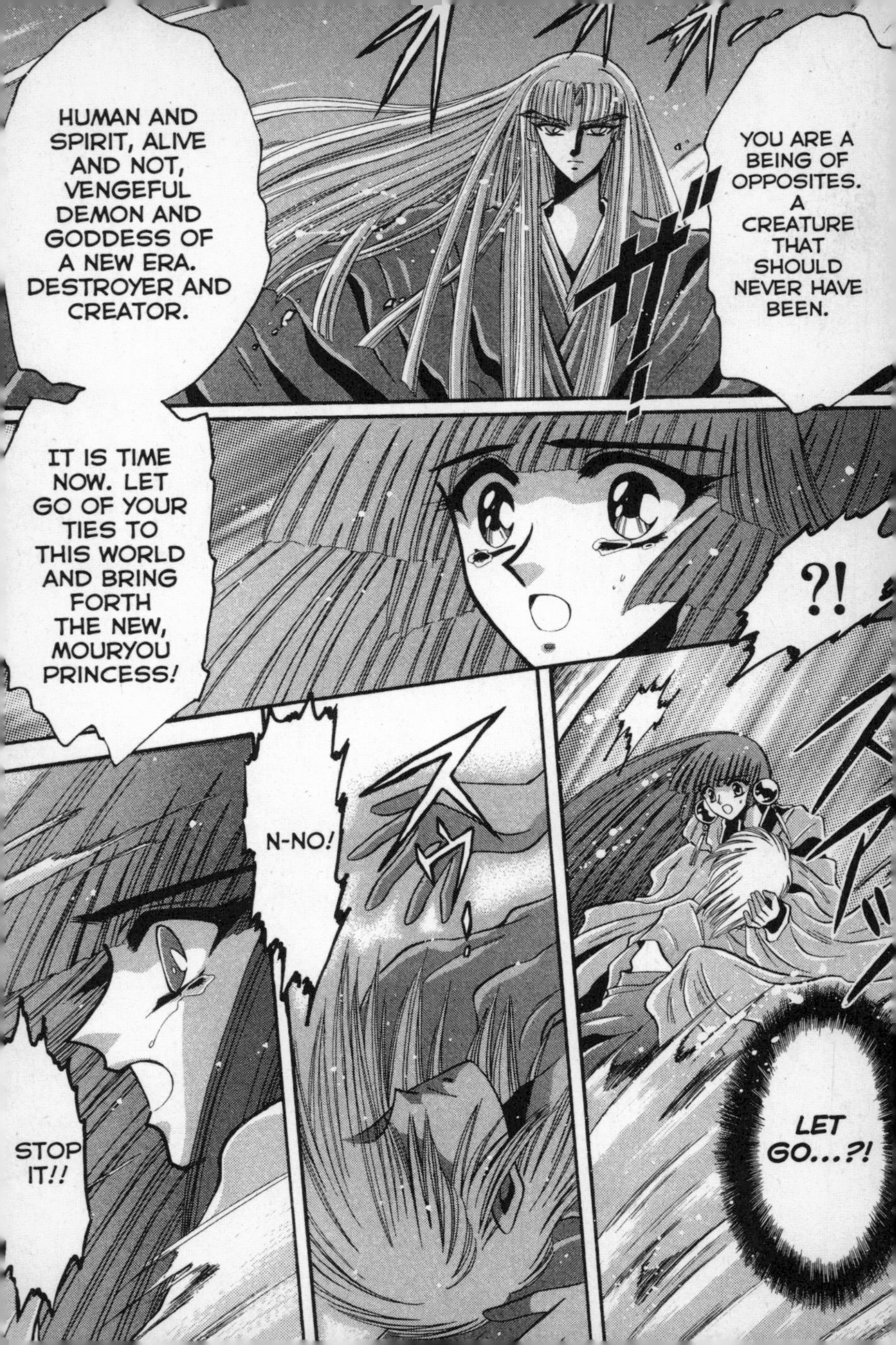
YOU ARE A BEING OF OPPOSITES. A CREATURE THAT SHOULD NEVER HAVE BEEN.
HUMAN AND SPIRIT, ALIVE AND NOT, VENGEFUL DEMON AND GODDESS OF A NEW ERA. DESTROYER AND CREATOR.
?!
IT IS TIME NOW. LET GO OF YOUR TIES TO THIS WORLD AND BRING FORTH THE NEW, MOURYOU PRINCESS!
LET GO...?!
N-NO!
STOP IT!!

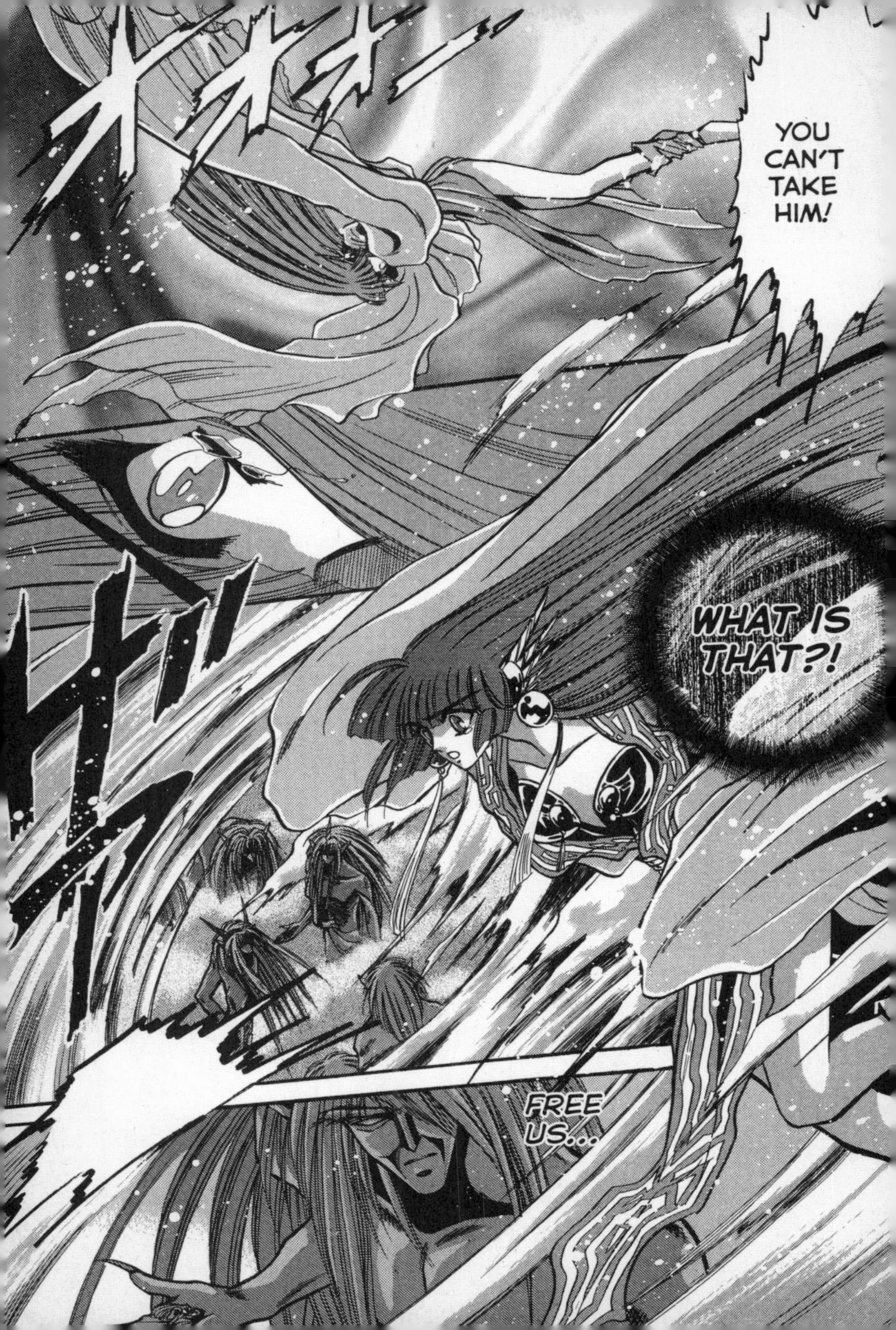
YOU CAN'T TAKE HIM!
WHAT IS THAT?!
FREE US...

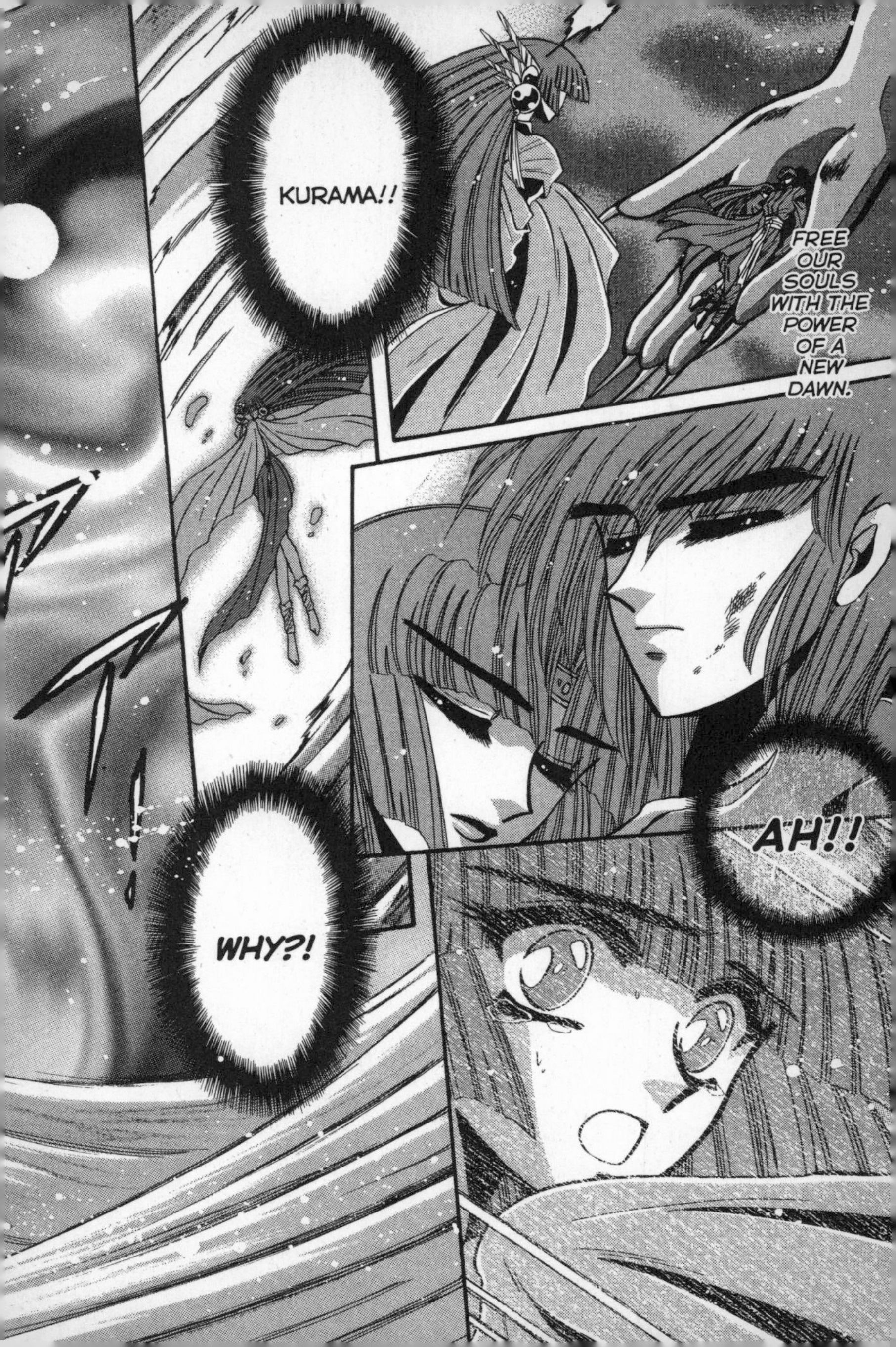
FREE OUR SOULS WITH THE POWER OF A NEW DAWN.
AH!!
KURAMA!!
WHY?!

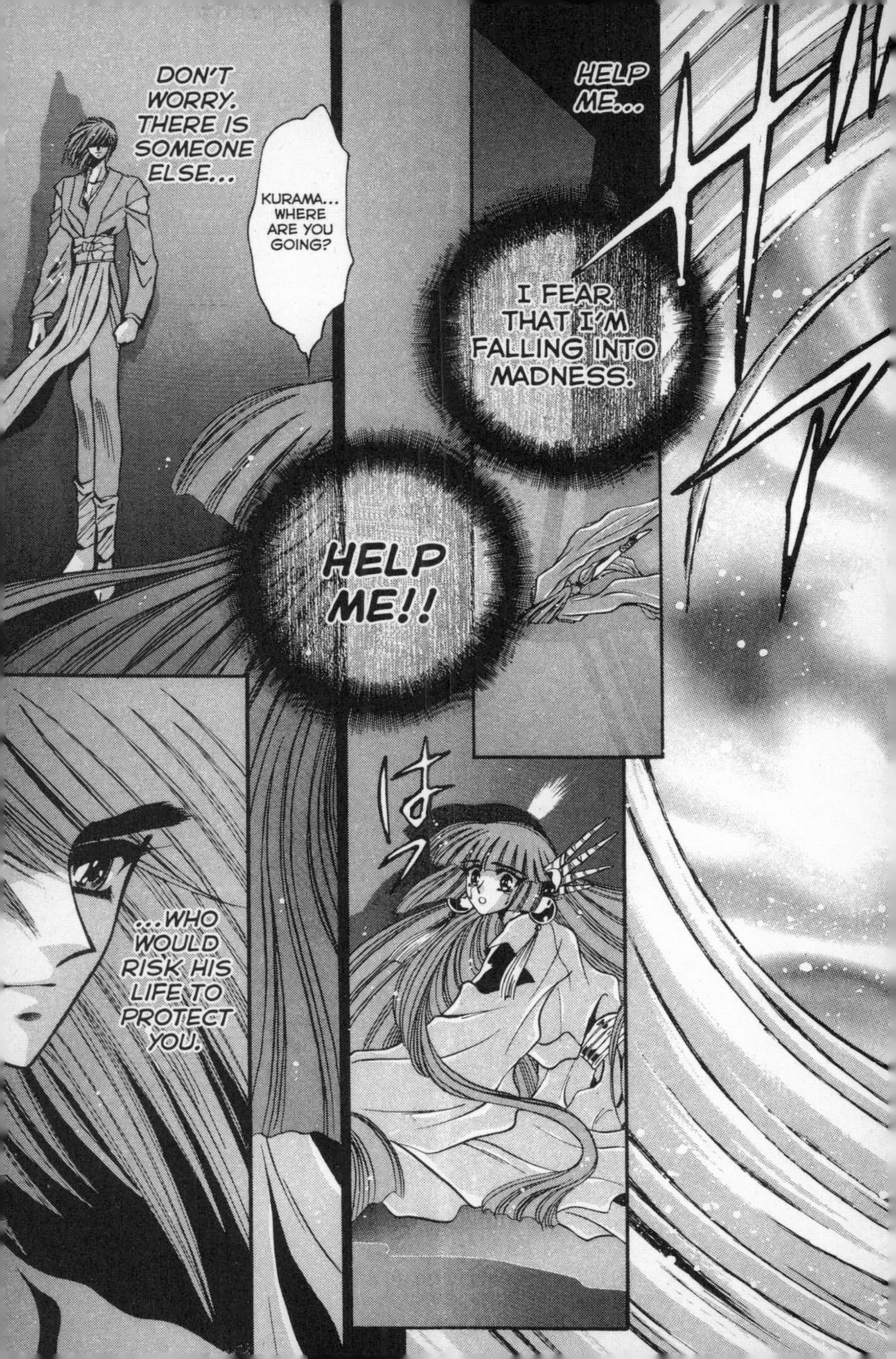
HELP ME...
I FEAR THAT I'M FALLING INTO MADNESS.
HELP ME!!
KURAMA... WHERE ARE YOU GOING?
DON'T WORRY. THERE IS SOMEONE ELSE...
はっ
...WHO WOULD RISK HIS LIFE TO PROTECT YOU.

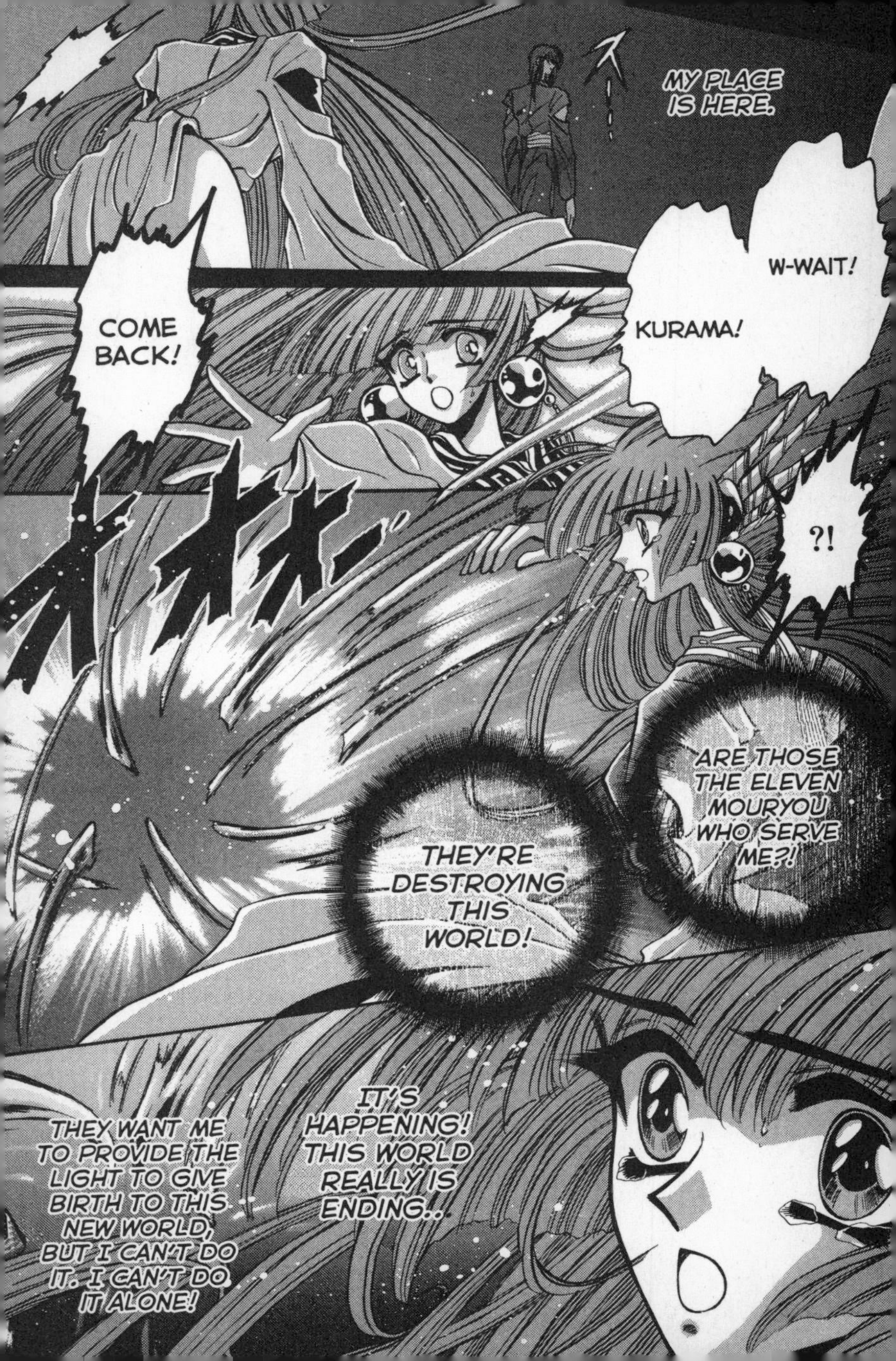
MY PLACE IS HERE.
W-WAIT!
KURAMA!
COME BACK!
?!
オオオー
ARE THOSE THE ELEVEN MOURYOU WHO SERVE ME?!
THEY'RE DESTROYING THIS WORLD!
IT'S HAPPENING! THIS WORLD REALLY IS ENDING...
THEY WANT ME TO PROVIDE THE LIGHT TO GIVE BIRTH TO THIS NEW WORLD, BUT I CAN'T DO IT. I CAN'T DO IT ALONE!

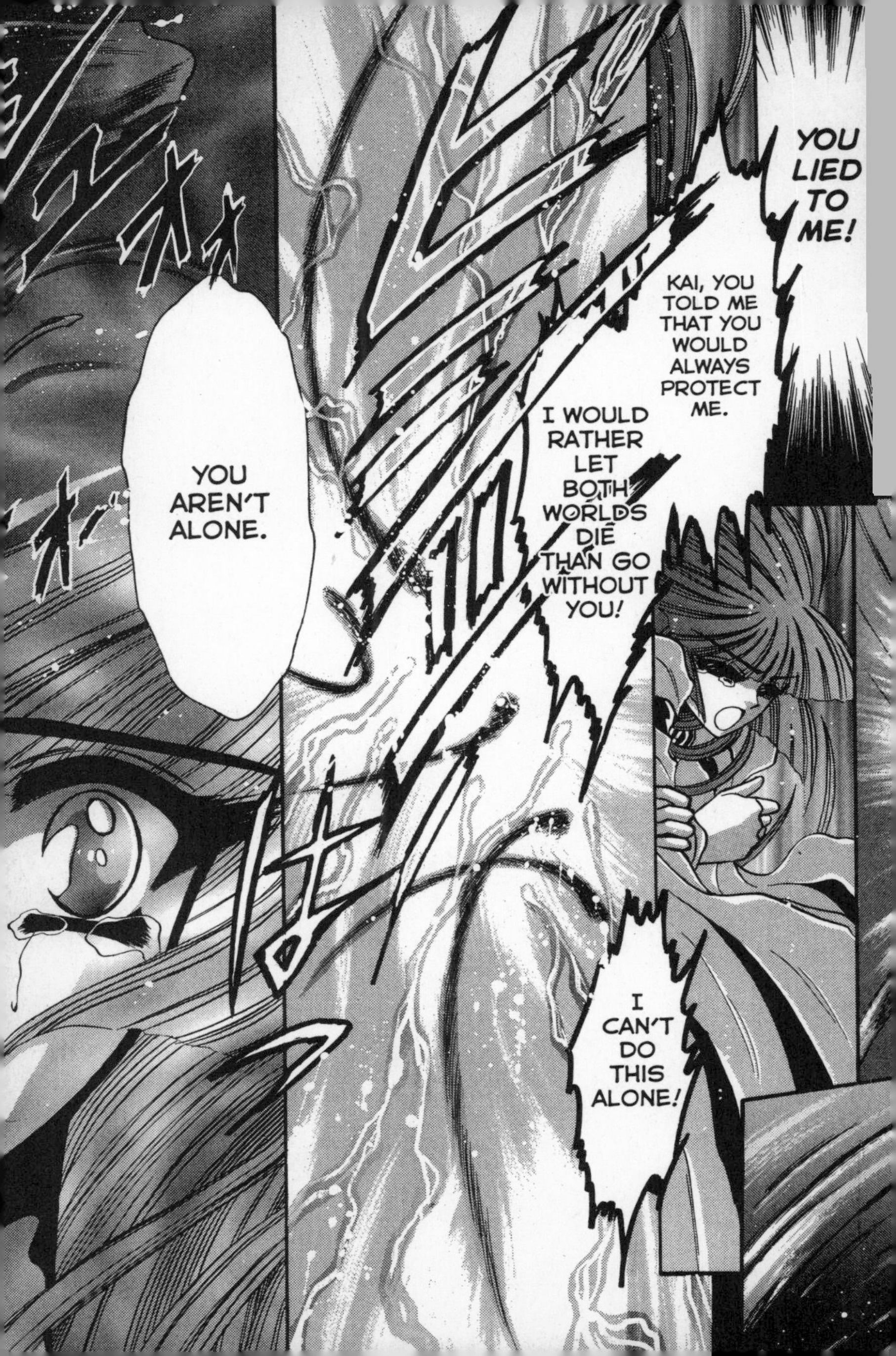
YOU LIED TO ME!
KAI, YOU TOLD ME THAT YOU WOULD ALWAYS PROTECT ME.
I WOULD RATHER LET BOTH WORLDS DIE THAN GO WITHOUT YOU!
I CAN'T DO THIS ALONE!
YOU AREN'T ALONE.

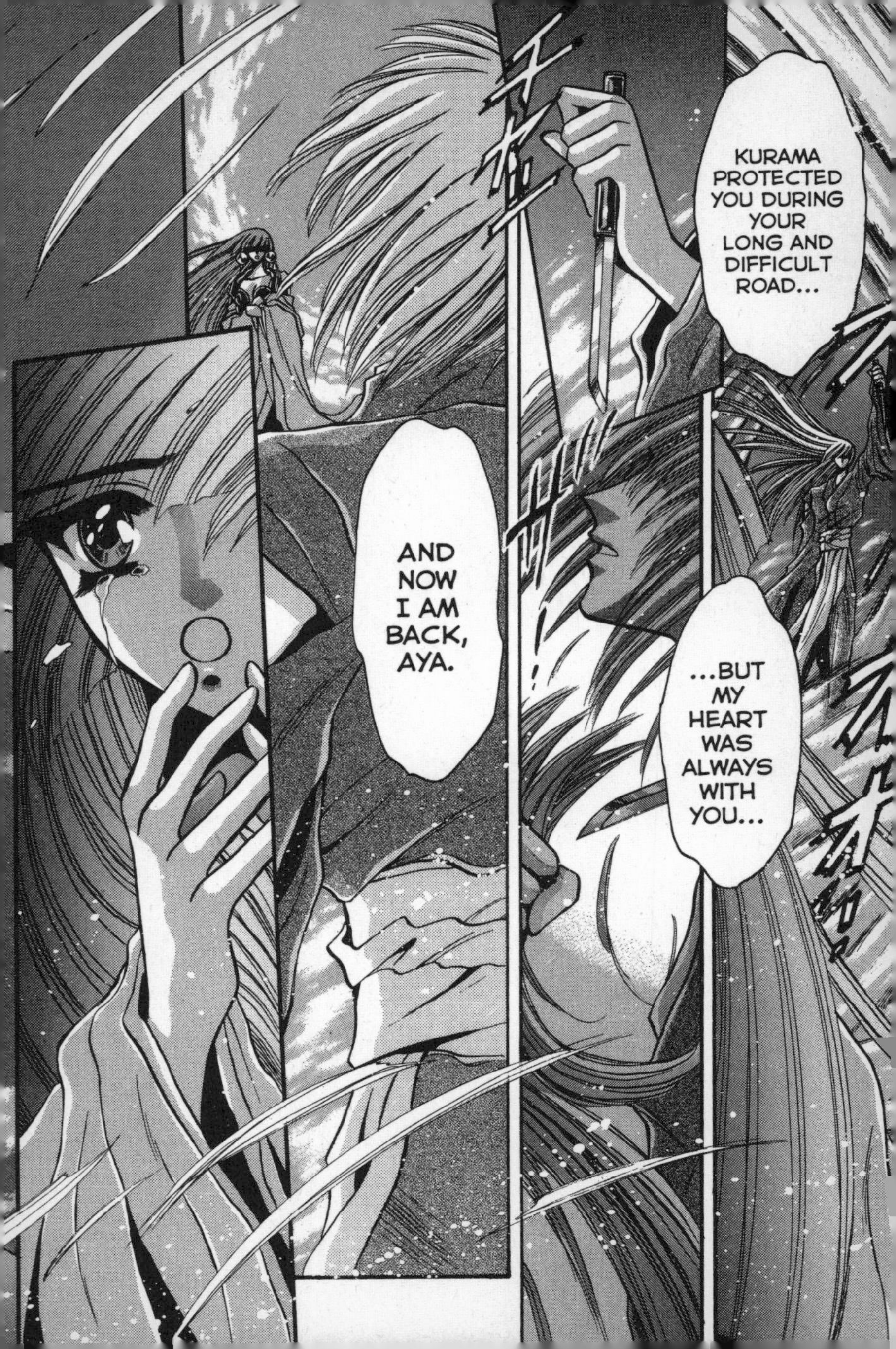
KURAMA PROTECTED YOU DURING YOUR LONG AND DIFFICULT ROAD...
...BUT MY HEART WAS ALWAYS WITH YOU...
AND NOW I AM BACK, AYA.

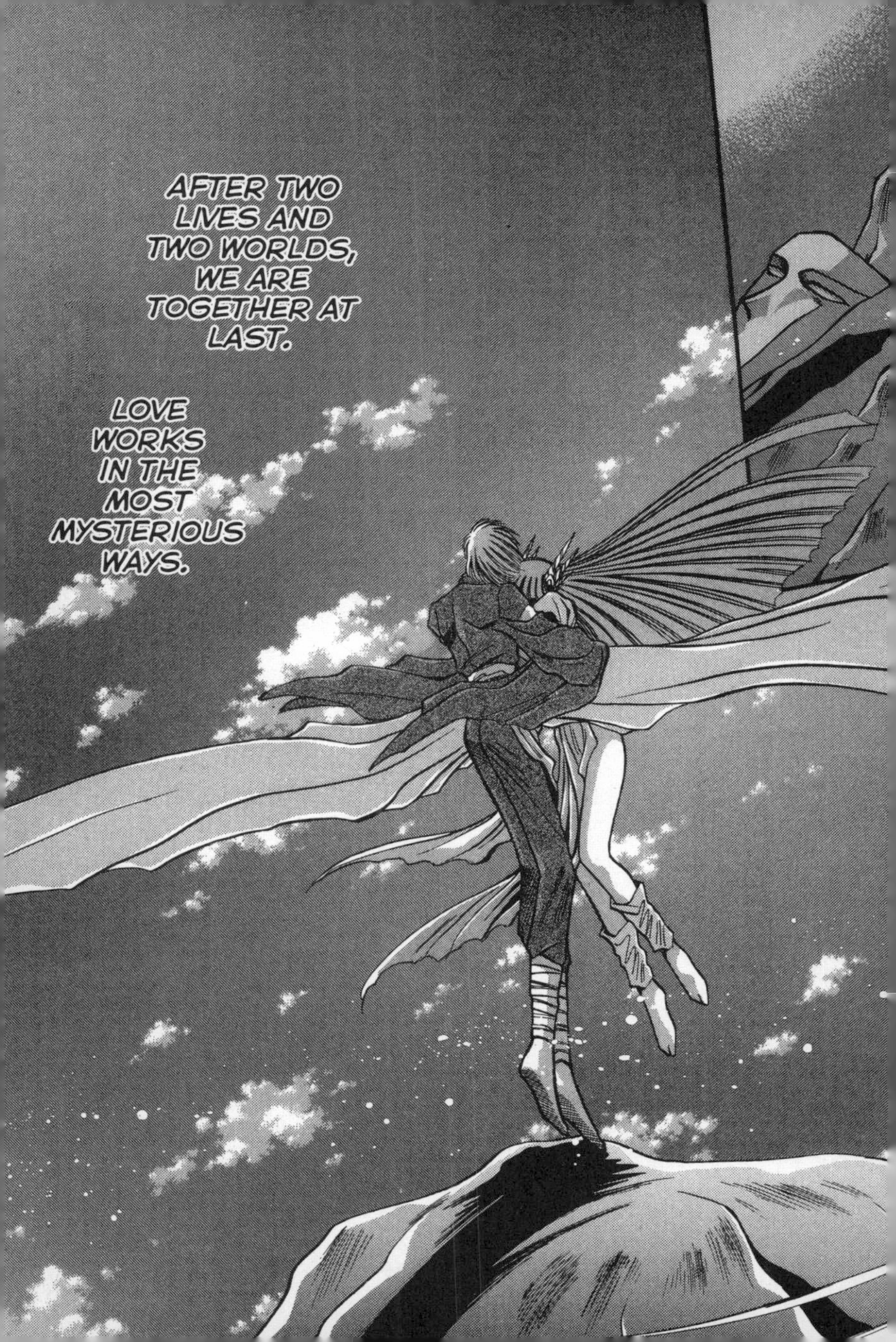
AFTER TWO LIVES AND TWO WORLDS, WE ARE TOGETHER AT LAST.
LOVE WORKS IN THE MOST MYSTERIOUS WAYS.

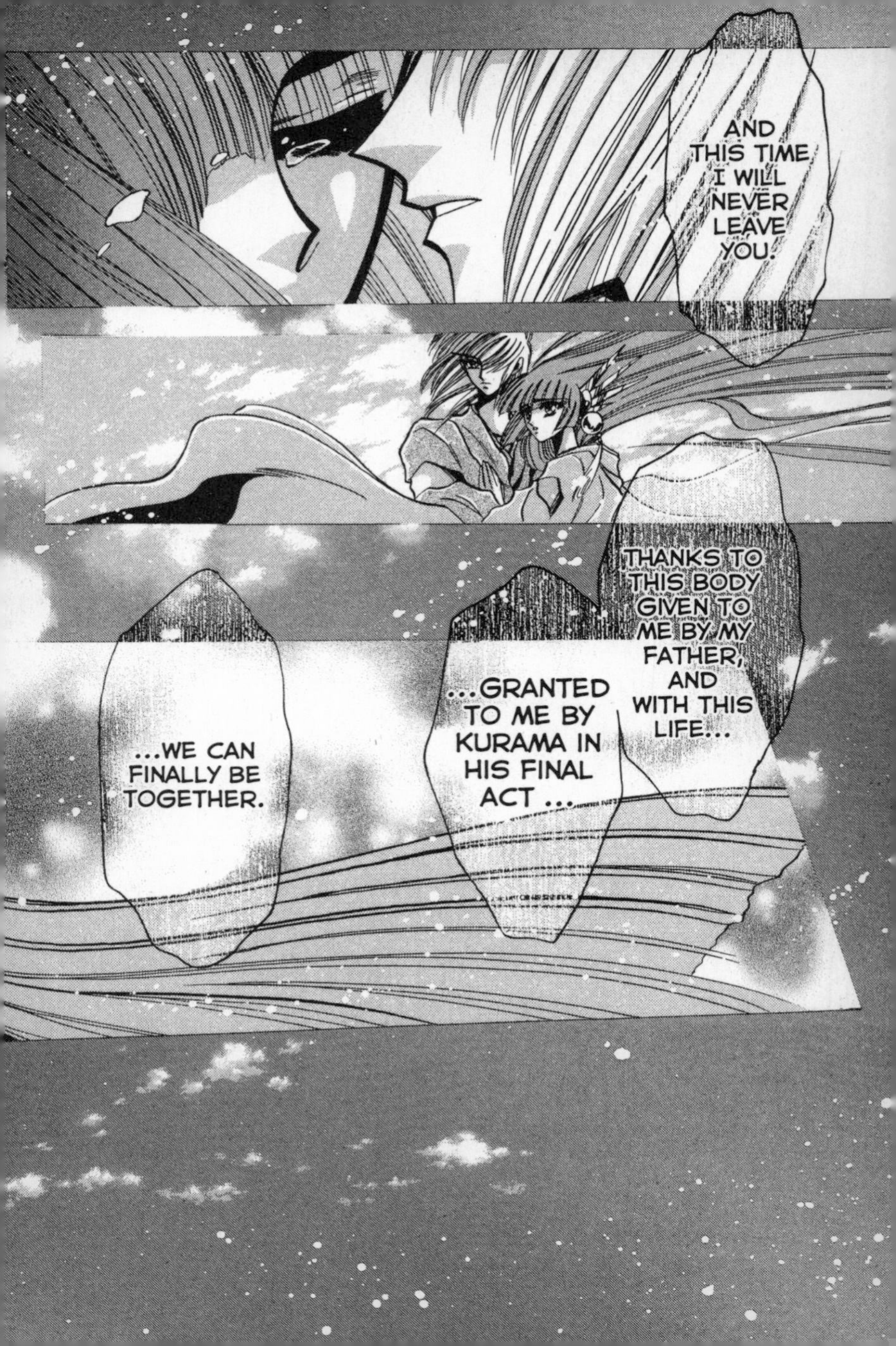
AND THIS TIME I WILL NEVER LEAVE YOU.
THANKS TO THIS BODY GIVEN TO ME BY MY FATHER, AND WITH THIS LIFE...
...GRANTED TO ME BY KURAMA IN HIS FINAL ACT ...
...WE CAN FINALLY BE TOGETHER.

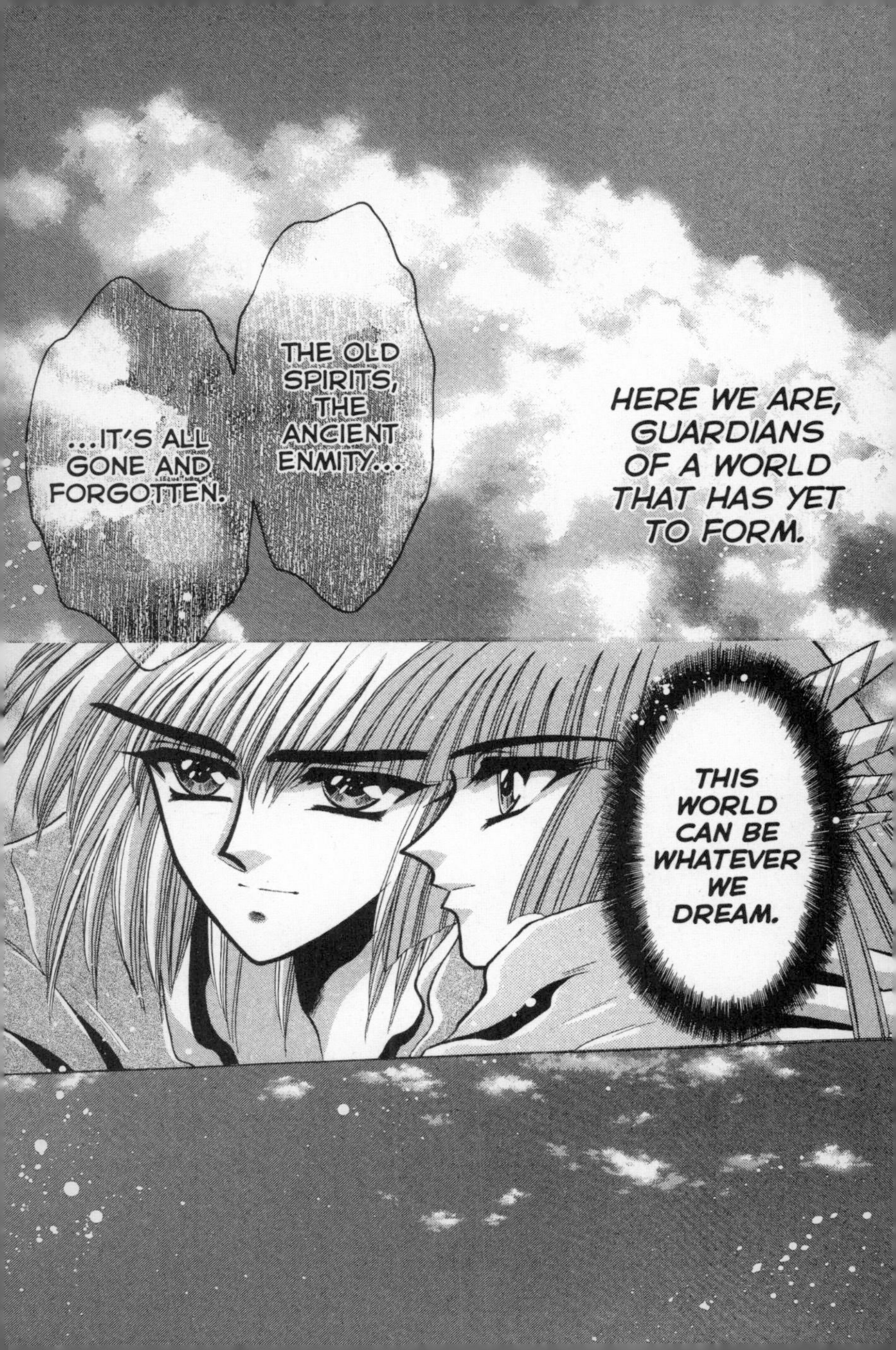
HERE WE ARE, GUARDIANS OF A WORLD THAT HAS YET TO FORM.
THE OLD SPIRITS, THE ANCIENT ENMITY...
...IT'S ALL GONE AND FORGOTTEN.
THIS WORLD CAN BE WHATEVER WE DREAM.

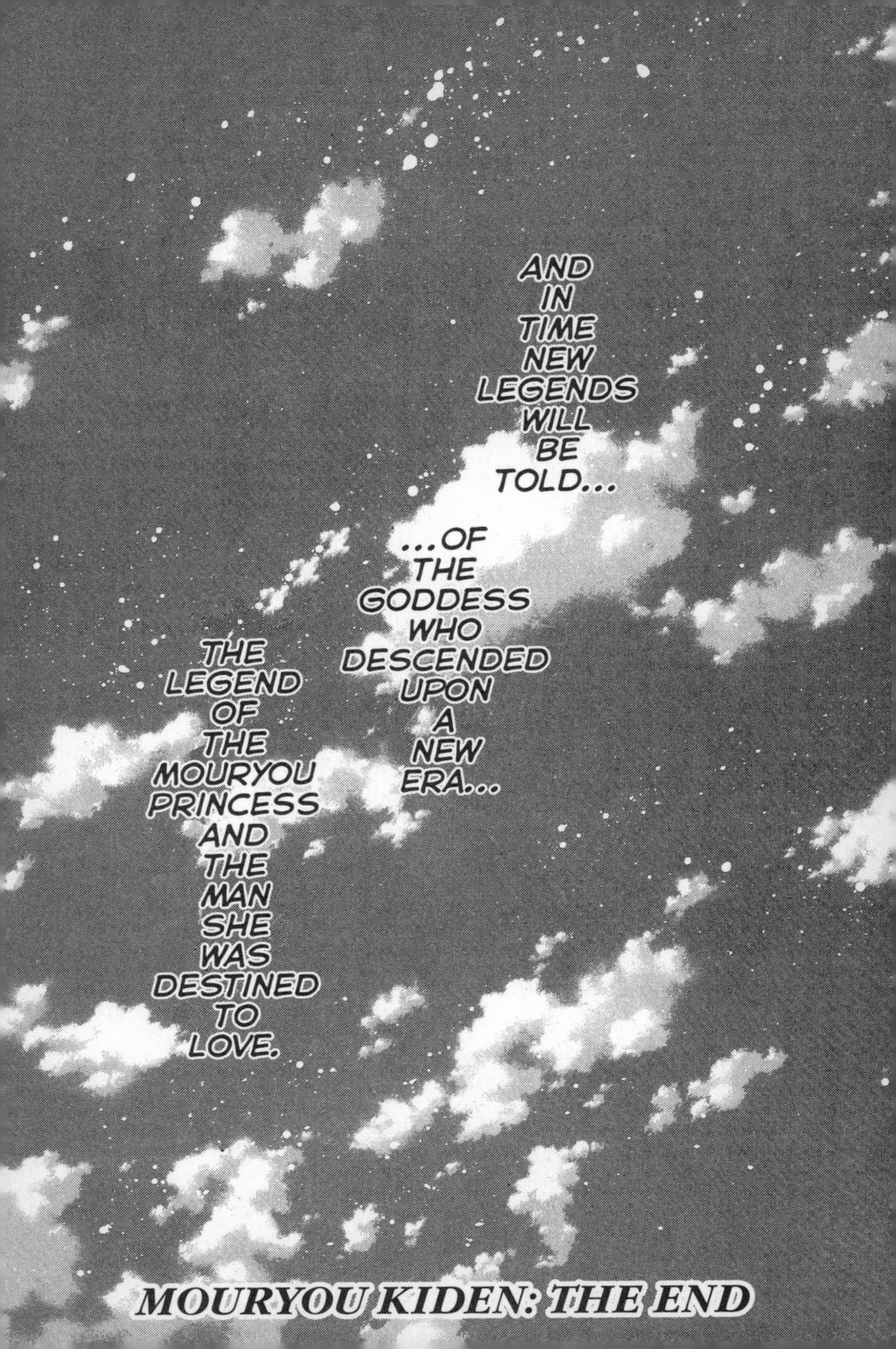
AND IN TIME NEW LEGENDS WILL BE TOLD...
...OF THE GODDESS WHO DESCENDED UPON A NEW ERA...
THE LEGEND OF THE MOURYOU PRINCESS AND THE MAN SHE WAS DESTINED TO LOVE.
MOURYOU KIDEN: THE END

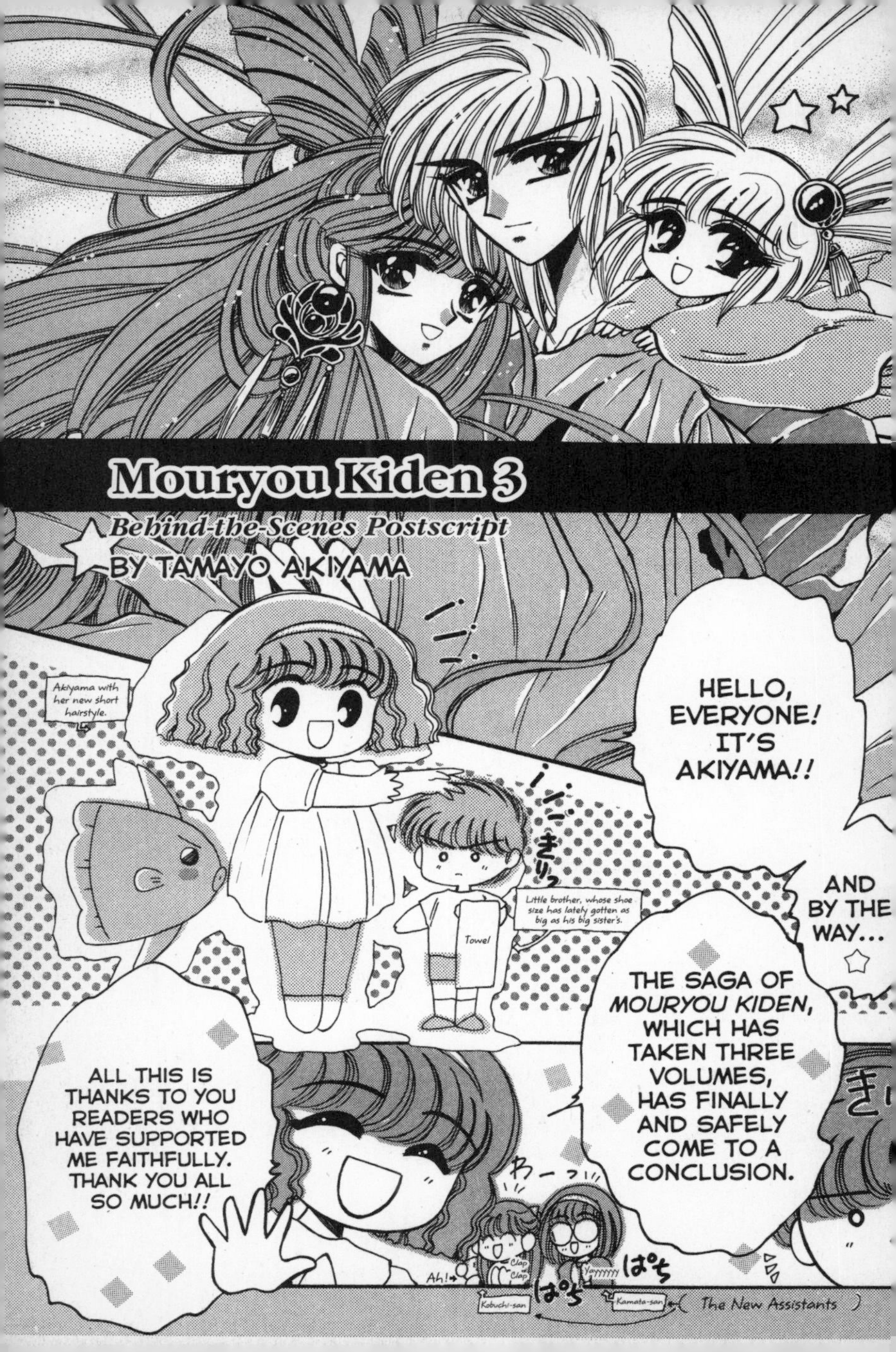
Mouryou Kiden 3
Behind-the-Scenes Postscript
BY TAMAYO AKIYAMA
HELLO, EVERYONE! IT'S AKIYAMA!!
きりっ
Little brother, whose shoe size has lately gotten as big as his big sister's.
Towel
Akiyama with her new short hairstyle.
AND BY THE WAY...
THE SAGA OF MOURYOU KIDEN, WHICH HAS TAKEN THREE VOLUMES, HAS FINALLY AND SAFELY COME TO A CONCLUSION.
ALL THIS IS THANKS TO YOU READERS WHO HAVE SUPPORTED ME FAITHFULLY. THANK YOU ALL SO MUCH!!
わーっ
Yayyyyyy
ぱち
ぱち
Clap Clap
Ah!
Kobuchi-san
Kamata-san
(The New Assistants)

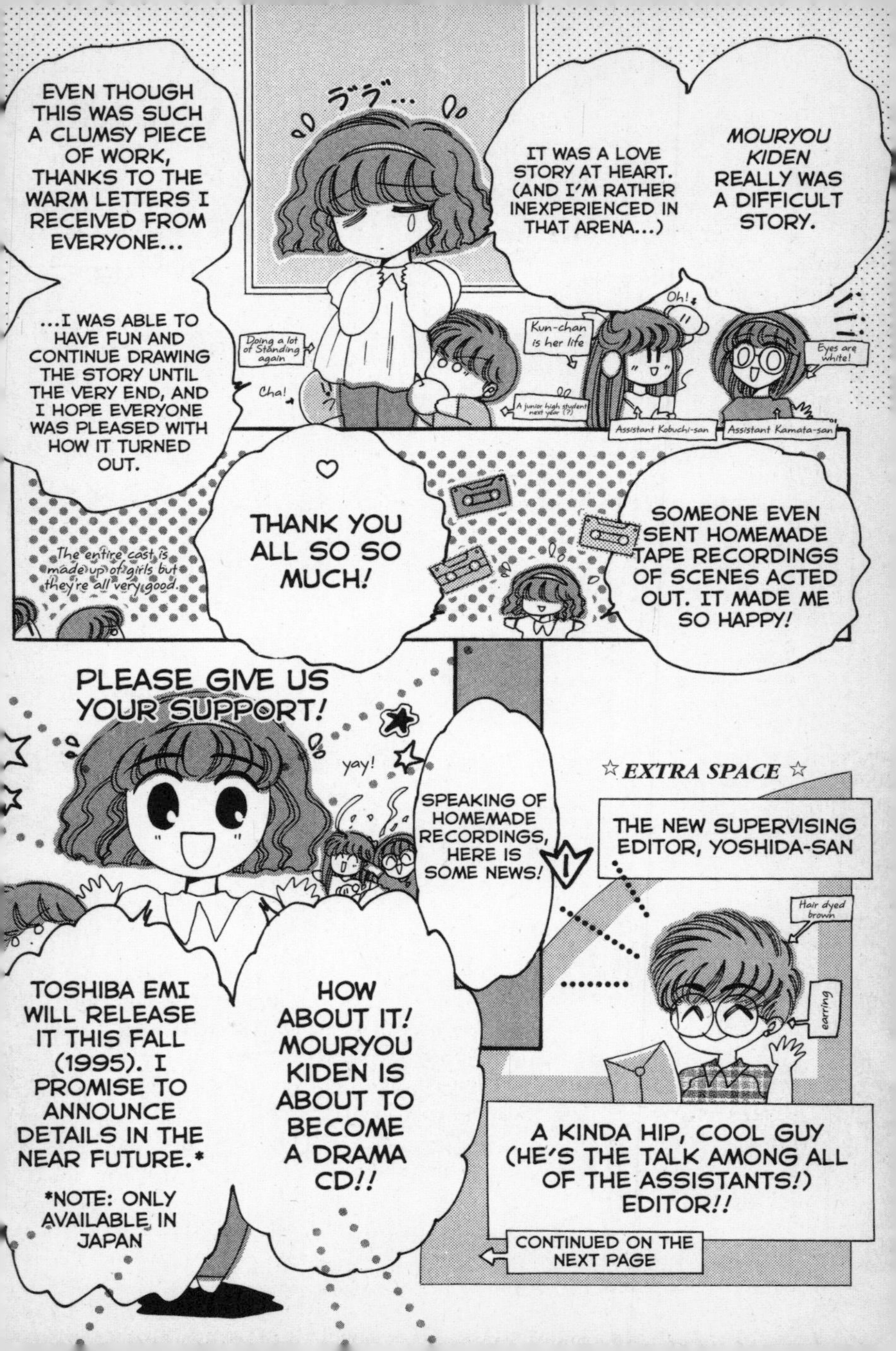
MOURYOU KIDEN REALLY WAS A DIFFICULT STORY.
IT WAS A LOVE STORY AT HEART. (AND I'M RATHER INEXPERIENCED IN THAT ARENA...)
ラ゛ラ゛...
Oh!
Eyes are white!
Assistant Kamata-san
Kun-chan is her life
Assistant Kobuchi-san
A junior high student next year (?)
Doing a lot of Standing again
Cha!
EVEN THOUGH THIS WAS SUCH A CLUMSY PIECE OF WORK, THANKS TO THE WARM LETTERS I RECEIVED FROM EVERYONE...
...I WAS ABLE TO HAVE FUN AND CONTINUE DRAWING THE STORY UNTIL THE VERY END, AND I HOPE EVERYONE WAS PLEASED WITH HOW IT TURNED OUT.
SOMEONE EVEN SENT HOMEMADE TAPE RECORDINGS OF SCENES ACTED OUT. IT MADE ME SO HAPPY!
THANK YOU ALL SO SO MUCH!
The entire cast is made up of girls but they're all very good.
SPEAKING OF HOMEMADE RECORDINGS, HERE IS SOME NEWS!
PLEASE GIVE US YOUR SUPPORT!
yay!
HOW ABOUT IT! MOURYOU KIDEN IS ABOUT TO BECOME A DRAMA CD!!
TOSHIBA EMI WILL RELEASE IT THIS FALL (1995). I PROMISE TO ANNOUNCE DETAILS IN THE NEAR FUTURE.*
*NOTE: ONLY AVAILABLE IN JAPAN
☆ EXTRA SPACE ☆
THE NEW SUPERVISING EDITOR, YOSHIDA-SAN
Hair dyed brown
earring
A KINDA HIP, COOL GUY (HE'S THE TALK AMONG ALL OF THE ASSISTANTS!) EDITOR!!
CONTINUED ON THE NEXT PAGE

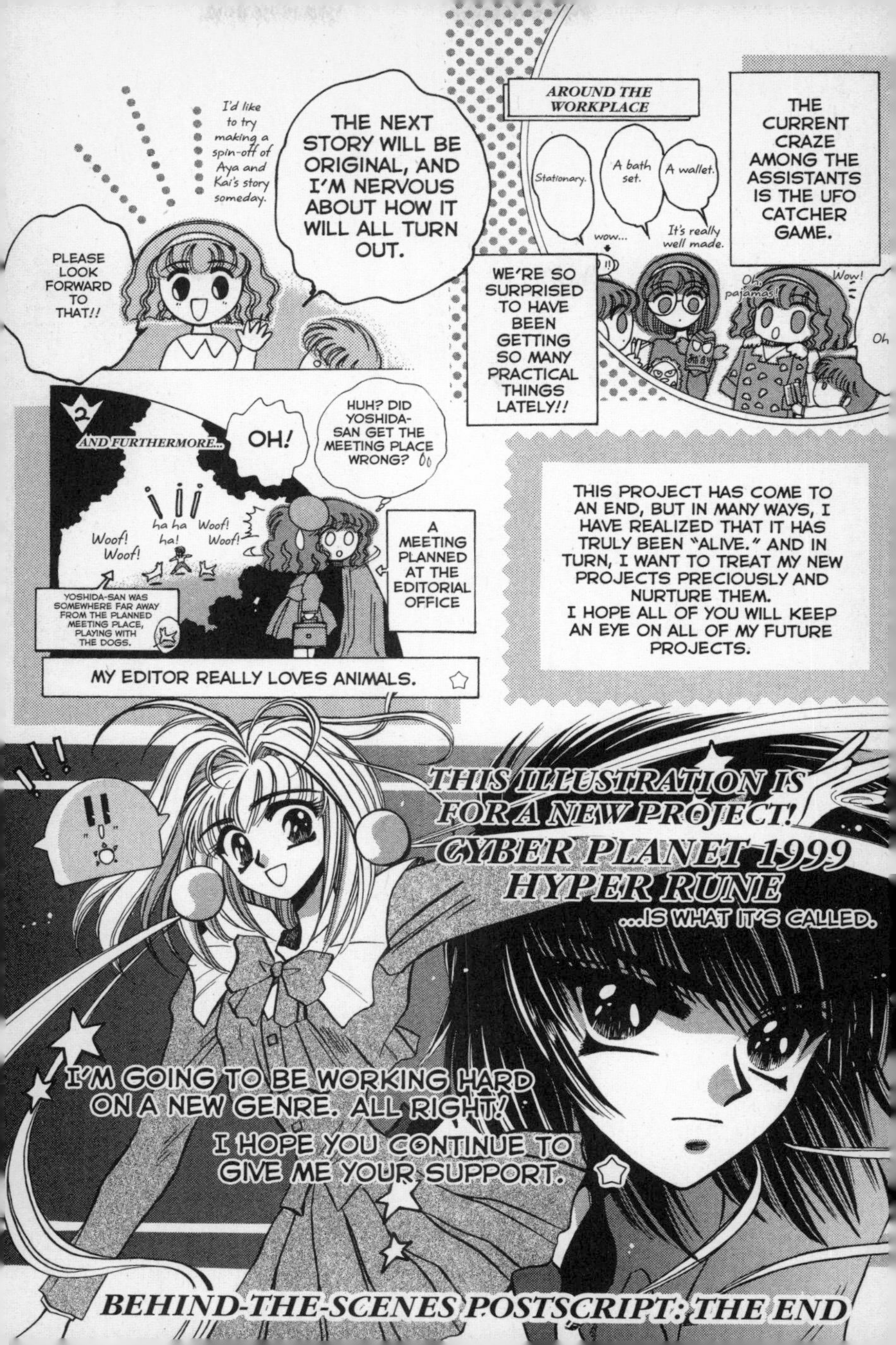
AROUND THE WORKPLACE
THE CURRENT CRAZE AMONG THE ASSISTANTS IS THE UFO CATCHER GAME.
A wallet.
A bath set.
Stationary.
It's really well made.
wow...
WE'RE SO SURPRISED TO HAVE BEEN GETTING SO MANY PRACTICAL THINGS LATELY!!
Wow!
Oh, pajamas!
Oh
THE NEXT STORY WILL BE ORIGINAL, AND I'M NERVOUS ABOUT HOW IT WILL ALL TURN OUT.
I'd like to try making a spin-off of Aya and Kai's story someday.
PLEASE LOOK FORWARD TO THAT!!
THIS PROJECT HAS COME TO AN END, BUT IN MANY WAYS, I HAVE REALIZED THAT IT HAS TRULY BEEN "ALIVE." AND IN TURN, I WANT TO TREAT MY NEW PROJECTS PRECIOUSLY AND NURTURE THEM.
I HOPE ALL OF YOU WILL KEEP AN EYE ON ALL OF MY FUTURE PROJECTS.
2
AND FURTHERMORE...
HUH? DID YOSHIDA-SAN GET THE MEETING PLACE WRONG?
OH!
A MEETING PLANNED AT THE EDITORIAL OFFICE
Woof! Woof!
ha ha ha!
Woof! Woof!
YOSHIDA-SAN WAS SOMEWHERE FAR AWAY FROM THE PLANNED MEETING PLACE, PLAYING WITH THE DOGS.
MY EDITOR REALLY LOVES ANIMALS.
THIS ILLUSTRATION IS FOR A NEW PROJECT!
CYBER PLANET 1999 HYPER RUNE
...IS WHAT IT'S CALLED.
I'M GOING TO BE WORKING HARD ON A NEW GENRE. ALL RIGHT!
I HOPE YOU CONTINUE TO GIVE ME YOUR SUPPORT.
BEHIND-THE-SCENES POSTSCRIPT: THE END

BECK: MONGOLIAN CHOP SQUAD

OT
OLDER TEEN
AGE 16+

ROCK IN MANGA!

Yukio Tanaka is one boring guy with no hobbies, a weak taste in music and only a small vestige of a personality. But his life is forever changed when he meets Ryusuke Minami, an unpredictable rocker with a cool dog named Beck. Recently returned to Japan from America, Ryusuke inspires Yukio to get into music, and the two begin a journey through the world of rock 'n' roll dreams! With cameos of music's greatest stars—from John Lennon to David Bowie—and homages to supergroups such as Led Zeppelin and Nirvana, anyone who's anyone can make an appearance in *Beck*...even Beck himself! With action, music and gobs of comedy, *Beck* puts the rock in manga!

HAROLD SAKUISHI'S HIGHLY ADDICTIVE MANGA SERIES THAT SPAWNED A HIT ANIME HAS FINALLY REACHED THE STATES!

©Harold Sakuishi

FOR MORE INFORMATION VISIT: WWW.TOKYOPOP.COM

TOKYOPOP SHOP

WWW.TOKYOPOP.COM/SHOP

HOT NEWS!

Check out the
TOKYOPOP SHOP!
The world's best
collection of manga in
English is now available
online in one place!

ARCANA

TOKYO MEW MEW A LA MODE

WWW.TOKYOPOP.COM/SHOP

MBQ and other
hot titles are
available at
the store that
never closes!

MBQ

- LOOK FOR SPECIAL OFFERS
- PRE-ORDER UPCOMING RELEASES!
- COMPLETE YOUR COLLECTIONS

MBQ © Felipe Smith & TOKYOPOP Inc. Arcana © SO-YOUNG LEE, DAIWON C.I. Inc. Tokyo Mew Mew a La Mode © Mia Ikumi & Kodansha.

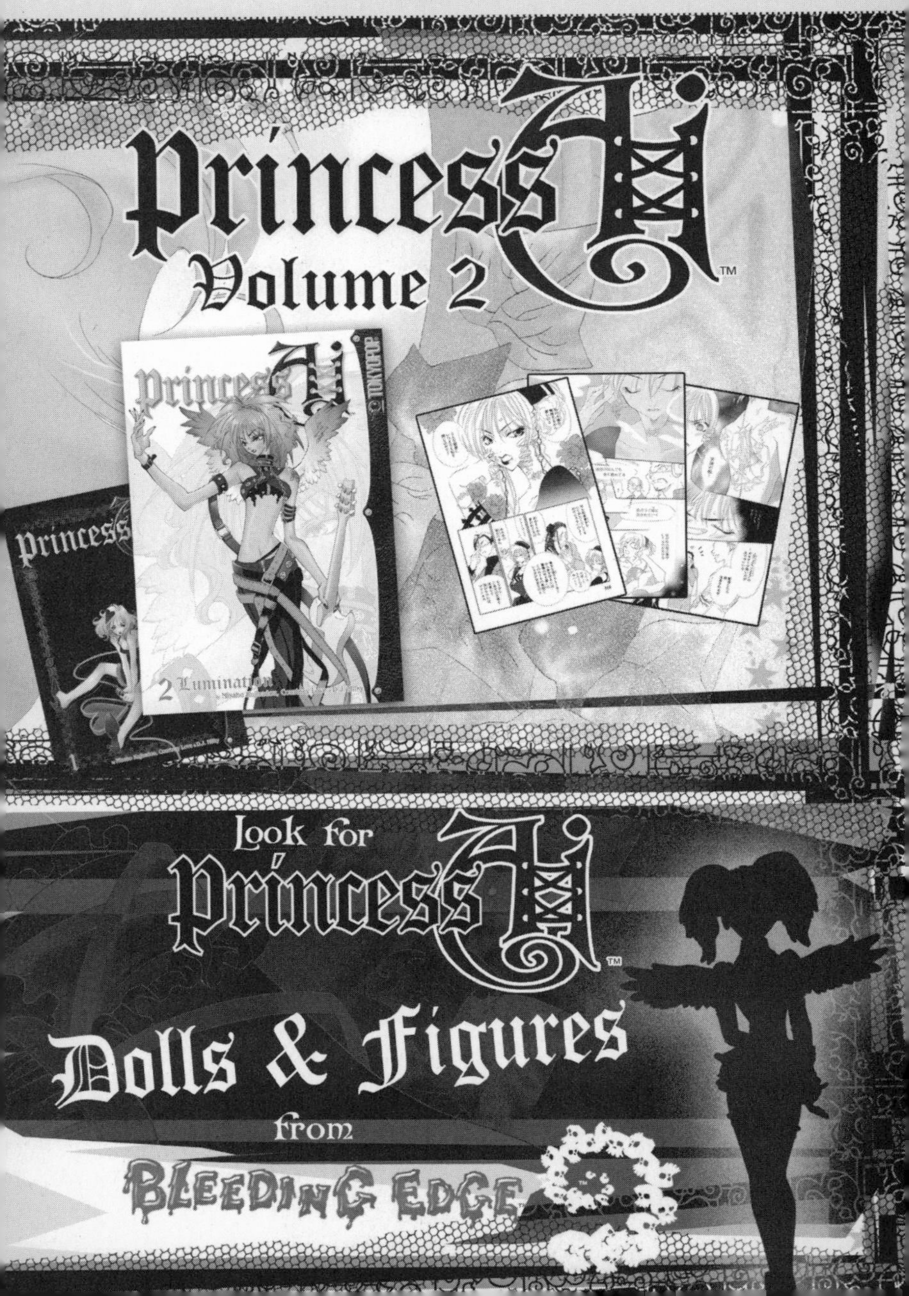

Princess Ai™
Volume 2
Look for
Princess Ai™
Dolls & Figures
from
BLEEDING EDGE

PRINCESS AI

A Diva Torn from Chaos
A Savior Doomed to Love

⋆ Volume 2

Lumination

Ai continues to search for her place in our world on the streets of Tokyo. Using her talent to support herself, Ai signs a contract with a top record label and begins her rise to stardom. But fame is unpredictable—as her talent blooms, all eyes are on Ai. When scandal surfaces, will she burn out in the spotlight of celebrity?

TEEN
AGE 13+

Preview the manga at:
www.TOKYOPOP.com/princessai

EDITORS' PICKS

BY YONG-SU HWANG
AND KYUNG-IL YANG

BLADE OF HEAVEN

Wildly popular in its homeland of Korea, *Blade of Heaven* enjoys the rare distinction of not only being a hit in its own country, but in Japan and several other countries, as well. On the surface, Yong-Su Hwang and Kyung-Il Yang's fantasy-adventure may look like yet another "Heaven vs. Demons" sword opera, but the story of the mischievous Soma, a pawn caught in a struggle of mythic proportions, is filled with so much humor, pathos, imagination—and yes, action, that it's easy to see why *Blade of Heaven* has been so popular worldwide.

~Bryce P. Coleman, Editor

BY MIWA UEDA

PEACH GIRL

Am I the only person who thinks that *Peach Girl* is just like *The O.C.*? Just imagine Ryan as Toji, Seth as Kiley, Marissa as Momo and Summer as Sae. (The similarities are almost spooky!) Plus, Seth is way into comics and manga—and I'm sure he'd love *Peach Girl*. It has everything that my favorite TV show has and then some—drama, intrigue, romance and lots of will-they-or-won't-they suspense. I love it! *Peach Girl* rules, seriously. If you haven't read it, do so. Now.

~Julie Taylor, Sr. Editor

Blade of Heaven © YONG-SU HWANG & KYUNG-IL YANG, DAIWON C.I. Inc. Peach Girl © Miwa Ueda.

BY BUNJURO NAKAYAMA
AND BOW DITAMA

MAHOROMATIC: AUTOMATIC MAIDEN

Mahoro is a sweet, cute, female battle android who decides to go from mopping up alien invaders to mopping up after Suguru Misato, a teenaged orphan boy... and hilarity most definitely ensues. This series has great art and a slick story that easily switches from truly funny to downright heartwarming...but always with a large shadow looming over it. You see, only Mahoro knows that her days are quite literally numbered, and the end of each chapter lets you know exactly how much—or how little—time she has left!

~Rob Tokar, Sr. Editor

BY KASANE KATSUMOTO

HANDS OFF!

Cute boys with ESP who share a special bond... If you think this is familiar (e.g. *Legal Drug*), well, you're wrong. *Hands Off!* totally stands alone as a unique and thoroughly enjoyable series. Kotarou and Tatsuki's (platonic!) relationship is complex, fascinating and heart-wrenching. Throw in Yuuto, the playboy who can read auras, and you've got a fantastic setup for drama and comedy, with incredible themes of friendship running throughout. Don't be put off by Kotarou's danger-magnet status, either. The episodic stuff gradually changes, and the full arc of the characters' development is well worth waiting for.

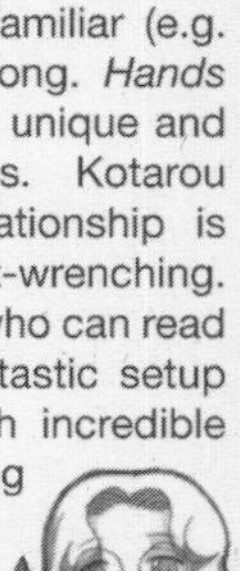

~Lillian Diaz-Przybyl, Jr. Editor

Mahoromatic: Automatic Maiden © Bunjuro Nakayama/Bow Ditama. Hands Off! © Kasane Katsumoto.

STOP!

This is the back of the book.
You wouldn't want to spoil a great ending!

This book is printed "manga-style," in the authentic Japanese right-to-left format. Since none of the artwork has been flipped or altered, readers get to experience the story just as the creator intended. You've been asking for it, so TOKYOPOP® delivered: authentic, hot-off-the-press, and far more fun!

DIRECTIONS

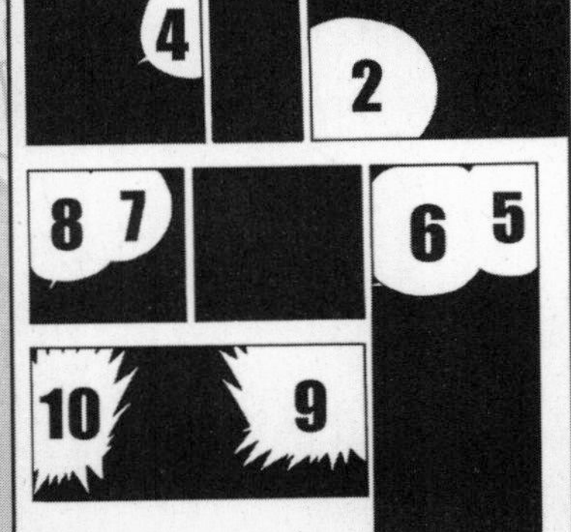
1
2
3
4
5
6
7
8
9
10

If this is your first time reading manga-style, here's a quick guide to help you understand how it works.

It's easy... just start in the top right panel and follow the numbers. Have fun, and look for more 100% authentic manga from TOKYOPOP®!

100% AUTHENTIC MANGA

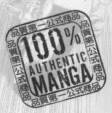